Motoring Reference Manual

CANADIAN DRIVER'S HANDBOOK

Published by The Reader's Digest Association (Canada) Ltd.
in conjunction with
the Canadian Automobile Association

CANADIAN DRIVER'S HANDBOOK
Edited and designed by St. Remy Press Inc.

Editor	Kenneth Winchester
Art Director	Pierre Léveillé
Research Editor	Caroline Miller
Researchers	Geneva Bennett Cosette Gauthier
Writers	Brian Parsons Carol Smith Dianne Thomas
Copy Editors	Peter Des Lauriers Heather Lawson
Illustrator	Elayne Sears
Indexer	Christopher Blackburn
Administrator	Denise Rainville
Consultants	H. G. Ronson, P. Eng. Sidney E. Swallow, SAE
Technical Assistance	Canadian Red Cross Society Pierre Champoux, Transport Canada Henk De Vries, Petro-Canada Skid Control Schools Direction générale des publications gouvernementales, Québec Ford Motor Company of Canada, Ltd. General Motors of Canada, Ltd. Martineau Walker Richard Poirier St. John Ambulance United States Department of Transportation

The acknowledgments and credits
that appear on page 224
are hereby made part of this copyright page

FIRST EDITION
ISBN for *Canadian Driver's Handbook:* 0-88850-128-5
ISBN for *Motoring Reference Manual:* 0-88850-133-1
Printed in Canada 85 86 87 / 5 4 3 2 1

 is the trademark of the Canadian Automobile Association

About the *Canadian Driver's Handbook*

In Canada today some two million of us own cars, and annually we drive almost 200 billion kilometres (124 billion miles) on 1 million kilometres (621,000 miles) of roads. We depend on our automobiles for everything from shopping and commuting to weekend getaways and summer-long vacations. Yet how many of us wish we could make driving safer, less expensive, and more enjoyable? For example, do you know where your PCV valve is located, and when it should be changed? How do you check for dangerously worn tires, a clogged air filter, or a leaking exhaust? Which headache remedies should you avoid when you are behind the wheel? How many drinks are "too many?" What are the tricks to making driving with young children more pleasurable? What temporary repairs can you make when faced with an overheated engine, a dead battery, or a broken belt?

Picture yourself in one of the following emergency situations—would you know what to do next?
- Thick smoke pours from under the hood.
- Your right wheels go off the pavement.
- You start to skid on a rain-soaked highway.
- You run into a thick patch of fog and cannot see.
- Your engine conks out on a busy highway.
- A car comes at you head on.

Whether you are a veteran motorist or student driver, the *Canadian Driver's Handbook* offers easy-to-find answers to these and most other questions you may have about driving, maintaining, and *enjoying* your car.

The *Canadian Driver's Handbook* is really two books. The 224-page *Motoring Reference Manual* is organized into three mini-guides to better driving, maintenance, and emergencies. The 72-page *Car Logbook*, tucked inside the other pocket, provides a ten-year record of fuel, oil, maintenance, and repair costs, plus specially designed forms for recording car data, emergency phone numbers, and accident details.

Within these pages, weekend mechanics interested in saving money by doing their own routine maintenance will find a wealth of practical how-to tips and techniques. There is even a glossary of automotive terms—from accelerator to Zerk fitting—that is designed to save you time and trouble when talking to mechanics. Holiday drivers will find practical advice on planning a car vacation, owning a recreational vehicle, and keeping children happily amused. Young drivers will learn the facts on drinking, drugs, and driving, and how to get the best deal on a new or used car. Even veteran motorists will pick up new techniques—for driving in rain, fog, and snow, and for squeezing the most kilometres from a litre of fuel, for example. To challenge newfound skills or refresh old ones, there is a driving I.Q. test on pages 88–91, and an emergencies quiz on pages 210–211.

Be sure to follow all safety tips and **Caution** warnings, especially when maintaining or repairing your car, and take the time to study the Emergencies section *before* you need this advice at the scene of an accident.

Car care can be dangerous

Working on your car can lead to serious injury unless you observe certain basic precautions. Most of the fluids used in a car are poisonous, corrosive, flammable, or explosive. Many automotive parts become red-hot during normal operation. They can cause severe burns if touched accidentally and can set off a fire or explosion if they come into contact with flammable materials. The potential for injury is great when you work on a car.

Nevertheless, millions of car owners have performed much of their own maintenance and repair work for years without serious injury. The key is to develop careful work habits, to observe basic safety rules, and to work slowly and deliberately, thinking through each action or step and its possible consequences before you perform it.

Skinned knuckles and minor cuts and burns are a normal part of car repair. Always keep a first-aid kit and a fire extinguisher handy. Never work on a car alone. An adult should always be nearby in case emergency help must be summoned quickly.

Throughout this book, specific safety precautions are given under the heading **Caution**. These special warnings should be strictly observed. So should the general precautions described on pages 98-99, which can help you avoid damage to your car and injury to yourself.

Motoring Reference Manual

Better Driving: Pages 6–95

Part I of *Canadian Driver's Handbook* is a refresher course in defensive driving. This section begins by telling you how to buy or sell a car, and exactly what are your rights and responsibilities on the road. Next, a series of spreads demonstrates proper techniques for city, country, and highway driving, and explains how to cope with rain, wind, fog, and Canadian winters. Here, too, is advice on automobile safety, drugs and alcohol, fighting fatigue, traveling with kids, fuel economy, trailering, and car touring.

Maintenance: Pages 96–159

Part II is filled with information designed to keep your car out of the repair shop and on the road. In these pages you will learn about routine maintenance and repair for the engine, drive train, exhaust, suspension, steering, brakes, tires, transmission, electrical system, bodywork, and interior. Follow do-it-yourself steps to interpret engine noises or trace leaks, "read" tire treads for signs of suspension problems, perform a lubrication job, and change your own oil. And, if a job is too complicated, learn how to shop for a garage.

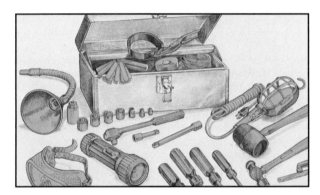

Emergencies: Pages 160–224

Part III provides information that can be indispensable, even lifesaving, in the event of a highway emergency. Here are techniques to help you drive out of trouble, or lessen the consequences if collision is unavoidable. Step-by-step illustrations show how to make roadside repairs, jump-start a battery, or change a tire. The first-aid guide shows what to do until help arrives—how to deal with stopped breathing, bleeding, broken bones, burns, and other injuries; how to move a casualty; and what to pack in a car first-aid kit.

Car Logbook

In the other pocket of *Canadian Driver's Handbook* is the 72-page *Car Logbook*—a lifetime diary for your car. It is designed to be used each time you fill up or service your car. There is a ten-year maintenance calendar, fuel economy charts to provide a month-by-month breakdown of gas and oil costs, plus a table to compute fuel consumption in both litres/100 kilometres and miles per gallon. From these records you will learn how your car is performing, save money by keeping it in top shape, and spot minor problems before they become major expenses.

PART I

Drive safely—and save gas

Better Driving

Our love affair with the automobile

When John Moodie imported the first automobile to Hamilton, Ontario in 1898, fellow citizens lined the streets to scoff and jeer at the noisy oddity. The fact was that most Canadians simply believed that an invention as impractical as the automobile would never catch on.

The first horseless carriages sprang from the inspiration of taking a steam-powered vehicle off the railway tracks and putting it on carriage wheels. Soon, other models appeared that were powered by electricity, the rage of the 1890s. Electricity was clean, quiet, and easy to use, but had one fatal flaw— the batteries ran down every few kilometres. The gasoline car, introduced around 1900, was rough, dirty, noisy, and cantankerous. But it had a gutsy appeal, and would run all day, given enough gas. With the introduction of the electric starter in 1912, which made operating an automobile safe and simple for anyone, the gasoline car's supremacy was assured.

Between 1900 and 1933, more than 125 different makes rolled out of Canadian sheds, garages, and factories. The McLaughlin Carriage Company, which first derided the horseless carriage, saw the way of the future in 1908 and became the McLaughlin Motor Car Company. One of the firm's models was designed along the lines of a yacht, boasting a copper-riveted mahogany body, brass lamps, and wicker seats. Toronto's *Motoring* magazine sniffed that the 1913 models included everything "except the bundle of bank notes to pay running expenses."

The early motorist had to dress for the sport. Men sported caps, goggles, and boots; women draped themselves in ankle-length dusters and veiled hats.

The transition from horse to horseless was far from painless. Many a neophyte careened toward inevitable collision, pulling on the steering wheel as though it were the reins of a horse, and shouting "Whoa!" Encounters between automobiles and horse-drawn carriages were common, usually ending with the carriage in the ditch and the motorist vanishing in a cloud of dust. Enemies of the automobile scattered broken

---

"Get out and get under"

With few garages and no one but a conniving farmer to offer a tow, every driver had to be his own mechanic. A wise motorist always carried tins of extra fuel and water, horse-nail pullers, rawhide tire bandages, chains, tow rope, a block and tackle, a lantern, two or three spare tires, and a complete set of tools.

Repair tricks were primitive but ingenious. To prime a carburetor, the motorist blew into the gas tank vent, then plugged it with a matchstick. Wide, stout planks were carried to reinforce rickety bridges or provide traction on muddy roads. Honey and water made a passable antifreeze when alcohol or glycerine was unavailable. To check the battery, a driver simply placed his tongue on one of the terminals—a slight prickly sensation indicated that the battery was charged.

The first person to cross Canada by car was Thomas W. Wilby. On August 27, 1912, he backed his Reo Special into the Atlantic near Halifax. After driving 6,760 kilometres (4,200 miles), and traversing western Ontario by ferry, he reached Victoria on October 18, and emptied a bottle of Atlantic water into the Pacific.

glass and tacks on the road, buried hay-mower blades, and strung wire across roadways. Enterprising farmers dug, watered, and camouflaged mudholes in the road and waited around the corner for unsuspecting victims. When a car fell into the trap, the farmer would offer to hitch up his mules and free the motorist—for $5.

The anatagonism of a resentful public was the least of the early motorist's worries. "Roads" were often mere cowpaths or wagon tracks; pavement was usually dirt or clay mixed with manure. A driver had to be prepared for mud, rocks, swamps, tree stumps, sand, potholes, and washed-out bridges. Signposts were few and far between, but breakdowns were frequent—every 15 to 30 kilometres on a rough road.

Winter driving was for the truly adventurous. Most Canadian roads were snowbound from December until May, and winter starts were doubtful, at best. A hot water bottle around an icy carburetor helped on occasion; pouring gasoline on the engine pipes and igniting it was effective, if dangerous. One driving manual suggested cutting a hole in the firewall to allow heat from the engine compartment to warm the passengers.

In self-defense, motoring pioneers began to band together to form automobile clubs, the first in Hamilton and Toronto in 1913. At the time, legislation reflected the animosity felt toward motorists. Drivers who exceeded the Westmount, Québec speed limit of 9 mph in 1907 were slapped with a $20 fine. Prince Edward Island went so far as to ban motor vehicles completely.

Officially, motor clubs lobbied for fair legislation and better roads, drew maps, erected road signs, and organized emergency road services. (Unofficially, they dunked mischievous farmers in their own mudholes.) Through their efforts, the dream of a road that would traverse the country—as the railway had done in the previous century—began to emerge.

The crusade was taken up by Dr. Perry Doolittle, president of the Canadian Automobile Association from 1920 until his death in 1933. An avid motorist and inventor (his "Doolittle detachable ring" facilitated tire changing), the good doctor campaigned long and hard for an "All-Red Route" across Canada. In 1925, he and photographer Ed Flickenger crossed the country by automobile in 40 days. Where there were no roads, the men fitted flanged wheels to their Model T and traveled by rail.

By 1946, highway construction had proceeded far enough for Brigadier R. A. Macfarlane and Kenneth MacGilliveray to drive from Cape Breton Island to Vancouver entirely on Canadian roads. In 1949, the Trans-Canada Highway Act was passed and, in 1962, Dr. Doolitle's dream was realized. Canada's national road—the world's longest—stretched 7,821 kilometres (4,860 miles) between St. John's and Vancouver.

Choosing the right car for you

How do you decide which is the best vehicle for you and your family? First, establish the price range you can afford (including sales tax and other charges) and stay within it. Second, determine your needs and choose the car, truck, or van within your price range that will best serve those needs.

If it's to be a family car it must be able to carry everybody comfortably. For camping and hauling a lot of gear a station wagon might be best. Do you live in hilly country? Will you pull a trailer? You'll need plenty of power. Are you a salesman clocking 2,500 kilometres (1,500 miles) a month on the freeways? You'll value dependability. Are you in the market for a weekend sports runabout, an easy-on-the gas commuter, or a first car for your teenager?

Body style

The size and body style of the vehicle you pick should be determined by the number of passengers and the amount of cargo you normally carry, how much comfort you want, and how far you will drive in a year.

Sedans, both two- and four-door models, tend to resist drafts and rattles better than other body types because of their roof-to-floor pillars. A two-door sedan is usually less expensive and slightly quieter than one with four doors, but some people may find it a struggle getting in and out of the rear seat. Because children can accidentally open rear doors, many four-door sedans now have "child-proof" rear-door locks, which cannot be opened from the inside. As a rule, a sedan costs less initially than a hardtop, but depreciates a little faster.

Hardtops have no pillars to obstruct side vision. Their sleek, open look may increase the resale value, but hardtops can be noisier than sedans, have less headroom and knee-room in the rear, and may provide less protection in some accidents.

Size up the right car

Interior and trunk capacity	Advantages	Disadvantages
Minicompact: 4 passengers; less than 2.4 m³ (85 ft³)	Excellent for city driving; maneuverable; easy to park. Lowest fuel consumption of any type of car; some models claim 4.8 L/100 km (59 mpg) with diesel engine and manual transmission.	Poor passenger protection in a collision. Highway performance only fair due to small engine. Back seat cramped for adults on long trips. Limited trunk space. Fewest available options.
Subcompact: 4 passengers; 2.4–2.8 m³ (85–100 ft³)	Advantages of minicompact plus added trunk space and back seat legroom. Low insurance rates, depreciation, and annual maintenance costs. Excellent fuel economy, especially with diesel.	Many minicompact disadvantages. Can be noisy and cramped for four passengers on long trips. Lack of power for towing, although some manufacturers offer optional larger engine. Few options.
Compact: 4–5 passengers; 2.8–3.1 m³ (100–110 ft³)	Many advantages of smaller cars, but less road noise and more available options, including better highway performance with larger engines. Good all-round car for small family.	Fair protection in a collision. Insufficient power for towing larger trailer. Limited passenger legroom. Headroom sometimes sacrificed for style. Harsher ride than larger cars.
Midsize: 5–6 passengers; 3.1–3.4 m³ (110–120 ft³)	Good compromise between large car and compact. Wide choice of engine sizes and options. More luggage and passenger space, less noise than smaller cars. Fair fuel economy.	Higher initial cost than for smaller cars. Mediocre fuel economy on models with large engines and power options. Higher maintenance costs. Somewhat harder to maneuver and park.
Full-size: 6 passengers; 3.4 m³ (120 ft³) or more	Generally best highway performance and passenger protection in collisions. Best size for towing trailers. Most options available and largest passenger and cargo space for an automobile.	Higher fuel, insurance, and upkeep costs than for smaller models. Limited maneuverability, even with power steering and brakes. Requires large parking space. Highest depreciation.
Van: 5–9 passengers; 3.4–4.5 m³ (120–220 ft³)	Most cargo and passenger space; can be converted to a recreational vehicle complete with beds, stove, and sink. Good for towing trailers. Fair fuel economy with smaller engine.	Full-size vans difficult to park and maneuver because of size. Poor fuel economy with larger engines. Difficult to heat and cool evenly. Mini-vans sacrifice cargo room for ease of handling.

Station wagons, which account for some ten percent of North American car sales each year, are more versatile than sedans or hardtops. Their large cargo space can be enlarged even more by folding down the rear seat. But the seat and tailgate often rattle, while the interior may be noisy and hard to heat and cool evenly. Station wagons cost more to buy and operate than sedans, but have a slower rate of depreciation.

Hatchbacks combine sedan advantages with station wagon convenience. A rear door, hinged at the roof, gives wide-open access to the cargo area, which expands when the rear seat is folded down. If you sometimes need extra cargo room but seldom require the seating capacity of a station wagon, a hatchback is a good choice.

Vans, which were once strictly commercial vehicles, have become popular as family transportation. Their cavernous interiors can be fitted with two or three bench seats to accommodate up to nine people, or left open to haul cargo. However, vans are more difficult to park and maneuver than cars, and more expensive to operate. New "minivans" seek to combine large-vehicle cargo space and small-car economy.

Sports cars and *coupes,* with seats for two (although "2 + 2" coupes can carry two children as well as two adults) and little space for cargo, are not practical family transportation. They appeal mostly to car buffs.

Convertibles may have room for four or more people. (A *roadster* is a two-passenger convertible.) Although the folding top provides an open-air feeling unmatched even by a sunroof, it may prove too drafty and noisy at expressway speeds. Convertibles can be less safe than sedans and hardtops in some kinds of accidents, and are more vulnerable to thieves and vandals.

Engines

The standard engine for a given model will usually be powerful enough for highway driving with moderate loads. However, if you drive on hilly roads, tow a trailer, or equip the car with air conditioning and power windows and seats, you will probably need a bigger engine. Although a smaller engine is generally cheaper to buy, run, and maintain, if it doesn't have the power to match the car's size and weight, it may prove costlier in the long term than a larger engine which doesn't strain under its load.

The *diesel engine* usually lasts many thousands of kilometres longer than a gasoline engine, but can be more expensive to maintain. Unlike the gasoline engine, the diesel has no ignition system or carburetor. Instead, diesel fuel is injected at high pressure into combustion chambers above the cylinders. There the mixture is so compressed that its heat ignites the fuel. A diesel engine will give slightly better fuel economy than a gasoline engine of comparable size.

On the minus side, you will pay more for the diesel-powered model of a car than for the gasoline model. Because diesels are hard to start in cold weather, you will need a block heater. In fact, a diesel won't start at all at $-15°C$ ($-5°F$) unless you have installed a block heater and a battery warmer, kept it in a heated garage, or added a fuel conditioner when you filled up. Compared to gasoline engines, most diesels tend to accelerate more sluggishly and idle more noisily. Although it's a little cheaper than gasoline, diesel fuel may be hard to find in remote areas.

The *turbocharged engine* can deliver more power on demand than an engine of the same size with no turbocharger—and without sacrificing much fuel economy. Exhaust gases—normally wasted—are recycled to spin a turbine connected to a compressor. The compressor pumps extra fuel and air into the cylinders at very high pressure to boost the engine's power, particularly when you accelerate or drive at high speeds. At one time found only in high-priced sports cars, turbocharged engines are now available in many regular automobiles.

Front-wheel drive. Because the weight of its engine is over the traction wheels, and because it is *pulled* by its front wheels rather than being *pushed* by its rear wheels, a car with front-wheel drive handles better than one with rear-wheel drive, particularly around curves and on slippery roads.

Making your "short list"

1. Analyze the type of driving you do (city, country, highway, commuting, weekend tours, shopping trips), and the distance you travel in a typical year.

2. Determine the usual number of passengers in your car.

3. Familiarize yourself with cars and options available; read car ads and articles in auto magazines and consumer publications.

4. Decide on the price range that you can reasonably afford.

5. Narrow your list down to three or four models and thoroughly examine each one, both on the lot and on the road.

6. Ask your insurance agent about your choices. What are the differences in insurance costs?

Getting the best deal

If you are thinking of buying a new car, first ask yourself if it's really your best buy. Certainly there are advantages to owning a new car rather than a used one. But do these benefits justify the high initial cost and depreciation loss you will have with a new car? If you drive less than 10,000 kilometres (6,000 miles) a year, you might be better off with a two- or three-year-old car in good condition that has been driven less than 40,000 kilometres (25,000 miles).

On the other hand, a new car may be a good choice if you...

• have not only a down payment that equals at least 25 percent of the total price (or a car of equivalent value to trade in or sell), but also the license and insurance fees;

• drive approximately 1,600 km (1,000 mi) or more per month;

• put dependability at the top of your list of concerns;

• drive far from home on vacations, or do a lot of highway driving;

• don't mind spending extra money for a new car, even though its value will decrease in the first year by as much as a quarter of the purchase price.

Once you have resolved to buy a new car, do your homework before you set foot in a showroom. This will increase your chances of getting a fair deal. Read consumer studies and statistics for specific makes and models. Compare prices and decide what you can realistically afford.

If you are a typical motorist, you haven't had much practice in the art of buying new cars. When you shop, remember that you are dealing with experts who sell cars every day. They are looking for high profits, so don't allow yourself to be oversold.

Dealers in Canada are not required to display window stickers showing suggested retail price (although most do this). However, they should be prepared to show you the *dossier*. This lists the manufacturer's suggested retail price for the basic vehicle plus the price for each piece of installed optional equipment. It also includes an estimate of fuel consumption.

You can determine what a particular car cost the dealer—the wholesale price—and therefore how much of the sticker price is profit or dealer markup. As a rule of thumb, subtract ten percent from the list price (excluding options) for minicompacts and subcompacts, 20 percent for midsize and large cars (including vans), and 25 percent for luxury and sports cars. Add half of the total list price of your chosen options. You now have the wholesale price. Subtract this from the list price to find the dealer markup—your bargaining room.

Be prepared to bargain for the best price. Even if a deal sounds good, visit at least two other dealers. For effective comparison shopping, get detailed price quotes in writing. Make sure the quote includes separate figures for the car, options, sales tax, freight and delivery charges; that it is valid for at least a few days; and that it has been approved and signed by the sales manager. But you shouldn't sign anything until you have finished shopping around. After the quote is written, ask the dealer to make you a trade-in offer on your old car.

Trade-ins

Whether you decide to trade or sell your old car, you can take steps to increase its value. Clean and polish it inside and out. Check the condition of your engine. Since an easy start-up is extremely important, invest in a tune-up or a new battery if necessary.

Smart private buyers and car dealers will want a mechanic to inspect a used car. You might be wise to have a CAA inspection center, or other qualified garage, look over your car. Some defects, which you might be able to correct inexpensively, can kill a sale or dramatically lower the trade-in value.

Know in advance what your car is worth, and look around for the best trade-in offer. You will probably get more money for your car by selling it privately than by trading it in. Once you have a buyer, don't accept anything but cash or a certified cheque.

The test drive

Before you make up your mind about any car, road-test it for at least an hour (the salesperson should come, too). Better still, try to borrow a demonstrator for a weekend or, if you can afford it, rent a similar model for a couple of days. Make sure that the car you test has the same engine and transmission you plan to buy.

Confirm that the dealer has insured the car. Then try to take your test run over a course that includes as many different driving challenges and kinds of roads as possible—hills, bumpy stretches, a fast, flat highway, and stop-and-go city streets. Drive at night or in foul weather if you can. Do some backing up and parking. Take your family along (or the number of passengers you normally carry), and load the trunk if possible. This will tell you whether the car is comfortable and roomy enough. Assess the vehicle for safety, performance, and convenience.

Before making your decision

It is important to have confidence in your dealer. You should know whether a particular dealer has a reputation for reliable and honest service. Ask friends about their experiences; consult your local CAA club and the Better Business Bureau.

Consider the dealership's location. A lower price offered by an out-of-town dealer could be offset by the inconvenience of having to venture far from home for regular service, not to mention emergency repairs. However, a local dealer may honor a warranty—depending on its terms—regardless of where the car was bought.

When contemplating different cars, study each company's warranty. Compare the extent of parts covered, the time limits, and distances allowed. Learn what your obligations are to perform regular maintenance chores such as tuneups and oil changes. Most warranties tie you to the dealer's service department for routine maintenance. Remember, dealer service is usually the most expensive.

The buy-sell agreement

When you have finally selected your car and negotiated the best deal, the salesperson will prepare a written sales agreement—an offer to purchase—describing the car and listing the options you ordered, the sales price plus all taxes and additional fees, trade-in allowance, and finance terms (if any). Make sure the agreement clearly states that the dealer will return your deposit if the deal falls through or if you refuse to accept delivery of a car that isn't exactly as described in the sales agreement.

Study the dealer's terms for repairs and inspection prior to delivery. The agreement can include a firm delivery date and specify a penalty or other provisions that will apply if the date is not met. Ask that anything you don't like be changed or deleted before you sign. Once you and the sales manager sign the agreement, it is final and binding (except where grace periods apply).

Inspecting your new car

When your new car is delivered, check the window sticker carefully. The equipment listed should match your sales agreement. Don't pay for options you did not order. Inspect and test-drive the car. Look for nicks and dents. Make sure you have a spare tire and jack. Test everything—the engine, lights, radio, windshield washers, windows. Try the seat belts, turn on the heating and ventilation systems, open and close the doors, hood and trunk, making sure that all the locks and latches work smoothly. Check that the seats adjust properly.

Insist that the dealer correct obvious defects before you accept delivery. Don't hesitate to take the car back to the dealer later if other defects come to light. You may find it helpful to keep a list of faults as you discover them. Finally, read your owner's manual from cover to cover.

Financing

In deciding what you can afford to pay for your car, remember that you should have enough cash (or a trade-in) to cover at least 25 percent of the total purchase price—plus the cost of license and insurance. Don't plan to spend more than 15 percent of your net salary each month on car payments.

The simplest method of financing is to pay cash. The main advantage of this method is that the car is completely yours. Paying cash, however, has its hidden costs. The same amount of money left in a savings account would have earned interest or, if invested elsewhere, could have made a profit.

If you decide to finance your purchase, shop around for the best terms. In general, the smaller the amount of money borrowed, the lower the interest rate; and the shorter the duration of the loan, the less its total cost. The total cost is the amount borrowed plus all finance or interest charges. Because interest rates vary between one lending institution and another, the only way to find the lowest rate available to you is to shop around. Wherever you borrow, be sure to ask what the penalties are for late or skipped payments and whether there is a prepayment penalty if you pay off the loan before it is due.

Borrow against an insurance policy if you can; this is the most economical loan. Banks and credit unions offer loans at lower interest rates than finance companies do. Your car dealer will arrange a loan through a finance company, which collects your payments. It charges the going rate for the loan plus a fee for the dealer. This may be a convenient arrangement—about 50 percent of car buyers borrow through their dealers—but it isn't the cheapest.

Usually, in any form of financing where the vehicle itself is the security, it must be fully insured, particularly for collision. Before arranging financing, therefore, find out what the collision insurance rates would be for the new car, based on your age and driving record. You could find your financing costs sharply increased by a high premium.

Customizing your car

With some options, you can improve your new car's performance or add to its safety, convenience, and resale value. Others are merely stylish extras—to give your car a sportier or more elegant look. If certain options you want seem overpriced by the dealer, and you can't negotiate a lower price tag, shop for them elsewhere. Most department stores, auto-parts outlets, and specialty shops feature such items as radios, tape decks, and roof racks at bargain prices.

Once you have settled on a particular car, find out what is optional and what is stan-

dard. Some top-of-the-line cars may have virtually everything you could ask for as standard equipment. With some of the economy models, a back seat, carpet, or glove compartment may be extras.

List the options you must have and those that you would like if you can afford them. Useful station wagon options, for example, include deflector vanes, to prevent exhaust fumes, dirt, and dust from being sucked into the car; power tailgate window; rear-window defroster; luggage rack; and a fold-down third seat.

Accessories plain and fancy

1. Heavy-duty battery, for cars loaded with power accessories, also improves winter starting.

2. Power brakes reduce the amount of pressure needed to stop the car, a plus on heavier vehicles or when towing a trailer.

3. Disc brakes retain their stopping power better than drum brakes when hot or wet, and generally stop the car with less swerve.

4. Power antenna lets you retract the aerial at the touch of a button, to prevent damage, and adjust it up and down for the best reception as you drive.

5. Radio can be simply AM or FM, alone or in combination, or AM-FM stereo with or without tape deck. FM provides cleaner reception, but AM stations can be tuned in at greater distances.

6. Tape deck alone can be a desirable alternative to radio, as it does not depend on strength of signals. Once-popular eight-track cartridges are being replaced by compact cassettes. Automatic rewind and shut-off are useful.

7. Sunroof, manual or powered, is a popular alternative to a convertible top. If powered, repair can be expensive.

8. Intermittent windshield wipers can be set to sweep at preset intervals of 2 to 10 seconds. Useful when driving in drizzle.

9. Instrumentation package enables driver to monitor engine, provides early-warning system for possible problems. May include tachometer, ammeter, oil-pressure gauge, and temperature gauge.

10. Power steering makes it easier to maneuver, especially when parking, but can reduce the driver's "feel" of the road. Standard on larger cars; some smaller cars offer "power-assisted" steering.

11. Remote-control side mirror is convenient for adjusting the outside mirror from inside the car in bad weather or for families with several drivers. Can be a source of mechanical trouble.

12. Side moldings protect the finish from chipping and scratching when the door of another car is banged against it. Side moldings of resilient vinyl offer the best protection.

13. Tinted glass keeps the car interior cooler by cutting out some of the sun's hot rays. Usually part of an air-conditioning package. The darker the tint, however, the more nighttime vision is reduced.

14. Power windows are convenient for ventilation control when driving alone and for passing through toll booths, but require special caution when children are passengers. Windows do not operate unless the ignition key is switched on.

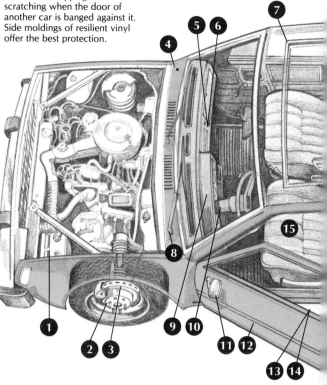

Some options, such as radios, automatic transmissions, power steering, power disc brakes, and radial tires, add to the car's re-sale value. Other power accessories, such as seats, windows, and sunroofs, add to a car's weight and fuel costs, can be expensive to maintain, and depreciate quickly. You may have a choice of upholstery; remember that leather-covered seats lose half their value in three years (so does chrome trim).

If you want a number of related options—added lighting convenience, for example—a *package* put together by the manufacturer may be the best buy. Often the carmaker can cut production costs by selling a group of related options such as dashboard gauges, extra trim, or winterizing accessories. Calculate what you would pay for individual items; a package may be worth the price.

You can, of course, buy a "stripped car" without a single option, but few people do. At the other extreme, if you load your car with every available option, you could easily double its cost. The options illustrated below are the most popular offered by carmakers to Canadian buyers.

15. Power seats are available with two-way, four-way, or six-way adjustments for drivers of various sizes. Changing position relieves fatigue on long trips. Repairs can be expensive.

16. Power door locks are a safety feature for drivers with small children.

17. Heavy-duty suspension is often part of an air-conditioning or towing package. This option gives better control at high speeds and on rough roads.

18. Rear-window defroster is available in two types. Electrically-heated wires on the glass are best for melting outside ice and snow. Blower-type defroster is best for removing interior condensation.

19. Magnesium wheels or other alloy wheels are expensive, but reduce the combined weight of the wheel and tire, thereby improving handling and fuel economy.

- **Lighting package** adds spots of illumination in various combinations: under the hood, inside the glove compartment and trunk, over the ashtray, and for map reading.

- **Vinyl roof**, although hard to clean and susceptible to deterioration and damage, adds extra style to the car. Dark vinyl tops absorb heat, placing an added load on air conditioning.

- **Rear speakers**, when combined with front speakers, enhance the sound of radios or tape decks. The driver can direct the sound to rear passengers so that front-seat passengers can converse, or vice versa.

- **Limited-slip differential** transfers power to one wheel if the other is spinning on ice or mud. Makes vary in efficiency; some are noisy, and others can cause fishtailing on slick roads.

- **Automatic speed control** maintains a preset cruising speed without driver intervention. Reduces fatigue on long trips, saves fuel on level stretches, and prevents speeding. Of no use for stop-and-go city driving.

- **Automatic transmission** is especially convenient for motorists who drive mostly in stop-and-go traffic, although it increases gas consumption. Can also reduce power somewhat on many small-engine subcompacts.

- **Air conditioning** is expensive and increases fuel consumption, often dramatically, but some drivers consider it a necessity for comfortable summer motoring. Requires a larger engine and regular maintenance. Repairs can be expensive.

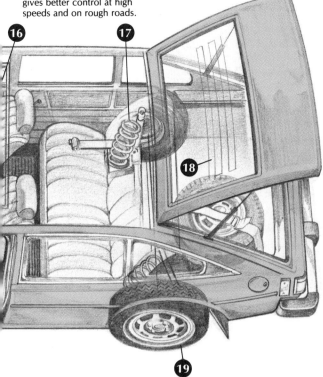

How to buy a used car

The cost of owning and operating a used car is only about half that of a new car—provided, of course, you don't buy a "lemon." One of the best ways to ensure against this is to do some initial research and to carefully shop around. A used car may be your soundest investment if:

• your travel is limited and local;
• yours is a two-car family;
• the car will be used primarily by a teenager or an infrequent driver;
• you have a limited amount to spend.

To begin your research, determine how much you want to spend and the type and size of car that best suits your needs (see pp. 10–11). Read the frequency-of-repair surveys and owners' reports in automobile magazines and consumer publications, including the CAA *Used Car Buyer's Guide*. Talk with your mechanic about which cars are the most trouble-free and inexpensive to repair. Your best buy is a vehicle in good condition with a lower-than-average odometer reading and a reputation for reliability.

New-car dealers are generally the safest source for used cars, offering the widest selection of late-model vehicles. However, they are also the most expensive source. Nonetheless, since most dealers have service and parts facilities, they will usually offer a used-car warranty.

Used-car dealers are most willing to accept trade-ins. Those without service departments will tend to sell a car "as is," and may not offer a warranty. You can minimize your risks by purchasing from a reliable dealer who has been in business for several years. When you buy from any dealer, you are legally entitled to request the name and address of the previous owner. Do so, and seek out information about the car's past performance and true condition.

Private owners can be a source of genuine bargains. The main drawback is that most private deals carry no warranty or guarantee. If the vehicle proves to have hidden defects, you have no legal recourse unless you can prove deliberate fraud. Check privately owned cars carefully, verify that the seller is really the registered owner of the vehicle, and make sure that there are no liens against the vehicle.

Rental and leasing companies and fleet sales of taxis, police cars, and government vehicles usually offer low prices. But these cars may have been driven long and hard, with questionable maintenance.

Repossessed cars in good condition are generally offered first to employees of the repossessing company. At auctions, you will probably be bidding against dealers, where the best deal you can expect will be the going wholesale price.

Wherever you shop for a used car, inspect the vehicle carefully for telltale signs of age or abuse. Variations in body color or a new paint job, for example, could mean that the car has been in a major accident. Worn pedals and steering wheel, or a sagging seat, point to wear and tear due to excessive driving. If there are scratches on the odometer face or holes in the plastic lens over the odometer, someone may have tampered illegally with the kilometre reading.

After you have inspected the car on the lot, road-test it as you would a new car. Start the car when the engine is cold. If the engine sputters or cuts out, a tuneup—or more—is needed. Test the shock absorbers on bumpy roads. Steer through winding curves to see how the car handles. The automatic transmission should not slip or hesitate as you shift gears. Unusual noises in the transmission, especially when accelerating, may point to expensive repairs. A car with a manual transmission should shift smoothly and quietly from low to high. Test the brakes; if the car pulls to one side, if the pedal feels spongy, or if you hear strange noises, something serious may be wrong. Do the odometer numbers move smoothly and properly? Test the parking brake on a steep grade.

Next, take the car to a garage or a CAA vehicle inspection center. Request a written estimate of the work that needs to be done, as well as the cost. Do not automatically reject a car with some flaws, but if you suspect it has been in a major accident, turn it down. Add the cost of repairs to the price, then decide if you are still getting a fair deal. Remember, the asking price is almost always higher than the vendor expects to receive, so be prepared to bargain.

Before you buy, inquire whether that model has been recalled, and if that particular vehicle has been repaired (and by whom). Simply call the manufacturer's customer-service office and give them the vehicle identification number. If the vendor will not permit an inspection or test drive, there is presumably something to hide.

You will usually receive a warranty from a new-car dealer, sometimes from a used-car dealer. Both may require that you return the car to the seller for any repair work covered. Be sure your warranty covers 100 percent of the cost of parts and labor. When a 50-50 warranty is offered, bills can be padded and you could end up paying for virtually all the work performed.

How much is it worth?

First, keep in mind how much you can afford. As with new cars, you should have enough cash to pay 25 percent down, plus license and insurance fees. Also budget up to 25 percent of the vehicle cost as a cushion for inevitable repairs.

Consult a used-car price book such as the FADA (Federation of Automobile Dealer Associations) *Canadian Red Book*. This monthly publication can be found in any public library or any financial institution that offers automobile loans. In it, you will find the wholesale and retail values of used cars. A car in bad condition or with a high odometer reading is worth less than the FADA wholesale price; a vehicle in excellent condition, with a low odometer reading, is worth more than the FADA retail price. Confirm your opinion by checking the newspaper classified ads for the average selling price of your make and model.

The buy-sell contract should clearly state:
- A full description of the vehicle, including the odometer reading.
- The full purchase price.
- The terms of payment.
- Trade-in allowance, if applicable.
- Any warranty or guarantee agreed upon. If a dealer claims to have installed new or rebuilt parts, these should be guaranteed.
- All repairs agreed upon by both parties, or a statement that the car is being sold "as is."
- The date of the agreement, and the names and addresses of both parties.

Read the agreement carefully, making sure all blank spaces are filled in or crossed out. The document is legally binding only when both signatures appear on it.

How to sell your car

Before you look for a buyer for your used car, get it ready and set a price. With a thorough cleaning, a mechanical check, and some attention to detail, you can increase the car's value by several hundred dollars. Timing can be crucial. Convertibles and sports cars, for example, are difficult to sell in the fall and winter, so wait until spring to put an ad in the paper.
- Clean the car inside and out—the body, windows, upholstery, carpet and floor mats, mirrors, tires, ashtrays, glove compartment, and trunk.
- A shiny, scratch-free finish can add value. Wax the body and polish the bumpers and hubcaps. Have any rust spots properly repaired and painted. If you have the entire car painted, however, some prospective buyers may assume you are covering up damage.
- Repair torn upholstery. You may also want to replace worn pedal covers and floor mats, although some buyers may interpret this as a sign that the car has had considerable—or even excessive—use.
- Clean up the engine compartment with an aerosol grease remover (but be sure to cover the distributor before you rinse) or have the engine steamed-cleaned.
- Check the levels of all liquids (brake, power-steering, clutch, and battery fluid, plus oil and water). If the engine oil is black and dirty, change it. Clean the battery terminals with a wire brush, and make sure the tires are properly inflated, including the spare. Check to see that the jack and spare tire are in place and that all lights are functioning.
- Consider having your car tuned so that the test drive will be a positive selling point for the prospective buyer.

Trading in on a new or used car is the simplest way to sell your vehicle, but you may not get the highest price. To obtain the best deal, show your car to several dealers, and bargain carefully with each of them before accepting an offer.

With a little extra effort, you can get the best price by selling privately. Place notices in local newspapers and classified-ad publications, some of which specialize in used automobiles. Your advertisement should be concise. Include the year, model, body style, condition, odometer reading (if low), major equipment (air conditioning, automatic transmission, AM/FM radio, for example), and telephone number. If you include the asking price in your ad, you will avoid answering many unnecessary telephone calls.

When showing the car, your honesty about its condition and defects will protect you against future complaints if the automobile proves defective in some way. If you have receipts for past maintenance repair, or a maintenance record such as that provided in the *Logbook*, the buyer will have greater confidence in your car. Should the buyer wish to test-drive the car, or have it inspected by a mechanic, go along.

Any loan you have on the car will have to be paid in full before you can transfer the car to a buyer. When the sale is made, insist on cash or a certified cheque. Then write a bill of sale and retain a signed copy.

To transfer the vehicle registration to the new owner, you must both go to a motor vehicle registration branch, taking along the license plates and registration. The buyer must pay the cost of a new registration, as well as the provincial sales tax.

Examine your coverage

In ten years of driving, chances are you'll be involved in at least one accident. Therefore your insurance coverage must be adequate. It will be determined, to some extent, by what you can afford.

Depending on where you live, rates for the same coverage can vary by as much as 70 percent from one company to another. Other cost factors include your age, sex, marital status, driving record, the type and age of your car, and the frequency of its use. There are often special discounts for nondrinkers, drivers over 65 years of age, drivers of compact cars, people with more than one car insured with the same company, drivers who have completed an accredited driving course, and drivers who have an accident-free record of more than five years.

Canadian car insurance protects you in Canada and the United States, but not elsewhere. If you plan to take your car outside North America, find out about insurance regulations from your representative well in advance. CAA members can obtain this information from their local club.

Automobile liability insurance covers damages to other people's properties and persons up to a specified amount. Also called "third-party liability" or "bodily injury and property damage" (BI and PD) coverage, this protection applies to accidents in which you are held responsible for causing property damage, or injury or death to innocent drivers, passengers, or pedestrians. But the minimum coverage required by law varies across Canada, from $50,000 to $200,000 (check with your agent or CAA club). If you are judged liable for an amount greater than your policy limit and you do not have additional coverage, you are personally responsible for the balance. Most companies, therefore, offer optional coverage, increasing third-party liability limits up to $2 million. A fourfold increase above your legal limit will add about 10 percent to your premium cost, a tenfold increase about 20 percent, and a twentyfold increase about 30 percent.

Every car owner in Canada must buy both BI and PD coverage. In Québec, the rules of settlement differ from those elsewhere in Canada. Québec motorists are insured against bodily injury liability by the government-owned Régie de l'Assurance Automobile. The fund is financed by levies attached to the yearly licensing fee. In addition, motorists' coverage for any property-damage liability is handled by the private insurance company of their choice. The Régie pays accident victims *regardless of fault*; legal action by an injured party to recover additional damages is not permitted. But if a motorist is innocently involved in an accident and seeks compensation for property damage, a claim must be filed with his or her private insurance company. By law, the company must make payments according to a legally determined scale. If a dispute arises, motorists must sue their own broker or agent, not that of the guilty party. The guilty motorist receives no property damage compensation unless he has collision insurance. Under certain circumstances, nonresidents may also be compensated for injuries sustained in an accident in Québec.

Protection against the indirect or long-term consequences of injuries to you and your family usually falls into two categories: accident benefits and medical payments insurance. This type of protection is available as *no-fault insurance*. Benefits are paid to you or your dependents regardless of who is responsible for the accident.

Accident benefits insurance provides some financial security in case of injury or death caused by an automobile accident, regardless of circumstances. This insurance will pay part of the medical or funeral expenses, a death benefit, or a disability income for any member of your family. It is compulsory across Canada except in Newfoundland and Prince Edward Island. In Québec, this kind of benefit is covered by the provincial liability insurance.

Medical benefit payments should take care of medical expenses which are not covered by your provincial or private health care plan. These benefits could pay for such "extras" as ambulances, special nursing care, or dental costs. The minimum amount offered varies from $2,000 in Nova Scotia, Prince Edward Island, and Newfoundland to $100,000 in British Columbia. In Québec, Ontario, Alberta, and British Columbia, medical benefits also cover special rehabilitation expenses.

Caution: If your provincial health insurance has lapsed, you will find help only if you reside in Québec. In the other provinces, accident benefits don't cover normal medical expenses.

Collision and comprehensive insurance, compulsory in Saskatchewan and Manitoba, protects you from financial loss. It is usually sold with a deductible amount chosen by the driver. The coverage is variously called collision, comprehensive, all-perils, or specified-perils insurance; each term has a slightly different significance.

The collision portion of your coverage will pay for repair or replacement of your car as a result of an accident, minus a deductible amount—usually $50 to $500. Choosing a higher deductible lowers your premium.

When your car is damaged, your insurance company has the choice of paying for repairing it or paying you its book value. If another driver is at fault, your insurance company will try to sue the driver responsible (or his or her insurance company) for compensation. Your insurer usually tries to recover your deductible at the same time.

Comprehensive insurance covers damages or loss of your car caused by anything other than a collision. It carries a deductible amount, usually $25 to $50. If your automobile is stolen, you are reimbursed, with no deductible charge, for the book value of the vehicle.

All-perils insurance combines comprehensive and collision insurance into a single policy with a single deductible. Specified-perils insurance covers specific mishaps only, including one or more of the following: fire, theft, lightning, wind, earthquake, hail, explosion, riot or civil commotion, falling aircraft, and rising water. If you have a special vehicle, such as an antique car, you may want to set its insured value by having it professionally appraised. This eliminates disputes about the compensation you should receive if the car is damaged.

Uninsured motorist insurance, which protects you from drivers who have no insurance, or insufficient insurance, is now included in all policies. It will make up the difference (to a specified amount) between your claim and the amount of liability insurance the other driver carries.

It pays to shop around. You could well be paying too much for your auto insurance—perhaps far too much. For one thing, insurance companies cover almost eight million vehicles annually and they are bound to make mistakes. For example, the accidental transposition of numbers, classifying you as 130 when you should be 013, would result in your insurance bill being four times higher than it should be. If in doubt, ask your agent to check and verify your classification.

The first step is to seek out a trustworthy insurance agent. One way of doing this is to base your selection on the experience of family and friends. Federal and provincial consumer services offices also provide guidance. CAA members can turn to their local club for expert advice and insurance coverage.

How well do you know your policy?

Car insurance policies—which are often couched in "legalese"—can be extremely complicated to understand. Are you familiar with what your insurance policy actually covers, and for how much? If you're like most people, you have never read your auto policy. In fact, you may not even possess a copy of the actual policy. Many Canadian insurers provide a copy of the policy only if it is requested.

Did you know, for example:

• If you have a claim against the insurance company for bodily injury, the company may be able to demand medical reports "as often as it reasonably requires" while the claim is pending. If you die, the insurer may have the right to order an autopsy to determine the exact cause of death.

• The insurance company probably doesn't have to pay if you rent or lease your car to someone else, if you use your car to carry explosive or radioactive materials, or if you use the vehicle as a taxi or sightseeing conveyance for pay. These circumstances all require additional coverage.

• If your policy carries an endorsement restricting occupant coverage in commercial automobiles and you carry more than three people in a pickup truck, you may not be covered. Never carry passengers in the back of a pickup; this practice is both dangerous and illegal.

• Your liability and accident-benefits insurance could be in effect if you borrow, rent, or lease a substitute vehicle while your car is being repaired or serviced, or if the car is lost, destroyed, or sold. But consult your insurance agent on this point if the repairs to your car are major and the substitute vehicle is to be used for some time.

• Your insurance company may be able to sue someone in your name, whether or not you agree to such legal action. In that case, if the insurance company has paid you for the damage caused by another driver, it is likely that it will sue to reclaim that money. It is legally entitled to sue in your name and to have your cooperation. If you refuse to cooperate, the company can sue you to get its money back.

These are just a few facts that may apply to you. If you don't have a copy of your policy, be sure to ask your insurance agent to send you one. A good agent should be willing to take the time to answer any questions you may have. Consumer inquiries are also answered by the Insurance Bureau of Canada, 181 University Avenue, 13th Floor, Toronto, Ontario, M5H 3M7.

How much is your car costing you?

After the purchase of your home, buying an automobile is likely to be your biggest single expenditure. In North America, the average car runs for ten years and 160,000 kilometres (100,000 miles), and has two to three owners.

The cost of a car can be broken down into two categories: the *fixed cost of ownership*, which you pay whether you use the car or not, and the *variable cost* of operating the car, which is determined by the distance you drive each year.

Fixed ownership costs include the purchase price (financing and depreciation, too), insurance, license and registration, parking fees, and garage rental. The purchase price is the highest cost. However, no matter when you sell or trade in your car, you will recover a portion of this investment. You can ensure maximum resale value by being conscientious about maintenance. If your car is a popular model with a good reputation for durability and fuel economy, the resale value will be high.

The part of your purchase price that cannot be recovered is depreciation—often the greatest expense of owning an automobile. Your car loses value most rapidly at the beginning of its life. A full-size domestic model depreciates about 25 percent in value when you drive it off the dealer's lot. After three years, it is worth about half the original list price, regardless of condition. Small cars and models with a reputation for reliability depreciate more slowly—about 35 percent in the first three years. After six or seven years, depreciation is no longer a major factor.

If you already own a car, it is probably cheaper to keep it than to invest in a new one. Insurance for your old car will cost less, and if the vehicle is more than four years old, the annual depreciation will be less than ten percent. However, maintenance costs rise over the years. You can safeguard against future problems by having a mechanic check your car, or by taking it to a vehicle inspection center. The Canadian Automobile Association operates such centers in most major cities. If the repairs will be more than half the value of the car, it is probably time to sell.

You can reduce a new car's depreciation if you buy at the end of the model year when extra discounts are available—the fact that the car is already one model-year old does not matter much if you plan to keep it for a long time.

You can further minimize depreciation by buying a used car in good running condition—with nearly half the depreciation gone and years of use left.

Insurance costs vary widely, depending on the amount of coverage you want; the make, model, and age of the car; the area in which you live; and your driving record (see pp. 18–19).

Finance charges are the interest you pay on an auto loan, or the interest you lose on money that is withdrawn from savings accounts or other investments in order to pay cash for a car.

Taxes and fees, including the annual registration fee and driver's license renewal fee, vary from province to province. In addition, when a car changes ownership, the buyer must usually pay sales tax and registration fees. In most places, you can save on sales tax by trading in your old car. In a trade-in, sales tax applies only to the difference between the trade-in allowance and the new-car price.

Your variable operating cost includes fuel, oil, maintenance, repairs, replacement parts, and tires. These expenses depend on the make and model of your car as well as on the distance you drive annually. A look at your individual operating costs, as recorded in the *Car Logbook*, can reveal possible ways of saving money.

Fuel expenditures are determined by the size of engine, its condition, the way the car is driven, and the grade of fuel used. Power brakes and steering, and particularly air conditioning, increase fuel consumption. By calculating your engine's fuel consumption, you can spot minor problems before they become major repairs. Always use the grade of fuel recommended by the manufacturer; it is a false economy to use too low a grade of fuel, wasteful to use a higher grade.

Oil must be added to the engine as necessary in order to maintain and prolong its life. Consumption of oil can vary significantly, even between two cars of the same model. Buying cheap oil and putting off an oil change will cost you money in the long run.

Maintenance, repair, and replacement costs also depend on the type of car, and can be an area for potential savings. For maximum safety, make sure your car is serviced at regular intervals. Costs vary from one garage to another; compare your savings in relation to the standard of workmanship you receive.

The annual cost of tires can vary tremendously, depending on distance driven, your driving habits, and the type of tire you use. Careful driving and maintenance, including proper inflation and rotation, can extend tire life considerably. Radials can last twice as long as conventional bias-ply tires.

How to calculate your ownership costs

Work sheet

1. Purchase price .... $_____
2. Sales tax on purchase.. $_____
3. Monthly installment payments (if any) .... $_____
4. Cost of a tire that fits your car... $_____
5. Price of fuel (per litre) .... $_____
6. Price of oil (per litre) .... $_____
7. Annual insurance premium.. $_____
8. Annual CAA membership fee .... $_____
9. Estimated daily parking cost .... $_____
10. Provincial annual registration fee.. $_____
11. Provincial driver's license fee .... $_____
12. Mechanic's hourly labor charge in your area .... $_____
13. Kilometres driven per year .... _____

Annual ownership costs

14. Depreciation (average over 10 years: 10% of original cost)..................... $_____
15. Insurance (line 7 above) .... $_____
16. Registration fees (lines 10 and 11) .... $_____
17. Finance charges (12 × line 3).. $_____

Annual operating costs

18. Fuel cost (annual litres × line 5)... $_____
19. Oil (annual litres × line 6) .... $_____
20. Tires × line 4 .... $_____
21. Maintenance and repairs.. $_____
22. Parking (250 × line 9, or actual days parked × daily cost)................... $_____
23. Total cost per year (add lines 14 through 22)................................... $_____
24. Cost per kilometre driven (line 23 ÷ line 13) .... _____ ¢

Average annual cost of owning and operating a car in Canada

Size of car	Variable costs (for 15,000 km or 9,320 mi, including gas, oil, maintenance, and tires)			Fixed costs (including insurance, license, depreciation)	Total costs (fixed and variable)
	Total	Per km	Per mile		
Standard 8-cylinder	$1,846	12.31¢	19.81¢	$4,655	$6,501
Standard 6-cylinder	$1,659	11.06¢	17.80¢	$4,179	$5,838
Compact	$1,459	9.73¢	15.65¢	$3,562	$5,021
Subcompact (standard transmission)	$1,295	8.63¢	13.90¢	$2,625	$3,920

How the law affects you

Whether you are a motorist or a pedestrian, highway regulations allow you to travel from one place to another with the least possible risk. In most cases, creating and enforcing motor vehicle and traffic laws is the responsibility of the provincial governments. All the provinces are members of the Canadian Conference of Motor Transport Administrators (CCMTA). This ensures the consistency of traffic regulations across Canada, and establishes reliable standards for roadway signs, signals, and markings.

As guidelines for driving behavior, traffic laws help you predict how other drivers will act. Although these rules of the road take some of the guesswork out of driving, good drivers nonetheless compensate for the faults of others. The rules below apply on all types of roads in Canada and most of the United States.

The basic rule of defensive driving, to be followed at all times: As a motorist, you should not proceed unless the road ahead is clear, and you should steer clear—and even stop—whenever necessary to avoid a possible collision.

You are entitled to assume—to a reasonable extent—that other drivers will observe the rules of the road, but you cannot stake your life on this. Everyone makes mistakes at one time or another, and the law says that it is the responsibility of the *last* person who could avoid an accident to do so.

Caution signs. A yield sign tells you that you must slow to whatever speed "due care" demands in present circumstances. This includes coming to a full stop to yield to any traffic that might constitute an immediate hazard. "Slow" signs, warning of turns, hidden intersections, or other possible hazards should be treated in the same way as flashing yellow lights.

Changing lanes. Indicate well in advance your intention to change lanes, and move only when there is room. Make sure the other lane is clear not only beside you but also behind you and ahead of you. On highways, the far right-hand lane is normally reserved for the slowest traffic (such as trucks) and for vehicles entering or exiting; the left-hand lane is reserved for passing. Any lanes in between are for through traffic moving at the average speed (see pp. 36–39).

Emergency vehicles are not exempt from the rules of the road. In emergencies they acquire the right-of-way over other vehicles. When you hear a siren or see the flashing lights of a police car, fire engine, ambulance, or other emergency vehicle, you must pull over to the right and stop, making sure you are clear of any intersection. It is an offense to follow a fire engine answering an alarm by less than 15 metres (50 feet).

Funeral processions must also respect the rules of the road. Vehicles in such a cortege must obey all traffic signals unless given clearance by a police officer.

Overloading occurs when a driver is crowded or when his vision is obstructed. Use common sense and the manufacturer's recommendations when loading your vehicle with baggage or passengers. Otherwise, you may be stopped by any police officer who considers your vehicle to be unsafe.

Passing involves overtaking another vehicle on its left, after making sure that the road is clear in both directions and signaling your intention. Passing on the right is permitted *only* when the driver ahead is making a left turn on a one-way street, or on roads or highways marked for multiple lanes. Passing is forbidden when a solid white or yellow line is on your side of the center line. It is usually illegal to pass on a curve, at an intersection or railway crossing, and on a bridge or in a tunnel.

Pedestrian crossings require an extra measure of defensive driving. The law protects a pedestrian who is using the crossing. At controlled intersections, a pedestrian must obey the signals, but once lawfully in the intersection, he or she has the right-of-way. Some provinces have pedestrian crosswalks at which all traffic in both directions must yield to a pedestrian. In some places, a pedestrian crossing in the middle of the block can be found guilty of jaywalking.

Police directions, including instructions from a traffic officer and an order to pull over and stop, supersede traffic signals and must be obeyed.

Railway crossings. Where flashers, flags, or other signals warn of an approaching train, you are required to stop more than 4.5 metres (15 feet) from the tracks.

Right-of-way rules, require one person to yield and let the other proceed first.

1. When two vehicles approach or enter an uncontrolled intersection at the same time, the driver on the right has the right-of-way unless otherwise posted.

2. Pedestrians crossing legally at intersections or on marked crosswalks have the right-of-way.

3. Drivers intending to turn left must yield the right-of-way to vehicles approaching from the opposite direction.

4. A vehicle leaving a driveway or alley must yield the right-of-way to vehicles on the street and pedestrians on the sidewalk.

5. When changing lanes, you must yield to any vehicle that is passing or is close enough to present a hazard.

Remember that having the right-of-way does not relieve you of the responsibility to do your utmost to avoid an accident.

Safety guards and flagmen are posted at intersections close to schools and highway construction sites. The rules of the road oblige you to obey their signals.

School buses. A motorist coming from *either* direction must stop when a school bus has its light flashing and is taking on or letting off children. The only exception is if the bus is on the other side of a divided highway.

Seat belts. Statistics prove that seat belts save lives, and carmakers are now obliged to install government-approved restraint systems in all new cars. The combination of lap and shoulder belts gives by far the best protection, provided they are properly adjusted (see pp. 64–65). Children up to age five should be strapped into approved car beds or car seats. The use of seat belts is mandatory in most provinces.

Signaling other drivers is required when you intend to stop or suddenly decrease your speed, to turn left or right, to change lanes, to leave the roadway, or to set your vehicle in motion from a parked position. Signals must be given well in advance by turn signal, stoplight, or hand and arm to allow other drivers to adjust their course. Never signal with your horn or headlights.

Speed limits, whether you see the signs or not, oblige you to drive at a reasonable and prudent speed. Even where signs are posted, you must drive at a safe speed for existing conditions, including snow, rain, fog, darkness, heavy traffic, and fatigue. Signs posting maximum speeds are sometimes supplemented by others setting minimum speeds or warning of restricted speed zones ahead. In some areas, there is a separate limit posted for night driving.

Stopping on a highway, if absolutely necessary, should involve pulling completely off the road onto the shoulder—if there is one. The safest course is to turn into a driveway or parking area.

Stop signs direct you to come to a full stop before entering an intersection. You are required to halt before reaching the painted stop line or crosswalk, and to yield to any pedestrian or vehicle close enough to constitute an immediate hazard. You may proceed through the intersection—with caution—only when the coast is clear.

Tailgating—following another vehicle too closely—is an offense. If you hit a vehicle from the rear, even in bumper-to-bumper traffic, you are considered guilty until proven innocent. A safe daytime following distance is two seconds, or about one car length for each 16 km/h (10 mph) of speed.

Traffic lights. A green light means that you may proceed through an intersection or turn left or right unless otherwise prohibited. When turning, you must yield to oncoming traffic and pedestrians, unless the light is flashing green (which indicates that oncoming traffic is facing a red light). Where a green light and a "walk" signal appear together, the pedestrian has the right-of-way.

When approaching a yellow light you may proceed with caution through the intersection—but only if you have insufficient time to stop safely. The yellow light is to clear the intersection, not to warn of an impending red light so that you can rush through.

A flashing yellow light signals you to slow down and proceed with caution; it indicates a potential hazard. Never shrug off this warning, even if you already know it marks a spot where other traffic must stop.

A red light means that you must stop until the signal changes. In some provinces, unless a sign indicates otherwise, you can turn right on a red light after first coming to a full stop and yielding the right-of-way to all traffic and pedestrians.

A red light in combination with a green arrow means that you can proceed only in the direction of the arrow. You need not come to a full stop but you must yield the right-of-way to other traffic.

A flashing red light has the same meaning as a stop sign. You must come to a full stop, yield to approaching traffic, then proceed cautiously into the intersection.

Turning. Having signaled, move cautiously as far to the left or right as possible in preparation for your turn. If making a left turn, you must yield to oncoming traffic. Whether turning right or left, you must first yield the right-of-way to pedestrians using the intersections lawfully.

U-turns are generally permitted where there is a long, unobstructed view with no traffic hazards, though regulations vary widely. Avoid making a U-turn on hills, curves, busy streets, and intersections with traffic signals.

Unmarked intersections, with no traffic signs, should be treated in the same way as intersections with four-way stop signs. You must yield to a vehicle or pedestrian entering the intersection. If two vehicles arrive at the same time, the driver on the right has the right-of-way.

British Columbia to Ontario

	BRITISH COLUMBIA	**ALBERTA**
Speed limits	Open highway, 80 km/h (50 mph) or as posted; residential and business districts, 50 km/h (30 mph); school and playground zones, 30 km/h (20 mph)	Open highway, 100 km/h (60 mph) during the day, and 80 km/h (50 mph) at night or as posted; urban areas, 50 km/h (30 mph) or as posted; school zones in urban areas, 30 km/h (20 mph), and in rural areas, 40 km/h (25 mph)
No passing zones	Indicated by a solid line on the right side of the center line	Indicated by a solid line in the center of the highway
Passing on the right	Prohibited, except on a one-way street, a multilane highway, or where a preceding vehicle is turning left	Permitted where there are two or more lanes on the same side of the center line
Right turn on a red light	Permitted after a complete stop, unless prohibited by a traffic sign	Permitted if not prohibited by a sign
Left turn on a red light	Permitted after stopping and yielding to other vehicles or pedestrians, and only when turning left onto a one-way street	Permitted at the intersection of two one-way streets, if not prohibited by a sign
Stops for railway crossings	Required as posted	Required as posted
Stops for school buses	Vehicles must stop for a bus with flashing red lights at the front and rear	Vehicles must stop for a school bus until the bus driver signals to proceed or the bus lights have stopped flashing
Highway parking	Prohibited	Prohibited. A vehicle on a jack must not be left unattended on a highway
Dimming headlights	Required when approaching an oncoming vehicle within 150 m (500 ft), or when following a vehicle within 150 m (500 ft)	Required when approaching an oncoming vehicle within 300 m (1,000 ft), or when following a vehicle within 150 m (500 ft)
Auxiliary driving lights	Two fog lights and two spotlights are permitted	Fog lights are permitted below headlight level, but they should not be less than 40 cm (16 in.) from the ground; spotlights are permitted
Seat belts	If a vehicle is equipped with seat belts, the driver and passengers must wear them	No regulation
Studded tires	Studded tires permitted from October 1 to April 30	Permitted
Windshield stickers	Permitted only if driver's view is unobstructed	No regulation

SASKATCHEWAN	MANITOBA	ONTARIO
Open highway, 80 km/h (50 mph) or as posted. Local speeds set by municipalities	Limited access highways, 100 km/h (60 mph); other highways, 90 km/h (50 mph) or as posted; urban areas, 50 km/h (30 mph) or as posted	Open highways, 80 km/h (50 mph) or as posted; cities, towns, villages, and built-up areas, 50 km/h (30 mph) or as posted; on some four-lane highways, 100 km/h (60 mph)
Indicated by a solid line in the center of a highway with marked lanes	Indicated by a solid line in the center of the highway	Indicated by a solid line in the center of the highway, and by a sign with a red circle and slash displaying one vehicle overtaking another
Permitted on a divided highway with at least two lanes	Prohibited, except on highways where the lanes are marked	Permitted when the vehicle is turning left, on one-way streets, and on streets and highways with two or more lanes in each direction
Permitted after a complete stop, except where otherwise posted	Permitted unless otherwise posted	Permitted after a full stop, unless otherwise prohibited
Prohibited	Permitted from a one-way street onto a one-way left, unless otherwise posted	Permitted from a one-way street onto another one-way street, after stopping and yielding to other traffic
Required when signal is given or as posted	Required as posted	Required as posted. Speed limit over the crossing, 30 km/h (20 mph)
Vehicles must stop for a school bus with alternating red lights	Vehicles must not pass a school bus that is loading or unloading, except on a divided highway	Vehicles must stop for a school bus when its red lights are flashing
Permitted on the right-hand shoulder as far as possible from the center	Prohibited on the roadway	Prohibited
Required when approaching an oncoming vehicle within 150 m (500 ft), or when following another vehicle within 60 m (200 ft)	Required	Required when approaching an oncoming vehicle within 150 m (500 ft), or when following another vehicle within 60 m (200 ft)
Fog lights are permitted; one spotlight is permitted	Fog lights are permitted. Residents must have special permits for spotlights	Fog lights are permitted; one spotlight is permitted
Front and back seat belts must be used in cars that are equipped with them	No regulation	If a vehicle is equipped with seat belts, both driver and passengers must use them
Permitted	Studded tires permitted from October 1 to April 30	Prohibited
Permitted only if driver's view is unobstructed	Permitted if driver's view is unobstructed	Permitted only if driver's view is unobstructed

Québec to Newfoundland

	QUEBEC	NEW BRUNSWICK
Speed limits	Autoroutes, 100 km/h (60 mph); outside cities, towns, and villages, and on numbered roads, 90 km/h (55 mph); other hard-surfaced roads, 80 km/h (50 mph); gravel roads, 70 km/h (45 mph); earth roads, 60 km/h (40 mph); earth roads in cities, towns, and villages, 50 km/h (30 mph)	Open highway, 80 km/h (50 mph), unless otherwise posted; cities and towns, as posted; residential or business districts, 50 km/h (30 mph)
No passing zones	Indicated by a single or double continuous line in the center of the highway	Indicated by a single solid yellow line on the right side of the center line
Passing on the right	Prohibited, except when passing another vehicle waiting to turn left	Permitted where the vehicle ahead is making a left turn, or on roads with two or more lanes of traffic moving in each direction
Right turn on a red light	Prohibited, unless a green arrow under a red light indicates a right turn permitted	Permitted after stopping and yielding to other vehicles and pedestrians if not prohibited by a traffic sign
Left turn on a red light	Prohibited, unless a green arrow under a red light indicates a left turn permitted	Prohibited
Stops for railway crossings	Required as posted. Stop should be 6 m (20 ft) from the track	Required as posted
Stops for school buses	Vehicles on an undivided roadway must stop for a school bus loading or unloading passengers. At such times, school buses must display flashing red lights	Vehicles must stop for a school bus displaying alternately flashing red lights
Highway parking	Prohibited	Permitted
Dimming headlights	Required when approaching an oncoming vehicle within 150 m (500 ft), or when following another vehicle within 60 m (200 ft)	Required when approaching an oncoming vehicle within 150 m (500 ft) and when following a vehicle within 60 m (200 ft)
Auxiliary driving lights	Fog lights are permitted; spotlights are prohibited	Fog lights are permitted but headlights must be turned off; one spotlight permitted
Seat belts	Driver and front-seat passenger must wear seat belts in cars built in or after 1974	No regulation
Studded tires	Permitted from October 15 to May 1, for vehicles under 2,268 kg (5,000 lb)	Permitted from October 16 to April 30
Windshield stickers	Permitted only if driver's view is unobstructed	Permitted only if driver's view is unobstructed

NOVA SCOTIA	PRINCE EDWARD ISLAND	NEWFOUNDLAND
Open highways, 80 km/h (50 mph) or as posted; residential and business districts, curves, intersections and school zones, 50 km/h (30 mph)	Designated open highways, 90 km/h (55 mph); other highways, 80 km/h (50 mph) or as posted; business districts and school zones, 60 km/h (40 mph); urban districts, 50 km/h (30 mph)	On paved portions of the Trans-Canada Highway, 90 km/h (55 mph); on other paved highways, 80 km/h (50 mph); unpaved roads, 60 km/h (40 mph); unpaved roads through settlements, 50 km/h (30 mph); municipalities, school zones, places of public assembly, as posted
Indicated by a solid yellow line on the right side of the center line	Indicated by a solid white line in the center of the highway	Indicated by a solid yellow line on the right side of the center line
Permitted when the vehicle ahead is signaling for a left turn, or when two or more unobstructed lanes are available	Permitted on one-way streets and multilane highways	Permitted only when the vehicle ahead is turning left or when two or more unobstructed lanes are available
Permitted, unless otherwise posted, after a full stop	Right turn permitted, unless otherwise posted	Permitted after a complete stop, unless otherwise posted
Prohibited	Left turn prohibited, unless otherwise posted	Prohibited
Required as posted	Required as posted	Required as posted
Vehicles must stop for a school bus with flashing red lights	Vehicles must stop for a school bus displaying alternately flashing lights	Vehicles must stop for school buses loading and unloading on roads outside St. John's and Cornerbrook. Vehicles may pass when the bus resumes movement
Prohibited	Prohibited	Prohibited
Required when approaching an oncoming vehicle within 150 m (500 ft), or when following another vehicle within 60 m (200 ft)	Required when approaching an oncoming vehicle, or when following another vehicle within 150 m (500 ft)	Required when approaching or overtaking another vehicle within 150 m (500 ft)
Two fog lights permitted; two spotlights permitted	Two fog lights permitted; one spotlight permitted	Fog lights are permitted when weather conditions warrant their use; spotlights can be used only when the vehicle has stopped
No regulation	No regulation	No regulation
Permitted from October 15 to April 30	Studded tires permitted from October 1 to May 1	Permitted from November 1 to April 30
Prohibited, except for inspection or other official stickers	Prohibited, unless authorized	No regulation

Pre-start routine and steering

Habits are easy to pick up—and often difficult to break. Make sure the habits you adopt for driving are good ones; it will be hard to correct them once they are established. The following eight pages present important guidelines on pre-starting and steering, braking, passing, gear-changing, and parking. If you are a new driver, take the time to study this section. If you are a veteran motorist, review it as a check against the habits you have developed over the years.

Good driving begins with a quick pre-start routine *before* you turn on the ignition. Before entering the car, look around it for anything from wayward pets to broken glass. Check the pavement for fresh leaks and trace their source before you move the car. Look for underinflated or damaged tires. Check for recent damage to the car body and to see that the front, side, and rear lights are clean. In winter, make sure that the entire car is clear of snow.

Periodically, and before each long trip, test the lights, turn signals, and emergency flashers. Check the engine oil level, the battery fluid, the windshield washer fluid, and the radiator coolant. Inspect all hoses, belts, and cables, and cast an eye around the engine compartment for any telltale signs of wear or leakage. Once inside the car, you should perform a few quick checks before starting the engine *(below)*.

Ten steps before you drive

1. Place the key in the ignition—but wait until you have completed all ten steps before starting it.

4. Check that the inside front, side and rear windows are clean and clear of frost or condensation.

7. Adjust the heating, ventilation or air-conditioning controls *before* you drive off. Always drive with at least one window opened a crack to provide fresh air and prevent exhaust buildup.

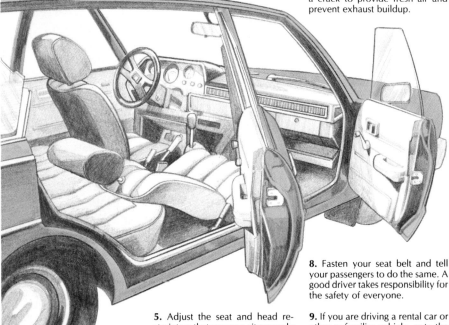

8. Fasten your seat belt and tell your passengers to do the same. A good driver takes responsibility for the safety of everyone.

2. Make sure all the doors are closed securely and locked. This will help keep you and your passengers safely inside—and unwelcome strangers outside.

5. Adjust the seat and head restraint so that you can sit squarely behind the steering wheel. You should be able to grip the wheel firmly at the 10-and-2-o'clock position. Make sure that you can reach the floor pedals easily. Position the head restraint at a point just above your ears.

9. If you are driving a rental car or other unfamiliar vehicle, note the location of gauges and indicator lights so that you can refer to them quickly. Be sure that you can operate all controls and switches easily without taking your eyes off the road.

3. Store all packages in a secure place to prevent them from shifting around, possibly causing injury or interfering with your driving. Make sure they do not block your field of vision.

6. Set the rear-view mirrors so that you have to shift only your eyes—not your head—for maximum visibility. Always set the mirrors *after* the seat is adjusted. Use the day or night setting as needed.

10. Make sure the car is in *Neutral* (or *Park*) and the parking brake is set before you start the engine. Remember to signal, check the rear-view mirrors, and look over your shoulder to check the blind spot before you pull out into traffic.

The steering "clock"

To begin a hand-over-hand turn to the right, grip the wheel firmly in the 10-and-2-o'clock position.

When your right hand reaches 6 o'clock, release it and cross over the left hand to 10 o'clock.

When the turn is completed, reverse the sequence.

Steering and tracking

As soon as the car is in motion, you must be able to keep it heading in the desired direction—this is called *tracking*—by responding with constant steering corrections. Your ability to maintain steering control depends on two key factors: directional control—the ability of a car to hold a straight line; and cornering ability—the ability of a car to round a curve without loss of precise control. Poor directional control and cornering ability can be the result of road or weather conditions; such poor handling may, however, signal problems with the car—in its suspension or steering system, for example. How the vehicle is loaded can also influence tracking. The higher and heavier the load, the less stable the vehicle will be.

For the best steering control when tracking in a straight line or through a slight turn, grip the outside rim of the steering wheel at the 10-and-2-o'clock position. Focus as far ahead as possible in the center of the path you intend to take—you will tend naturally to steer in the direction you look. If you stare too close to the car, you will miss gradual changes in your position and track poorly. Beginning drivers frequently make the mistake of using the middle of the hood or edges of fenders to steer by. It is better to use an imaginary line down the middle of your intended path of travel.

Crosswinds, uneven road surfaces, low tire pressures, passing trucks and excess wheel play can all cause a car to wander. Steering corrections must begin as soon as the car starts to move from its intended path. Some drivers wait too long, allowing the car to move farther off course than necessary. As a result, the driver may overcompensate by turning the wheel too far in the opposite direction, necessitating a second steering correction. This can lead to a "sawing" mo-

tion as the driver turns the wheel back and forth. Correct adjustments, while very slight, should become automatic as you learn to look down the road.

To track smoothly through a sharp turn, use the hand-over-hand steering technique illustrated above. Look through the turn to where the road straightens out again, and allow sufficient room for the back of the car to clear the inside of the turn. Keep in mind, especially when driving a truck or hauling a trailer, that the rear wheels take a different path (with a smaller radius) than the front wheels in a turn.

When the front of the car reaches a point halfway through the turn, start to recover, and return the wheels to their straight-ahead position. If you hesitate during recovery, the car will start to oversteer, requiring corrective steering.

Backing up is a simple maneuver if you think of the rear of the car as the front whenever the transmission is in *Reverse*. Turn your head and body to the right until you can see clearly through the back window (don't rely on your mirrors alone for backing up). Place your right hand and arm over the back seat. Then grasp the top of the steering wheel with your left hand and select the point to which you want to steer.

If you want to back up in a straight line or make slight adjustments, simply move your left hand and the steering wheel slightly left or right in the direction you want the rear of the car to move. To back up around a corner, turn your head and body in the direction of the turn so that you can see clearly through the rear and side windows. Keep your hands at the 10-and-2 position and use the hand-over-hand steering method. Again, turn the steering wheel in the direction you want the back of the car to follow.

Braking, turning, and passing

Many factors—road surface, tire condition, weather, and your speed—determine stopping time and distance. As a driver, you must be constantly aware of these factors and adjust your speed accordingly. To stop a vehicle a driver must do three things:

• Recognize a need to stop (this is called *perception time*).

• Release the gas pedal and move to the brake (*reaction time*).

• Depress the brake pedal and bring the vehicle to a stop (*braking distance*).

The purpose of *controlled braking* is to minimize the third factor—to stop the car in the shortest possible distance without losing directional control. This is accomplished by applying pressure to the brake pedal without making the wheels *lock* (stop turning). Under most conditions, apply firm, steady pressure to the brake pedal. However, under the stress of trying to stop quickly, drivers often overreact and lock the wheels. If one or more of the wheels lock and the car starts to skid, reduce brake pressure momentarily so that all wheels start to roll again. Brake again with steady, moderate pressure.

Use your brakes gently and sparingly. Extended hard braking builds up heat, which reduces stopping power. Repeated hard braking can produce a condition called *brake fade*, in which the brake linings get so hot that they lose their ability to keep the wheels from turning (disc brakes are far less susceptible to fade). To avoid fade, braking should start well in advance of a stop. The amount of pressure should be just enough to bring the car to a smooth, steady stop.

Wet linings also affect braking ability and can double the distance needed to come to an emergency stop. This condition can be caused by condensation (especially in humid weather), or when brake drums are flooded by surface water. If you drive in heavy rain or through a deep puddle, pump your brakes gently; the friction will generate enough heat to evaporate any moisture.

When determining your speed and position in traffic, observe other vehicles around you. For example, if the vehicle ahead has a sagging rear end or other suspension problem, it will need more space to make a rapid, controlled stop. When you are stopped at a light, you might notice a bald or under-inflated tire on a nearby vehicle—both will increase stopping distances. Overloaded vehicles, trucks, buses, and campers require greater stopping distances, and will have more difficulty holding a straight line while braking. The braking ability of motorcycles is good at lower speeds. However, at highway speeds braking is complicated by the risk that the rider may lose control and skid.

How to take a curve

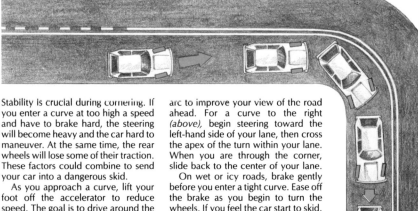

Stability is crucial during cornering. If you enter a curve at too high a speed and have to brake hard, the steering will become heavy and the car hard to maneuver. At the same time, the rear wheels will lose some of their traction. These factors could combine to send your car into a dangerous skid.

As you approach a curve, lift your foot off the accelerator to reduce speed. The goal is to drive around the bend under constant throttle—neither speeding up nor slowing down—to keep the car balanced. As you exit the turn, accelerate slightly.

When driving on a multilane highway, stay in the center of your lane throughout the turn. On a two-way road, you can "flatten" the turning arc to improve your view of the road ahead. For a curve to the right *(above),* begin steering toward the left-hand side of your lane, then cross the apex of the turn within your lane. When you are through the corner, slide back to the center of your lane.

On wet or icy roads, brake gently before you enter a tight curve. Ease off the brake as you begin to turn the wheels. If you feel the car start to skid, let up on the accelerator and steer in the direction of the skid to recover. Remember that the more the wheels are turned, the more they will act like plows. If a sharp turn is necessary, turn the steering wheel a little at a time, rather than steering sharply all at once.

Proper passing procedures

Passing—particularly in two-way traffic—is one of the most demanding maneuvers that a motorist makes. It need not be a dangerous, white-knuckle experience provided you follow the correct procedures for passing safely. The first rule is to recognize where *not* to pass. Never pass as you approach a curve, the crest of a hill, a railroad crossing, an intersection, an underpass, or a narrow bridge. In all these cases your vision will be at least partially obstructed. Never pass if there is a solid stripe dividing the road, and never pass just because the driver ahead signals you by. Despite his good intentions, he may inadvertently lead you into a dangerous trap.

Three-lane, two-way roads are particularly hazardous. If such a road is otherwise unmarked, the first car into the center (passing) lane from either direction has the right of way. Use the center lane only for passing, and return as quickly as possible to the right lane.

Avoid leapfrogging. There are few things more annoying than a driver who slows down after passing and forces the trailing driver to hit his brakes or do a leapfrog of his own. When you return to the right lane after passing, maintain a steady speed at least as fast as the car you just passed.

When passing on a two-lane road you may realize that an oncoming car is traveling much faster than you first thought. This is a classic emergency situation: You must decide whether to gun the accelerator or fall back into line. The correct response is to brake firmly and pull back into the right lane.

Passing on a multilane highway

Is your path clear? Identify a four-second planned path while maintaining a two-second following distance behind the car ahead. If you are tailgating, there is simply no way to see around the car ahead. If you are following a large truck, the huge blind spot directly behind it won't allow the driver to see you.

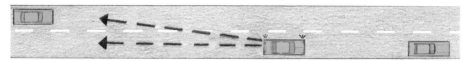

Check the mirrors. Is there anything in, or approaching, the lane you wish to enter? Early signaling of your intentions will reduce the chances of a following car pulling out as you begin your maneuver. Just before moving, check over your shoulder and confirm that there is a four-second gap in the new lane.

Change lanes quickly. Your passing speed should not be more than 16 km/h (10 mph) faster than the speed of the vehicle you are passing. If you have to drive faster, you're probably passing unsafely (unless the other vehicle is moving much too slowly). When you are well past the other vehicle, use your right turn signal and glance back over your right shoulder before returning to the lane.

Passing on a two-lane highway

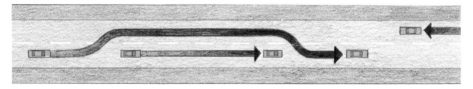

Passing on a two-lane road is a hazardous maneuver. In addition to the checking required for a lane change, you must now also watch for cars coming toward you. As a result, you must make critical time and distance judgments. Do you have time to complete your pass and return to your lane? If you increase your speed to pass another car at highway speed, it will take approximately 9 to 10 seconds to complete the pass. If you and the approaching car are both traveling at 90 km/h (55 mph), the total distance covered will be about 0.5 km (.3 mi). This means that to pass safely, you will need almost 0.8 km (.5 mi) between you and the oncoming vehicle.

Although it is difficult to measure these variables, there is a useful guide to determine a safe time and distance gap at highway speeds. When you start to pass, any oncoming vehicle should be far enough away so that it appears to be standing still. Assuming that the road is straight, the vehicle will appear to be motionless at distances of 0.8 km (.5 mi) or more.

Shifting gears

The combination of brake, gas, clutch, and shift lever may seem confusing at first, but with practice the various steps will become second nature. Before starting the engine, shift into *Neutral* and set the parking brake. Push the clutch to the floor with your left foot, and keep it there as you turn on the ignition (this reduces engine load).

With the clutch depressed, shift into first gear. Press down on the brake pedal with your right foot and release the parking brake. Remember to check the rear-view mirrors and to look back over your shoulder to your blind spot. Signal your intention to move out into traffic.

Let the clutch up slowly until it reaches the *friction point* (the point where the clutch first takes hold). Hold it there momentarily. Move your right foot from the brake to the accelerator and press down gently. Slowly let the clutch up the rest of the way. Always keep your eyes on your path of travel; *never* look down at your feet.

Once you have the car moving ahead smoothly in low gear—at about 25 km/h (15 mph)—you are ready to change to second gear. Without taking your eyes off the road, press the clutch pedal to the floor and release the accelerator pedal. Move the shift lever through the neutral position and into second gear. Release the clutch pedal as far as the friction point and hold it there for an instant while you press down on the accelerator. Release the clutch pedal all the way.

From stop to start in first gear

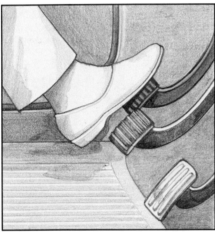

1. Push the clutch pedal to the floor. Shift into first gear and release the parking brake.

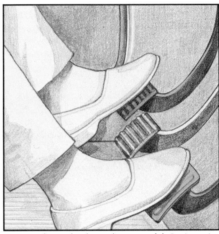

2. Press down slowly on the gas pedal. Begin easing up gradually on the clutch.

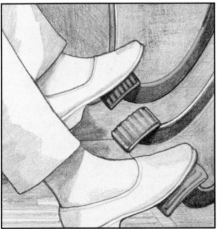

3. Ease up on the clutch until the friction point is reached. Slowly give the car more gas.

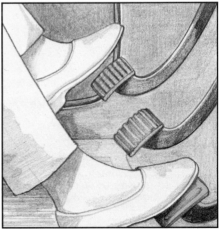

4. Release the clutch as the car begins moving. Press down on the accelerator to pick up speed.

The same procedure applies to shifting into third, fourth and fifth (overdrive) gears. Since each car and engine combination is different, consult your owner's manual for the speed ranges recommended for each gear. Divide the maximum speed given for each gear by two to get the approximate speed for gear changing. The friction point for first and reverse gears is more pronounced than it is for second, third, or fourth gears. With the higher gears, the car has more momentum and thus less resistance when shifting.

Sometimes it is necessary to *downshift*—to go from a higher gear to a lower one. Downshifting increases the engine's power and decreases the car's speed. This is necessary when ascending steep hills, moving slowly in heavy traffic, or turning corners. You may also want to downshift on long, steep, downhill roads, to make use of the braking power of the lower gears.

To downshift from third to second gear, for example, release the gas pedal and press the brake pedal. Press the clutch pedal to the floor, then shift from third into second gear. (If you are going uphill, shift quickly and do not brake; otherwise you will quickly lose momentum.)

The cardinal rule for driving with a manual transmission is *never ride the clutch pedal*. Driving with the pedal partly depressed wears out the clutch rapidly. When you stop for a traffic signal on a hill, do not ride the clutch to keep the car from sliding back; this is a sure way to ruin the clutch. Instead, depress the clutch pedal completely and hold the car with the brake.

Unfortunately, few people use their car's gears properly. One of the commonest mistakes is being in the wrong gear—a dangerous and uneconomical habit. It is hazardous because if you are in too high a gear, it is difficult to escape from a situation that requires quick acceleration. It is wasteful because you will use more gas and strain both the engine and transmission.

Experience and "feel" will tell you when to shift. Do not try to reach the maximum speed in each gear before shifting. Listen to the engine and change gears when it begins to labor. Most cars will apparently start off easily in second gear, but you should always use first gear to minimize clutch wear and prevent engine strain. For maximum economy, drive in top gear whenever possible (see diagram at right). In general, a car will consume as much fuel moving the first 20 m (66 ft) from a stop as it does to cover 0.5 km (1/3 mi) at 60 km/h (40 mph) in top gear.

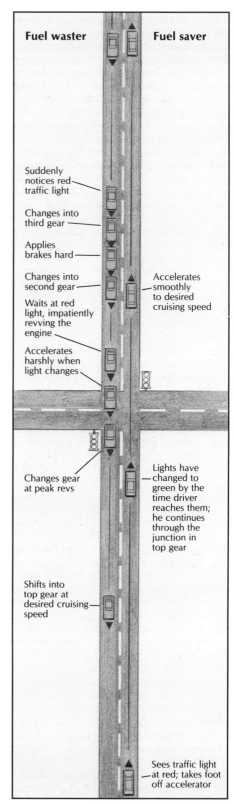

Fuel waster — **Fuel saver**

Suddenly notices red traffic light

Changes into third gear

Applies brakes hard

Changes into second gear

Waits at red light, impatiently revving the engine

Accelerates harshly when light changes

Changes gear at peak revs

Shifts into top gear at desired cruising speed

Accelerates smoothly to desired cruising speed

Lights have changed to green by the time driver reaches them; he continues through the junction in top gear

Sees traffic light at red; takes foot off accelerator

The art of parking

Parking ranks high among the challenges of driving. With practice, however, no one should have to circle the block endlessly looking for a "better" spot.

Angle and perpendicular parking are the maneuvers most often required in parking lots and shopping centers. Although the procedures are simple, they must be performed slowly and carefully to avoid ending up with a scratched or dented fender.

Once you spot an empty space, signal your intention to turn. Check the rear-view mirrors and watch for cars backing out of adjacent spaces. Approach the empty space slowly, at a distance of about 1.5 m (5 ft) from the line of parked cars into which you plan to move (about 2 m if you are parking perpendicular to the curb). As your leading fender draws even with the space, turn sharply. Be mindful of the rear quarter of your car on the side you're cutting. Move slowly into the parking space, straightening the wheels so that the car is centered between adjacent vehicles. Be sure that there is enough room for you and your passengers to open the doors without banging any cars next to you. If the car is not squarely parked, back out carefully and reposition it.

When you exit from an angle or perpendicular parking space, your side and rear visibility will be extremely limited. As a result, you must proceed slowly when backing out into traffic. Once you have shifted into *Reverse* and the car begins to move, keep your foot poised over the brake pedal. Check constantly to the side and rear for vehicles, pedestrians, and obstacles. Use your mirrors, but don't trust them completely. Pay special attention to your blind spot—an inattentive pedestrian may be walking there. Back straight out until your windshield is in line with the rear bumper of the cars parked on each side. Turn sharply so that you do not back into the opposite lane of traffic. Be sure that the front bumper will not strike the rear of the adjacent car. When you have cleared the space, turn the steering wheel rapidly in the opposite direction to straighten the front wheels. Stop, shift into *Drive* or first gear, and move forward, remaining alert for other cars backing up. Keep in mind that nearly five percent of all urban accidents result from cars leaving parking spaces or driveways.

With practice and adherence to a five-point procedure (facing page), *parallel parking* need not intimidate you. The key is to judge if a parking space is large enough—usually a distance at least 1.5 m (5 ft) longer than your car. Learn to turn sharply while the car is moving slowly; it is easier on both you and the car's steering than turning the wheels when the car is stopped.

To leave a parallel parking space, signal your intention, check the mirrors, and look over your shoulder to the blind spot. Turn sharply as you move forward, leaving the space at a 45-degree angle to the curb. Make sure the front bumper has room to clear the car parked ahead. Once the steering wheel is in line with the rear bumper of the car ahead, recover it and straighten out the front wheels. Watch for approaching traffic, especially from the rear.

When parking on a hill, a simple procedure must be followed to keep the car from rolling away. To park facing downhill, move forward slowly, turning first away from the curb, to give the inside front wheel clearance, then sharply toward the curb. Stop when the inside front wheel touches the curb without rolling over it. Remember that to move from this parked position, it will be necessary to back up slightly to give the inside front wheel clearance to turn.

To park facing uphill, move forward slowly, turning the wheels sharply to the left as far as they will go. Move about 1 m (3 ft), then stop. Allow the car to roll back slowly until the inside front tire touches the curb. Where there is no curb, turn the front wheels sharply in the *opposite* direction (toward the side of the road). Then, if the parking brake slips, the car will back off the road rather than swing into traffic. Whenever you park on a hill, be sure that the car is in first gear or *Reverse* (or *Park*), and that the parking brake is set securely.

You should not stop, park, or leave your vehicle on a highway when it is possible to do otherwise. If you must stop on the road, regulations require that your vehicle must be visible for at least 125 m (400 ft) in each direction. If you become stranded beside a multilane highway, place flares or warning triangles behind the vehicle. On a two-lane highway, also put an additional signal *ahead* of the vehicle to warn oncoming traffic (see pp. 172–173).

There are areas where no parking is permitted. The obvious locations are designated by signs and/or curb markings. Never park on a crosswalk, in a loading zone, or at a bus stop. Resist the temptation to "stand" in a no-parking zone while you run a quick errand. This practice invites both parking tickets and theft. Know the laws in your province and community regarding the distances you must park from intersections, fire stations, fire hydrants, and railway crossings.

Five steps to parallel parking

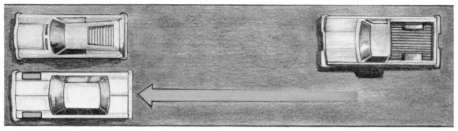

1. Signal a stop, checking the rear-view mirrors. Pull up exactly parallel to and about 1 m (3 ft) away from the car ahead. This starting position is important, so check it carefully.

2. Shift into *Reverse* and back up slowly, steering sharply to the right until the car is at a 45-degree angle to the curb and the steering wheel is in line with the rear bumper of the car ahead.

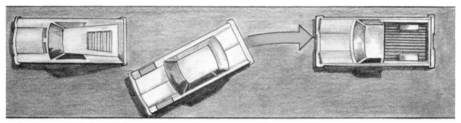

3. Straighten the front wheels while continuing to back up slowly until the right front bumper is in line with the rear bumper of the car ahead. Your right rear wheel should be about ¹/₂ m (18 in.) from the curb.

4. Keep backing up slowly, steering sharply to the left. Make sure the right front bumper has enough space to clear the car ahead. Stop when the car is parallel to the curb without rubbing against it.

5. Shift it. *Drive* and move forward slowly, straightening the wheels. Stop midway between the cars ahead and behind. If you are parking on an incline, position the wheels before leaving the car.

Predict and react to highway traffic

The basic rules of defensive driving—stay alert, concentrate, anticipate—require special application when you are traveling at high speeds. Common highway hazards range from tailgaters and truck convoys to stranded vehicles and hitchhikers (see pp. 38-39). Coping with these situations requires efficient management of both time and space. On the road you must constantly adjust your speed and position in response to other traffic. You should:

• *identify* important elements such as other vehicles, pedestrians, and road conditions;

• *predict* potential conflicts in your path of travel, or hazards in other directions;

• *decide* on the best course of action to safely avoid the hazard;

• *act* by braking, steering, or accelerating out of trouble (or a combination of these).

Defensive driving is more than a matter of carefully positioning your car in relation to front and rear traffic *(below)*. It also requires *lateral* or side positioning. This means keeping as much space as possible between your vehicle and other traffic or obstacles on both sides—at least a car width (2 m or 6 ft) at highway speeds.

It is also essential to simplify situations when you are faced with several hazards at the same time. For example, you should

Managing time and space

1. Maintain at least a two-second gap between your car and the vehicle ahead. To determine this following distance, select a roadside marker such as a signpost or telephone pole. As the car ahead passes the marker, begin counting "one-thousand-one . . . one-thousand-two." If you have passed the sign before counting two seconds, slow down, then test yourself again. In poor weather, at night, or in heavy traffic, increase this margin to three or four seconds.

2. Plan for the unexpected by having an escape route. As you drive, identify an immediate path of travel. This is where you want to be four seconds from now. Next, select an alternate path—where you would steer if your immediate path was suddenly blocked. If the car ahead makes a panic stop, for example, can you safely steer to the right or left? This four-second gap is best determined by counting, and is more accurate than the older method of estimating car lengths.

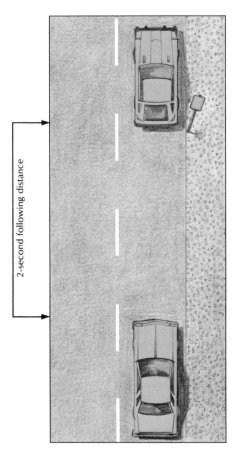

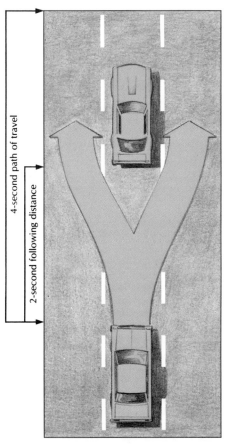

adjust your speed to avoid meeting a large truck on a narrow overpass, particularly if you suspect that the surface will be slippery there. Then, if either your car or the truck begins to skid, you will have room for evasive action without risking an accident.

At times, however, separating hazards is not so easy. If a car suddenly swerves into your lane, you may have to brake enough to avoid a collision, but not so hard that you will be rear-ended by a following vehicle. Resolving these two hazards into a single course of action involves compromise, something a motorist must do constantly on a busy highway or in city traffic.

When choosing your path of travel, ask yourself these four questions:
• Does your lane provide the best visibility? Position yourself to permit a minimum 12-second line of sight.
• Do you have sufficient space on each side? You should have a safety margin of at least one car width.
• Does your lane have the smoothest flow of traffic? This path usually has the most space and best visibility.
• Do you have an escape route (or, better still, two alternatives)? It's better to drive out of trouble than to instinctively slam on the brakes when trouble threatens.

---

3. Look farther down the road, too. An adequate visual lead time is necessary for choosing an immediate path of travel. Your advance warning should be at least 12 seconds, and may increase to 20 or 30 seconds for high-speed driving. You will need this much time to pass another vehicle, for example, but should not do so unless you can see what lies ahead. If there is a knot of traffic or a stalled car, or if you are approaching your exit, you will have time to react.

4. If a curved stretch of highway is uncrowded, you can "straighten it out." Instead of following every curve, choose as straight a line as possible, cutting from shoulder to center line, if necessary. This will reduce the actual distance you travel and the amount of fuel you use. On the road below, the difference in length between routes A and B is about seven percent. Always signal lane changes, watch for other cars coming from behind, and never cross the center line.

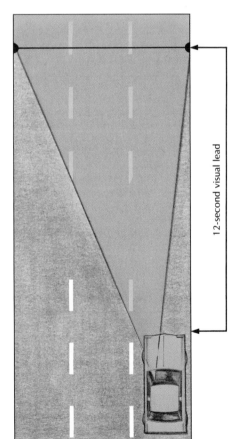

12-second visual lead

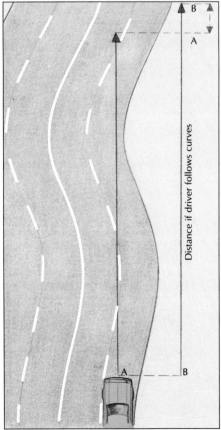

Distance if driver follows curves

High-speed defensive driving

Contrary to popular belief, this country's controlled-access highways are the *safest* roads to drive. (The fatality rate for Canadian highways is about half the national average for all roads.) However, these high-speed routes present special challenges and demand quick, sure judgments.

If you are unfamiliar with the route, prepare for a highway driving trip by studying a road map beforehand. Then you won't have to rely completely on sometimes misplaced or misleading road signs, which will distract you from watching the road. Jot down route and exit numbers (including the towns where they are located), as well as key checkpoints along the way.

As you drive down the entrance ramp to enter a highway via an acceleration lane, signal your intention to merge with highway traffic. If there is a car ahead of you, don't make your move until that driver has merged

successfully. Do not come to a full stop on the entrance ramp unless absolutely necessary—you will disrupt drivers behind you and risk a rear-end collision.

Select a gap in the flow of traffic large enough to ensure that you will not block traffic, and move in quickly. (If there is a stop sign rather than an acceleration lane, you will need to wait for a longer gap in traffic.) Before you merge, try to accelerate to a speed not lower than 16 km/h (10 mph) under the minimum limit for the highway. If the posted minimum speed is 70 km/h, for example, you should enter the highway at a speed of at least 55 km/h. Once you have merged, don't lag behind the flow of traffic.

To exit, move into the right lane at least 1.5 km (1 mi) before the exit, and signal your intention well ahead of turning. Do not risk passing a slower vehicle within this distance from the exit. Note the posted ramp speed,

A bird's-eye view of highway hazards

Tailgaters are an annoying and dangerous highway hazard. Move to the right lane, reduce your speed, and signal the vehicle to pass. Do not brake; instead, switch on the emergency flashers to activate your brake lights.

A **hitchhiker**, anxious for a lift, has one foot on the pavement. When driving on a highway, scan the shoulder for such smaller hazards, not just cars and trucks. Do not stop unless it is an obvious emergency.

Passing on the right can be both dangerous and illegal. Instead of waiting for the other vehicle to return to the right lane, this impatient motorist has slipped by on the right side. The other driver is now in his blind spot.

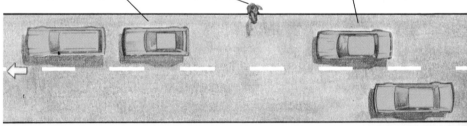

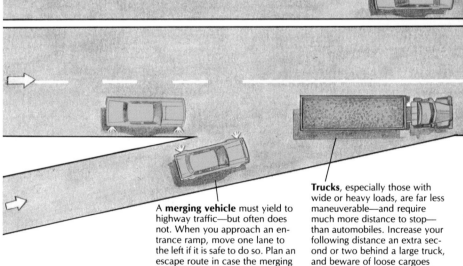

A **merging vehicle** must yield to highway traffic—but often does not. When you approach an entrance ramp, move one lane to the left if it is safe to do so. Plan an escape route in case the merging car swerves in front of you.

Trucks, especially those with wide or heavy loads, are far less maneuverable—and require much more distance to stop—than automobiles. Increase your following distance an extra second or two behind a large truck, and beware of loose cargoes such as sand, gravel, or wood.

and be prepared to brake for a tight curve. Vehicles entering and exiting the highway are sometimes forced to merge in a *weaving lane (below)*. Be especially careful of vehicles crossing your path at high speed here—from the left if you are entering the highway; from the right if you are exiting.

At 100 km/h (60 mph), you will need approximately 100 m (328 ft) to stop on a dry, smooth road. Be able to anticipate a possible hazard far beyond that distance. Watch not only the car directly in front of you, but also the cars beyond. Often a car much farther down the road will tip you off to the first signs of trouble with a flash of brake lights or a cloud of dust. Use your mirrors (and check your blind spot) constantly. If you are driving at a speed of 80 km/h (50 mph), a car that you spot 100 metres behind you and moving at 110 km/h (70 mph) will be able to overtake you in a matter of seconds.

Drive with the flow of traffic unless, of course, the cars around you are speeding. Check your speedometer frequently; a clear stretch of highway or steep downgrade will invite speeding. Be a loner in highway traffic. Don't drive beside other cars except to pass, and especially don't hold a position in another car's blind spot. Avoid convoys—several cars or trucks driving together at high speed. A swerve or panic stop by one of them could mean disaster. If a convoy or tailgater approaches you from behind, lift your foot off the accelerator to slow down (do not brake) and let it pass quickly.

Stay to the right on all highways, with two exceptions. On a multilane road, you may use all but the far left lane for normal driving. And as you approach an expressway entrance, move one lane to the left if traffic permits to make room for those drivers trying to merge from the right.

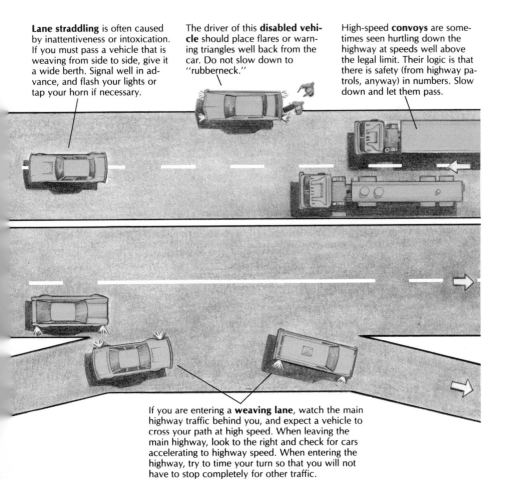

Lane straddling is often caused by inattentiveness or intoxication. If you must pass a vehicle that is weaving from side to side, give it a wide berth. Signal well in advance, and flash your lights or tap your horn if necessary.

The driver of this **disabled vehicle** should place flares or warning triangles well back from the car. Do not slow down to "rubberneck."

High-speed **convoys** are sometimes seen hurtling down the highway at speeds well above the legal limit. Their logic is that there is safety (from highway patrols, anyway) in numbers. Slow down and let them pass.

If you are entering a **weaving lane**, watch the main highway traffic behind you, and expect a vehicle to cross your path at high speed. When leaving the main highway, look to the right and check for cars accelerating to highway speed. When entering the highway, try to time your turn so that you will not have to stop completely for other traffic.

The urban obstacle course

Most drivers spend a large part of their time in city traffic, where they are likely to encounter every traffic situation from the serenity of a quiet residential neighborhood to the madness of a downtown traffic jam. The keys to safe city driving are patience, courtesy, and the assumption that something unexpected can happen and probably will.

Short trips, stop-and-go driving, and slow speeds are hard on a car. You use the brakes more frequently driving around town than on longer trips. On short trips the exhaust system does not get hot enough to evaporate the moisture that has condensed in the muffler and tail pipe, encouraging rust. Slow driving tends to increase carbon buildup in the engine, particularly if you use regular gasoline. Your tires may rot before they wear out. After five years, the rubber valve stems may start to leak; this may be the case if your tires gradually lose their air pressure, even after being properly filled.

One way to keep your car running well is to take it out on the highway once a week and drive a few kilometres at the legal speed limit. Premium (high-octane) gasoline will help burn off excess carbon and should improve engine performance. Remember that the amount of time your car is driven is as important as the distance driven in determining the frequency of oil and filter changes, lube jobs, and tune-ups.

Observation and anticipation are crucial skills in congested downtown traffic. You need to be aware of many things at once: other vehicles, pedestrians, parked cars, cyclists, traffic lights, road signs, and intersections. Keep your eyes moving; you will need to rely heavily on your peripheral vision to take in everything around you. Develop the habit of checking the rear-view mirrors, as well as your blind spot, at least once every 15 seconds—urban traffic patterns change quickly and with little warning.

Be especially cautious at intersections. If you are turning, move into the correct lane well in advance. If you find that you are hemmed in the wrong lane by surrounding traffic, do not change lanes abruptly. Drive on until you can turn off, go back, and make the maneuver safely.

If you see that cars are blocking your way on the other side of an intersection, do not begin to cross, even though you may have a green light or the right-of-way. Wait until your way is clear to prevent blocking cross traffic, even if you must wait out another red light. While moving forward in traffic, avoid race-and-brake driving, which annoys other drivers and wastes gas.

Many pedestrians who are involved in accidents have never driven, and so have never learned how much time and distance is needed to stop a moving vehicle. It is your responsibility as a driver to stay on the lookout for pedestrians, who are both vulnerable and unpredictable, and allow them enough time to cross the street. An adult may take five or six seconds to cross, a child seven or eight, while an older person may need eight to twelve seconds. Elderly strollers may also suffer from impaired eyesight or hearing loss and can be expected to react more slowly. A blind person, recognized by a white cane or seeing eye dog, *always* has the right-of-way.

Most pedestrian accidents in busy downtown areas occur at intersections, where drivers often fail to stay alert for people on foot. Instead, they give most of their attention to traffic signals or other cars. The greatest number of pedestrians are struck by a vehicle just as they step into the street. The car is most often in the lane closest to the sidewalk and is usually driving straight through the intersection. The driver, who has anticipated a safe path through the crossing, is unable to respond fast enough when a pedestrian suddenly steps out into traffic. Adding to the problem is the pedestrian's failure to accurately judge the speed of traffic and the amount of time needed to cross the street. Drivers can cope with such situations by reducing speed, covering the brake, and watching for sudden movement.

Watch the car ahead of you; rear-end collisions are the most common type of city driving accident. Be aware, too, of the *type* of vehicle you are following. Taxis and buses may pull out into a line of traffic or stop unexpectedly; delivery trucks often double park without warning; motorcycles and mopeds may weave unpredictably; emergency vehicles may make sudden U-turns.

Cyclists must follow some of the rules for motorists, and some of the rules for pedestrians. They are more limited in their ability to steer and stop than many drivers believe, and must cope with more problems. For example, such things as railway crossings, gravel, storm drains, and puddles present major hazards for cyclists, who may swerve in front of you to avoid them. Give bicycles as much leeway as possible, moving into the left lane on a four-lane roadway.

Suburban streets create special traffic problems. Here, most accidents occur in the middle of the block. Meter-readers, postal employees, or delivery men, all concentrating on their jobs, are apt to walk into your path. Residents may step into the street while mowing lawns or sweeping their sidewalks. Dogs are often unleashed and may chase your car. The absence of sidewalks in many suburban residential areas forces pedestrians of all ages to walk on the road itself, and encourages children to use the street as a playground.

Childhood pedestrian accidents peak between the ages of five and six years. These children often dart out into the street with no thought to traffic. Motorists, on the other hand, are often unaware of the cues that should make them especially alert for children. Driving in residential areas should trigger a type of scanning called *ground search*. Slow down and search for movement under and around parked cars, trees, bushes, and fences. And remember that behind every ball that bounces into the street a child is likely to follow.

A minute in downtown traffic

City streets can seem like an endless obstacle course. Drivers must be alert to traffic movement, pedestrians, and potential hazards. In the space of a few seconds, they must take into account many of the following situations:

1. A taxi that could suddenly swing into traffic.

2. A group of pedestrians who may carelessly become jaywalkers.

3. A jaywalking pedestrian.

4. A tailgater who is too close to the car ahead.

5. A parked car, which may be blocking your view of a pedestrian or road sign.

6. A child playing with an unleashed dog—either could dart into the street.

7. A driver who has jammed on his brakes.

8. An ambulance entering the intersection.

9. An elderly pedestrian in the intersection.

10. A stopped school bus about to discharge children.

11. A cyclist who may swerve to avoid a storm drain or pothole.

12. A delivery truck emerging from a blind alleyway.

Rural roads—slow but scenic

The extensive network of country roads and secondary highways that crisscross Canada are seldom as peaceful and relaxing to drive along as they may seem. Concentration and anticipation are required to cope with twisting highways, unpaved roads, animals, slow-moving farm vehicles, and other familiar country hazards.

In most parts of Canada, the law requires that you reduce speed on open access country roads, no matter how clear your path. (For provincial speed regulations, see Rules of the Road, pp. 24–27). However, slower speeds will allow you to sightsee. If you want to savor a particular bit of scenery, find a safe place where you can pull over. Driving too slowly can be as dangerous as speeding—an impatient driver may try to pass when it isn't safe to do so. Besides, driving demands all your attention.

Curves, rises, and dips in country roads will often restrict long-distance visibility, making it difficult to maintain a 12-second line of sight. Sunlight through overhanging trees can cast deceptive shadows, especially if you are wearing sunglasses. Trees and hedges by the roadside may block your view of an intersection, driveway, or road sign, or disguise a soft shoulder. As you drive, scan the road ahead for advance warning of any upcoming dangers. A break in roadside foliage may tell you that you are approaching an unmarked driveway; skid marks before a bend indicate that the turn may be sharper than you think. You may be able to spot the line of an access road across a field ahead, or hear an approaching train before you actually see the crossing.

Be alert to signs. However battered or faded the signs may be, believe all warnings of such hazards as curves, hidden drives, narrow bridges, and animal crossings. Remember that country road signs are often obscured by trees, knocked askew, or missing altogether. Watch for reduced-speed signs close to towns, intersections, and schools. Occasionally the limits they impose seem unreasonably low, but it is better to crawl along for awhile than to risk a speeding ticket—or to hit a child.

The center line provides important information about the likelihood of a hazard ahead. Where this line changes from a series of dashes to a solid single or double line, proceed with greater caution and do not try to pass. The word "slow" painted on the road is always there for a good reason and should never be ignored.

Reduce your speed in trouble spots. As you approach an intersection, the crest of a hill, or even a gentle curve, let up on the gas momentarily. Around the corner may be a slow-moving tractor or stopped school bus. This won't slow you down very much, but it will reduce the reaction time necessary to move from the gas pedal to the brake if you have to stop unexpectedly. Use your horn, if necessary, to warn oncoming traffic when approaching blind, narrow curves or underpasses. On a hill, always give the traffic going up the hill priority, particularly heavy vehicles. Do not try to pass on a hill, unless there is an extra lane for that purpose.

The design and condition of country roads vary considerably, and you should adjust your speed accordingly. Never trust a shoulder until you have determined that it will support the weight of your car, and that you won't become mired in mud. When pulling off the road, watch out for drainage ditches, which may be hidden by weeds or snow. Secondary roads often suffer severe frost damage and are repaired less frequently than main highways. After a hard winter the edges may be crumbling, the paved surfaces potholed and cracked. Farm machinery which has been working in muddy fields will lay a slippery trail of mud along an otherwise dry roadway.

Clouds of dust churned up on dirt roads will obscure your vision and that of drivers behind you. Slow down until you can see clearly through your rear window. Gravel and other rough surfaces are hard on tires; the faster you drive, the faster they will wear out. In addition, flying stones thrown up by spinning tires can chip your paint or puncture your exhaust system.

Weather affects country roads much more than well-traveled highways. After a prolonged period of hot, dry weather a shower can produce extremely slippery conditions. Autumn leaves on a damp road will have the same effect. On a cold winter morning when the sun has melted the snow in places, watch for icy patches where trees shade the road. When driving in ski country after a snowstorm, don't expect secondary roads to be plowed as early as major routes.

Strong winds, which push vehicles around and strew fallen branches across the road, are a common cause of accidents on country roads. The swaying of roadside trees will warn of strong winds. If you see a car ahead veer suddenly to one side, brace yourself for gusts of wind at that point. When emerging from a protected stretch of highway into an open area, be prepared to compensate for sudden crosswinds by turning the steering wheel toward the gust.

Tractors, animals, and adventure highways

Tractors and other slow-moving vehicles are familiar sights on country roads—and are involved in at least ten percent of all rural auto accidents. During the fall, harvesters are often used around the clock, so they could be met on roads between fields at any time of the day and night. However, even the best and most modern tractors will move considerably slower than the average family car. Their drivers may be oblivious to traffic approaching from behind, especially if they are wearing ear protection. Before passing, signal your presence to the driver with horn and headlights and, preferably, wait for some indication that he has seen you before proceeding. By law, all slow-moving vehicles must display a special warning sign—a fluorescent red triangle with a dark red border.

Animals. The behavior of large animals, even normally docile cows, is unpredictable, and a collision could cause serious damage. Even if the animals are being tended, slow down well in advance and let them pass. When approaching a horse and rider, slow down and be prepared to stop if necessary. Drive past the horse slowly and give it as wide a berth as possible. Wild animals are a particular hazard in mountainous and forested areas, especially at night. The best defense against such accidents is the same kind of ground search recommended for driving in residential areas. Use your judgment before swerving to avoid an animal on the road. The options aren't pleasant, but often the lesser evil is to hit an animal rather than risk a skid or collision with another car.

Northern roads link the Trans-Canada Highway and other southern routes with remote settlements —and offer vacationers a bit of adventure. The best-known Northern route is the Alaska Highway, which stretches 2,436 km (1,514 mi) between Dawson Creek, B.C., and Fairbanks, Alaska (1,900 km are in Canada). From Grimshaw, Alberta, the Mackenzie Highway reaches north across 940 km (584 mi) of prairie and forest to Fort Simpson, N.W.T. The Dempster Highway touches the Arctic Ocean at Tuktoyaktuk, N.W.T. Both car and driver must be well prepared for this wild and remote country. Have your vehicle fitted with a protective underbody shield and front screen, carry at least two spare tires, and take along a first-aid kit, flares, tool kit, and a reliable road map.

The special demands of darkness

Although the total number of accidents that occur is smaller after dark than in the daytime, the number of traffic fatalities is *higher*, and the ratio of deaths to kilometres driven is three times greater. Nighttime accidents are most often linked to four factors: inattention, fatigue, drinking, and poor visibility. When you drive in darkness, your depth perception and, therefore, your reflexes and judgment are severely limited. However, you can train yourself to "see" in the dark, anticipate hazards, and compensate for the bad habits of other drivers.

Allow your eyes to adjust to darkness before driving at night, particularly if you are leaving a brightly lit place. It will take half an hour before you are able to see at 80 percent efficiency, and up to an hour before your night vision is at its best. If you are tired, don't drive; your reaction time will be significantly slower than when you are rested and alert. If drowsiness overcomes you while you are driving, pull over and rest.

Are you one of the 20 percent of drivers with a vision problem? Have your eyes checked if you find night driving particularly strenuous. You may be afflicted with anything from tunnel vision to nyctalopia—night blindness—which could make night driving difficult and dangerous. Your doctor might recommend that you avoid driving altogether after dusk.

At night, until objects are illuminated by headlights, you will see them as silhouettes against the darkness, or by the shadows they cast against a dimly lit background. You may miss a pedestrian who is dressed in dark clothing, or an object which does not reflect enough light to be visible. Focus on the edge or outline of anything you spot—you will perceive it more sharply than if you look directly at it. Develop the habit of using your peripheral (outer) vision, which is less affected by darkness than central vision.

Be especially alert around dusk. At this in-between time the sky is still fairly bright, but objects begin to merge with their shadows. (Dawn light will have the same effect.) Turn on your lights even though you may think it is too early in the evening. In fact, traffic safety experts now recommend driving with lights on *at all times* (see below).

As darkness descends, move your eyes constantly as you scan the road ahead. By shifting your line of sight every few seconds, you will widen your field of view and

High beam or low beam?

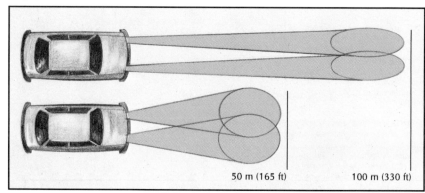

50 m (165 ft)   100 m (330 ft)

Most headlights on high beam and in good working order light up the road for about 100 m (330 ft) ahead. Low beams illuminate about half that distance, and are directed downward so as not to blind oncoming drivers. However, low beams have a slightly wider field, which is an advantage on twisting country roads. As a rule, drive with your high beams for maximum visibility unless you are within 150 m (about 500 ft) of another vehicle. The quality of the light emitted by the headlight depends more on the cleanliness of the lens and the brightness of the reflector mirror than on the wattage of the bulb. Modern headlights, of great optical precision, must also be aimed and adjusted periodically (see pp. 130–131).

Many safety experts and consumer groups now recommend using low-beam headlights *whenever* you drive, day or night. Professionals, such as bus drivers, have followed this practice for years, not to see better, but to be seen by others. Although remembering to turn headlights on—and off—in broad daylight might seem inconvenient, their use would reduce daytime accidents in Canada by an estimated 20 percent.

Never use your headlights to "talk" to another driver: to signal your intention to pass, slow down, or pass, or to invite the other driver to do so. If either driver misinterprets the message, a serious accident could result. Rely instead on turn indicators, brake lights, and hand signals.

Keep your eyes moving

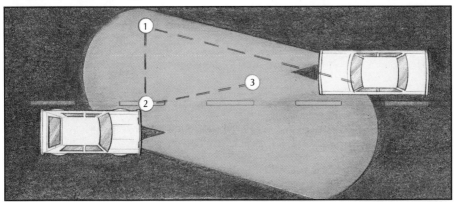

The *three-point scan (above)* is an effective technique to minimize glare and reduce eye fatigue. Focus on a point toward the right side of your lane (1), higher than where the light meets the pavement. Then glance across to the left (2), to a point alongside the approaching vehicle (avoid looking directly into the headlights). Complete the triangle by shifting to a point midway between your car and the oncoming vehicle (3). Remember, too, that your headlights illuminate *only* the road directly in front of the car. When rounding a curve *(right)*, slow down and anticipate what lies ahead.

sharpen your perception of detail. Avoid focusing on one point, particularly the taillights of the car ahead, for more than a few moments. Lights, road signs, or a reflective center line can have a hypnotic effect.

Keep your windows clean. A dirty windshield will not only restrict your vision, but will also increase the glare of oncoming headlights. Try not to smoke while driving at night. It will cloud the passenger compartment and smudge the windshield if the car is not properly ventilated.

Increase your following distance at night, and allow a greater margin of safety when overtaking and passing. You may find it useful to follow another car on a poorly lit or unfamiliar road, but maintain a following distance of at least three or four seconds (see pp. 36–37). Most important, don't "overdrive" your headlights. You must be able to stop within the distance illuminated. Use low-beam headlights when another vehicle approaches (as the law requires), regardless of what the other driver does.

Your headlights help you to see and be seen by other drivers. Whenever possible, use your high beams for night driving, low

beams for dusk, dawn, and fog. Switch to low beams when following another car, and when approaching the crest of a hill—you could dazzle and disorient a driver coming from the other side.

Do not try to judge the distance of an oncoming vehicle from the size and spacing of its headlights. The lights of a compact car will be closer together than those of a truck, for example, and will make the smaller vehicle seem farther away. When you spot a single headlight, play it safe and hug your side of the road. It is probably a motorcycle, but could also be a large car or truck with a missing left headlight.

Keep your headlights as clean as your windshield. Dirt can cut their effective illumination by half. Should your headlights go out, pull off the road immediately. Loss of one light usually means a burned-out bulb. Drive carefully to the nearest service station and have it replaced. If both lights fail, a faulty fuse may be the cause. If a replacement fuse does not solve the problem, you will need to call an emergency road service or drive slowly, with flashers on, to the nearest garage.

Taming wet weather hazards

Rain and fog can drastically reduce both visibility and traction. Driving in bad weather is also fatiguing; concentration becomes difficult in a pounding rain or thick fog. Both can drown out surrounding traffic noises, and muffle the sounds that warn a driver of other vehicles. Switch on your low beams in rain or fog, not to see better, but to be seen by others. (Many expert drivers use their headlights at all times, regardless of weather conditions.) Don't hesitate to use your horn to warn other motorists of your presence, especially when turning left, rounding a sharp curve, or entering a multilane highway. Increase your following distance from two to at least three or four seconds. Slow down, to a crawl if necessary, and pull over when conditions become too treacherous. In lightning storms, stay in your car. The insulation provided by the rubber tires will protect you from electric shock.

Rain can limit vision so much that you cannot see the edges of the roadway or the car ahead. Keep the windshield and windows as clean as possible. Turn on the defroster and fan, or open the windows slightly, to keep them from fogging up with condensation. To avoid smearing the windshield, wait until it is completely wet before turning on the wipers (or use the washers). Heavy rain can overload the wiper blades, allowing an almost continuous sheet of water to flow over the windshield. Reduce your speed even more to compensate.

In the first 30 minutes of even a light shower, water mixes with the dust and oil on the pavement to make the surface dangerously slick. In heavy rain a car's tires can actually begin to ride up on a thin layer of water. This phenomenon, called *hydroplaning,* begins at about 55 km/h (35 mph); at 90 km/h (55 mph) your tires may lose their traction entirely (see pp. 170–171). Bald tires are particularly dangerous because their treads are not deep enough to drain surface water. Instead, the water forms a wedge between tire and road. This loss of traction results in lack of control.

Drive with a firm but gentle touch in wet weather. Avoid jerky starts or stops, or sharp turns that could trigger a skid. If you must negotiate a deep puddle, drive very slowly. Hitting still water at high speeds is like hitting a brick on the road—the impact could jerk the car into a skid. Reducing your speed will also keep water from splashing under the hood and possibly stalling the engine. If you do stall, try to coast out of the puddle and off the road to dry out the engine. Wipe the spark plugs, cables, coil wire and the inside of the distributor cap with a rag, or use a moisture-dispersant spray.

Bad-weather lighting

Using too little—or too much—light is the most common error of driving in bad weather. Rain and fog particles both reflect and scatter light. Never use parking lights on their own in these conditions—moisture in the air will disperse this weak illumination and effectively render the car invisible *(right, top).* On the other hand, do not use high beams in rain or fog, because a large proportion of their light will be reflected back into your eyes. Low beams, which shine down onto the road surface, are most effective *(bottom).* Before entering patches of fog, flash your brake lights to warn other drivers that you are slowing down.

If you drive frequently in poor weather, consider a pair of fog lights (check provincial regulations first). Fog lights should be mounted low on the vehicle, but not so close to the ground that they will become coated with road dirt. The right beam should be angled slightly to the curb; the left beam directed so that it illuminates the center line without dazzling oncoming vehicles.

Stopping distances on wet roads

The type and condition of your tires will greatly affect your stopping distance on wet roads. The tire's grip depends on the weight of the tire as well as on the adhesion between the rubber and the pavement. Abrupt changes of direction or speed transfer weight from one tire to another, further upsetting the handling and braking balance. The comparisons below are based on an emergency stop made from 100 km/h (60 mph), and allowing a reaction time equivalent to 18.5 m (60 ft)—the minimum distance it will take to recognize a hazard and apply the brakes.

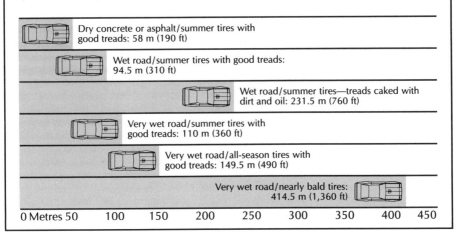

Dry concrete or asphalt/summer tires with good treads: 58 m (190 ft)

Wet road/summer tires with good treads: 94.5 m (310 ft)

Wet road/summer tires—treads caked with dirt and oil: 231.5 m (760 ft)

Very wet road/summer tires with good treads: 110 m (360 ft)

Very wet road/all-season tires with good treads: 149.5 m (490 ft)

Very wet road/nearly bald tires: 414.5 m (1,360 ft)

0 Metres 50   100   150   200   250   300   350   400   450

Fog can descend rapidly and unexpectedly. It not only reduces visibility, but also distorts the appearance of objects. A dense fog can be frightening and disorienting as familiar landmarks and driving situations become suddenly unfamiliar. Be aware of the psychological as well as the physical limitations of driving in fog.

The density of fog determines how much vision is limited. It can be as slight as an early-morning haze, or so dense that it is difficult to see even the front of your car's hood. Spotty fog is especially hazardous because its density can change abruptly. You may be driving at high speed with good visibility and, before you can react, the fog can become extremely thick. Your 12-second visual lead could, in an instant, be cut by 80 percent, or eliminated completely. Another problem is that dense fog will cause moisture to accumulate on the windshield without you realizing that visibility has been reduced. Occasional use of the wipers will prevent this.

In many cases, you will be forewarned of fog. If you see ground fog in a field or ditch beside the road, chances are you'll soon run into a patch on the road itself. Early morning mists are soon burned away by summer sun, but tend to linger in spring and fall. Slow down and be ready to turn on your lights if they are not already on.

Once into a patch of fog, watch your speedometer. The disorienting effect of fog often lulls motorists into driving too quickly for prevailing conditions. Never use high beams—the droplets of water will reflect the light and bounce it back into your eyes. Open a window to prevent condensation and to help you hear the sounds of traffic.

Increase the gap between you and the car ahead. Although it may seem helpful to follow the taillights of another vehicle, particularly a large truck with a better view of the road, it will be difficult to judge following distance accurately. Another problem is that fog appears deceptively thin in the wake of a large vehicle. Above all, don't be lured into one of those 10- or 20-car convoys that swoop through fog, each car following the taillights of the car ahead. Chain collisions are a particular hazard in fog—a recent disaster in California involved 234 vehicles.

When visibility drops to three or four car lengths, pull off the road completely and wait for the fog to lift. Don't leave your driving lights on—you may be rear-ended by a driver who thought you were still moving. Instead, use your emergency flashers.

In case of an accident, get everyone out of the car immediately and well away from the highway. If you stay behind to help, listen carefully for the sound of approaching vehicles. Place flares or warning triangles well back from a vehicle stranded in fog (see pp. 172–173), and switch on your emergency flashers.

Preparing for winter's worst

Your car must be running at peak efficiency to meet the challenges of a Canadian winter. Any preventive measures taken in the fall will pay off once temperatures drop, and will help prolong the life of your vehicle. Of course, you are safest to avoid driving altogether in bad winter weather. But if you must drive, make sure your car is properly prepared and outfitted.

Tires. Steel-belted radial snow tires have several advantages over bias-ply tires. While conventional tires tend to stiffen at below-freezing temperatures, radial tires remain flexible to −15°C (5°F). Radials also offer less rolling resistance—and therefore better handling—on dry pavement. And new "four-season" radials can be left on all year long. For best traction, mount radial snow tires on all four wheels. Your car's cornering performance will benefit, as well as straight-ahead traction and stopping. Never mix radial and bias-ply snow tires; the combination may seriously impair handling. Studs improve traction dramatically on snow and ice, but their use is restricted in most provinces.

Cooling system. Severe cold taxes the car's heating and cooling system. In the fall, inspect all hoses, radiator connections, and heater components (132–135). If any part is corroded, worn, loose, or damaged, have it replaced. Consider replacing your thermostat with a "high-range" thermostat, which will remain closed until the engine has warmed up. A grille cover will retain heat under the hood, to help keep the engine and heater at proper operating temperatures.

When flushing or topping up the system, add enough antifreeze to protect the engine down to the lowest temperature expected in your area. If you do not drain the system, check the coolant with a hydrometer, and add antifreeze if necessary. A year-round mixture of 50 percent antifreeze and 50 percent water is generally recommended. A higher concentration of antifreeze actually *raises* the coolant freezing temperature.

Electrical system. For quick, reliable starts in cold weather, begin with a good battery (pp. 128–129). Even a battery that was reliable all summer long will lose half its power once the temperatures dip below freezing. If the case is cracked or if it will not hold a charge, replace the battery with a new one. If you live in a particularly cold area, buy a

---

Winter tire choices

All-season tire is usually a radial with an "aggressive" tread that is a compromise between summer and snow treads. It is useful on dry roads or light snow, but does not provide sufficient traction on heavy snow or slippery ice.

Snow tire has wide, ribbed treads that bite through loose upper layers of mud, snow, slush, or gravel. On dry roads, however, snow tire has a smaller contact area and tends to wear out more rapidly than conventional tire.

Chains provide the best traction on snow and ice, but they can damage tires. Use them only for short distances at low speeds. Steel-link chains, with or without cleats, are the most common type. Make sure chains fit your tires.

Keeping your engine warm

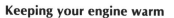

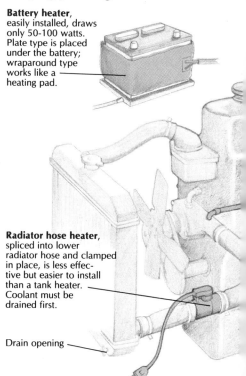

Battery heater, easily installed, draws only 50-100 watts. Plate type is placed under the battery; wraparound type works like a heating pad.

Radiator hose heater, spliced into lower radiator hose and clamped in place, is less effective but easier to install than a tank heater. Coolant must be drained first.

Drain opening

battery with at least 20 percent more cold cranking power than that normal.

Next, be sure that the other electrical components are in good condition. Check the spark plugs and cables, distributor, starter, and the various headlights, bulbs, and fuses. Replace any wiring that has frayed or cracked insulation. Once the ignition system is tuned up and winterized, finish the job by applying waterproofing solution to all exposed ignition wires.

Fuel system. Check the fuel filter and replace it according to the schedule in the owner's manual. Any clogging will thin the air-fuel mixture—the opposite of what is desired in winter. Clean or replace the air filter and PCV filter if necessary (pp. 114–115).

To prevent ice from forming in the carburetor or fuel line, add a container of fuel-line antifreeze (usually isopropyl alcohol) to your tank every second or third fill-up. If your car must stand outside in temperatures below −20°C (−4°F), add fuel-line antifreeze with each tankful. Keep the tank more than half full at all times, to reduce icing.

Brakes. Perform a fall test on your brakes by driving on a dry, straight road. The brakes should not grab, drag, make noise, or pull the car to one side. With the car standing still and the engine idling, press the brake pedal firmly. If the pedal feels spongy, there may be air in the hydraulic line. If the pedal fades, you may have leaks in the master cylinder, hydraulic lines, or wheel cylinders (see pp. 122–123). Finally, have your mechanic inspect all brake linings.

Exhaust system. The danger of carbon-monoxide poisoning to you and your passengers is greatest in winter, when most driving is done with the windows closed. To prevent this hazard, give the exhaust system a thorough inspection and replace any part that is leaking or shows signs of corrosion. Make sure that all clamps holding the tail pipe and muffler are tight and in good condition.

Winter car kit. Carry the following items in your car, so that you can handle almost any winter emergency: flashlight, flares, booster cables, bag of sand or salt, traction grid, scraper and brush, matches and candles, blanket, shovel, extra hat and warm gloves, windshield-washer fluid, and first-aid kit (see pp. 186–187).

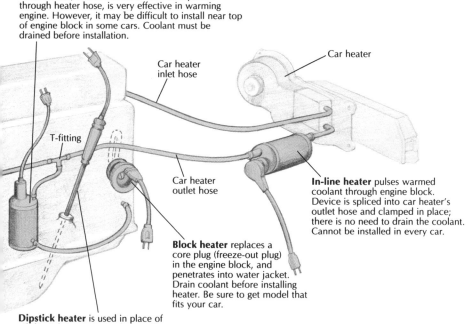

Tank heater, which warms coolant as it passes through heater hose, is very effective in warming engine. However, it may be difficult to install near top of engine block in some cars. Coolant must be drained before installation.

Car heater

Car heater inlet hose

T-fitting

Car heater outlet hose

In-line heater pulses warmed coolant through engine block. Device is spliced into car heater's outlet hose and clamped in place; there is no need to drain the coolant. Cannot be installed in every car.

Block heater replaces a core plug (freeze-out plug) in the engine block, and penetrates into water jacket. Drain coolant before installing heater. Be sure to get model that fits your car.

Dipstick heater is used in place of oil dipstick to warm crankcase oil. (Dipstick must be replaced before starting car.)

Caution: Diagram illustrates locations of various engine heaters. Do not install more than one heating device on your engine unless recommended by a mechanic.

On the go through ice and snow

Before setting out in poor weather, check the weather forecast and road conditions so that you know what to expect en route. Clean the snow off the windshield, windows, hood, roof, trunk, headlights, and taillights so that it won't slide down onto the windshield or swirl up suddenly to block your vision. A push broom is most effective for clearing off heavy snow—you may want to keep one in the trunk for this purpose. Clean the dirt off all lights front and back, and make certain the exhaust isn't clogged with snow or slush. If the windshield is coated with ice, start the car and let the defroster melt it while you scrape. In a pinch, a credit card will serve as a substitute scraper.

In our cold climate, an under-the-hood heater is a good investment for any car that is not parked or stored in a warm garage. A $50 heater will soon pay for itself by easing start-ups and reducing engine wear. An engine block heater is the most efficient but also the most expensive. Battery warmers and dipstick heaters are simpler and less expensive (see pp. 48–49).

To prevent battery drain when starting the car, make sure that the heater-defroster fan and the lights are off before turning the key. Cold temperatures drastically reduce battery power, so don't run the starter too long. If the engine doesn't catch immediately, turn off the ignition, wait a few seconds, then try again. You may need to make several attempts—wait a moment between each. Don't pump the gas or you may flood the engine (see pp. 178–179).

Let the motor run for a minute or two before starting off, but do not let it idle for too long. It may be tempting on cold mornings to let the car warm up for several minutes while you finish breakfast, but excessive idling harms the engine. Check your owner's manual for the length of warm-up time recommended for your car. Engines of cars with both automatic choke and automatic transmission tend to race when you first start up. Wait a few minutes until the engine has regulated, especially before driving on a slippery surface or in heavy traffic.

Accelerate slowly, avoiding sudden turns which may trigger a skid. Inexperienced drivers often make the mistake of speeding off too quickly on slippery surfaces. If yours is a manual transmission, accelerating in second gear instead of first will give you better traction on an icy surface. With automatics, drive in *High* to reduce wheelspin.

If you are unaccustomed to winter driving, sharpen your reflexes by practicing in a safe area—such as an empty parking lot. Learn to "read" the road by observing the way your car handles in various conditions. Gently tap your brakes occasionally to test for traction on snow, ice, and freezing rain.

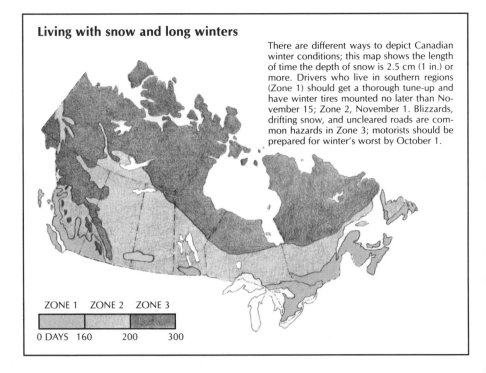

Living with snow and long winters

There are different ways to depict Canadian winter conditions; this map shows the length of time the depth of snow is 2.5 cm (1 in.) or more. Drivers who live in southern regions (Zone 1) should get a thorough tune-up and have winter tires mounted no later than November 15; Zone 2, November 1. Blizzards, drifting snow, and uncleared roads are common hazards in Zone 3; motorists should be prepared for winter's worst by October 1.

ZONE 1   ZONE 2   ZONE 3

0 DAYS   160   200   300

Stopping on snow and ice

Stopping distances increase and traction decreases in winter. The chart below compares how tires and chains perform in an emergency stop made from 32 km/h (20 mph) on two common winter road surfaces: loosely packed snow and glare ice. Charts are useful, but only experience can improve your winter driving skills. With practice, you can learn to judge road surfaces and adjust your speed accordingly. Check the tread depth of winter tires frequently. Note that snow tires actually have slightly *less* traction on ice than summer tires do.

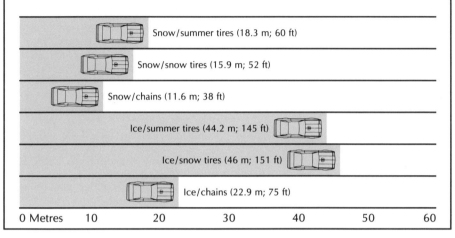

Snow/summer tires (18.3 m; 60 ft)
Snow/snow tires (15.9 m; 52 ft)
Snow/chains (11.6 m; 38 ft)
Ice/summer tires (44.2 m; 145 ft)
Ice/snow tires (46 m; 151 ft)
Ice/chains (22.9 m; 75 ft)

0 Metres   10   20   30   40   50   60

Stopping distances can be many times greater on a slippery surface than on a smooth, dry road. Soft snow on a dry road provides fair traction; hard-packed snow slightly less. Most dangerous is a light snow cover on glare ice. The dusting of snow may fool you into thinking traction is good when, in fact, stopping distances will increase dramatically.

Both sun and wind affect snow coverage. Watch for icy patches on bridges, overpasses, and elevated roadways (which often freeze before other road surfaces), beneath underpasses, and in shaded areas. Conditions will be most dangerous when the temperature hovers around the freezing point; they can change abruptly with a sudden shift in temperature.

If drifting or falling snow limits daytime visibility, switch on your low beams so that other drivers can see you. (Many safety-conscious professionals drive with their headlights on, day or night, regardless of weather conditions.) Focus your eyes as far ahead as possible. Avoid staring into oncoming headlights; look to the right side of the road, watching the approaching vehicle out of the corner of your eye. During a storm, shift the direction and focus of your vision regularly. Falling snow and the rhythmic movements of your wipers can have a hypnotic effect.

When descending a steep incline, reduce your speed, shift into a lower gear (*Second* on automatics), and avoid hard braking. The key to climbing a steep, slippery hill is to keep the car's wheels from spinning. Pick up as much speed as you safely can before you reach the hill, then use the extra velocity to help carry you over the crest. If the rise is so steep that downshifting is necessary, shift to the next lower gear (or *Second*) before you reach the hill; downshifting halfway up the hill may cause the wheels to spin.

Remember that stopping distances increase sharply on ice and snow. Gently pump your brakes on a slippery road, rather than braking harshly. Press down slowly on the pedal, hold for a second or two, then ease up before the wheels lock. If the car skids, let up on the brakes immediately. On front-drive cars with manual transmissions, shift down through second into first gear when slowing on icy surfaces and let the engine brake the car. After driving through slush or a deep puddle, pump your brakes gently a few times to dry them out. If you must pull over, choose the safest place to do so. Be especially careful of narrow shoulders on country roads—your tires could sink into a snow-filled ditch.

If you travel long distances in snowy country during the winter, take along emergency equipment including warm blankets, extra food, a thermos of soup or coffee, and a supply of candles. Should you become stranded in a storm, a lighted candle and a blanket can keep you fairly comfortable while you wait for snow-clearing equipment.

Sure starts and improved traction

1. The proper way to start most cars in cold weather is to depress and release the gas pedal just once and turn the key. Any more than that could flood the engine. If it is flooded, put the gas pedal slowly to the floor and hold it there while turning the key.

2. Low temperatures can reduce a new battery's power by as much as 50 percent—older batteries by as much as 70 percent. To restore part of your battery's capacity, remove it from the car, take it indoors, and let it warm up overnight away from any heat source. A better solution is to invest in a block heater—and if this is not sufficient, a plate-type or wraparound battery warmer.

3. If your car won't start after a night in cold, damp weather, check under the hood to see if moisture on the spark plug cables, distributor cap, or coil wire is causing the problem. Dry them with a rag, or use a moisture-dispersant spray (available at auto-parts stores and a useful item to carry in your car). A hair dryer may also do the trick.

4. Have the coolant level checked regularly and renew it every two years. By that time the coolant's anti-corrosive properties will have broken down. Also check the level of windshield washer fluid, and be sure it has the proper concentration of antifreeze.

5. Lubrication is a vital part of winter maintenance. The right kind of engine oil for cold weather (see your owner's manual) will improve your car's starting performance and protect the engine's moving parts against wear. A thorough grease job will shield the suspension and steering systems against the corrosive effects of slush mixed with road salt. You can also protect your car each winter by coating the underside with used engine oil. A correctly lubricated steering system will help ensure responsive handling. On rear-drive cars, make sure the oil in the differential is at the proper level—severe strain is placed on the differential when one of the wheels spins, a common occurrence when traction is poor.

6. When the temperature is below freezing, add a drop of ethylene glycol antifreeze (never alcohol) to the valves when inflating your tires. Moisture in the air inside the tire or air pump can freeze the valve open and cause slow leaking.

7. You can thaw a frozen lock with an aerosol that squirts a mixture of alcohol and lubricant into the keyhole. Or use a match or cigarette lighter to heat the key before inserting it into the frozen lock. To avoid burning yourself, wear gloves or hold the key with pliers. Never use hot water to thaw a lock; it will cool and refreeze.

8. Keep your gas tank as full as possible during the winter months to minimize condensation in the tank, which can lead to fuel-line freeze-up. With rear-drive cars, the extra weight of a full tank will also improve traction on slippery roads.

9. Keep your car wheels as straight as possible when moving through deep snow, especially when leaving a parking space. The more the wheels are turned, the more they will tend to plow, banking up the snow to block your way. If a turn is necessary, edge around gradually, backing up and moving forward several times rather than trying to swing out in one motion.

10. When you use traction devices to get out of snow, keep driving until you reach a clear spot and know you won't be stuck again if you stop. To save a long walk back to retrieve the grids, attach them to the back bumper with short lengths of cord (rear-drive cars only). Drag them with you until you are free, then store them back in your trunk until you need them again.

11. Keep two or three candles (plus matches) in your glove compartment. If your car breaks down and you are stranded, the candles will provide heat for several hours—and may save you from freezing. Run your engine a few minutes every 15 minutes or so, but do not leave it running. Otherwise, you run the risk of carbon monoxide poisoning from exhaust gases that leak into the passenger compartment. Leave a window open slightly for ventilation.

12. To prevent the wheels of a rear-drive car from spinning when stuck in snow, lightly apply the parking brake as you accelerate. Keep your hand on the brake release, and disengage the brake once the car is in motion and traction is regained.

13. Before leaving your car outside on a stormy night, cover the windshield with a heavy plastic or burlap bag. Close the car doors on the edges of the cover to hold it in place. In the morning, sweep off the heavy snow, then peel off the plastic and ice together.

Getting unstuck

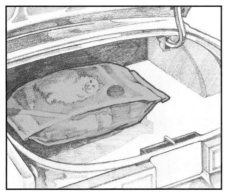

If yours is a rear-drive car, carry extra weight over the drive wheels in poor weather (this can reduce fuel economy, however). A couple of sandbags or a large bag of cat litter in the trunk is a good idea, as the sand can be used to provide extra traction on ice. Place the weight in the forward part of the trunk.

A traction grid—with the help of a jack—can sometimes be used to free a spinning wheel. Use a scissors jack or hydraulic jack (a bumper jack is more likely to slip) and dig the snow away so that the jack rests on bare earth or pavement. In an emergency you can use sand, roofing paper, or twigs for traction.

Rocking is generally the easiest way to move a vehicle that is mired in snow. Point the front wheels straight ahead, and shift back and forth between first gear (*Low* on automatics) and *Reverse*. Give the car enough gas to move it without spinning the wheels, which will bury them deeper in the snow.

If all else fails to free your car from deep snow, try a length of strong chain and a winch, which can be rented for less than the cost of a tow. Wrap the chain around a sturdy tree and hook one end of the winch to the car frame, the other end to the chain. Take up the winch gradually, until the car is on clear ground.

14. Even if there is no snow, cold-weather driving can be difficult and dangerous. Ice can form anywhere, even on a road you think is well plowed and sanded. At night ice that has melted and refrozen is often indistinguishable from dry pavement. It's safest to assume that the road ahead is icy and reduce your speed accordingly.

15. Regular tires are dangerously inadequate for winter driving. Put on your snow tires well before the first snow falls. (The chart on page 51 shows the difference in stopping power between tire types.) Studded tires are best in glare-ice conditions but are of little value in other conditions. A full set of chains may serve you better for emergency use.

16. Park your car, or back it into your garage, so that the battery is accessible should you need a boost. Carry a set of heavy-duty jumper cables in case you need to get—or give—a boost (see pp. 184–185).

17. Take a few extra precautions when driving long distances in winter. Don't travel alone unless absolutely necessary. Tell a relative or friend where you are going, what route you will take, and approximately what time you expect to reach your destination or stopovers along the way. Arrange to notify someone that you have arrived safely. Note telephone numbers of emergency road services and keep a few quarters in the car for emergency phone calls.

Sunshine and Sunday drivers

Once winter storms have subsided and the snow has melted, driving takes on new appeal. Down come the convertible tops and out come the Sunday drivers. Keep in mind that there are far more drivers on the road during summer months; as a result traffic fatalities reach their peak in June, July, and August. Summer is also a time for tourists who are unfamiliar with local roads, traffic conditions, and provincial highway regulations. Although warm-weather problems seem small in comparison to winter hazards, some can spoil even the best-planned road trip. The following advice will help keep summer driving as pleasant as it should be.

Spring maintenance

Your car will have taken a cruel beating during a typical Canadian winter. When the weather warms, check the fluid levels for the battery, brakes, transmission, and power steering. Inspect the engine hoses and belts for wear, and have them replaced if necessary. When changing summer tires yourself, check and adjust the air pressure. Replace the air filter if it is dirty or clogged, and have the engine oil changed. Look for signs of rust beneath the car, especially in the exhaust system.

Driving in sunlight

A driver must be aware of the vision problems caused by bright sunlight. The eye adapts slowly to changes in light intensity; sudden glare can temporarily blind a motorist, or make light-colored or shaded objects difficult to distinguish. A long drive in bright sunlight can cause visual fatigue.

Sunglasses will effectively reduce glare under certain conditions. Be sure to choose good lenses which will not distort images or color. Test the lenses by moving them up and down and from left to right; then rotate them. Watch for distortion and any waviness in lines that should appear straight.

Brown- and grey-tinted lenses are most effective in screening bright light; with a green element added, they will also protect against infrared radiation. Photochromic lenses automatically adjust to changing light conditions. However, their darkening effect may also be triggered by a drop in temperature. (In addition, they take longer to lighten than to darken.) Polarized lenses are particularly effective in cutting reflected glare, although light absorption is less than with other lens types. As a rule, choose the lightest tint that seems comfortable.

Other tips

It can be more comfortable to drive barefoot on a hot summer day, and it's not illegal, as many people think. Bare feet may even give you more sensitive control of the pedals.

Dark vinyl upholstery can raise the temperature inside the car by 5°C (9°F) on a sunny day. To keep the passenger compartment cool, drape a light-colored blanket or beach towel over the seats, lower the visors, and park in the shade if possible.

Don't keep the rear window of a hatchback or station wagon open for ventilation while you drive—it will suck poisonous exhaust fumes into the car. If you must keep the rear window open to carry a large item, close all other windows and turn on the fan.

Wash and wax for added protection

Sunlight and warm summer weather can actually harm your car's finish. Ultraviolet light can cause oxidation—a chemical breakdown in paint pigment which gives the finish a dull, chalky appearance. Crazing, a maze of hairlike cracks, may appear on metallic or refinished surfaces when the paint shrinks under a hot sun. Bird droppings can permanently stain the finish if not wiped off immediately.

A thorough wash and wax treatment will not only improve your car's appearance, but will also protect it from the damaging rays of the sun. Park in a shaded area, and use plenty of water from a hose or bucket. Use a car-wash soap or mild detergent if your car is particularly dirty; anything stronger may damage the finish. Wipe with a soft towel or sponge, then rinse thoroughly. Spray the underbody and inside the wheels with a strong stream of water to loosen any dirt, mud, or sand trapped under the chassis. To remove bits of hardened tar or bug and bird marks, hold a cloth saturated with cooking oil over the spot until the blemish lifts off. Give the surface a final wipe with a clean, dry towel or chamois.

Now is the time to clean out and touch up any small dents, scratches, or rust spots before the damage spreads (see pp. 148–149). Use paint sparingly, and wait until it has dried completely before waxing.

Apply paste or fluid car wax (never use floor wax) with a soft, damp cloth, rubbing in a circular motion until the entire body is evenly covered with a thin film. (Read the directions first; some waxes are applied one section at a time.) Press down vigorously on the cloth to remove any oxidized paint. When the wax has dried to a dull haze, give the finish a final rubdown to a lustrous, protective shine. If the paint is severely oxidized, you may want to use rubbing compound before waxing. It contains fine abrasives for deeper cleaning, and will help restore the original color of the finish.

If your car overheats

Overheating occurs either because of a mechanical fault or because more heat accumulates than your engine can normally disperse. Stop-and-go driving in hot weather is a common cause, particularly if you have air conditioning and it is on.

As soon as you see the temperature gauge begin to rise into the warning zone (or the warning light goes on) turn off the air conditioning to decrease the load on the engine. However do not stop and turn off the engine—although it will shed built-up heat, it won't have the help of the water pump to circulate coolant.

When you are in a lineup, stay at least 3 m (10 ft) behind the car ahead so that its hot exhaust doesn't blow onto your radiator. Try not to ride the brakes, which will also increase engine load. Lag behind the car ahead in heavy traffic, and move up slowly when the gap widens to several car lengths. If possible, leave the crowded highway and move onto a less congested route. If you can drive at a moderate speed with the air conditioner off, your car will probably cool off by itself (provided there is no mechanical problem). Have your coolant level checked.

If you can't escape traffic and the temperature gauge continues to rise, shift into *Neutral* and rev the engine to speed up the water pump and fan. As a last resort, turn the heater and the fan on *High* to draw heat away from the engine.

If the cooling system does boil over, pull off the road immediately and turn off the engine. Wait until you can open the hood without being burned—15 or 20 minutes if necessary. Carefully check for leaks, burst hoses, a broken drive belt or other obvious faults. Check the coolant recovery tank to see if the system still has sufficient fluid. Most reservoirs indicate two levels; the upper one is for a hot engine. If you find no mechanical problems, remove the radiator cap *(right)* or recovery tank cap (refer to your owner's manual for the exact location) to check the coolant level and top it up.

If your car is equipped with an electric fan, pull over at the first sign of overheating. Leave the engine running while you open the hood and check the fan. If it has stopped, the switch or the fan motor may be defective (replacing the fuse may help). With an air-cooled engine, loss of power and a hot engine smell will warn of overheating. Pull off the road, let the engine cool, and check for mechanical problems (see pp. 174–175). **Caution:** Beware of hot or moving engine parts as well as escaping steam.

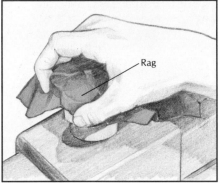

To relieve steam pressure, wrap a rag around the radiator cap. Without pressing down, turn the cap counterclockwise to the first stop—steam should escape from the overflow hose. Wait for the pressure to subside before turning the cap further. **Caution:** Stand away from the cap and be prepared to jump back quickly; keep your feet away from the overflow.

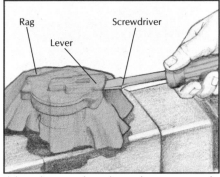

If the radiator cap has a lever, place a rag over the cap, and use a screwdriver to lift the lever through the rag. The rag will absorb some of the overflow and keep you from being scalded. Wait until the pressure is released before opening the cap.

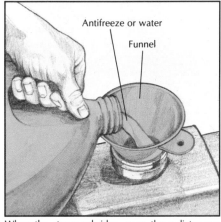

When the steam subsides, press the radiator cap down with the rag, turn and remove. Allow the system to cool, then top up with coolant mixture. If antifreeze is unavailable, use water alone, but add antifreeze as soon as possible.

Getting the most from a litre of gas

Once you have purchased your car, you no longer have any control over its fixed costs—financing, insurance, license and registration fees. On the other hand, variable costs—especially fuel—will *increase* the more you use your car and the "harder" you drive it. Reduced traction in rain, snow, ice, and on poor road surfaces will increase fuel consumption an average ten percent. Driving into a 30 km/h headwind has about the same effect on fuel economy as increasing your speed by the same amount. Driving style is an important factor: different drivers using the same vehicle over the same road conditions in identical weather may find that their gas consumption varies by as much as 20 percent. To help beat the odds in this economy game, take note of the following tips and techniques:

1. Avoid short trips as much as possible. Combine errands, especially during the winter months when your car consumes more fuel warming up. Remember, it takes energy to heat the engine to operating temperature and on short trips the choke provides a rich air-fuel mixture.

2. Plot your course. Travel when traffic is light if you can, and choose a route with a minimum number of stops. If you commute, listen to local traffic reports before setting out; you may save time and gas by avoiding congestion.

3. Accelerate smoothly, avoiding jackrabbit starts, which waste fuel and cause extra wear on your tires.

4. If you have a manual transmission, get into high gear as quickly as possible. Traveling at 80 km/h (50 mph) in fourth gear (2,500 rpm) uses less gas than traveling at 50 km/h (30 mph) in third (also 2,500 rpm) because the engine turns fewer revolutions per kilometre. An automatic transmission will shift up earlier if you ease up on the gas pedal as your speed increases.

5. Check your tires every week or so with a reliable tire gauge to make sure they are properly inflated. Underinflated tires offer more resistance to the road surface, which results in reduced fuel economy and stiffer handling. Radial tires provide better traction than standard bias-ply tires, thereby reducing fuel consumption. "Energy saver" tires are inflated to higher pressures than radials, which make the tires harder and reduces rolling resistance even further. Special rubber compounds are used to soften the harsh ride which can result from higher inflation pressures. **Caution:** Do not mix radial and bias-ply tires. Serious handling problems can result from mismatched tires.

6. Slow down. Don't exceed the speed limit, no matter how clear the road ahead. By staying within the 100-km/h (60-mph) highway speed limit (instead of allowing the speedometer to creep up to 110) you can decrease gas consumption by ten percent. By slowing to 90 km/h (55 mph), you will save an additional ten percent.

7. Maintain a steady speed on the highway. Varying your speed by as little as 8 km/h (5 mph) can increase fuel consumption by ten percent, depending on engine size. Avoid changing lanes unless you must pass another car or make an exit.

8. Drive smoothly to avoid unecessary braking. Accelerate gently as you gather speed to pass another vehicle. Ease up on the gas pedal, without braking, as you merge back into the right lane.

9. When traveling at high speeds, drive with the windows rolled up (leave one cracked open for ventilation, however) to reduce aerodynamic drag.

10. Empty your trunk; unnecessary additional weight will increase fuel consumption. Remove that bag of sand you used for extra traction during the winter as soon as the snow has melted.

11. Anticipate stops and avoid them where possible. When approaching a red light at an intersection, for example, take your foot off the gas pedal and coast so that the light has time to change before you reach it. It takes about 20 percent less fuel to accelerate to cruising speed from coasting speed than from a full stop.

12. Hills can temporarily increase fuel consumption by up to 30 percent. When driving up a steep grade, allow your car to slow rather than depress the gas pedal further to compensate for the incline. Allow your car to reach the legal limit on the way down before applying the brakes.

13. Turn off the engine whenever you will be stopped for more than a few minutes. An idling engine can use about one-half litre (one pint) of gas every five minutes.

14. If you must pack luggage atop your car, streamline to save fuel. A poorly packed roof rack will raise consumption by 12 percent at 30 km/h (19 mph), and by 20 percent at 100 km/h (60 mph). A well-packed rack will cut this loss in half, although even an empty roof rack will increase fuel use by five percent. To streamline your load, select luggage that is best suited to the size and shape of the roof rack. Arrange it in steps, with the shortest items in front. Cover the packed bags with a tarpaulin 2$\frac{1}{2}$ times longer and wider than the rack, tuck in the edges, and secure it with rubber shock cords or rope.

15. Don't just say "Fill 'er up." Service station attendants will "top off" the tank to the brim and often spill some gas in the process. Every time you accelerate or turn a corner, fuel will spill out of your over-full tank. Fill it only to the first "click," when the pump shuts itself off. When you drive with a full tank, you are also carrying the additional weight of gas.

16. Use the air conditioning as little as possible. Merely having a system in your car adds extra weight and can reduce fuel economy by as much as six percent in small cars. When in use, it can increase consumption by as much as 20 percent (in stop-and-go driving conditions). The average air-conditioned car will use approximately 340 more litres (90 gallons) per year than an identical car without this option.

17. Use *Neutral* when stopped. If you have an automatic transmission, slip the gearshift into *Neutral* to reduce stress on the torque converter and save fuel. If the car has warmed up and the engine still races, have your mechanic adjust the choke.

18. In winter, if your car takes a long time to warm up, or if it never reaches peak operating temperature, try fitting the grille with a protective cover (or partially cover the radiator with particle board). This radiator "blanket" will help prevent frigid air from over-cooling your engine.

19. Be patient with a diesel engine. Diesels, which rely on high compression rather than spark plugs to ignite the air-fuel mixture in the cylinders, are sometimes balky in winter. Do not try to start the engine until the indicator signals that it is ready. Otherwise, fuel will pass through the engine unburned.

20. Keep a record of your fuel consumption and maintenance (see the *Car Logbook*). Make fuel saving a challenge; try to improve your consumption with each fill-up.

21. The effect of weight on fuel economy is the most important reason to buy the smallest and lightest car that will suit your driving needs. The heavier the car, the more power it needs to accelerate, climb hills, and overcome rolling resistance. A 45-kg (100-lb) reduction in vehicle weight can reduce fuel consumption by about one percent. Aerodynamic shape is also important. Other factors being equal, a car with a small front end—which will cut through wind resistance like a wedge—will deliver the best fuel economy. Conversely, air resistance is *increased* by such features as vinyl tops, bumper guards, extra mirrors, ornamental hood fixtures, and towing accessories.

22. Finally, the easiest way to cut down on fuel consumption is to use your car less. Share a ride with a friend, form a car pool at work, and, once in a while, take the bus.

Accessories: Fuel savers or wasters?

When you are shopping for a new or used car, keep in mind that a small car with a well-matched engine will deliver the best fuel economy. But there are other factors which affect fuel economy: vehicle weight, aerodynamic drag, transmission, and accessories. The chart below lists popular options which will affect your gas consumption. Consider this savings—or loss—when you buy a new or used car.

Energy-efficient option	Little or no effect	Decreased fuel economy
Small engine	Power steering	V-8 engine
Diesel engine	Power brakes	Automatic transmission
Manual transmission	Cruise control	4-barrel carburetor
Overdrive (manual or automatic)	Exterior trim	Sun roof
Smaller carburetor	Fuel injection	Permanent roof rack
Low-ratio differential	Magnesium wheels	Air conditioning
Radial tires	Heavy-duty suspension	Power windows
Fuel economy gauges	Power antenna	Power seats
Engine heater	Air dam or spoiler	Automatic starters
Torque converter lock-up	Bias-ply tires	Convertible top
Aerodynamic aids	Auxiliary headlights	Towing accessories

Illness, drugs, and driving

Even if you are in excellent health and peak physical shape, a temporary illness, minor ailment or disability can inhibit your driving skills. Think carefully before driving when you are "under the weather" or on medication—you may be endangering yourself and other drivers.

Colds, flu, and allergies. Even the relatively mild symptoms of colds, flu, and allergies can be debilitating enough to affect driving. Stuffiness, aches, fever, and other familiar symptoms can dull your senses, lower your concentration, and increase reaction time. Minor illness can sometimes also affect your vision. In the time it takes to sneeze or cough, you may drive a significant distance, effectively blind and with minimum control.

Aches and pains. Minor aches and pains associated with colds, tension, or fatigue will make you restless and uncomfortable while driving. When this occurs, shorten your driving time, or pull over and rest. A few roadside exercises may help (see p. 61).

It is unwise to drive if you are in severe pain. A toothache or stomach cramps may be dangerous if they reduce your concentration. Such distractions, combined with emotional anxiety, are certain to impair your judgment and slow your response rate.

Stiffness and orthopedic problems. Stiffness and pain in the joints will make driving both uncomfortable and tiring. A cushion or backrest may sooth minor backache—a common complaint of long-distance drivers. However, chronic orthopedic problems may reduce flexibility and limit your capacity to react quickly in an emergency. If persistent orthopedic problems affect your driving, consult your doctor.

Visual problems. Any permanent or temporary sight problem will impair your ability to perceive, interpret, and react quickly to a highway situation. If you notice any change in your vision, or have trouble reading signs or judging distances (especially at night), have your eyes checked. If your driver's license stipulates that you must wear glasses, never drive without them. If you are susceptible to such conditions as tunnel vision or poor depth perception, your doctor may advise that you avoid driving after dark.

Hearing problems. Deafness or poor hearing is as dangerous as poor eyesight. With reduced hearing, a driver is cut off from the noise of traffic, which provides valuable clues about what is happening around him. Additional mirrors are usually required to compensate for lack of hearing.

Heart problems. Consult your doctor before driving with a heart condition. The exertion and everyday frustrations of driving could trigger a serious heart attack.

Reaction time: the critical margin

If you take more time to react to an emergency because of visual impairment, lack of concentration, or other effects of illness or drugs, you will use up more stopping distance as well. If you must drive when you are ill or on medication, allow yourself an extra margin of safety. The chart below illustrates how reaction times vary with physical condition. A rested, alert driver will take less than a second to move his foot from the gas to the brake pedal; a tired driver, 1 to 1.5 seconds; and a driver who is ill or under the influence of drugs or alcohol, 2 seconds or more.

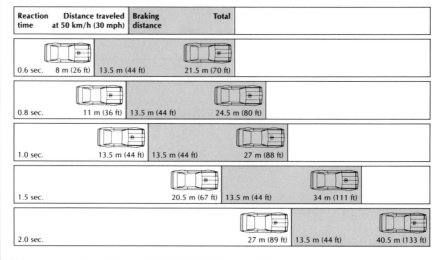

Reaction time	Distance traveled at 50 km/h (30 mph)	Braking distance	Total
0.6 sec.	8 m (26 ft)	13.5 m (44 ft)	21.5 m (70 ft)
0.8 sec.	11 m (36 ft)	13.5 m (44 ft)	24.5 m (80 ft)
1.0 sec.	13.5 m (44 ft)	13.5 m (44 ft)	27 m (88 ft)
1.5 sec.	20.5 m (67 ft)	13.5 m (44 ft)	34 m (111 ft)
2.0 sec.	27 m (89 ft)	13.5 m (44 ft)	40.5 m (133 ft)

Chronic illnesses. In some ways a chronic ailment is easier to handle and less of a threat to driving ability than a temporary or acute one. With a chronic ailment, you are well aware of your limitations and can take measures to compensate. Ask your doctor about driving limitations and emergency procedures in the event of an attack. For example, mild cases of diabetes which can be controlled with diet will not seriously affect driving ability. Epileptics may be authorized to drive if they haven't experienced attacks for a given period of time. Anti-convulsant drugs, often taken by epileptics, can have dangerous side effects, however.

Emotional problems. An argument before you get in the car or a problem at work can subtly but definitely affect the way you drive. Stress, anxiety, tension, insomnia, and depression, even in mild form, will restrict your ability on the road. However, any drug that you take may have side effects more serious than the problem itself. Again, if in doubt, consult your doctor, particularly if dizziness and fatigue are possible side effects of a prescribed treatment.

The age factor. Age will affect vision (particularly night vision), stamina, and reaction time. If you are over 50, watch for signs that your eyes are not what they used to be and have them examined regularly. Be aware of your physical limits, and don't overextend yourself on long car trips.

Physical handicaps. Mechanical devices designed to compensate for disabilities can be installed to give a handicapped person full control of an automobile. Hand-controlled brake and accelerator levers, for example, are used by drivers who do not have the use of their legs. With such adaptation, there is no reason why a handicapped person cannot become a skilled driver.

Common drugs and their side effects

Amphetamines and other stimulants:
These drugs stimulate the central nervous system to keep a person awake and alert. Some drivers, particularly long-haul truckers, may take stimulants to prolong the time they can remain behind the wheel without rest. Amphetamines are also found in decongestants, cold remedies, and diet aids.

Driving dangers:
Stimulants can give a driver a false sense of alertness and self-confidence, which may encourage willingness to take risks. They will mask fatigue, preventing a driver from being aware of its effects. When the drug wears off, dizziness or exhaustion often occurs.

Sedatives and tranquilizers:
These drugs depress the central nervous system, slowing heartbeat and breathing. They are used in the treatment of tension, nervous disorders, emotional problems, alcoholism, high blood pressure, epilepsy, and insomnia. They may also be found in muscle relaxants.

Driving dangers:
Sedatives and tranquilizers can cause drowsiness and can severely limit a driver's ability to concentrate. Lack of coordination, dizziness, blurred vision, and confusion are potential side effects. In combination with alcohol, barbiturates can cause severe depression, dangerously slow the heart rate, and even kill.

Narcotics:
Narcotics are depressants, and are used to relieve pain and induce sleep. Continued use may lead to addiction. Many non-prescription cough and cold remedies sold in Canada contain a common narcotic, codeine.

Driving dangers:
Drowsiness, visual impairment, confusion of thought, lack of concentration, and delayed response are all side effects of narcotics.

Antihistamines:
Antihistamines are used to treat allergies, colds, flu, and skin conditions. Many common preparations contain an antihistamine. If in doubt as to the contents or possible side effects of a drug, ask your doctor or pharmacist for advice.

Driving dangers:
Many antihistamines cause drowsiness, blurred vision, lack of coordination, and fatigue.

Antibiotics:
Antibiotics are widely used to treat many kinds of infections, from skin rashes to sore throats.

Driving dangers:
Potential side effects include dizziness, drowsiness, ringing in the ears, headache, nausea, and vomiting.

Illegal drugs:
LSD and mescaline are strong hallucinogens which can produce drastic mind-altering effects. Marijuana is a mild hallucinogen which can act either as a stimulant or a depressant, depending on the strength of the dose, the user's mood, and his experience with the drug. Cocaine acts as a stimulant, producing a feeling of euphoria in small doses and violent stimulation and hallucination in greater quantities.

Driving dangers:
Not only is it illegal to possess and use such drugs, it is also against the law to drive while under their influence. They will have various effects depending on whether they are narcotics, stimulants, or depressants. An additional danger is that a user has no way of knowing the strength or content of an illegal drug.

If you can't fight, rest

Fatigue is second only to alcohol as a factor in automobile accidents, particularly those involving a single car. A driver numbed by fatigue may swerve suddenly to avoid a real or imagined obstacle, or be blinded by the dazzle of oncoming headlights. A long journey, particularly on a straight and monotonous highway, will further aggravate fatigue. Even a commuter, driving the same stretch of road day after day, may fall victim to boredom and inattention.

Fatigue can result from a number of causes: physical exertion, prolonged mental activity, stress, or lack of sleep. When fatigue sets in, your awareness is dulled, your attentiveness diminishes, and responses become slower and less accurate. If you are suffering from a cold or are emotionally upset, you will be even more susceptible to lethargy. If you use a prescribed or over-the-counter drug, be aware of potential side effects. Many such drugs induce drowsiness. Even the weather can affect you—the atmospheric disturbances associated with heavy storms can make you irritable, susceptible to headaches, and accident prone.

The symptoms of fatigue may be subtle. You may doze off behind the wheel while driving at night, only to be awakened by a blaring horn or the headlights of an oncoming car. However, fatigue usually sets in gradually, with several warning signs: drowsiness, eyestrain, stiffness, disorientation even on a familiar route. If you find yourself gritting your teeth, hunching your shoulders, or clutching the steering wheel tightly, pull off the road and rest.

Your car is well equipped to help keep you comfortable and alert as you drive. Adjust the seat so that you are the proper distance from the steering wheel, and can reach the pedals without stretching. Body position is crucial to good driving. Maintain a natural, upright position behind the wheel; keep your back straight and your head up. In normal driving, your knees and elbows should be slightly bent, and your hands resting naturally on the steering wheel. The correct driving position will provide a commanding, all-around view and leave you relaxed, yet alert (below).

Adjust the temperature control and vents to keep the passenger compartment slightly cool. A warm car will make you drowsy. Make sure the car is well ventilated so that plenty of fresh air is circulated. Open a window if you feel the interior becoming too hot and stuffy.

Cruise-control devices enable a driver to maintain a preset speed without using the gas pedal. You regain control of the car's speed simply by tapping on the brake. Not having to concentrate on the accelerator may be more comfortable, but it may also make you less attentive. Switch off the device occasionally.

When setting out on a long trip by car, especially at night, keep the following tips in mind to minimize fatigue:
• Make sure that you are well rested before you start.
• Avoid eating a heavy meal or consuming alcohol before you leave. Both will make you drowsy and slow reaction times.

The proper position

Sit comfortably erect while driving, squarely behind the steering wheel. Position your hips firmly in the hollow of the seat, with your back straight and shoulders squared. Adjust the seat so that your eye level is well above the steering wheel—use a seat cushion if necessary. Grip the wheel firmly with your hands positioned comfortably at the 10-and-2 position.

Clear field of vision

Feet can easily reach pedals

Hands at 10-and-2-o'clock position

Legs and arms are relaxed, uncrowded

Seat is upright and properly adjusted

Your feet should easily reach the pedals when your knees are slightly bent. Don't wear shoes with high heels or platform soles for driving—they may catch between the pedals. Finally, fasten your seat belt for additional safety and comfort. The shoulder and lap belt will keep you from shifting during turns or bouncing with every bump and dip in the road.

• Do not travel too long without food. Eat lightly but frequently—picnic stops and coffee breaks are good ideas.

• Avoid traveling in the early morning when your level of alertness is low, after a long, hard day at work, or at the time of night when you usually go to bed.

• Wear comfortable, loose-fitting clothes.

• Find and fix the source of any unnecessary noise (see pp. 140–141). A steady rattle or creak can be irritating and distracting, not to mention dangerous.

• Never drive for more than two or three hours without a break. Stop more often if you are an inexperienced driver or are unaccustomed to long car trips.

• Deliberately vary your speed from time to time. Glance in the mirrors occasionally and shift your line of sight. Listen to the radio set to a volume which does not obliterate the noise of other traffic. Tune in a talk show rather than quiet music.

• When alternating shifts with a second driver, make it a rule to change every two hours, whether you feel tired or not. This will enable you to cover longer stretches at a time with less fatigue.

• Don't attempt to drive for more than six hours a day, even if you are sharing the driving with a companion.

• You will be most susceptible to fatigue on the third day of a long trip. At this point you will be at your lowest ebb—unwound from the tensions at home, but not yet refreshed. You may be irritable, and any arguments, particularly in the car, increase the risk of accident. If possible, plan to spend this day resting or sightseeing.

• If you see another car behaving erratically, perhaps due to the tiredness of the driver, do not startle him with a sudden horn blast or flashing of lights.

• If you begin to show symptoms of fatigue while driving, and find yourself relying on conversation or the radio to stay alert, pull over and rest. A short walk or a few exercises *(below)* may revive you. If not, take a nap or quit for the day.

Roadside exercises

1. To relax your arms and shoulders, clasp your hands behind your back and swing your arms up as high as you can, then down. Repeat this motion several times. Let your arms dangle, then shrug your shoulders.

2. To loosen cramped foot and leg muscles, extend one leg in front of you while you sit. Stretch your heel out and your toes toward you. Change to the other leg after a few stretches. Then clench and unclench your toes a few times. Rotate your foot clockwise, then counterclockwise several times.

3. To relieve a stiff neck, bend your head back as far as possible, then let it drop forward onto your chest. Slowly trace the outline of a figure eight with your chin as shown. Repeat this exercise several times.

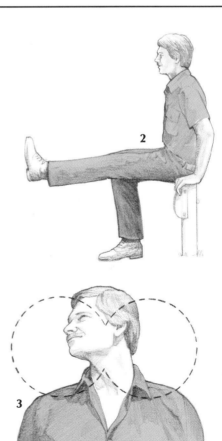

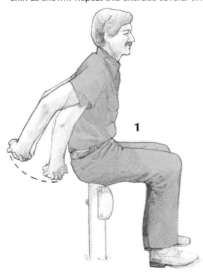

The high price of alcohol

Alcohol is a factor in nearly half of all traffic accidents. The chances of being killed on the road are almost 50 times greater for a driver who has been drinking than they are for a sober driver. Some people can "hold" a few drinks; others are impaired after only one. The safest thing to do is simply to avoid the dangerous combination of alcohol and driving—completely. If you do drink before you drive, use your common sense. Know your limit and do not exceed it. Be aware of the effects of alcohol and watch for signs of impairment in yourself and others. When you know that you have been affected, wait until the alcohol level in your blood drops before you take to the road.

Alcohol is a depressant that works on the brain and central nervous system. It affects everyone, but how it affects *you* depends on your weight, sex, physical condition, mood, personality, your rate of intake, and whether or not you have eaten.

Alcohol is carried by the bloodstream to the brain, where it soon begins to affect both your perception and coordination. One drink will often bring on a pleasant feeling of euphoria, and sometimes fatigue. The higher brain functions, which control reason and judgment, are the first affected. Learned responses, especially new skills, are impeded. (This is one reason why young drivers are particularly susceptible to the effects of alcohol.) After two or three drinks, you may find it difficult to concentrate on more than one task at a time; you may find yourself staring at a single object rather than glancing around at your surroundings as you would do normally. Vision will be further affected if you continue to drink. You will have trouble judging how far one object is from another, or images may become blurred. As the alcohol level in your bloodstream rises, your muscle coordination will next become impaired. Habitual tasks will become major challenges, and familiar sounds unrecognizable. High levels of alcohol will eventually cause loss of consciousness and, under certain conditions, even death.

Elimination of alcohol, unlike absorption, is a slow process. Your body needs an hour or more to rid itself of the alcohol contained in one drink. If you consume three drinks in an hour, it will take at least three hours to detoxify. Remember that when you stop drinking, the alcohol level in your bloodstream will continue to rise until your body begins to process and eliminate it. Exercise, fresh air, coffee, or a cold shower may have a short-lived psychological effect, but they cannot accelerate the elimination process. The only cure for overindulgence is time.

Practiced drinkers may learn to "hold their liquor"—to control their speech and actions enough to appear relatively normal after drinking. Even if you learn to control your behavioral response to alcohol, you cannot reduce its debilitating effects on your senses.

Legal measurement of sobriety is expressed as a BAC (blood alcohol concentration) index—the number of mg of alcohol

Finding your BAC limit

The charts below show the estimated BAC levels for men and women after consuming one to ten drinks. Calculations are based on ideal body weights. Since women have a higher proportion of body fat than men, equal amounts of alcohol will cause a higher BAC level in a woman than in a man of the same weight. Locate your estimated BAC reading on the appropriate chart by comparing your body weight to

Women ideal body weight (lb.)	Number of Drinks									
	1	2	3	4	5	6	7	8	9	10
100	50	101	152	203	253	304	355	406	456	507
125	40	80	120	162	202	244	282	324	364	404
150	34	68	101	135	169	203	237	271	304	338
175	29	58	87	117	146	175	204	233	262	292
200	26	50	76	101	126	152	177	203	227	253
225	22	45	68	91	113	136	159	182	204	227
250	20	41	61	82	101	122	142	162	182	202

per 100 mL of blood. The current legal limit for a driver in Canada is 80 BAC. Anyone driving, or in charge of a vehicle—you may simply be sitting behind the wheel of your car in your own driveway, keys in hand—with a BAC over 80 is committing an offense under the Criminal Code. If you are stopped by police and asked to take a breathalyzer test, and you refuse, the consequences are the same as those for driving while impaired. If you show signs of impairment, even though your breathalyzer reading is under 80, you can still be charged. Even a first offense brings a criminal record, and a fine of up to $2,000 or six months in prison.

The effects of alcohol on specific driving skills begin well before the legal limit. A BAC level of 40 will affect the speed of your response to visual stimuli, which is crucial in defensive driving. Distances between objects will become distorted, and the speed of moving vehicles will be harder to judge. Night vision can be severely impaired, particularly in older drivers. Eye movements become sluggish, and the quick scanning required for driving in darkness becomes difficult. By reducing your concentration, alcohol will narrow your field of vision.

With your coordination and observation skills impaired, your reaction time will increase dramatically. You may miss a hazard up ahead. Your steering may become clumsy, and you will have difficulty judging your speed. It is inevitable that you will make more driving errors than usual.

To limit the effects of alcohol, drink slowly to allow your body time to eliminate the alcohol. Have something to eat; drinking on an empty stomach will accelerate alcohol absorption. If you are tense, tired, or recovering from an illness, limit your intake even further. Tension or anxiety may also delay the apparent effects of alcohol. Do not have a second drink thinking the first has had no effect. And never combine drinking and drugs. Even nonprescription medicine may produce dangerous side effects in combination with alcohol.

Tips for hosts
• Use a shot glass to measure out standard amounts of liquor. You will help your guests keep track of their own intake.
• Don't offer drinks without food.
• Mix the drinks yourself, or put someone in charge of the bar. Don't let your guests help themselves.
• Stop serving drinks at least an hour before the party ends, and encourage guests to linger. Bring out more food and offer nonalcoholic beverages.
• Watch the woman who says she is drinking less than her male companion because she's the one who will drive home. A woman will become impaired on less alcohol than a man.
• If one of your guests has had too much to drink, don't allow him to drive home. Arrange a lift, call a cab or, if necessary, have him stay overnight.

the number of drinks you have had. The body eliminates alcohol at a rate of approximately 15 mg per hour. To calculate your precise rate of sobriety, multiply the number of hours since your first drink by 15.

Subtract this number from the reading below. One drink equals: one shot of 80 proof liquor *or* one 350-mL (12-oz) bottle of beer *or* 150 mL (5 oz) of red or white table wine.

Men ideal body weight (lb.)	Number of Drinks									
	1	2	3	4	5	6	7	8	9	10
100	43	87	130	174	217	261	304	348	391	435
125	34	69	103	139	173	209	242	278	312	346
150	29	58	87	116	145	174	203	232	261	290
175	25	50	75	100	125	150	175	200	225	250
200	22	43	65	87	108	130	152	174	195	217
225	19	39	58	78	97	117	136	156	175	195
250	17	35	52	70	87	105	122	139	156	173

Buckle up to stay alive

During your lifetime, you stand an alarming fifty-fifty chance of being injured—however slightly—in a car accident. Wearing a seat belt, however, can cut these odds in half. To be sure, you can reduce this risk by driving carefully, by never mixing drinking and driving, and by maintaining your car in top running order.

Two collisions actually occur during an accident—the first, when your car hits another vehicle or an obstacle; the second, the *human collision*, when the driver and passengers strike the dashboard, windshield, or seat back. A collapsible steering wheel or padded dashboard will absorb some of the impact, but when a person strikes the windshield or door frame, it is the body that suffers the full force of the collision.

Unrestrained passengers may also endanger each other during an accident. A driver can suffer serious neck and spinal injuries when hit by a rear passenger; fatal head injuries can occur when passengers bump heads with heavy force; and one passenger thrown sideways may push another out the door or window.

Serious or fatal injuries can occur even when a car is traveling at low speeds. In a 50-km/h (30-mph) collision, a passenger will hit the interior of the car—or another passenger—with more than a *tonne* of force. When held securely in place by a seat belt, that passenger can withstand this otherwise irresistible force.

Seat belts have been mandatory in Canadian cars since 1971, and in most provinces it is now illegal to drive without wearing them. Although the value of seat belts has been proven time and again in laboratory tests and accident studies, most Canadians still do not wear them. Unfortunately, several myths persist despite scientific evidence to the contrary:

Seat belts are uncomfortable and restrictive. Carmakers have developed one-piece lap and shoulder belts that are both comfortable and effective. Newer systems are fitted with locking retractors which wind up the slack in loose or unused seat belts. During normal driving, this allows passengers to bend forward and sit comfortably. In the event of a panic stop or collision, the

How a seat belt works

0.0 seconds—car hits object

Without seat belt: 0.1 seconds—car stops; **0.11 seconds**—passenger hits windshield

With seat belt: 0.1 seconds—car and passenger stop together.

When a car hits a solid object head-on, it stops abruptly. Traveling at 50 km/h (30 mph), it will come to a full stop within $1/10$ of a second of impact. The front of the car will buckle as the vehicle absorbs the force of the collision. As a result, the passenger compartment comes to a more gradual stop than the front of the car, and will remain undamaged. Instead, it is damaged by the person striking it with his head or body. A passenger inside the car will be traveling at the same speed and, if unrestrained, will continue to move forward after the vehicle has stopped. The second collision occurs when the person hits the windshield or dashboard. Within $1/100$ of a second, he will absorb the full force of this impact. Unlike the car, which may crumple up to half a metre before stopping, a person must come to a stop over a very short distance—three to five centimetres.

Seat belts prevent the human collision. When restrained by lap and shoulder belts, which are fastened to the car frame, a passenger is better able to "ride down" a crash *with* the car. The person has an additional $9/100$ of a second to stop—a small but lifesaving margin of safety—and is prevented from being pitched into the windshield or dashboard.

retractor will automatically lock and hold the person in his seat. By keeping the driver upright and squarely behind the wheel during sharp turns, over bumpy roads, or during unexpected stops, seat belts actually increase driving comfort.

Back-seat passengers do not need to wear seat belts. Seat belts will hold passengers securely in their seats in the event of an accident—and prevent them from hitting the inside of the car or each other. Rear seat belts dramatically reduce the chance of head injury, the most common cause of death in vehicle collisions.

It is better to be thrown clear of a collision. The world outside the car is very dangerous for a fast-moving, unprotected human body. Risk of injury and death is far greater for a passenger who is thrown out of the car than for one who remains belted in the vehicle. About one-quarter of all crash fatalities occur when the victims are thrown from the car and hit the pavement or another vehicle. An estimated 80 percent of these deaths could have been prevented if the victims had been properly buckled up.

A seat belt can trap you in a burning or submerged vehicle. If you are wearing a seat belt during an accident, your chances of remaining conscious are ten times better than if you were unrestrained. You can then unbuckle your seat belt in moments and react to any further emergency.

Seat belts are unnecessary at low speeds or for short trips. Half of all traffic deaths in Canada occur at speeds of 65 km/h (40 mph) or less, and within a few kilometres of the victim's home. An unbelted passenger risks death in collision at speeds as low as 30 km/h (19 mph).

You can adequately protect yourself during an accident by holding the steering wheel, or by bracing yourself against the dashboard. Accidents occur too quickly and unexpectedly for passengers to prepare themselves. Impact occurs with such bone-crushing force that only a restraint system can provide adequate protection.

Seat belts are useless at high speeds. Seat belts are designed to make serious accidents survivable. Although they may not prevent injury, they could save your life.

How to wear a seat belt

For greatest comfort and security, make sure that your seat belt is properly adjusted each time you drive. The lap belt, which will absorb most of the force of impact, should fit snugly across your hips, well below your abdomen. The shoulder belt—your protection against head and chest injury—should be slack enough to put your fist between your chest and the belt. Always wear the upper belt over your shoulder and across your body, never under your arm. Never wear a shoulder belt without a lap belt.

There has been much controversy over whether or not pregnant women should wear seat belts. However, studies have shown that, in an accident, the greatest danger to an unborn child is the death of the mother rather than his or her own injuries. Thus, for maximum safety, pregnant women should always wear both the lap and shoulder belts at all times. Be sure that the lap belt fits very low around the pelvic bone, well below the abdomen, so that there is no pressure on the unborn child.

Protecting the young passenger

Many parents do not realize how dangerous a car can be for a child, or how severely a child can be injured in an otherwise minor accident. Even a sudden stop or turn, or the child's unrestrained movement within the car, can result in injury. An unharnessed 4.5-kg (10-lb) infant may be thrown forward with a 136-kg (300-lb) force. By buckling your child into a correctly installed child-restraint system, even for short trips, you can greatly improve his or her chances of coming through an emergency injury free.

Because of their size and stature, children are far more vulnerable than adults. Their heads are larger and heavier in proportion to their bodies—and their centers of gravity higher—so that they are more likely to be thrown headfirst into the dashboard or out of a window with the force of a collision or sudden stop. Severe head injuries often result in death or crippling brain damage. As well, children's bones are soft and have not had time to grow and develop; their pelvic bones and ribs provide poor protection for internal organs.

The safest place in a car for a child is in an approved restraint system installed in the back seat (the center of the back seat unless your car has bucket seats). Child restraints are specifically designed to spread the force of a collision across the strongest parts of a child's body, and to limit head movement. All of the numerous models on the market have been tested to ensure that they meet or exceed stringent federal safety standards. Before buying a child restraint, check the manufacturer's label—required by law—which describes how the seat should be used, and confirms that it complies with safety standards.

Infant restraints, suitable for babies who cannot hold their heads up without effort, face the rear of the car. The 9-kg (20-lb) limit generally specified for these restraints is somewhat misleading. Infant carriers provide extra protection against whiplash and head injuries. Babies need this protection until their neck muscles are strong enough to withstand stress. It is wise, therefore, to use an infant restraint until the crawling stage—up to nine months or even a year.

Child restraint seats face forward and are secured against the back of the rear seat. Manufacturers generally recommend this system for children weighing 9–18 kg (20–40 lb). Children who are over the recommended limit can stay in a child restraint seat as long as the tops of their ears do not reach above the seat. There is a danger of whiplash once a child is too tall for the seat.

Safety for infants . . .

When driving with a baby under one year, use a rear-facing infant restraint. For maximum safety, secure the restraint in the center of the back seat. Accident statistics show that the rear-facing position provides the best protection from windshield and dashboard contact (if placed on the front seat), as well as whiplash.

An infant restraint consists of a molded plastic shell, upholstered padding, and a safety harness. The system is secured to the car seat by the car lap belt, and is designed to hold a baby in a semi-reclining position. Take note of the angle recommended by the manufacturer; if the restraint is tilted too much, the child may slide out should the car stop suddenly. Adjust all the straps snugly, including the crotch strap.

When carrying a very small baby in an infant restraint, place a towel or rolled-up blanket beside the head to prevent it from rolling from side to side. Once the child can sit comfortably without support (usually by the crawling stage), he is ready to graduate to a child restraint seat.

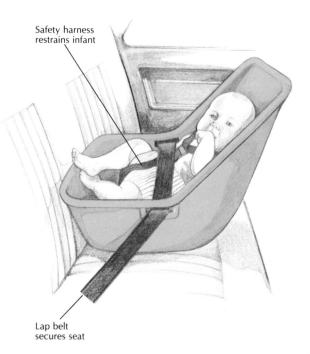

Safety harness restrains infant

Lap belt secures seat

Convertible seats can be used as rear-facing infant restraints for babies, and converted to front-facing child restraints to accommodate older children.

A *booster seat,* with or without arms, will help position the car lap belt safely over the hips of an older child, below the soft stomach area. It will also raise the child up high enough to see out the window.

Select a car seat that fits both your child and your car—and plan on spending $50–100. If you are considering a second-hand restraint, remember that a few years ago there were models on the market which would not meet today's standards. Don't buy a model that is no longer sold.

All child-restraint systems are attached to the seat of a car using the car seat belts, which in turn are bolted to the car frame. Read the manufacturer's instructions carefully before installing a child restraint, and follow them carefully; any variation could endanger your child.

Front-facing restraint seats also require a tether strap, which is fastened to a bracket bolted to the car body. This strap, which prevents the seat from pitching forward, must be installed properly.

Some child-restraint systems have several positions, not all of which are safe for driving. Check the directions carefully. Fasten the harness straps snugly, so that you can fit no more than two fingers between a strap and your child. Check the harness each time you buckle the child into the seat, and adjust it for different weights of clothing.

For an infant, anything other than an infant restraint is dangerous. If you must travel when a restraint is unavailable, the safest place for the baby is in an infant carrier on the rear floor, with the head facing toward the center of the car.

A young child can sit on the floor in the back if a restraint is unavailable. Or you can strap a toddler into a seat belt so that it fits low over the hips, touching the thighs. If the shoulder belt touches the face or neck, tuck it behind the child's back, not under the arm (it could break a rib if the child is thrown forward).

Never carry a child in your lap while riding in a car. The force of a collision will wrench the youngster from your arms no matter how tight your grip. It is also dangerous to buckle two children together, or worse, a child and an adult. The two children could be thrown together and bang heads with injurious force; the adult could crush the child, or cause pelvic injuries by pressing with adult force on the seat belt.

. . . and older children

A child restraint seat is designed to protect a child who can sit alone, and who weighs at least 9 kg (20 lb). The restraint faces forward and is secured to the car seat by both the car lap belt and a tether strap anchored to the car frame. A child restraint system should be used in the back seat only, away from the potential dangers of the dashboard and windshield.

Make sure that all straps fit snugly, especially over the child's shoulders. Some models provide an additional chest strap, which prevents the harness from slipping off the child's shoulders. Do up this strap at armpit level, no higher. Keep the crotch strap as short as possible, to hold the lap strap low across the child's thighs and away from the delicate abdomen area. The crotch strap also prevents the child from slipping down and out of the harness.

Never wrap your child in a blanket before seating him in a restraint—this will interfere with the straps. In cold weather, dress your child in heavy clothing, secure him in the restraint, then cover him with a blanket if necessary.

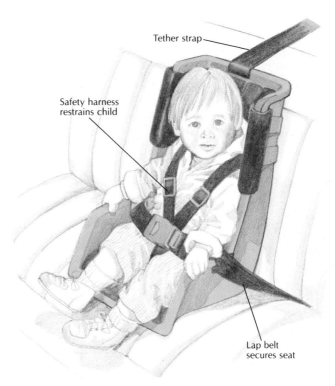

Tether strap

Safety harness restrains child

Lap belt secures seat

Patience plus good planning

A comfortable and occupied child is a happy traveler. Since long-distance driving can be tedious for children, plan ahead for a comfortable ride that includes rest stops, toys, games, and snacks.

A child who is too warm or too cold will soon become cranky, so dress youngsters for temperatures inside the car. Also make sure you have the appropriate safety restraint for the age and size of each child, whether it is an infant seat, child seat, or lap and shoulder belts (see pp. 66–67).

How often you stop for a rest will depend on the ages and dispositions of your young passengers. A good rule of thumb is to plan a break of 20 minutes or so for every two hours of driving. Don't just sit in a restaurant; let the kids run around and burn some of their pent-up energy.

Organization is important. Pack food and drinks in the car, rather than in a cooler in the trunk. Choose snacks that are healthful and practical, from juice and teething biscuits to fruits, nuts, and cheese for older children. If you keep the sugar and caffeine content down, your children will remain calmer. Picnics are not only fun, but also less expensive than highway restaurant meals. And you will have better control over your child's nutrition. Keep other travel needs, including tissues and non-spill cups, close at hand. Decide in advance what games you will play in the car, then pack the needed equipment.

Infants (birth to one year)

While younger babies tend to sleep in the car, infants six months to one year can be more unpredictable. Because teething, crawling, separation crises, and other traumas come and go, your tiny passenger may be content and cheerful—or impossible.

Traveling with a baby takes special planning and packing. Take along an assortment of teething toys and simple picture books (with cardboard pages for little fingers). For infants in the back seat, tape a colorful picture to the seat they're facing to make their view more interesting.

Entertain your baby with a coffee can filled with an assortment of safe, baby-size items. Include ping-pong balls, small blocks, plastic farm animals, and spongy bath toys. Open the can and let baby choose one, then demonstrate what the toy does or says. Some babies pull toys from the can until it's empty; others enjoy putting the toys back after each "find." For baby's self-entertainment, take a piece of dye-proof yarn or ribbon and tie several plastic toys to the car

Most three- to six-month-olds enjoy musical toys, and bright, simple rattles attached to the car seat.

Puppets are especially good for entertaining restless toddlers, as are short, simple stories and sing-alongs.

seat. Then you can drive without having to constantly retrieve dropped toys.

Toddler (one to two years)

Some parents claim that this is the toughest age for traveling, and prefer to depart *after* their child is asleep and gently placed in the safety restraint. Children this age want to assert their independence, not sit quietly in a car seat. Some families keep boxes of car toys packed away, for use only on trips. Keep these toys out of sight in the front seat, and hand them back, one at a time, as the child's interest in the last toy begins to fade. You can also add variety to your children's

When toys lose their magic, entertain your two- to four-year-old with games such as "Simon says."

Play the "alphabet game" with older children by finding each letter on road signs, billboards, and trucks.

attention span. Since children this age can become bored and restless, frequent stops are a help. A rest stop will give you and your child a new topic of conversation. ("Listen to the sounds; do you hear a plane? Smell the air; maybe a dairy is nearby.") A stop at a fruit and vegetable stand or scenic lookout can break the monotony, too. At this age, children are fascinated with nature. Give them a small box or bag for collecting such treasures as pine cones, leaves, flowers, rocks, and shells.

Pack a toy bag filled with dolls to dress and undress, and visit the library to stock up on books. Keep youngsters busy with a clipboard, paper or coloring books, and crayons (avoid indelible markers). Teach them colors and shapes; show them how to draw passing scenes and how to scribble to music on the radio. Instead of leaving the modeling clay at home, spread it over a large book—it makes a perfect ground cover for plastic zoo animals and dinosaurs.

Play "Simon says" by demonstrating first. Think of new and funny positions, then let your child be the leader. Teach them simple preschool songs like "Old McDonald" and "Row, Row, Row Your Boat." Or let each child pick a color, then sing out when he sees a car of that color. Tell stories, too, and let the children help. Take turns describing the scene, character, and situation; let everyone think up silly adventures. At this age, however, you're best to avoid scary stories.

The involved traveler (ages five and up)

With their longer attention span and wider variety of interests, five- to eight-year-olds can benefit from a simple lesson in geography or local history. Plan to stop at interesting spots along the way, and carry a Frisbee or soccer ball for your youngsters to play with at rest stops.

Help your older children feel involved in the trip planning by letting them pack their own toy bag (give them guidelines for the number and size of toys they can reasonably fit in). You might also consider a portable cassette player, with favorite stories and music, and a travel bingo game. (If you can't find such a game in the stores, make one with squares indicating things to spot from the car—brown cows, yellow flowers, red barns, and stone houses.) In the "animal game," simply count the number of animals on your side of the road. As your children get older, teach them how to read a road map, then let them help you plan the route and navigate. They'll develop a valuable skill *and* keep occupied.

snacks by placing them in interesting containers such as plastic Easter eggs, glass jars, or colorful boxes.

Children are more susceptible to car sickness than adults, so keep a few sickness bags handy. If motion sickness is a problem, restrict your child's eating to a light meal two hours before departure. Another option is medication, but be prepared for the side effects—your child could become drowsy or cranky at an inconvenient time.

The talking traveler (two to four years)

Your two- to four-year-old is a talkative, interested passenger with a relatively short

Protecting against theft

More than 100,000 cars are stolen each year in Canada. In the greater Montréal area alone, nearly 10,000 vehicles are reported missing, not to mention the thousands more that are broken into. Many are gone for good, either dismantled for replacement parts or re-registered with false papers. Those vehicles that are recovered have often been vandalized or stripped.

Many motorists are careless when leaving their cars, forgetting that unlocked doors and open windows will make a break-in easy even for an amateur thief. Never leave your car unlocked, and never leave the keys in the ignition. (In some areas such neglect is illegal and subject to fine.) Also avoid placing inviting parcels in full view on the seat of your car. Stash them out of sight in the trunk before leaving the vehicle.

But these precaution won't hamper a determined thief armed with the proper tools. This expert can unlock your car door, remove the ignition lock, and start the engine within two to three minutes.

Even if your car is fully insured, its theft can mean significant financial loss and inconvenience. Your insurance company will cover only the depreciated value of a stolen vehicle, not the cost of a new car, and any deductible on your policy will reduce the amount paid to you. Unless your policy states otherwise, you will have to pay for your own transportation during the 90-day period in which the insurance company must process your claim. If your car is found during these three months, it will be returned to you as is. Your policy will cover obvious damage and vandalism, but you will receive no compensation for abuse to your vehicle. Thus, depending on your circumstances, you may find it worthwhile to invest in extra protection for your car, whether a sturdier ignition lock or an elaborate alarm system.

Anti-theft systems and accessories currently on the market in Canada vary widely in price and method of operation. They do not all offer protection to the same degree, or against the same dangers. Determine your requirements before installing a security system. Your 12-year-old car may seem unattractive to a thief, but your new cassette deck may need additional protection.

Standard car door and ignition locks are easily jimmied or removed. You can install a

Anti-theft accessories

Theft-proof ignition lock may not deter experienced thieves, who are familiar with this simple device and can "hot wire" the ignition in other ways.

Krook lock links the steering wheel with the brake or clutch pedal. It is easy to fix and unlock, but will not deter the serious thief. The lock can be jimmied, sawn through, or the steering wheel bent to release it.

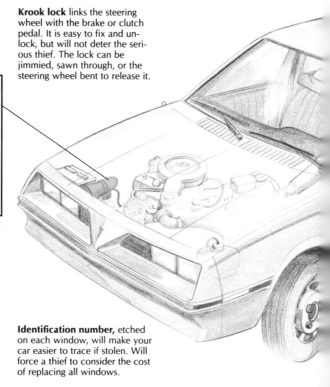

Siren alarm (above) blares when thief opens hood, trunk, or doors. More effective than car horn in alerting passersby.

Hood lock replaces a standard hood catch. A wise precaution if you install a security device under the hood.

Removable radio or tape deck slides out of frame in dashboard, can be hidden in trunk or taken with you. Likewise, expensive speakers can be removable.

Identification number, etched on each window, will make your car easier to trace if stolen. Will force a thief to consider the cost of replacing all windows.

better-quality ignition lock, buttonless door locks (to prevent opening with a coat hanger), and supplementary locks for the steering wheel and car wheels. Although these devices may not stop a determined professional thief, they will discourage most amateurs. Window etching is another effective deterrent. Even if the car is stolen, the indelible personal identification number (or serial number of your car), which is marked on each window, makes the vehicle easier to trace. The thief must destroy or replace the windows to resell the car.

You can install an alarm system in various parts of the car (such as under the hood or in the trunk). It is activated when you remove the key from the ignition (a time delay of 30 seconds or so allows you to leave the vehicle without setting off the alarm). Some systems are set by a hidden switch which can be inside or outside the car. All alarms include a detector, which may be a pendulum switch, vibration or infrared sensor, mechanical switch, or voltage detector; and a warning device—usually a mechanical siren or electrical alarm. In simpler systems, the car horn itself may be the warning device. However this type of alarm may not warn passersby that something is amiss (other than a stuck horn), and the horn is usually easily accessible and quickly disconnected.

A circuit breaker or fuel-line interruptor can be installed to cut off the electrical or fuel supply to your car should a thief attempt to drive it away. However, the car must then be serviced before it will start again—a disadvantage with a false alarm. Some professional thieves carry their own batteries, and will be undeterred by an electrical interruptor system.

Complex alarm systems must be installed by a professional (who will also offer a guarantee), but in many cases you can install a simple security device yourself. It's wise to first consult an alarm specialist, who can guide your choice, explain the operation of the system, and offer a few installation tips.

A good alarm system should last the life of your car. Some parts may need replacing during that time, particularly switches, which tend to corrode. Install a supplementary power source for the alarm, as well as a hood lock to prevent a thief from opening the hood to cut battery cables or siren wires.

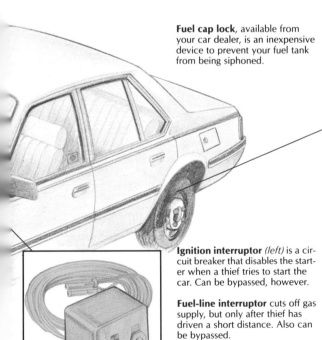

Fuel cap lock, available from your car dealer, is an inexpensive device to prevent your fuel tank from being siphoned.

Wheel locks (above) prevent theft of wheels by locking them in place. Recommended for cars with alloy wheels, prized by car thieves. One lug nut per wheel is locked in place, can be removed only with special "key."

Ignition interruptor (left) is a circuit breaker that disables the starter when a thief tries to start the car. Can be bypassed, however.

Fuel-line interruptor cuts off gas supply, but only after thief has driven a short distance. Also can be bypassed.

Replacement buttons for the door locks have straight, smooth shafts that can't be easily lifted with a coat hanger.

Alarm sticker advertises that you have installed an alarm device in your car. May encourage a professional thief who is familiar with your system, but is more likely to discourage burglary.

Killjoy system disconnects fuel ine, brakes, and ignition all at the same time. Will discourage even professional thieves, who must reactivate all three systems or tow the car away.

In search of a safe automoblle

In the early days of the automobile, little thought was given to passenger safety. On many early vehicles, bumpers, windshield wipers, and even headlights were options rather than standard equipment. Our high-speed, car-in-every-garage way of life has changed all that. The car that you buy in the not-too-distant future will meet new, even stricter safety standards as a result of recent innovations. Vehicle safety programs in North America, Europe, and Japan have sought to develop attractive, comfortable cars with four important goals in mind:

• increased protection for passengers in a variety of severe crashes;
• a high level of protection for pedestrians;
• fuel conservation;
• reduced exhaust emissions.

Since 1974, three major Research Safety Vehicles (RSVs) have been designed and built in North America. The Calspan RSV, featuring an advanced turbocharged engine, was designed to protect occupants at crash speeds of over 64 km/h (40 mph) in front collisions, and over 72 km/h (45 mph) in side collisions (with the help of air bags). An anti-skid braking system improves wet-pavement stopping performance by 25 percent. A plastic foam front end and an aluminum hood significantly reduce injury to pedestrians at speeds of up to 32 km/h (20 mph), and lower the car's weight.

Volkswagen's RSV is a Rabbit look-alike that combines the crashworthiness of a safety vehicle with remarkable fuel economy. This prototype delivers a fuel consumption

Anatomy of a research safety vehicle

• **Body** is made of thin sheet metal with hollow sections filled with lightweight polyurethane foam. This construction surrounds passengers with a crash-absorbent "sandwich" wall.

• **Roof** is protected by pillar supports and a roll bar.

• **Engine.** This RSV is equipped with a 1.6-litre, four-cylinder engine and a five-speed manual transmission. Fuel consumption is 7.2 L/100 km (39 mpg).

• **Gull-wing doors** provide easy access to front and rear seats, and are less likely to be crushed in most side-impact collisions than conventional doors.

• **Rear body, fenders, and hood** are made of flexible polyurethane to reduce cosmetic repair resulting from minor accidents.

• **Vision.** Wide glass areas give the driver an unobstructed view for 325 degrees.

• **Seats.** Body-molded seats reduce fatigue and work with restraint systems to minimize injury.

• **Suspension and brakes.** Four-wheel independent suspension and hydraulically assisted disc brakes provide 30 percent more stopping power than those of an average car. A radar braking system signals the driver if the car is too close to the vehicle ahead, and will automatically apply the brakes if a high-speed crash is imminent.

figure of 4.7 L/100 km (60 mpg)—twice the fuel economy standard set for cars to be sold in the U.S. in the mid-1980s. Passengers are protected in 64 km/h (40 mph) crashes by Volkswagen's passive-restraint system, in which seat belts buckle automatically when the doors are closed. Each belt is connected to a gas-powered piston, which pulls it tight around the wearer the instant a collision begins.

The third RSV (pictured below) is a sleek, gull-winged prototype developed by Minicars, Inc., under a safety program sponsored by the U.S. Department of Transportation. Its hollow, foam-filled frame is designed to provide protection in 72- to 80-km/h (45- to 50-mph) collisions, and eliminate 75 percent of the serious side-impact injuries.

Developing the car of the future is a painstaking and expensive process. The single Volkswagen RSV cost well over $500,000 to design and produce. Calspan's six-year contract to develop a "practical, producible, energy-efficient vehicle" (with Chrysler as the main subcontractor) amounted to more than $8 million. Although these vehicles are many years away from the showroom, some of their innovations are finding their way into production models. Governments, too, are studying and updating safety vehicle standards based on this research. The Volpe-Jamieson Agreement, for example, was updated and signed in 1984. In this pact, Canada and the U.S. guarantee an exchange of safety research findings that will someday make the roads safer for all drivers.

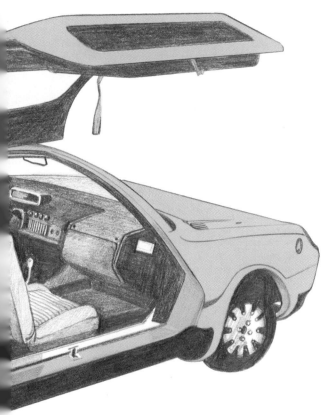

- **Bumpers,** front and rear, are made of resilient foam covered by flexible urethane to resist 13-km/h (8-mph) collisions with no damage. At speeds of 13 to 32 km/h (8 to 20 mph), front-end crashes will result in structural damage only to a bolt-on, replaceable section for quick repair.

- **Trunk.** Approximately 0.37 m³ (13 ft³) of space is equivalent to that of a standard compact car.

- **Dashboard controls** include a digital display that monitors fuel level, speed, engine rpm, and temperature in "normal" and "emergency" modes; a citizens band radio for weather and emergency information; and heater/air conditioner controls.

- **Air-bag restraints**—which inflate automatically within 0.025 second of impact—protect front-seat passengers in 80 km/h (50 mph) front collisions.

- **Lap and shoulder belts** protect rear-seat passengers in 65 km/h (40 mph) collisions.

- **Lightweight alloy wheels** improve handling performance. Advance Concept Tires (ACT) can roll even when deflated, eliminating bulky spares and roadside tire changes.

- **Size and weight.** Interior space is equal to that of the average compact car (3 m³ or 106 ft³). However, the total weight of 1,135 kg (2,500 lb) is the same as that of today's subcompact cars.

21 tips to reduce the risk

Traffic accidents claim more lives than war. During the Second World War, almost 33,000 Canadians died of battle injuries. But 130,000 Canadians have been killed on our roads since the first national records were compiled in 1950, and that figure grows by 5,000 to 6,000 each year. One out of every 20 drivers can expect to be in a traffic collision this year. The cost, in terms of medical expenses, car repairs, and loss of productivity, is a staggering $2.5 billion.

Driving, as pleasurable and convenient as it can be, is also risky business. "Drive defensively" is an oft-repeated phrase, but a true one. Be constantly on the lookout for the other motorist, expect the unexpected, and remember the following tips:

1. Don't drive a sick automobile. If it takes longer to stop than usual, if it pulls to one side when you're braking, if there is too much play in the steering wheel—have it fixed immediately. Learn the routine facts of maintenance: how much air is supposed to be in the tires (crucial for good traction; see pp. 102–105), how to tell if the engine needs oil (see pp. 112–113), how to check your brake-fluid level (your life may depend on a couple of teacups of fluid; see pp. 122–123). Get out at the gas station to make sure the attendant makes a thorough check under the hood, or do it yourself. Follow your car's maintenance schedule, and record maintenance and repair jobs in the *Car Logbook*—even those you perform yourself.

2. Enforce a family rule: If the car is moving, everybody's seat belt must be fastened. No exceptions. However, adult seat belts are not suitable for small children. Depending on their size and weight, children should be buckled in a front- or rear-facing safety restraint (see pp. 66–67). Confine children to the back seat if possible. Don't carry sharp or heavy objects on the same seats with children. In a sedan, don't put anything on the shelf under the back window. In a sudden stop, even a camera, flying forward at the original speed of the car, can kill. Put groceries in the trunk or on the floor.

3. Never leave small children alone in the car. If you leave children old enough to obey and remember, put the transmission in *Park*, apply the parking brake, and take the ignition key. If the car has power windows that can operate with the ignition off, be certain that your child can be positively trusted not to play with them. Power windows have strangled small children.

4. Drive smoothly. Weaving in and out, cutting in on other drivers, spurting through narrow gaps in traffic, abrupt changes in direction—all are accident makers. Driving too fast or too slowly can cause trouble, too. Both result in unnecessary passing—by you or by other drivers. If someone is anxious to get around you, don't compete, even if he or she is in the wrong.

5. Signal your intentions. Whether slowing down, turning, or changing lanes, use your brake lights and turn signals early enough to let other drivers know well in advance what you are going to do. Use your horn sparingly, but use it if necessary—not to complain but to communicate and attract attention.

6. Allow plenty of room. Maintain a stopping distance of at least two seconds behind the vehicle ahead at all times (see pp. 36–37). Under poor conditions, stretch this margin to four seconds. There are also side benefits to this two-second rule. Your line of vision is now increased and you can spot potential hazards in the traffic flow much sooner. You have more time to avoid potholes and debris on the roadway. In mud or slush, your windshield won't get quite as dirty.

7. Keep cool. Be patient and tolerant at the wheel. You are more likely to have an accident when you're angry or tense; the same is true of the other driver. Anything you do to upset him will increase the chances of an accident. Courtesy is contagious. Even a small gesture such as letting a motorist get out of his driveway into traffic will put at least two drivers in a safer frame of mind.

8. Leave a margin for error; mistakes are made by the best of drivers. Allow extra room to permit evasive action if the other driver makes a misjudgment or has reflexes dulled by fatigue or alcohol. In traffic, observe the vehicles around you and compensate for any erratic behavior by other drivers by giving them a wide berth.

9. Beware of what psychologists call "mental set." Some drivers, even those with good eyesight, fail to take appropriate notice of certain things. An example is the motorist who seems unaware of any vehicle smaller than his. He may actually observe a motorcycle or a bicycle, but it doesn't register as a potential hazard; he doesn't "see" it. By concentrating on whatever is in your field of vision, your eyesight will actually become sharper. The ideal is relaxed concentration.

10. In passing situations, a car coming straight at you on a two-lane road looks much the same doing 100 km/h (60 mph) as it does doing 50 km/h (30 mph). When in doubt, don't pass. When you *do* pass, do it quickly. Never pass more than one vehicle at a time, especially on two-lane roads.

11. When an approaching driver leaves his high beams on, don't get even by turning yours on. Why should *both* of you be blinded? Reduce your speed, maintain a steady path of travel, and avoid looking directly into the oncoming headlights. Use the three-point scan to improve night vision (see pp. 44–45).

12. Cargo stowed on your roof rack can pose a fatal hazard for another driver. If you are carrying cargo, tie it down securely. Never drive close behind a car with a roofload of baggage or furniture, or a truck carrying loose gravel or such deadly cargo as structural steel or long timbers.

13. If you are descending a hill and a heavy truck looms up behind, run ahead of it until you are on the flat or can find a place to pull off. If a heavy truck comes very close with lights flashing on a downgrade, he may have lost his air brakes—and with them, his air horn.

14. Whenever you find yourself squinting, relax your facial muscles and take a deep breath or two. The extra oxygen not only helps you relax, but also can sharpen your vision momentarily. Blinking can relieve eye tension, too. In the fraction of a second that eyelids close, the muscles of the pupils get a rest. Occasional blinking also keeps the eyes moist and clean.

15. Learn to shift your eyes in quick, continuous movements. Shifting your line of sight back and forth, and up and down, widens your field of vision and sharpens perception of detail. Do not focus on one point, particularly a light, for more than a few moments. You can easily lull yourself into a hypnotic state by staring at something, even for a short time.

16. Two hands are required to steer an automobile, and they should be opposite each other—in the 10-and-2-o'clock position. According to statistics, if you drive with one hand at the top of the wheel you will be at least 50 percent less effective in dealing with an emergency.

17. Everyone who must drive in snowy conditions should learn how to handle a skid by actual practice—on a driving-school skidpan if possible, or in a deserted parking lot. Basically, you must release the brake pedal and steer in the direction of the skid to regain control (see pp. 170–171). This maneuver seems natural in a rear-wheel skid but frighteningly unnatural in a front-wheel skid. Only practice will improve your reflexes in this type of emergency.

18. Windshield washers used at high speed in extremely cold weather can instantly glaze the windshield with ice. The air blast can evaporate the alcohol content of the fluid, leaving only water to hit the glass. If the outside temperature is cold enough to make this a possibility, use the washers at low speed or pull off the road.

19. When driving long distances at night, plan to get an early start, rather than a late one after work. If you must leave straight from work, get some extra sleep the night before. Schedule a food or rest stop every 90 minutes to two hours, and even more often if you are tired. Substitute light snacks at these stops for heavy meals, which can be almost as stupefying as alcohol. Caffeine—in coffee, tea, and soft drinks—will help keep you awake, but only for a limited time.

20. An experienced motorist never gets into a strange car and drives away without taking a few seconds to familiarize himself with the controls. It can be disconcerting, and even dangerous, to reach for the headlights and turn on the windshield wipers.

21. The only safe driver is one who anticipates, and so almost never gets into a situation requiring violent braking or rapid acceleration. In an emergency, there is no time to think: an accident can be all over in less than a second; an emergency lasting two seconds is a long one. So memorize some emergency decisions. For example:
• If swerving to avoid hitting an animal will put you in the path of an oncoming car, hit the animal. This alternative is unpleasant, but will avoid more serious damage or injury to you or other motorists.
• If you hear a tire squeal, you're doing something wrong: accelerating too hard, braking too hard, going too fast in a curve.
• If in doubt, swerve to the right. Running off the road into a ditch or stationary obstacle is almost always preferable to hitting another moving vehicle.

Problem-free touring

The key to enjoyable, trouble-free traveling is planning. Your car is essential to your family's well-being, so first make sure it is in excellent running order. The commonest causes of on-the-road breakdown are problems with tires and electrical and cooling systems, so have your car inspected by a mechanic before you set out. Before—and during—the trip, check the tire pressure, belts, hoses, and battery and oil levels. (You can do this yourself.) Each morning, look under the car for any telltale leaks and have any suspected defects inspected immediately.

Are your travel papers in order? Find out well in advance what documents you will need. Depending on your destination, you may require a passport, visas, international driver's license, certificates of inoculation, or standard identification papers.

If you are entering the United States, a driver's license is no longer sufficient. You must now present proof of citizenship, such as a passport or birth certificate. Otherwise, you could be fined up to $2,000. Mexico requires proof of citizenship and a tourist card (obtainable at a Mexican consulate, at a travel bureau, or through your travel agent). Since health regulations often change without notice, check all requirements prior to departure with Health and Welfare Canada, the International Association for Medical Assistance to Travellers (IAMAT), or the consulates of the countries you will be visiting.

Check the terms of your provincial health insurance plan and determine whether you should invest in additional private coverage. If you are taking your own car on the trip, do not forget to carry your vehicle registration and insurance certificate. Finally, before you depart, contact your local Canadian Automobile Association member club or the service department of your car's manufacturer to determine the location of service networks along the route you plan to take.

For most travelers, *expense* is the most important part of planning a trip. Calculate the total cost of a car vacation in advance by considering:
- cost of transportation (fuel, toll charges, car rental, air transportation, other);
- accommodations, meals, tips;
- insurance (extra medical coverage, travel coverage, if applicable);
- documents (special documents for your car, international driving permit, visas);
- recreation and entertainment costs (entrance fees to museums, amusement parks, and other attractions; tickets to special events; rental charges for boats, bicycles, or ski equipment; gifts and souvenirs).

If you're traveling outside Canada, keep abreast of daily exchange rates and how they affect your budget.

Car rentals are available almost everywhere in North America, and in most large cities overseas. Although nearly all U.S. rental agencies permit you to hire a car in one city and leave it in another without additional charges, there is usually a fee for this convenience in Canada. Rates vary widely; if you plan to do a lot of driving in a short time, look for rental companies that charge by day rather than by distance driven.

Before you rent, check the deductible clause in the insurance coverage. Some companies set deductibles as high as $500 which, in the event of an accident, could drain your family's vacation fund. For a premium—an extra few dollars a day—the company's collision insurance will cover the deductible amount. If you rent frequently, inquire about adding a clause in your own insurance that will cover you no matter what car you drive.

Whenever you travel by plane, train, or bus and plan to rent a car when you arrive at your destination, consult your local CAA club before your departure or check with your carrier. Many carriers offer a discount if you combine your travel with a car rental. At an airport, do not simply limit your inquiries to car-rental agencies that have counters in the terminal building. A telephone directory may help you find a company offering better rates, plus transportation to the pickup point.

Taking your car abroad? In addition to your provincial driver's license and vehicle registration, you may need a *carnet* (an official customs document required of motorists crossing European borders), an international driving permit, and a Canadian nationality driving plate with "CDN" on it. Applications for the *carnet* and the international permit are available only from the CAA and its member clubs. Anyone may apply for this documentation.

While planning an overseas trip, look into insurance regulations as well. Many countries, including all of Europe, require proof of insurance before your car can cross their borders. For a European trip, it may be wise to purchase the Touraide package offered to CAA members through an affiliate, the ANWB (Royal Dutch Touring Club). Help will then be a mere phone call away, whatever the crisis, and wherever you may be in Europe. In addition to roadside emergency service, you may receive extended credit, emergency cash, delivery of replacement parts, even chauffeur service.

Tailor-made travel

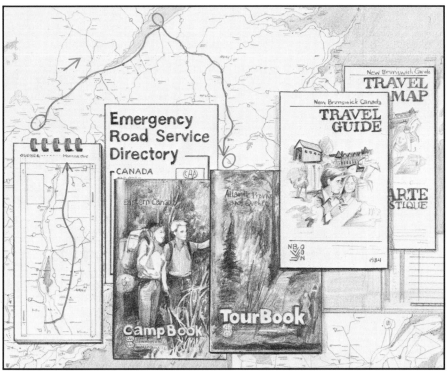

Custom-planned travel is a specialty of the Canadian Automobile Association. Their travel counselors can help you plan your itinerary and provide up-to-date city maps as well as information on lodging, campgrounds, restaurants, service stations, time changes, highway codes, and customs regulations. In addition to indicating the best routes to take (both the quickest and most scenic), the counselor can answer questions about things to see and do in the places you plan to visit. You will also receive advice about area hotels, motels, and restaurants, based on the CAA's own inspection and rating service.

If you are driving from Montréal to the Maritimes, for example, you can obtain a CAA travel package like the one pictured above. The CAA *TourBook* describes local attractions, and provides a detailed list of accommodations and restaurants in the region. The *Triptik* is a routing, tailored specifically to your needs on a series of up-to-date strip maps, plus travel and customs tips. The emergency road service directory lists CAA-approved garages along the way. The guide to campgrounds in eastern Canada is a directory of accredited camping and trailer sites. A full-size map of Atlantic Canada completes the package.

Brief yourself. The more you know about your destination, the more you will enjoy your trip. When you travel in North America, consult a good travel guide or the CAA's regional *TourBook* series. If your destination is a foreign country—or an unfamiliar region of North America—read up on the foods, customs, weather, and dress requirements, currencies, laws, and rules of the road. Investigate the import regulations of each destination. (Fruits and fresh meat cannot be transported across some borders; some countries will not allow your pet to enter; alcohol and firearms are restricted in many places.) You may also wish to purchase a language phrase book to make communication and direction-finding easier.

Plan for enjoyment. When you calculate your driving distances for each day, keep in mind that your averages probably won't match the maximum allowable speed. For most people, 500–600 kilometres (300–350 miles)—the distance between Montréal and Toronto—is a good average. Allow a rest stop every 150 kilometres (100 miles), and include time to stretch your legs whenever you stop for gas. Follow the roadside exercises on page 61 to relieve cramped muscles and sore backs.

In the car, try to adopt a comfortable driving posture. Watch for unconscious driving habits such as clenching your teeth, gripping the steering wheel too tightly, and hunching your shoulders. When you recognize these signs, it's time to pull over. Not only will you be more relaxed as you travel, you will also reach your destination more refreshed, ready to enjoy your stay.

Choosing an RV

A recreational vehicle (RV) can free your family from motel and restaurant expense, and allow you to enjoy the outdoors in a new, comfortable way. It is, however, a sizable investment. Will you use the RV enough to justify the expenditure? The average camper is used about 34 days a year. If you plan to use an RV less often than that, consider renting instead of buying.

To determine whether you really want to buy an RV and, if so, what type to look for, consider these RV "facts of life":

• What can you *really* afford? Multi-year finance plans are available, and RVs depreciate less rapidly than passenger cars. But, even with an attractive payment plan, it's still a large investment—perhaps second only to your house. One rule of thumb is not to spend more than ten percent of your monthly family income on RV payments.

• Where do you want to go? Depending on the size of your RV, your travel may be restricted by tunnels, low bridges, and narrow country roads.

• How maneuverable is the vehicle? Even the best-designed RVs are more difficult to park, steer, and stop than a car. You will have to acquire specialized driving skills.

• Are you prepared to deal with the defective wiring, clogged sinks, and housecleaning that goes with RV ownership?

• How big is your family? Imagine everyone going to bed or having meals. What about privacy for dressing, and bathroom location?

• What about family transportation? Passengers cannot ride in a trailer as they can in vans and motor homes. However, you can establish a convenient "base camp" with your trailer while you sightsee around the area in your car, which will consume a lot less fuel than a heavy RV.

• What will be your additional operating costs for gasoline, propane, electricity, storage, insurance, and maintenance?

It's a good idea to rent before buying. Talk to RV owners about their dealers, and the advantages and disadvantages of their vehicles. Look for a single warranty and a sound service agreement. Then inspect the dealer's service department to ensure that promises about repairs can be kept.

Finally, if you decide in favor of a trailer, make sure your car or truck is powerful enough to pull the load. Have your CAA inspection center or a reliable mechanic check the vehicle. Consider having an oversize radiator or transmission cooler installed to prevent engine overheating. Trucks must be checked to make sure they can carry the weight of a camper top *plus* passengers.

Under canvas or over a truck

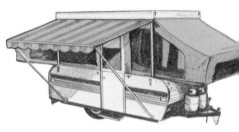

Tent trailers, the cheapest and simplest RVs, fold down into a compact, low-profile box on wheels which can be towed by almost any kind of vehicle. Available with soft canvas or hard fiberglass tops, tent trailers sleep two to six adults. These RVs may require electrical and sewage hookups. Units can be well appointed, with gas or propane stove, mini-refrigerator, toilet, and heater. Look for zippered rather than permanent doors and windows. Better models have leveling jacks for parking on uneven terrain.

Buying a used RV

A new trailer, camper, or motor home loses up to 30 percent of its value as soon as it leaves the lot. In subsequent years, however, an RV will depreciate more slowly than a car. As a result, more than one-quarter of the RVs sold each year are used.

Latches on cupboards should be secure. If not, food and dishes may tumble out on sharp turns or sudden stops.

Insulation should keep the interior walls of a heated trailer warm, with no cold spots.

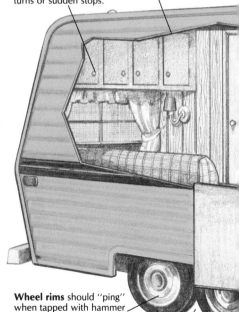

Wheel rims should "ping" when tapped with hammer or wrench; cracked wheels make a dull sound.

Brakes and bearings should be clean and dry, with no sign of unusual wear.

Motor homes are self-contained, roomy, and often luxurious, but expensive to buy and operate. The smallest are *van conversions* suitable for weekend camping and two to four adults. The largest models have room for up to ten people, with extra weight-carrying dual rear wheels and tandem axles. Don't buy a motor home with more built-in cupboards than you will need—they raise the vehicle's center of gravity and reduce maneuverability. A skylight will add light and increase ventilation.

Truck campers provide living space in a separate unit that either slides onto the bed of a pickup truck or is bolted directly to the truck chassis. The slide-in models from 2.4 to 3.6 m (8 to 12 ft) are most popular, and offer sleeping room for as many as six people—with two in the compartment over the cab. There is also room for closets and overhead cabinets, but these can make the truck top-heavy if overloaded. Chassis-mounted truck campers allow for a larger "box" and lower center of gravity.

If you're considering buying a trailer *(below)*, the first thing to check is the tongue weight (the pressure the trailer exerts on the car hitch). If it exceeds 68 kg (150 lb), you will need to have a special load-leveling hitch installed.

If you are buying from a dealer, get a warranty. (All you can demand from a private seller is proof of ownership and a bill of sale.) Look for the labels of the CSA (Canadian Standards Association) and the CRVA (Canadian Recreational Vehicles Association).

Roof should have reinforced joints and adequate headroom.

Leaky roof produces interior stains around the ceiling, top ventilator, and windows.

Windows and doors should open and close easily and not rattle.

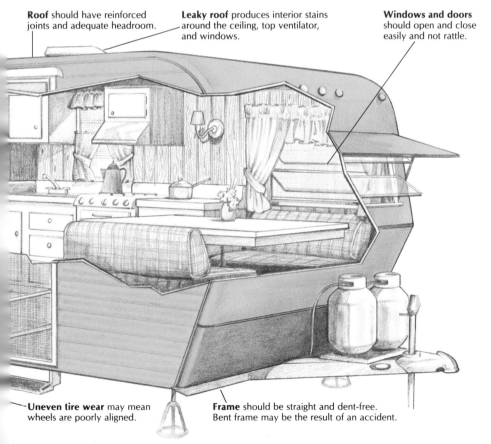

Uneven tire wear may mean wheels are poorly aligned.

Frame should be straight and dent-free. Bent frame may be the result of an accident.

How to pull anything—safely

Before towing anything with your car or truck, check with your dealer or manufacturer for your vehicle's towing capacity, and have a qualified garage install a hitch. Welding the hitch to your car frame is a job for a professional; doing it yourself can be dangerous and may well void your warranty. The hitch installation should include safety chains and an electrical outlet for the trailer taillights, stoplights, and turn signals.

Before each trip and after every stop, check the following:
• The trailer and car should be level when hitched. Heavy items should be packed low and near the center of the trailer.
• The hitch should be securely attached to the tow vehicle. Look for loose welds, broken bolts, missing nuts, and stress cracks in the hitch supports.
• All trailer lights should be working.
• The load-equalizing system and mirrors should be properly adjusted.

• There should be no passengers or pets in the trailer while it is moving.
• All tires should be in good condition and properly inflated.

Before you venture onto the highway, practice towing maneuvers on an empty parking lot, where mistakes won't lead to an accident. On the road, be aware of your added length and reduced maneuverability. Accelerate slowly and evenly to save gas and reduce engine strain. Pass only when absolutely necessary, and be sure you have enough clear distance before you start. Do not pull back into the right lane too quickly; the trailer could start to fishtail. Use your side mirrors, but do not rely solely on their incomplete view. Remember that drivers you pass may not expect to see a trailer behind your vehicle. Try to anticipate their actions by driving defensively.

To ensure you are driving at a safe following distance, allow a car and trailer length

The right hitch

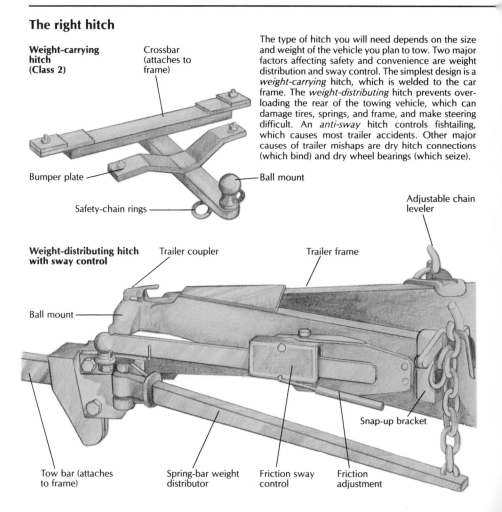

Weight-carrying hitch (Class 2)

Crossbar (attaches to frame)

Bumper plate

Safety-chain rings

Ball mount

The type of hitch you will need depends on the size and weight of the vehicle you plan to tow. Two major factors affecting safety and convenience are weight distribution and sway control. The simplest design is a *weight-carrying* hitch, which is welded to the car frame. The *weight-distributing* hitch prevents overloading the rear of the towing vehicle, which can damage tires, springs, and frame, and make steering difficult. An *anti-sway* hitch controls fishtailing, which causes most trailer accidents. Other major causes of trailer mishaps are dry hitch connections (which bind) and dry wheel bearings (which seize).

Weight-distributing hitch with sway control

Trailer coupler

Trailer frame

Adjustable chain leveler

Ball mount

Snap-up bracket

Tow bar (attaches to frame)

Spring-bar weight distributor

Friction sway control

Friction adjustment

behind the vehicle ahead for each 16 km/h (10 mph) of speed. Alternatively, maintain a 3- to 4-second following distance (see pp. 36–37). When a large vehicle passes, you will feel the turbulence. Instead of braking to maintain control, adjust your steering. Be prepared to slow down for dips and bumps in the road; otherwise the rear of your trailer could drag bottom and be damaged. Do not drive too near the edge of the road; if the trailer's right wheel wanders onto the shoulder or curb, it could cause the car and trailer to fishtail.

Most trailers with a load capacity of more than 700 kg (1,540 lb) have their own electric or hydraulic braking system. This prevents the trailer from pushing the towing vehicle from behind at stops. Even with this second set of brakes, it is important to remember that stopping requires much more distance when pulling a trailer. Avoid high-speed passing lanes on highways and antici-

pate the need for sudden slowdowns or stops before they occur. If you must pull off the road, be sure the shoulder is firm enough to support both car and trailer.

Signal your intentions well in advance. When turning right at an intersection, take a position farther from the curb than you would with just your car. Keep the vehicle in a straight-ahead position until the front wheels are well beyond the corner. Then turn the steering wheel sharply right. Check the right side mirror to be sure the trailer wheels do not jump the curb. For a left turn, proceed even farther into the intersection than normal. Swing wide enough so that the trailer will not become jammed in traffic.

On uphill grades, keep up as much momentum as possible. If your car has a manual transmission, downshift *before* the hill. Driving downhill, change into a lower gear so that the engine can assist the brakes in slowing both the car and trailer.

Backing up

A few minutes behind the wheel will teach you that a car and trailer have certain special driving characteristics. Reversing is the maneuver which causes the most difficulty for the inexperienced trailer operator. It should be done slowly, preferably with the assistance of someone to guide you. Although an experienced driver can avoid backing up in most parking situations, it is an important skill to master. Tow your trailer to an empty parking lot and practice the technique before you set out on a long trip. Leave yourself plenty of room so that your mistakes will not lead to a dented fender.

First, walk behind the trailer to make sure the path is clear (don't rely on the mirrors; trailers have huge blind spots). It is important to back slowly, turning the steering wheel *right* to back to the left, and *left* to go right. Since this may seem unnatural at first, try this simple trick: place a hand at the bottom of the steering wheel with the car in *Reverse*. Then, when you want to back the trailer to the right, move your hand to the right. To back the trailer to the left, move your hand to the left. One error to avoid: Don't turn the steering wheel too far to either side (which may cause the trailer to jackknife).

Whenever you must back into a space where a turn is required, you will find it easier to back up so that the trailer turns toward the left side of the car, where you can see it over your left shoulder.

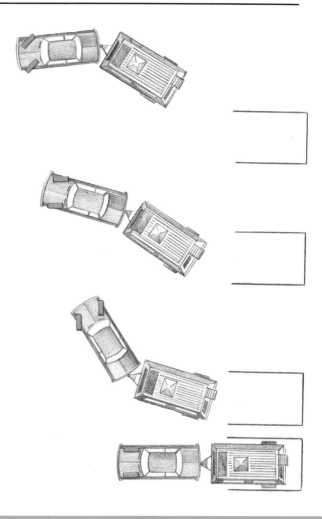

Car rallies for fun and competition

There must be few motorists who have not, at one time or another, fancied themselves as racing drivers. Perhaps this is why rallying is the most popular motor sport in terms of the number of enthusiasts who actually compete.

Navigational rallies can be fun-filled social events or serious contests. This type of rally, often organized by friends, social clubs, and charity groups, can range from cross-country tours to local scavenger hunts. Teams of two, a driver and a navigator, unravel their route by solving a succession of navigational clues. While the navigator racks his brains to decipher the paperwork, the driver may act as little more than chauffeur. Unmodified personal cars are used, and speeds usually average ten percent *below* the legal limit on the usual 100-km course.

Performance, or special stage, rallying is a competitive sport that emphasizes teamwork and driving skill. Each rally consists of a series of "special stages"—stretches of road that are considered particularly challenging. The course is usually a twisting dirt or gravel path strewn with bumps and ruts. Most rally enthusiasts thrive on excitement.

The more challenging the route—especially in snow, mud, or fog—the greater the fun. While rocketing through special stages, participants' speeds can exceed 210 km/h (130 mph).

All special stages in Canada are held on either private roads or public land (often provincial forests) closed to other traffic during competition. Most rallies are run "blind"—participants are unfamiliar with both the route and the roads over which it passes.

Special stages are connected by "transit stages"—sections of public road that take competitors from the finish of one special stage to the start of another. The objective in the transit stage is to drive at or below the speed limit, finishing in *exactly* the assigned amount of time. Early or late arrivals are penalized.

Competing two-person crews start out one or two minutes apart, with their elapsed driving time recorded to the tenth of a second at various checkpoints along the route. At the finish line, the times for each stage are totaled. The crew that has completed the entire rally in the shortest time—and with the fewest penalties—is declared the winner.

A checklist of rally equipment

1. Lights. Although original headlights must remain, competitors may add up to four auxiliary headlights. A single switch must operate all high-beam headlights and auxiliary lights.

2. Tires. Much competitive rallying takes place on loose surfaces, so tires must stand up to pounding as well as provide vital traction. Serious competitors use several sets, and change all four tires as road conditions vary.

3. Wheels must be the same diameter as the originals, and up to 2.5 cm (1 in.) wider.

4. Suspension, which must withstand constant pounding, tops the list of permitted modifications, although the standard suspension mounts must remain.

5. Hood lock. The engine compartment cover must open without a key from outside the passenger compartment.

6. Engine. Belts and hoses should be in new condition. Certain performance modifications are permitted, but safety modifications have top priority.

7. Emission control devices, such as the catalytic converter, must be intact and functioning properly.

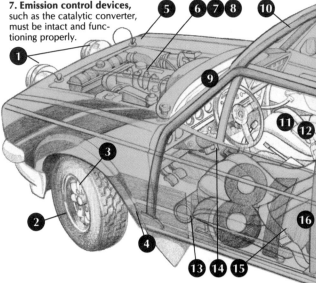

8. Drive shaft must be original and unmodified. However, the housing and mounts must be reinforced to withstand jolts.

9. Windshield must be laminated safety glass; all other windows, tempered safety glass.

10. Roll bar is mandatory in all sanctioned rallies.

11. Standard equipment for your particular car model, such as radio, heater, and rear-window defogger, must be in working order.

In Canada, running times for stage rallies average 8 to 12 hours, traversing an average 200 km (125 mi) in special stages, and 500 km (300 mi) in all. Each participant must be a member of a rally club affiliated with Canadian Automobile Sport Clubs, Inc., the governing body of motor sport in Canada.

In competitive rallying, teamwork is essential. The co-driver navigates by following instructions listed in a specially prepared route book and calling them out to the driver. Simple arrows indicate the direction and severity of turns; landmark information provides visual checkpoints; distances between instructions are given. Experience, instinct, and fast reactions make for a good team. Front-runners, for instance, often speed confidently toward a blind hill because they have already noticed the direction of a grove of trees beyond. In addition, each participant must be his or her own mechanic. A flat tire, broken drive belt, or burst hose must be repaired on the road, with whatever tools or materials are at hand.

Equally important is the performance of the car itself. Rally cars must be production-line models, with most standard equipment in place. Approved additions and alterations are limited—most modifications add to safety rather than performance. For example, roll bars and high-powered spotlights are permitted, but the gearbox may not be modified.

In Canada, only a handful of rally cars are sponsored by car manufacturers; most are privately owned and driven by amateur competitors. If you want to get into the sport, be prepared to spend $5,000 to $15,000 for a used rally car and, if you become a real enthusiast, $40,000 for a world-class vehicle. Or you can convert an off-the-lot car into a rally vehicle; your conversion bill will add up to about $3,000. For aspiring international competitors, the cost of equipment—from extra tires to special seats—often exceeds the price of the car.

Risky as it may sound, rallying—even performance rallying—is one of the safest types of motor sport. This is in large part because competitors must wear helmets and safety harnesses, and because cars are generally four-cylinder, standard models to which full roll bars and other safety gear have been added *(below)*.

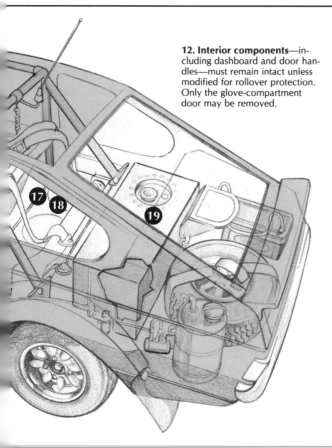

12. Interior components—including dashboard and door handles—must remain intact unless modified for rollover protection. Only the glove-compartment door may be removed.

13. Fire extinguisher is mandatory, and must be readily accessible to seated crew members at all times.

14. Circuit breaker, capable of instantly disconnecting all electrical circuits, must be spark-proof.

15. Safety harness must be worn by both driver and co-driver, and attached to the structural frame.

16. Seats. Most drivers prefer hard bucket seats; co-drivers often have a reclining seat. Both seats must be securely mounted to prevent seat movement in the event of a rollover.

17. Tools must be securely stowed but readily accessible. Drivers may need to find the jack quickly, possibly at night.

18. First-aid kit and warning devices (such as flares and reflector signs) must be carried in the car at all times.

19. Fuel tank and lines. The fuel tank area must be separated from the passenger compartment by a fuel-resistant and fire-retardant plate.

"Reading" the road

Signs, signals, and markings are important because they give you crucial information that affects your driving decisions. Always remember that traffic signs have standard shapes and colors, each with specific meanings. If you are aware of these, you can begin to "read" a sign before you get close enough to actually see the words and symbols. Regulatory signs, which prohibit or require specific acts, are generally rectangular in shape. If you fail to obey such signs, you are breaking the law. Warning signs, usually diamond-shaped and yellow, tell you what to expect on the road ahead. Information and service signs inform you about your route and the travel services along the way. In recent years, internationally recognized symbols have begun to replace written signs.

Regulatory signs

Stop. Always red and octagonal (eight-sided). Full stop required.

Yield. Triangular. Give right-of-way to traffic on intersecting road.

Do not enter. Red circle with white bar. Turn back immediately.

Speed limit

MAXIMUM
50

Maximum speed limit 50 km/h (30 mph).

Minimum speed limit (used on highways) 60 km/h (37 mph).

Speed zone ahead. Slow to posted speed of 50 km/h (30 mph).

Prohibition

No U-turn. Red circle and slash indicates prohibition.

Access prohibited for trucks (such as in residential areas).

Do not pass. Narrow road or other unsafe section.

Crossing

Pedestrian crossing. Yield right-of-way to person crossing here.

Playground crossing. Yield right-of-way to children.

School zone. Blue and white. Watch for children.

Route markers

Numbered primary and secondary highway.

Expressway. Numbered provincial highway.

Trans-Canada Highway. Route number varies across country.

Road services (symbols may appear in combination)

Service station. Open 24 hours a day when posted.

Diesel fuel available. Indicated by an inset D.

Restaurant or snack bar. Often open 24 hours a day.

Lodging. Hotel or motel at intersection. Open year-round.

Restaurant and lodging. Both open year-round.

Campsite. Federal, provincial, or private campground facilities.

Other signs

Alignment marker. Indicates a change in roadway direction to left or right.

Hazard marker. Pass on either side of obstacle, usually a median or other divider.

Tourist information available at this exit; a good place to stop for road directions.

Hospital. Blue (or green) and white. In an emergency, follow the arrow.

Low overhead. Clearance of obstruction (underpass, bridge, or tunnel) given in metres.

Weigh station. All commercial trucks must stop and be weighed ahead, unless station is closed.

Warning

The familiar diamond-shaped *warning* sign is one of the most common signals on Canadian highways. It provides an advance warning of permanent or temporary hazards, from falling rocks to construction.

Divided highway begins. Traffic flows on either side of division.

Road narrows. Traffic merges into fewer lanes or single lane.

Winding road. Several curves less than 150 m (500 feet) apart.

Signals ahead. Reduce speed and be prepared to stop or yield.

Advance stop sign warns of stop ahead at distance indicated.

Railway crossing ahead. Be prepared to stop before crossing.

Rough road surface ahead. Reduce speed and watch for bumps.

Slippery when wet. Reduce speed and avoid sudden turns.

Steep hill ahead. Angle of grade sometimes indicated.

Truck entrance ahead. Construction site or truck terminal.

Construction ahead (yellow or orange). Watch for flagman.

Road ends. Black and yellow checkerboard.

Pavement ends and unimproved surface begins.

Fallen rock hazard. Possible obstruction ahead.

Flooded roadway. Possible hydroplane danger.

Traffic lights

The three-lens red, yellow, and green light found at many intersections is a familiar part of life for drivers. Traffic lights control the flow of traffic and designate who has the right-of-way at a specific time and location. The standard sequence of the signals in North America is green-yellow-red-green. For quick recognition when partly screened from view (and for drivers who are color blind), signals also have standard positions. Vertically, the red light is on top, the yellow in the middle and the green at the bottom. When signals are placed horizontally, the red is at the left, the yellow in the middle and the green at the right. Often, they can also be identified by shape. In standard configuration, the red light is square, the yellow light is diamond-shaped, and the green light is a circle. Unfortunately, traffic lights are so common that they are often taken for granted, or their signals misunderstood.

RED

Stop before entering the intersection or crosswalk (or before the stop line). Most provinces permit a right turn on red after coming to a full stop and yielding to traffic and pedestrians.

YELLOW

Do not enter the intersection. Driving through an intersection on a yellow light is hazardous because cross traffic may be preparing to move. However, unless you can safely stop without blocking the intersection or risking a rear-end collision, it may be safer to continue.

GREEN

Go (when safe to do so). If you are waiting at or approaching an intersection when the light turns green, yield to any cross traffic or pedestrians already in the intersection.

ARROW

You may proceed in the direction of the arrow. A green arrow permits movement only in the direction indicated, and only after yielding to pedestrians and cross traffic.

FLASHING RED

A flashing red light has the same meaning as a stop sign and must be obeyed in the same way. It appears at hazardous intersections where there is not enough cross-street traffic to justify a traffic light.

FLASHING YELLOW

A flashing yellow light indicates a potential hazard; proceed with caution. Since this signal may be used in a variety of locations—such as intersections, fire station areas, or school zones—you should determine its meaning before choosing a proper response.

FLASHING GREEN

You may proceed with caution (usually a left turn); opposing traffic is facing a red light.

FLASHING ARROW

You may proceed in the direction of the arrow; opposing traffic is facing a red light. A flashing yellow arrow means that you must first yield right-of-way before turning.

Pedestrian signals

Walk. Pedestrians may proceed across the intersection.

Flashing don't walk. Pedestrians in the street may continue.

Steady don't walk. Pedestrians must not enter the intersection.

How do you measure up?

Being alert and competent behind the wheel can increase your self-confidence, your passengers' comfort and the safety of all. How do *you* rate as a driver? This is a matter not only of your belief in your own abilities, but also of how you behave toward other road users—and how safely you handle unexpected situations.

The questions on these two pages were designed to get you thinking about your driving—and how you might even be able to improve it. Answer them to the best of your knowledge and judgment. Then compare your answers with those on pages 90–91.

1. You are approaching a set of traffic lights which are red. You are still some distance away from them and see a small line of traffic waiting. What will you do?
a. Ease off the power to slow the car gradually, waiting for the lights to change.
b. Maintain your speed so that following cars will not be tempted to tailgate.
c. Brake early so that you can accelerate when the lights change.

2. You are driving along a narrow highway. Suddenly, a car pulls out from a road at the right and proceeds directly in front of you. What should you do?
a. Downshift through the gears.
b. Brake hard, then release the brakes, then brake hard again.
c. Slam on the brakes.

3. When sudden car trouble forces you to drive more slowly than other traffic, the safest thing to do, after you have moved to the right lane and switched on your flashers, is:
a. relax and enjoy the scenery until you can find a garage;
b. check your rear-view mirrors more frequently than you normally do;
c. concentrate on the road ahead.

4. You are driving in the first light rain after a long dry spell. You should drive:
a. as usual;
b. with extreme caution;
c. as you would in any rainy weather.

5. You are driving around a curve that veers to the left. For maximum stability, you should:
a. keep your speed constant through the bend, leaving it at the same speed at which you entered it;
b. take your foot off the accelerator;
c. accelerate slightly and try to leave the bend a little faster than you entered it.

6. You are driving through bumper-high flood water. You should use:
a. a high gear;
b. a low gear.

7. You are planning to pass a large moving van on a two-lane highway. Before starting the maneuver, you should:
a. switch on your left turn signal, then check in the mirrors to see that all is clear before moving out of your lane;
b. check your mirrors before you switch on your left turn signal.

8. You are driving on a highway in high winds. Exposed stretches of the road are:
a. the main hazard to watch for;
b. one of several hazards to consider.

9. As you pass a slow farm truck, your speed ought to exceed the truck's by about:
a. 8 km/h (5 mph);
b. 24 km/h (15 mph);
c. 40 km/h (25 mph).

10. You are driving at night in a thick fog. It is best to:
a. follow the rear lights of another vehicle;
b. rely on your own perceptions.

11. You are driving along a narrow road with cars parked on both sides. The road is effectively wide enough for only one vehicle to pass. At the far end of the road, another car appears, headlights flashing. What do you do?
a. Accept the invitation and drive forward.
b. Stop and wait to see what the motorist does next.
c. Invite the other driver to come first by flashing your headlights.

12. When you are driving in fog:
a. yellow lights penetrate fog better than white ones;
b. white lights penetrate better.

13. You are approaching an intersection where crossing traffic is controlled by stop signs, and your view is partially blocked by a truck waiting to turn left from the lane next to yours. What should you do?
a. Maintain your speed, since you have the right-of-way.
b. Slow down, and be prepared to stop in case vehicles or pedestrians unexpectedly emerge from the hidden area.
c. Come to a complete stop, and wait for the truck to complete its turn before you proceed.

14. When driving at about 80 km/h (50 mph) in moderate traffic, you spot a board lying across the road, directly in your path. Since you have no time to avoid it by slowing down and changing direction gradually, it is best to:
a. try to hit it as squarely as possible;
b. brake and steer sharply;
c. try to steer around it, but don't brake.

15. You are driving up a snow-covered hill. You should shift into:
a. the highest gear suitable for the gradient;
b. the lowest gear suitable for the gradient.

16. The best way to avoid being involved in a rear-end "chain collision" is to:
a. maintain four car lengths between you and the car ahead;
b. maintain at least a two-second following distance;
c. keep an eye on the car ahead of the one you're following.

17. Your car becomes stranded in a blizzard. It is better to:
a. stay with your car;
b. walk to safety.

18. Your car is first in line at an intersection where the light is about to turn green. You should:
a. avoid holding up traffic behind you by making sure you're ready to move out as soon as the light changes;
b. take at least a second to move your foot from brake to gas after the light changes, then move out slowly.

19. You are worried about your friend, who has been drinking, and is now leaving a party to drive home. You should:
a. make him wait one hour;
b. give him two to three cups of coffee;
c. call a taxi, or invite him to stay overnight.

20. You are driving at night. You should dim your headlights when following another vehicle at less than:
a. 50 metres (164 feet);
b. 100 metres (328 feet);
c. 150 metres (492 feet).

21. Since many accidents happen because one or both drivers "didn't even see the other car," you decide to buy a highly visible car. You choose one that is:
a. white with a shiny, black-vinyl top;
b. "fire-engine" red;
c. bright yellow.

22. Driving alone, you are unable to find a legal parking space near the store where you must pick up a large, heavy package. You:
a. park your car in a no-parking zone in front of the store, and put your flashers on;
b. keep looking for a space, or arrange for someone to go with you to run the errand while you drive around the block.

23. Your most important quality is:
a. fast reaction;
b. good anticipation.

24. You must drive a long distance. This is best done:
a. between midnight and dawn;
b. during the day.

25. You arrive at an intersection at the same time as two other motorists—one on the cross street to your left and one to your right. Who has the right-of-way?
a. You do.
b. The motorist to your left.
c. The motorist to your right.

26. You are driving at night, and the lights of oncoming traffic dazzle you. Putting on tinted glasses will:
a. allow you to see better;
b. impair your vision.

27. When stopping for a red light behind another car, you should always leave:
a. about 1 m (3 ft) between you and the car ahead;
b. about 2 m (6 ft);
c. about one car length.

28. You are driving straight into the late-afternoon sun on a cold winter day. What type of sunglasses are most suitable?
a. Photochromic sunglasses, which lighten or darken in response to sunlight.
b. Polarized sunglasses.

29. You are stopped at a traffic signal. The light changes while a pedestrian is still in the intersection. Who now has the right-of-way?
a. The pedestrian.
b. You do.

30. If you can't help driving when overtired, the safest course is to:
a. drive a bit more slowly than usual, open your window, and tune in a talk show;
b. drive at a safe speed, keep the temperature comfortable, and listen to music;
c. eat something to give you energy and have coffee before starting out.

Answers

1. a. By looking ahead you will have seen the red traffic light in good time. You will conserve fuel by easing off the power, thus staying in high gear for as long as possible.

2. b. The brakes are designed to stop the car; they, not the gears, should be used for this purpose. The technique of releasing the brakes just before they lock up, then quickly re-applying them, is the safest way to stop—particularly if the road surface is poor or slippery. Maintaining hard, steady pressure on the brake pedal could lock the wheels and cause a dangerous skid. (However, you should have spotted the side road earlier and been prepared for a vehicle to emerge.)

3. b. Be on the lookout for cars behind you, whose drivers may be inattentive. When traveling at high speeds, especially on winding roads, they can be dangerous. On multilane highways, watch for cars quickly changing into your lane—often without signaling—in order to exit at right.

4. b. You should be especially careful, because such light rain mixes with the oil and rubber deposits that accumulate on the road during a dry spell. They form an extremely slippery surface film which can also fill the treads of your tires. Allow plenty of room for braking under such conditions.

5. c. Progressive acceleration through the bend maintains the car's stability, although the amount of power should be carefully controlled. Once you see the end of the curve, accelerate smoothly but gently. To avoid skidding, never brake on a bend unless it is an emergency; even then do not brake any more than necessary.

6. b. There are two points to remember when driving through deep flood water or puddles: Keep the car moving, and prevent water from entering the engine or exhaust pipe. It is best to drive slowly to minimize the bow wave, and in first gear (*Low* on automatic transmissions) to keep the engine speed up.

7. b. Once you have decided on your course of action, you should always check your mirrors before making a signal of any kind. Make sure the other lane is clear immediately beside you, as well as ahead and behind.

8. b. There are several possible hazards to consider when driving in a high wind. Exposed stretches of road are, of course, susceptible to crosswinds. But you will also have to deal with sudden side gusts when you drive under bridges, and buffeting when you are passing or being passed by trucks. In all these cases it is important not to be panicked into making rapid or excessive steering corrections.

9. b. At 8 km/h (5 mph) faster, you would take too long to pass a slow-moving vehicle. However, at 40 km/h (25 mph), you would find it almost impossible to avoid a collision if the truck suddenly turned left or drifted across the center line.

10. b. It can be dangerous in fog to follow another driver's rear lights, for several reasons. You can become hypnotized and disoriented by the lights, or given a false impression of speed, which may result in your driving too fast. The fog in the wake of another vehicle is thinned by its passage, so you could be led to believe that the fog is thinner than it actually is. In addition, the driver in front may be going too fast for safety. Rely on your own perceptions of the conditions and drive at a speed which will ensure sufficient braking distance.

11. b. Headlight signals are very ambiguous and can be easily misinterpreted. The only safe meaning they can have is "I am here." Do not, therefore, assume that the other driver's headlight flash is an invitation until you observe what the driver does next. Never flash your own lights to convey a message.

12. b. White lights penetrate fog better than yellow lights. Yellow lights produce less glare, which may give an impression of good fog penetration.

13. b. Having the right-of-way does not relieve you of the responsibility to do all you can to avoid an accident. Whether your view is blocked or not, you are required by the highway code to yield to any vehicle or pedestrian close enough to constitute an immediate hazard. Treat this intersection as though it had a flashing yellow light. You may proceed—with caution—only when the coast is clear.

14. a. Take your foot off the accelerator and try to hit the obstacle as squarely as possible. It is better to get a hard jolt or a flat tire than to lose control of the car—a definite possibility if you swerve or brake hard or do both at highway speeds.

15. a. Select the highest suitable gear. But remember, if you use too high a gear, you will probably have to change gears partway up the hill—which could result in your getting stuck. If you use too low a gear, you could end up spinning your wheels because of the extra power you are giving them. With an automatic transmission, your best choice would be *Second* rather than *High* or *Low*.

16. b. You can estimate safe following distances more accurately in seconds than in car lengths. To determine the number of seconds between you and the car ahead, pick a stationary object near the road and, as the car ahead passes it, begin to count until *you* reach the object.

17. a. As a rule, if you are far from safety and the weather is bad, stay with your car. You will be better able to keep warm, and rescuers can more easily locate you in a stranded car than if you are wandering through the snow. When waiting in the car, keep moving and do not allow yourself to fall asleep. A single burning candle can provide enough heat to keep you from freezing.

18. b. That extra second can keep you safe from drivers who rush through a yellow light as it turns red. Although this is a violation, it does happen.

19. c. The safest course is to prevent your friend from driving for several hours, or overnight, until he is completely sober. Hot coffee, exercise, and fresh air may have a short-lived psychological effect, but will not accelerate the body's elimination of alcohol.

20. c. Dim your headlights when within 150 m (492 ft). Remember to dim them for oncoming traffic as well, even on divided highways.

21. c. Some fire departments have begun to paint their trucks yellow. Except against snow, red has proven hard to see on the road (especially at night or in fog), and two-toned cars tend to "disappear" into their surroundings.

22. b. Even with your flashers on, you may not park in a no-parking zone. If you do, you are risking a parking ticket.

23. b. Although fast reactions are very important, anticipation helps you avoid potential danger well in advance, *before* emergency situations arise.

24. b. Obviously, visibility will be better during daylight hours, and chances are that you—as well as other drivers—will be more alert at noon than at midnight. Statistics also show that your chances of being involved in an accident rise between dusk and dawn, partly because of the increase in the number of drinking drivers then.

25. c. When two or more vehicles approach or enter a controlled intersection at the same time, the driver on the right has the right-of-way. Therefore, the driver to your right may proceed first, followed by you and, finally, the driver to your left. But be careful: the driver on your left may not know the rules.

26. b. Never wear dark glasses when driving at night. To reduce the little light available after dusk by wearing sunglasses is to court danger. Instead, use the three-point scan to avoid staring directly into oncoming headlights (see pp. 44–45).

27. c. With a safety margin of one car length, you can see around the vehicle in front of you, or, if a car should come up too quickly from behind, you can move to one side or go forward a bit to avoid being hit.

28. b. Polychromic sunglasses are unlikely to be suitable for this task. Their darkening effect depends on the intensity of the light, which, in this situation, may not be bright enough. These lenses are also affected by temperature; if it is cold inside your car, they may not darken sufficiently. Polarized sunglasses will more effectively cut glare.

29. a. At controlled intersections, a pedestrian must obey the signals, but, once in the intersection, has the right-of-way.

30. a. Compensate for fatigue by driving more slowly than usual. Fresh air and conversation will help, but the effects of high-energy foods are only temporary.

How do you rate?
26–30 correct: Excellent. You are a thoughtful, defensive driver who should seldom have even a close call.
21–25 correct: Good. You have basic driving and safety skills.
16–20 correct: Fair. You may be an infrequent motorist who needs to refresh your skills and practice driver etiquette.
15 or fewer correct: Poor. You should consider taking a driving-safety course.

Directory of CAA offices

In the early 1900s, the typical Canadian motorist had to possess both patience and a sense of adventure. He was faced with poor roads, irate farmers, lack of road signs, and oppressive license fees (Québec charged a then-outrageous price of $5.00 for annual registration). In 1913, local motor clubs which had formed across Canada banded together in a national federation, the Canadian Automobile Association, to fight for better roads and more sensible highway laws.

CAA clubs now serve more than two million members, and continue to campaign for safer streets and highways. More than 40 years ago, the CAA organized the school safety program in Canada. This program now involves more than 100,000 patrollers, protecting the lives of some five million children on their way to and from school. Several clubs offer driver education services for both teenage and adult drivers. In a number of provinces, the CAA and its member clubs assist in the training of high school teachers who will later instruct pupils in driver education.

The CAA direct member services include the following:

• *Emergency road service* is provided by the club's own vehicles, dispatched 24 hours a day, seven days a week.

• *Technical services.* Several clubs perform vehicle inspections for members. For a fee, the vehicle is given a thorough, unbiased examination and a report of its condition is provided. CAA clubs also supply road reports, maintenance information, and other technical advice.

• *Approved auto repair service* assures members that more than 1,300 approved garages across Canada will perform guaranteed repair work at a reasonable cost.

• *Auto travel services* include personalized trip routings, tour books for areas to be visited, road maps, road service directories, and campground listings (see p. 77).

• *Club travel agencies* offer domestic and foreign travel services, including chartered and escorted tours, transportation and hotel reservations, car rentals, travel insurance, and traveler's cheques.

• *International services.* Through the CAA's affiliation in a worldwide chain of auto clubs that spans 100 countries and serves a combined membership of more than 45 million motorists, CAA members traveling abroad can obtain advice and services from any member club.

• *Community service.* The CAA monitors all legislation affecting motorists and represents its members' interests at various levels of government.

CAA member clubs

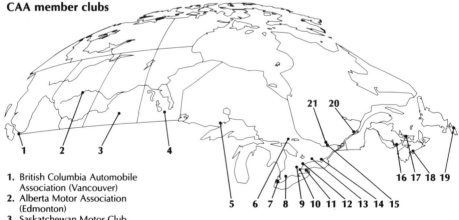

1. **British Columbia Automobile Association** (Vancouver)
2. **Alberta Motor Association** (Edmonton)
3. **Saskatchewan Motor Club** (Regina)
4. **Manitoba Motor League** (Winnipeg)
5. **OML Northwestern Ontario Club** (Thunder Bay)
6. **CAA-Sudbury**
7. **CAA-Windsor**
8. **OML Elgin Norfolk Club** (St. Thomas)
9. **CAA Mid-Western Ontario Auto Club** (Kitchener)
10. **Hamilton Automobile Club**
11. **OML Niagara Peninsula Club** (St. Catharines)
12. **CAA-Toronto**
13. **CAA-Peterborough**
14. **OML Eastern Ontario Club** (Kingston)
15. **OML Ottawa Club**
16. **Maritime Automobile Association** (Saint John)
17. **Maritime Automobile Association** (Charlottetown)
18. **Maritime Automobile Association** (Halifax)
19. **Newfoundland and Labrador Automobile Assoc.** (St. John's)
20. **CAA-Québec**
21. **CAA National Administrative Office** (Ottawa)

British Columbia Automobile Association

Provincial Headquarters:
BCAA
999 West Broadway
P.O. Box 9900
VANCOUVER, B.C.
V6B 4H1
Telephone: (604) 732-3911

Branch Offices:
BCAA
Southgate Shopping Centre
45905 Yale Road West
CHILLIWACK, B.C.
V2P 2M6
Telephone: (604) 792-4664

BCAA
Pine Tree Village, Unit 42
2991 Lougheed Highway
COQUITLAM, B.C.
V3B 6J6
Telephone: (604) 464-3311

BCAA
Scott 72 Centre
7325—120 Street
DELTA, B.C.
V4C 6P5
Telephone: (604) 594-2222

BCAA
243 Seymour Street
KAMLOOPS, B.C.
V2C 2E7
Telephone: (604) 372-9577

BCAA
2159 Departure Bay Road
NANAIMO, B.C.
V9S 3V5
Telephone: (604) 758-7377

BCAA
556 Baker Street
NELSON, B.C.
V1L 4H9
Telephone: (604) 352-3535

BCAA
755—6th Street
NEW WESTMINSTER, B.C.
V3L 3C6
Telephone: (604) 521-3791

BCAA
1605 Hamilton Avenue
NORTH VANCOUVER, B.C.
V7P 2L9
Telephone: (604) 986-1941

BCAA
512 Martin Street
PENTICTON, B.C.
V2A 5C7
Telephone: (604) 492-7016

BCAA
690 Victoria Street
PRINCE GEORGE, B.C.
V2L 2K4
Telephone: (604) 563-0417

BCAA
Lansdowne Plaza
116—4940 No. 3 Road
RICHMOND, B.C.
V6X 3A5
Telephone: (604) 278-4646

BCAA
1075 Pandora Avenue
VICTORIA, B.C.
V8V 3P7
Telephone: (604) 382-8171

Alberta Motor Association

Provincial Headquarters:
AMA
11230—110 Street
P.O. Box 3740, Station "D"
EDMONTON, Alta.
T5L 4J5
Telephone: (403) 474-8660

Branch Offices:
AMA
215 Bear Street
P.O. Box 1520
BANFF, Alta.
T0L 0C0
Telephone: (403) 762-2266

AMA
4700—17th Avenue South West
CALGARY, Alta.
T3E 0E3
Telephone: (403) 246-7900

AMA
532—10816 MacLeod Trail S.E.
CALGARY, Alta.
T2J 5N8
Telephone: (403) 278-3530

AMA
4807—50 Street
CAMROSE, Alta.
T4V 1P4
Telephone: (403) 672-3391

AMA
109 Street & Kingsway Avenue
P.O. Box 3500, Station "D"
EDMONTON, Alta.
T5L 4J5
Telephone: (403) 474-8601

AMA
150 Southpark Village
3803 Calgary Trail South
EDMONTON, Alta.
T6J 5M8
Telephone: (403) 438-4942

AMA
15819—87 Avenue
EDMONTON, Alta.
T5R 4E7
Telephone: (403) 484-1221

AMA
105—9911 MacDonald Avenue
FORT McMURRAY, Alta.
T9H 1S7
Telephone: (403) 743-2433

AMA
10828—100 Street
GRANDE PRAIRIE, Alta.
T8V 2M8
Telephone: (403) 532-4421

AMA
608—5th Avenue South
LETHBRIDGE, Alta.
T1J 4B9
Telephone: (403) 328-1181

AMA
2710—13 Avenue South East
Box 610
MEDICINE HAT, Alta.
T1A 7G5
Telephone: (403) 527-1166

AMA
9611—100 Street
Box 2256
PEACE RIVER, Alta.
T0H 2X0
Telephone: (403) 624-1175

AMA
2965 Bremner Avenue
RED DEER, Alta.
T4R 1S2
Telephone: (403) 346-6633

AMA
C5002—51 Avenue
Hartland Plaza
STETTLER, Alta.
T0C 2L0
Telephone: (403) 742-2357

Saskatchewan Motor Club

Provincial Headquarters:
SMC
200 Albert Street North
REGINA, Sask.
S4R 5E2
Telephone: (306) 543-5677

Branch Offices:
SMC
80 Caribou Street West
MOOSE JAW, Sask.
S6H 2J6
Telephone: (306) 693-5195

SMC
2002—100th Street
NORTH BATTLEFORD, Sask.
S9A 0X5
Telephone: (306) 445-9451

SMC
68—13th Street West
PRINCE ALBERT, Sask.
S6V 3E8
Telephone: (306) 764-6818

SMC
3806 Albert Street
REGINA, Sask.
S4S 3R2
Telephone: (306) 586-1844

Directory of CAA offices

SMC
321—4th Avenue North
SASKATOON, Sask.
S7K 2L9
Telephone: (306) 653-1833

SMC
300 Begg Street West
SWIFT CURRENT, Sask.
S9H 0K6
Telephone: (306) 773-3193

SMC
Weyburn Square
110 Souris Avenue
WEYBURN, Sask.
S4H 2Z8
Telephone: (306) 842-6651

SMC
159 Broadway Street East
YORKTON, Sask.
S3N 3K6
Telephone: (306) 783-6536

Manitoba Motor League

Provincial Headquarters:
MML
870 Empress Street
P.O. Box 1400
WINNIPEG, Man.
R3C 2Z3
Telephone: (204) 786-5411

Branch Offices:
MML
940 Princess Avenue
P.O. Box 1042
BRANDON, Man.
R7A 6A3
Telephone: (204) 727-1394

MML
Portage La Prairie Mall
P.O. Box 398
PORTAGE LA PRAIRIE, Man.
R1N 3B7
Telephone: (204) 239-6455

Ontario Motor League

Provincial Office:
OML-Provincial
2 Carlton Street, Suite 619
TORONTO, Ont.
M5B 1K4
Telephone: (416) 964-3068

Offices:
CAA-Toronto
320 Bayfield Street
BARRIE, Ont.
L4M 3C1
Telephone: (705) 726-1803

OML
181 Pinnacle Street
Box 264
BELLEVILLE, Ont.
K8N 5A2
Telephone: (613) 968-4733

CAA-Toronto
Bramalea City Centre
Unit 310
BRAMALEA, Ont.
L6T 3R5
Telephone: (416) 793-4911

OML
175 Hespeler Road
CAMBRIDGE, Ont.
N1R 3H6
Telephone: (519) 622-2620

CAA-Windsor
810 Richmond Street
P.O. Box 622
CHATHAM, Ont.
N6M 5K8
Telephone: (519) 351-2222

CAA-Windsor
7 Rattenbury Street
Box 560
CLINTON, Ont.
N0M 1L0
Telephone: (519) 482-9300

CAA-Peterborough
39 King Street West
COBOURG, Ont.
K9A 2M1
Telephone: (416) 372-8777

CAA-Sudbury
Espanola Mall
ESPANOLA, Ont.
P0P 1C0
Telephone: (705) 869-3611

OML
94 Gordon Street
GUELPH, Ont.
N1H 4H6
Telephone: (519) 821-9940

CAA-Toronto
5233 Dundas Street West
ISLINGTON, Ont.
M9B 1A6
Telephone: (416) 231-4181

OML
2300 Princess Street
KINGSTON, Ont.
K7M 3G4
Telephone: (613) 546-2679

OML
836 Courtland Avenue East
KITCHENER, Ont.
N2C 1K3
Telephone: (519) 576-1020

OML
1069 Wellington Road South
LONDON, Ont.
N6E 2H6
Telephone: (519) 685-3140

CAA-Toronto
Square One
100 City Centre Drive
MISSISSAUGA, Ont.
L5B 2C9
Telephone: (416) 275-2501

OML
4444 Drummond Road
NIAGARA FALLS, Ont.
L2E 6C6
Telephone: (416) 357-0001

CAA-Sudbury
300 Lakeshore Drive
NORTH BAY, Ont.
P1A 3V2
Telephone: (705) 474-8230

CAA-Windsor
150 First Street
ORANGEVILLE, Ont.
L9W 3T7
Telephone: (519) 941-8360

CAA-Toronto
64 Mississauga Street West
ORILLIA, Ont.
L3V 3A7
Telephone: (705) 325-7211

CAA-Toronto
340 King Street West
OSHAWA, Ont.
L1J 2J9
Telephone: (416) 723-5203

OML
Lincoln Fields Shopping Centre
1354 Richmond Road
Box 8350
OTTAWA, Ont.
K1G 3T2
Telephone: (613) 820-1890

CAA-Windsor
187—10th Street West
P.O. Box 518
OWEN SOUND, Ont.
N4K 5R1
Telephone: (519) 376-1940

CAA-Sudbury
Parry Sound Mall
70 Joseph Street
PARRY SOUND, Ont.
P2A 2G5
Telephone: (705) 746-9000

CAA-Peterborough
238 Lansdowne Street East
P.O. Box 1957
PETERBOROUGH, Ont.
K9J 7X7
Telephone: (705) 743-4343

OML
76 Lake Street
P.O. Box 144
ST. CATHARINES, Ont.
L2R 6S3
Telephone: (416) 688-0321

OML
1091 Talbot Street East
ST. THOMAS, Ont.
N5P 1G4
Telephone: (519) 631-6490

CAA-Windsor
1433 London Road
P.O. Box 100
SARNIA, Ont.
N7T 1P6
Telephone: (519) 542-3493

CAA-Toronto
334 Queen Street East
SAULT STE. MARIE, Ont.
P6A 1Z1
Telephone: (705) 942-4600

CAA-Toronto
1200 Markham Road
SCARBOROUGH, Ont.
M1H 3C3
Telephone: (416) 439-6370

OML
25 Peel Street
SIMCOE, Ont.
N3Y 1S1
Telephone: (519) 426-7230

OML
360 Caradoc Street South
STRATHROY, Ont.
N7G 2P6
Telephone: (519) 245-0530

CAA-Sudbury
1769 Regent Street South
P.O. Box 985
SUDBURY, Ont.
P3E 3Z7
Telephone: (705) 522-0000

OML
585 Memorial Avenue
THUNDER BAY, Ont.
P7B 3Z1
Telephone: (807) 345-1261

CAA-Toronto
2 Carlton Street
TORONTO, Ont.
M5B 1K4
Telephone: (416) 964-3111

CAA-Toronto
152 Yorkdale Shopping Centre
TORONTO, Ont.
M6A 2T9
Telephone: (416) 789-2611

CAA-Toronto
1871 O'Connor Drive
TORONTO, Ont.
M4A 1X1
Telephone: (416) 752-9080

CAA-Toronto
Commerce Court Postal Station
Box 111
TORONTO, Ont.
M5L 1K4
Telephone: (416) 365-1603

CAA-Toronto
875 Eglinton Avenue West
TORONTO, Ont.
M6C 3Z9
Telephone: (416) 785-0111

OML
540 Niagara Street
WELLAND, Ont.
L3C 1L8
Telephone: (416) 735-1100

CAA-Toronto
5740 Yonge Street
WILLOWDALE, Ont.
M2M 3T4
Telephone: (416) 223-1751

CAA-Windsor
1215 Ouellette Avenue
WINDSOR, Ont.
N8X 1J3
Telephone: (519) 255-1212

OML
976 Dundas Street
WOODSTOCK, Ont.
N4S 1H3
Telephone: (519) 539-5676

Hamilton Automobile Club

Headquarters:
HAC
393 Main Street East
HAMILTON, Ont.
L8N 3T7
Telephone: (416) 525-1210

Branch Offices:
HAC
431 St. Paul Avenue
BRANTFORD, Ont.
N3R 4N8
Telephone: (416) 756-6321

HAC
491 Brant Street
BURLINGTON, Ont.
L7R 2G5
Telephone: (416) 632-6772

HAC
125 Navy Street
OAKVILLE, Ont.
L6J 2Z5
Telephone: (416) 845-9680

CAA-Québec

Headquarters:
CAA-Québec
2600, boul. Laurier
STE-FOY, Qué.
G1V 4K8
Telephone: (418) 653-2600

Branch Offices:
CAA-Québec
1670, boul. Provencher
BROSSARD, Qué.
J4W 2Z6
Telephone: (514) 465-7770

CAA-Québec
1401, boul. Talbot
CHICOUTIMI, Qué.
G7H 4C1
Telephone: (418) 545-8686

CAA-Québec
456, boul. St-Joseph
HULL, Qué.
J8Y 3Y7
Telephone: (819) 778-2225

CAA-Québec
1200, ouest boul. St. Martin
LAVAL, Qué.
H7S 2E4
Telephone: (514) 668-2240

CAA-Québec
1425, rue de la Montagne
MONTREAL, Qué.
H3G 2R7
Telephone: (514) 288-7111

CAA-Québec
18, rue Ste-Anne
QUEBEC, Qué.
G1R 3X2
Telephone: (418) 692-4720

CAA-Québec
2433, ouest rue King
SHERBROOKE, Qué.
J1J 2G7
Telephone: (819) 566-5132

CAA-Québec
1295, rue Aubuchon
TROIS-RIVIERES, Qué.
G8Y 5K4
Telephone: (819) 376-9393

Maritime Automobile Association

Regional Headquarters:
MAA
335 City Road
SAINT JOHN, N.B.
E2L 3N6
Telephone: (506) 657-3470

Branch Offices:
MAA
193A Prince Street
CHARLOTTETOWN, P.E.I.
C1A 4R8
Telephone: (902) 892-1612

MAA
7169 Chebucto Road
HALIFAX, N.S.
B3L 1N5
Telephone: (902) 453-2320

MAA
869 Main Street
MONCTON, N.B.
E1C 1G5
Telephone: (506) 388-1225

Newfoundland and Labrador Automobile Association

NLAA
54 Kenmount Road
ST. JOHN'S, Nfld.
A1B 1W3
Telephone: (709) 726-6100

PART II

Troubleshooting and basic repair

Maintenance

How—and how not—to do it yourself

The modern car is designed and built to have a useful road life of at least 160,000 kilometres (100,000 miles) in Canada—a decade of driving for the average motorist—if it is kept in good repair.

When maintaining your car, it is more important to know *what* must be done, and *when*, than to know how to do it yourself. If you do not follow the manufacturer's maintenance schedules, you may void the warranty on a new car. A poorly maintained car, whether old or new, burns more fuel. An inexpensive maintenance job left undone will often lead to more expensive repairs. Neglecting oil changes may save a few dollars initially, but may eventually cause expensive engine damage.

Many maintenance items, such as those for tires and brakes, affect driving safety. A soft tire can throw your car into a skid when you brake suddenly. Incorrect air pressure also shortens tire life and can increase fuel consumption by as much as 15 percent.

Your owner's manual lists specific intervals between major and minor services required by your car. Make sure that all these jobs are done on time. Doing them yourself will not void your new-car warranty, provided you keep records and file receipts for new parts. The *Logbook* provides a yearly record for this purpose, with space to describe each maintenance or repair job, along with the car's odometer reading and the date. You may also find that self-adhesive labels are useful for recording such periodic maintenance jobs as oil or filter changes. Labels can be pasted on the inside of the glove compartment door or in the engine compartment.

Some maintenance and repair tasks are best left to a professional mechanic. Major overhauls and bodywork, wheel alignment and balancing, and repairs on the transmission, steering, brakes, and air conditioning require specialized tools and techniques.

There are many jobs, however, that you can perform yourself, even if you have never tried them before. If you follow instructions carefully, you may not complete a job as quickly as a mechanic, but you will likely do a better job. In the case of an air filter change, most professionals lift out the old filter, drop in a new one, and put the cover back on the housing. You can take extra time to carefully wipe out the housing with a rag, to check and replace the PCV filter, and to see that the wing nut that secures the cover is properly tightened.

You save money in two ways when you work on your car yourself. You do not have to pay labor charges, which currently average $30 per hour in Canada. Also, you can often get parts and supplies at lower prices than a garage will charge. Oil costs 25 to 50 percent less when bought by the case at discount or auto supply stores than it does when bought by the litre from a service station. Even greater savings are available on filters, fan belts, and spark plugs.

Tucked in the glove compartment of every new car, the owner's manual supplies all the necessary information about operating and servicing you car. Among other things, it explains the proper way to start the engine and change a flat tire; how to operate the heater; and when to lubricate and change the engine oil. The manual also lists such vital statistics as the capacity of the gas tank, recommended tire pressures, and the type of fuses required for the electrical system. The manual is must reading for every car owner. If you have lost yours, get another from the dealer.

Raise your car safely

Raising a car high enough to work under it safely can pose a problem for home mechanics. The bumper jacks and side-lift jacks that come with most cars are flimsy and should never be used for anything but changing a tire. A scissors jack is safer and easier to use. Post-type hydraulic jacks may not fit under your car or, if they do fit, may not raise the car high enough for jack stands to be put in place. A small version of a mechanic's floor jack is expensive but is a good investment if you use it often.

Before jacking up a car, park on level ground. Set the parking brake and put the transmission in gear (automatics in *Park*, manuals in *Reverse*). When raising both front or both rear wheels, center the jack under a solid jacking point, such as the differential housing or the lower suspension A-arms. Raise the car high enough to fit the jack stands under the frame, then lower the car onto them. For a light car, you will need 1.5-tonne jack stands; for a heavy vehicle such as a van, 2.5-tonne jack stands.

If the wheels need not hang free, you can raise the car by driving it up onto ramps. For safety, buy ramps that will support about 2.5 to 4 tonnes. Ramps must be at least 30 cm (12 in.) wide to accommodate most tires, and they must raise the car at least 45 cm (18 in.) off the ground to allow enough work space. Position the ramps directly in line with the wheels that are to be raised. With someone to guide you, drive slowly onto the ramps, being careful not to overdrive them or let the wheels slide off the sides. When the car is properly positioned, set the parking brake and put the transmission in gear (automatics in *Park*). When using either ramps or jack stands, use blocks of wood to chock the wheels that remain on the ground.

Caution: Never get under a car that is supported only by a jack—always use ramps or jack stands.

Planning your maintenance schedule

Every owner's manual provides a maintenance schedule tailored specifically to your make and model. In addition, some new cars come with a warranty service booklet that contains tickets meant to be torn out or validated when certain services have been performed. What these booklets do not stress is that you can perform the services and sign for them yourself without endangering your warranty, provided you use reputable parts and keep careful records and receipts.

At first, especially with a new car, you may want a dealer to perform semiannual or major service. But the only way to get weekly, visual inspections done at all is to do them yourself. These are similar to the pre-flight checks that every pilot must make before flying his plane, and they take only a few minutes. Making your own checks is also a practical way to get to know your car.

A few good habits will make the job easier. Stock the supplies you know you will need—items like filters, belts, and oil will not deteriorate in storage. However, never store gasoline in your home. Assemble all tools and materials and put them in a convenient place in the order you will need them.

The first time you perform a task, proceed slowly. Most important, work safely. Never work on a running engine unless the area is well ventilated. Beware of hot exhaust manifolds, muffler pipes, hoses, radiators, and other parts that run hot. Stay clear of fan blades and other moving parts; electric fans may start up even when the engine is off. Disconnect the battery ground cable whenever you work on the fuel or electrical system. And never work under a raised car unless it is on level ground and securely supported by jack stands or ramps.

A typical maintenance routine

Interval	Service or check
Every week (daily if traveling)	From the driver's seat: check fuel level (on the gauge), brakes, warning lights and instruments. Outside the car: check lights and signals (pp. 130-131), tires (visual check for pressure and tread wear, pp. 102-105), look for puddles under the car caused by fluid leaks (pp. 138-139), clean the lights and glass. Under the hood: check oil level (pp. 112-113), coolant (pp. 132-133), brake fluid (pp. 122-123)
Every month (or every 1,500 km/1,000 mi)	Check tire pressure with an accurate gauge (remember to check spare; see pp. 102-103). Check battery water (pp. 128-129), power steering fluid (pp. 108-109), and drive belts (pp. 134-135). Top up windshield washer fluid. Touch up chipped paint (pp. 148-149). Check fluid level in automatic transmission and differential (pp. 120-121)
Every 3 months (or every 5,000 km/3,000 mi)	Change engine oil (pp. 112-113). Check tire tread depth (pp. 102-103) and condition of all hoses and drive belts (pp. 134-135). Check exhaust system for leaks (pp. 116-117)
Every 6 months (or every 10,000 km/6,000 mi)	Change engine oil and filter (pp. 112-113). Check fuel filter, cooling system (pp. 132-133), oil level in manual transmission and free play in clutch pedal (pp. 118-119). Lubricate chassis fittings (pp. 110-111), door locks, and hinges (pp. 142-143). Check headlight aim (pp. 130-131). Have wheel alignment checked if tire wear indicates need (p. 104). Rotate tires (p. 105)
Every 12 months (or every 20,000 km/12,000 mi)	Inspect brakes (pp. 122-123) and adjust parking brake. Repack wheel bearings. Check oil level of steering gearbox (pp. 108-109). Check front-drive axle boots and air filter (pp. 114-115). Replace antifreeze and spark plugs. Tune engine with conventional ignition. Check emission controls and PCV valve, air conditioner (pp. 136-137), carburetor or fuel injection, and distributor cap and rotor. Thoroughly wash underbody to remove winter salt (do this each spring). Check for paint chips, dents, scratches, and body rust
Every 2 years (or every 40,000 km/24,000 mi)	Replace spark plugs, PCV valve, coolant hoses (pp. 134-135), antifreeze, automatic transmission filter and fluid (pp. 120-121), oil in manual transmission and differential (pp. 118-119), and brake fluid (pp. 122-123)
Every 3 years (or every 60,000 km/36,000 mi)	Replace spark plug cables if necessary. Check owner's manual for other specific long-term service requirements for your car, such as inspecting timing belt on overhead cam engines

The right tool for the job

A professional mechanic has thousands of dollars invested in hand tools because he has to repair virtually any part on any car. Having the right tool enables him to work faster and make more money. Because you will need only the tools to fix one or two cars, and speed is not crucial, you can handle most do-it-yourself chores with the auto tool set shown below. Such a kit will cost between $150 and $300. However, you do not have to buy everything at once. Start with a basic set of tools, then add to it as your interest, needs, and abilities grow.

Virtually every new engine, transmission, or other major component now installed in North American vehicles is made to metric standards. The do-it-yourself mechanic will sooner or later be confronted with metric nuts, bolts, and fluid capacities. Although many metric nuts and bolts seem to be about the same size, they are not interchangeable. Do not use metric wrenches on imperial nuts and bolts or imperial wrenches on metric nuts and bolts except in emergencies. A wrench that is only slightly too large is likely to round off the corners of the fastener and make it much more difficult to remove. Other tools such as ratchet extensions, punches, and chisels, whose exact sizes are not crucial to their function, are usually sold in imperial measure only.

Even a one-car garage can be turned into an automotive workshop if you can find another place to store all the bicycles, lawn

Shopping for tools

A good rule of thumb for buying tools is to let the job determine what you buy. Don't get more sophisticated or more elaborate tools than the task requires—unless you need the features for future projects. Never buy cheap tools—they are really no bargain. Most good name-brand hand tools are guaranteed for life; you will still be using them long after inferior tools have broken, possibly injuring you or your car. However don't rule out secondhand tools. You may get a perfectly good set at a bargain rate from someone who has tired of a hobby. If you need only a few tools, the best buy is often a small mechanic's tool set that includes a chest and a selection of tools at a price lower than that of buying the pieces individually. Check catalogs to see which sets contain what you want, and watch for sales.

You may also save money by buying a mechanic's test kit that includes a timing light, engine analyzer, compression gauge, pressure gauge and other test equipment.

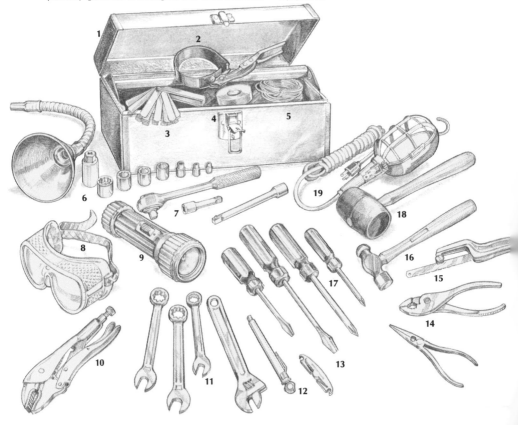

mowers, and garden tools that clutter most garages. Plan your work area so that you have easy access to your tools, lots of storage shelves, and plenty of counter space.

In a one-car garage, install narrow shelves or cabinets down one side only, and construct your major work area at the end. That way, there will be enough room to move around. Second-hand kitchen cabinets can sometimes be obtained free or very cheaply. Or build your own cabinets for a custom fit. A wall-mounted pegboard is the most efficient way to store the tools you use often. Discipline yourself to clean and put tools away after each job; the most elaborate storage system is pointless if it is unused. Well-ordered tools will speed your work.

Make your workshop as comfortable and pleasant as possible. Paint the walls with washable latex or oil-base paint—white or another light color will reflect as much light as possible. Scrub the concrete floor with a special concrete cleaner-etcher to remove grease and grime. Patch any broken spots, then seal the surface with two coats of epoxy resin concrete floor paint.

Install two double-tube fluorescent ceiling fixtures—one in the center of the garage and one over your workbench. A droplight is essential for working under your car's hood and chassis. Make sure the space is adequately ventilated. Keep a fire extinguisher and a first-aid kit in an accessible spot, and install a smoke alarm.

1. Tool box. A sturdy plastic or metal box will keep tools organized and protect them from wear and tear in your car trunk or garage. Should have tight catch and secure lock, especially if stored around children.

2. Oil-filter wrench. Adjustable strap wrench can spin off tight filters without damage. Other types are available.

3. Feeler gauge. Blade-type gauge is the most versatile for checking spark-plug gap, valve clearances, and other critical adjustments. Typical set has about 15 blades, graduated from 0.1 to 0.7 mm (0.002 to 0.030 in.).

4. Electrician's tape. Waterproof black tape is useful in emergencies for patching leaks, repairing hoses, wrapping wires, and making temporary repairs of all kinds.

5. Spare wire. A short length (1 or 2 m) of automotive wire may come in handy for replacing a frayed, broken, or shorted wire.

6. Funnel. An inexpensive plastic funnel is useful for adding or draining fluid, such as during an oil change or when backflushing the radiator. Add a flexible hose for hard-to-reach filler holes.

7. Socket wrenches. The heart of a socket wrench is the ratcheting drive handle, which reverses direction to tighten or loosen nuts and bolts. Sockets are available in various lengths and depths, in both metric and imperial sizes. Most useful is ⅜-inch drive with sockets ranging from 6 to 19 mm and ⅜ to ¾ in. Add 3-in. and 6-in. extensions, a U-joint connector, and a spark plug socket.

8. Safety goggles. Ventilated plastic eye protection should be worn whenever using a drill, grinder, or saw, or when working with the air-conditioning system.

9. Flashlight. Buy a small flashlight with alkaline or other heavy-duty batteries for emergency use.

10. Locking pliers. Versatile tool that can be used as pliers, adjustable wrench, or mini-vise.

11. Wrenches. The auto mechanic's most basic tools are wrenches. Sets range from ⅜ in. to ⅞ in. and 4 mm to 19 mm. Combination wrenches have an open-end wrench at one end and a box-end wrench at the other. Because it will fit a large number of sizes, an adjustable wrench is useful to have for emergencies. However it can slip off tight fasteners and round them off.

12. Tire-pressure gauge. Keep handy in glove compartment to check pressure on all tires, including the spare, at least once a month. Pencil-type gauge takes up little space; dial gauge is more expensive and bulkier but easier to read.

13. Fuse puller. Safely removes burned-out glass fuses without breaking them.

14. Pliers. The best pliers are made from high-carbon steel and are nickel-chrome plated. Most useful are common slip-joint pliers (for utility use) and long-nose pliers (electrical work). Never use slip-joint pliers to turn nuts or bolts—they will round off the corners.

15. Hacksaw. Mini-hacksaw works well in small quarters. Replacement blades are available with 18, 24, or 32 teeth per inch. Choose a blade that will always have at least two teeth in contact with metal being cut.

16. Ball-peen hammer. Use a machinist's hammer with 450- or 675-g (16- or 24-oz) head for general automotive work. Carpenter's claw hammers are not

recommended for use with steel punches and chisels.

17. Screwdrivers. The strongest screwdrivers are made of chrome-vanadium steel and are nickel-chrome plated. Include three flat-blade screwdrivers with ⅛ in., ¼ in., and ⅜ in. tips; Nos. 1, 2, 3, and 4 Phillips screwdrivers; and one stubby screwdriver of each kind for tight spots.

18. Soft hammer. Rubber or plastic mallet will not mar metal, so it can be used for replacing hubcaps and light bodywork repairs. Never use soft hammers to strike hard metals or chisels.

19. Worklight. Must be grounded and have a strong metal or plastic cage protecting the bulb. Some models plug into the cigarette lighter for emergency use.

Other useful tools:
Ventilated face mask
Wire cutting/stripping pliers
Torque wrench
Flat chisel
Center punch
Aluminum rule, 1 m or 1 yd
Pocket knife
Wire brush
Oil can spout
Pencil-type soldering gun
Oil-drain pan, 6-L (6-qt) capacity
Ramps or jack stands
Metal files
Large hacksaw and blades
Electric drill, ⅜ in.
Twist bit set
Drill attachments (sanding disc, polishing wheel, grinding wheel, wire brush)
Grease gun
Radiator coolant hydrometer
Battery hydrometer
Offset ratcheting screwdriver
Bench vise
Multi-function engine analyser (multi-meter)
Mechanic's creeper

Periodic Checks

Probably no other parts of your car are as abused, neglected, and misunderstood as your tires. Yet they rival the brake system as the most important safety device on your car. A tire and its rim form a compartment containing air under high pressure. The air carries 92 to 95 percent of the car's weight; the rest is carried by the tire itself. Tires must transmit the engine's power to the road, steer the car, cushion it against impacts, and provide traction and braking stability. They should be checked regularly for early signs of wear and tear.

Begin by inspecting the tread depth on the tires. If solid bars of rubber called "wear indicators" appear across the tread, your tire no longer provides traction and should be replaced. Check for unusual wear patterns (see p. 104). Measure the tread depth across the width of the tire in several places. You may spot uneven wear before the tread is completely worn away. Pry out any pebbles or pieces of glass with a screwdriver. If you find a nail, do not pull it out, but mark the spot with chalk and take the tire to a garage to be fixed. If a tire has a slow leak and you cannot find any cuts or foreign objects in the rubber, suspect a leaking tire valve or a damaged bead.

Each month check and adjust the air pressure in your tires, including the spare. Too little pressure causes tread wear, and can affect steering, reduce road-holding ability, and decrease the load the tires can safely carry. Underinflation can also increase fuel consumption and result in excessive tire flexing, which can lead to overheating and the risk of a blowout. Overinflation of tires will make them vulnerable to puncture and create a harsh ride. It also leads to rapid wear in the center of the tread, which results in reduced cornering ability.

The recommended tire pressures for your car are printed in the owner's manual and on a sticker inside the glove compartment or on the driver's door. You can exceed these pressures by about 20 kPa (3 psi) as long as the total is still under the maximum pressure given on the sidewall of the tire. In fact, the extra pressure may improve your car's fuel economy.

Remember to check the pressure only when the tires are cold. Pressure increases as the tires grow hot from driving—by as much as 40 kPa (6 psi). If you adjust the pressure when the tires are hot, they will be incorrectly inflated when they are cold. To verify that you have the right pressure, use an accurate pocket tire gauge. As you press the gauge down squarely onto the tire valve, the stem of the gauge pops out to indicate how much pressure is in the tire. If there is too much pressure, bleed some air by pushing down on the valve stem.

Gas station air pumps are usually set to the desired pressure by turning the handle at the side of the pump. Push the air hose nozzle firmly onto the tire valve; when the pump stops ringing, the pressure in the tire equals the setting on the pump. Don't rely solely on the pump reading; check the pressure with a pocket gauge.

When buying tires, you naturally want to get the best bargain possible. But don't let cost alone rule; tires are critical to safe driving. Your chief consideration should be to select tires best suited to your type of car and driving habits. For example, inexpensive bias-ply tires may be fine for around-town driving, but if you plan long, high-speed trips, consider spending additional money for the strength and durability of radial tires. However, never mix radials—which are constructed very differently from either bias-ply or bias-belted types—with other tires. The U.S. Government has developed a tire grading system based on tread wear, traction, and temperature resistance (the U.S. codes appear on many tires sold in Canada). "A" is the highest grade, "B" is intermediate, and "C" is the lowest rating. Tires made and sold in this country must show the National Tire Safety Mark (a maple leaf). This indicates that a tire has passed federal government stress tests. There are no government safety standards for retreaded tires, so there are both good and bad retreads on the market. Avoid them if possible.

Testing for tread depth

A tread depth of 1.5 mm (1/16 in.) or less is unsafe, and illegal in most areas. Measure the depth with a penny, as shown. If the top of the Queen's head shows, the tire is badly worn and should be replaced. Do not mix new and worn tires, however.

Anatomy of a tire

Every tire has three major components: the tread, the bead, and the casing (also known as the carcass). The tread is the patterned, outer surface of the tire which comes into contact with the road. The bead, reinforced with a strand of steel wires, secures the tire to the wheel rim. The casing, made of layers, or plies, of various materials, maintains the tire's shape when inflated. It is the way the plies wrap around the bead which determines the variety of tires available. In increasing order of durability these are:

Bias-ply. This most common—and least expensive—tire is made up of several plies of rubber-coated fabric. The threads, or cords, of these layers cross at an angle (or bias). The result is a tire with firm sidewalls suitable for moderate driving conditions. At faster speeds or during hard cornering, however, the tread elements tend to distort and overheat.

Bias-belted. This design uses the crisscross plies of a bias-ply tire, but has a stabilizing belt the same as the radial tire. The belt not only strengthens the tire, but also stiffens the tread and improves road handling.

Radial-ply. Most new cars are equipped with radial-ply tires, whose plies run at right angles (radially) to the center line of the tread. Directional stability is supplied by stiff belts of fabric, fiberglass, or steel. This construction reduces cornering wear and increases tire life. Radials are well-suited to high-speed driving, but may produce noise or roughness at low speeds.

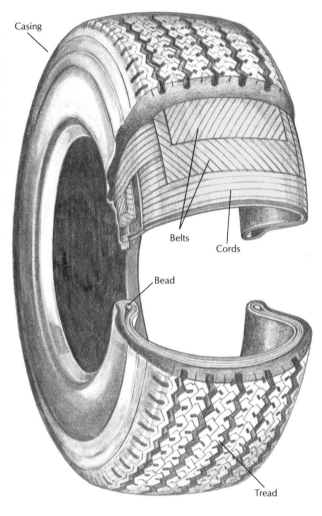

Casing

Belts

Cords

Bead

Tread

Tire profiles

Bias-ply. Though relatively inexpensive, bias-ply tires are rated below the other two types for tire life and fuel economy.

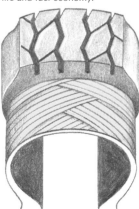

Bias-belted. Two or more belts under the tread of a bias-belted tire give additional protection and increase fuel economy.

Radial. Due to their lower rolling resistance, radial tires can give 5 to 7 percent better fuel economy than bias-ply tires.

How to read your tires

No tire is perfectly round or uniform. Each has heavy spots that can cause annoying vibrations at high speeds as well as abnormal tire wear. To compensate for irregularities in their construction, wheels and tires must be *dynamically balanced* by a tire dealer or garage with a machine that spins the wheel at high speeds.

It may be difficult to balance some wheel and tire combinations. In such cases, you should seek out an experienced shop with special equipment. The better balancing machines allow a wheel to be attached to your car's lug nuts or bolts. On less accurate machines, the wheel is simply clamped in place through its center hole. Special self-adhesive balancing weights should be used on aluminum or other alloy wheels. Have a problem wheel checked with and without the tire. If the wheel is badly out of balance or bent, it must be replaced.

After dynamic balancing, a problem wheel should be *afterbalanced* on the car. This procedure can reveal faulty hubs, brake rotors, brake drums, or wheel bearings.

Unbalanced wheels and tires can cause the steering wheel to shimmy and tires to wear unevenly, and in extreme cases may damage the wheel bearings. The wheels should be balanced every time a tire is mounted or replaced—such as when repairing a flat or mounting snow tires. If you plan to keep your car for several years, it pays to buy extra wheels for your snow tires from a tire store or wrecking yard. You can then install and remove your own snow tires without paying a mounting and balancing fee each spring and fall.

Severe skids or fast cornering can cause abnormal tire wear patterns that will eventually throw a tire out of balance. If the tire is seriously out-of-round, it must be replaced.

Your tires provide early-warning signs of alignment problems. If you car handles differently than normal, or tends to drift to one side or the other, first check for unequal tire pressure, which has the same effect as incorrect wheel alignment. Inflate all the tires to the correct pressure and check them with an accurate gauge. If this does not solve the problem, have the alignment checked by a garage that specializes in front-end work. If you continue to drive the car, misalignment will cause the tires to wear badly. You can usually feel a wear pattern before you see it. Slide your hand back and forth across the tread to feel for edges just beginning to feather. Also slide your hand around the circumference of the tire for 20 to 25 cm (8 to 10 in.) to check for uneven tread wear.

Tire wear patterns

Tread-wear indicators appear when only 1.5 mm ($\frac{1}{16}$ in.) of the original tread remains. Replace the tire immediately.

Wear at the tire's shoulders indicates underinflation, which can cause skids. Adjust the tire pressure.

Incorrect wheel camber causes wear at one edge of tire only; have the alignment checked.

Wear at the center of the tread points to overinflation, which reduces tire life. Adjust the pressure.

Cupping, or scalloping, of the tread is caused by an unbalanced tire or by faulty suspension.

Feathering of the tread is caused by excessive toe-in or toe-out; have the alignment checked.

Tire rotation: a twice-yearly puzzle

To promote even tread wear and increase the life of your tires, rotate them every 10,000 to 15,000 km (6,000 to 10,000 mi). Tire pressures should be checked after rotation. To use the chart below, read down the left column to find the number and type of tires on your car. Headings across the top indicate normal rotation, and snow tire removal and mounting in the spring and fall. Remember that at any given time only one procedure will apply to your car.

	Normal rotation	Snow tires (fall)	Snow tires (spring)
Four radial tires		Storage	Storage
Five radial tires		Storage	Storage
Four nonradial tires		Storage	Storage
Five nonradial tires		Storage	Storage

Smoothing out the bumps

The suspension system supports the weight of your car and its cargo, isolates the passengers from the bumps and dips in the road, and keeps the wheels in contact with the ground. This is all acomplished by means of springs and shock absorbers.

A spring is simply a device that returns to its original shape after being distorted. In a car suspension, springs are placed between the frame and each wheel. Three types of springs are used in various combinations. *Leaf springs* consist of several lengths of steel or fiberglass bolted together so that the spring is thicker in the middle (where the greatest force is applied) than at the ends. *Torsion bars,* connected rigidly to the frame and indirectly to the wheel, absorb shock by twisting. *Coil springs* are rods that have been wound into spirals—in effect, a coiled torsion bar. They absorb shock by compressing and extending.

Shock absorbers are attached to the suspension to dampen the motion of the springs and provide a more comfortable ride. Shock absorbers are misnamed—the shock is really absorbed by the springs.

Checking your car's suspension involves a few simple procedures. When all four tires are properly inflated and there is someone in the driver's seat, the car should sit level on flat ground. None of the corners should sag, and the front end should not be higher or lower than the rear unless the car's suspension has been deliberately modified (such as for trailer towing). If you suspect a spring problem, have a specialist check the suspension. Spring work requires special tools and equipment not found in the typical garage.

If your car handles badly, skitters across rough roads, or wallows up and down after a bump, the shock absorbers are probably worn. Original-equipment shocks seldom last more than 40,000 km (25,000 mi). Worn shocks may be replaced individually, not necessarily in pairs, unless the carmaker recommends otherwise.

For information on lubricating the suspension, see pp. 110-111.

Front suspension: steering the car

Almost all modern cars have independent front suspension, which means that each front wheel is linked separately to the frame. This allows the wheels to react independently to the road so that one wheel can go over a bump without lifting the whole car. The ride is more comfortable than with a solid-axle suspension because the whole car no longer responds to each variation in road surface, and handling is improved because both tires retain better contact with the road.

The front wheels must steer as well as respond to the road surface (and provide traction on front-drive cars). Ball joints, which can rotate in all directions, allow the wheels to steer left or right and move up and down simultaneously. A stabilizer bar is often set between the left and right wheels to reduce the car's tendency to lean towards the outside of a turn.

A popular type of independent front suspension is MacPherson strut suspension, which allows very little change in wheel camber (tilt) as the car goes over a bump. Although they are compact, MacPherson struts may cause added expense because in many cases the springs must be removed in order to service the shocks.

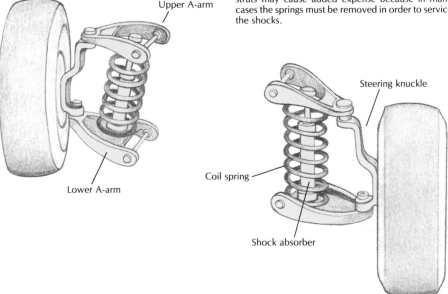

Upper A-arm

Lower A-arm

Steering knuckle

Coil spring

Shock absorber

Rear suspension: carrying the weight

Rear suspension, like that on the front wheels, is designed to keep the wheels in contact with the road and to give passengers a comfortable ride. However there are some important differences. The load carried by the front wheels—the engine and front end—is fairly constant. The rear wheels carry a load that varies with the number of passengers and amount of groceries, baggage, or other cargo. Rear springs must not sag too much under added weight, yet must not be too stiff without it. If your load fluctuations are large, or if you pull a trailer, consider installing adjustable shock absorbers.

While the front wheels must steer as well as move up and down, the rear wheels should remain straight at all times. Instead of the ball joints used in the front suspension, the rear wheels are attached to the axles in a way that keeps them constantly aligned, regardless of their up-and-down movement.

Another important difference between front and rear suspension is that in rear-drive cars the torque—the twisting force that powers the car—is transferred to the road through the rear wheels. The rear suspension must be strong enough to resist this torque while providing traction.

Two basic types of rear suspension are found on most rear-wheel-drive cars. *Live-axle rear suspension (below)* has an axle housing which runs the width of the the car and bounces up and down when either wheel hits a bump. *Independent rear suspension* allows each wheel to respond to the road separately.

Front-wheel-drive cars can use the simplest of all independent rear suspension systems because their rear wheels are neither driven nor steered. Many have flexible beam axles—a form of semi-independent rear suspension. Some trunk space may be lost to allow room for axle movement.

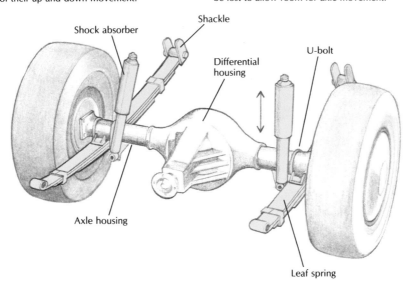

Shock absorber · Shackle · Differential housing · U-bolt · Axle housing · Leaf spring

Inside a shock absorber

All shock absorbers work in much the same way; only their internal valves and chambers vary. When the wheel hits a bump and moves up, so does the bottom tube of the shock *(compression)*. Fluid in the lower chamber is displaced through holes and valves into the upper chamber and reservoir. When the spring *rebounds,* fluid is forced back through the holes and valves to the lower chamber. If the shocks are too hard, the springs will not be able to properly absorb road shocks, and the car's ride will be harsh. If they are too soft, the springs will oscillate too much, resulting in excess body movement.

Since shock absorbers are normally replaced several times during a car's lifetime, most types are designed for easy installation by an average do-it-yourselfer. Although special tools are available at auto parts stores, most shocks can be removed or installed with ordinary socket, box-end, and open-end wrenches.

On cars with coil-spring front or rear suspension, the suspension arms must be supported before the shocks are removed; otherwise, the arms may drop under their own weight and damage the brake lines or the coil springs.

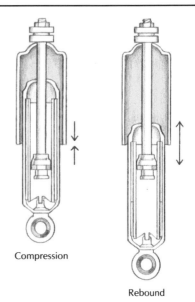

Compression · Rebound

Steering and handling checks

Thanks to your car's steering system, you can control a fast-moving vehicle 30 times your weight. This is accomplished by a set of components that lead from the steering wheel to the front wheels.

Because the steering wheel is a small lever (its radius is only about 17 cm, or 7 in.), the driver needs a mechanical advantage to steer a heavy vehicle. This advantage is provided by the *steering ratio*—the number of 360-degree turns of the steering wheel that are required to swivel the front wheels from lock to lock. A low ratio responds more quickly to the wheel but requires more power to operate than a high ratio.

The steering shaft runs inside the steering column, through the fire wall, and into the steering gearbox under the hood. Modern steering shafts are designed to collapse on impact to protect the driver in a collision. The steering gearbox converts the rotational motion of the steering wheel into the side-to-side motion of the wheels. The steering linkage is a series of rods running across the front of the car, which connect the front wheels to each other and to the steering box. Ball joints allow steering movements to be transmitted even as the suspension moves up and down over a bumpy road. Power steering adds hydraulic pressure to reduce the effort needed to steer heavier cars.

Steering problems are usually easy to spot but difficult to pinpoint. They are often the result of accumulated wear in all of the front-end parts. Making regular checks of the steering components *(right)* enables you to monitor wear as it occurs and simplifies the job of isolating problems that may develop and require repair. When you drive, be alert to signs that the car is not handling as easily as it should. For example, there should be little or no play in the steering wheel. Tire wear (pp. 104-105) is also a good early-warning indicator of front-end problems.

If you have jack stands or wheel ramps, raise the car and have a helper apply the brakes. Push and pull each front wheel from side to side. More than 0.5 cm (¼ in.) of play indicates wear in the ball joint, linkage, or bearing. Watch as your helper turns the steering wheel. The motion should be smooth, with no scraping. Next, examine each linkage part, and shake to check for looseness. Inspect the idler arm and Pitman arm for worn bushings (which can cause the car to wander on the road), excess play in the steering wheel, and wheel shimmy. The idler arm and Pitman arm should have little or no vertical play.

Servicing steering components should usually be left to a good garage and skilled mechanics. Special tools and precise workmanship are often required. After any service or repair that requires disassembly of front-end parts, have the front wheels realigned. And remember that regular lubrication can extend the life of steering and suspension parts.

Front-end alignment

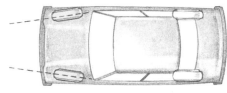

Toe-in

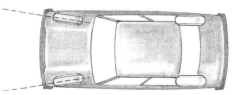

Toe-out

Wheel alignment refers to the relationship between the front suspension, steering, wheels, and frame. Five angles are involved in alignment; the optimum is a compromise between between tire life, fuel economy, and handling. For example, maximum economy and tire life are achieved if the tires are perfectly upright and parallel to the direction of travel. But a car steers better if its tires run at a slight angle. However, this causes them to scuff along the pavement a bit as they roll, which reduces tire life and increases fuel consumption slightly.

The most common alignment problem is excessive toe-in or toe-out *(above)*. Toe-in means that the front of the wheels are closer together than the rear. Some toe-in is desirable—it counteracts the tendency of rear-drive cars to toe-out under power. When the car is moving at highway speeds, toe-in disappears and the wheels roll straight. Conversely, toe-out is sometimes used in front-drive cars to counteract their tendency to toe-in under power. Some toe-out on turns is necessary for all cars because the inner wheel must turn at a sharper angle than the outer wheel. However, wheels that toe-in or toe-out at highway speeds will result in uneven tire wear (see p. 104) and poor handling.

Another important angle is *camber*—the inward or outward tilt of the wheels. Zero camber means the wheels are perpendicular to the road. If the wheel tilts out, camber is said to be *positive*. If it tilts in, the camber is *negative*. Front wheels often have a little positive camber in order to provide stable handling in turns.

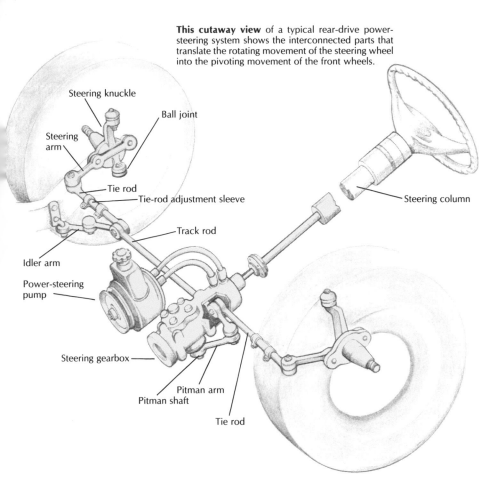

This cutaway view of a typical rear-drive power-steering system shows the interconnected parts that translate the rotating movement of the steering wheel into the pivoting movement of the front wheels.

Steering knuckle

Ball joint

Steering arm

Tie rod

Tie-rod adjustment sleeve

Steering column

Track rod

Idler arm

Power-steering pump

Steering gearbox

Pitman arm

Pitman shaft

Tie rod

Adding steering fluid

Manual steering fluid in cars made by GM, Honda, Volkswagen, and Chrysler (1975 and later models) should last the lifetime of the vehicle. The level in other cars should be checked once every six months. As a rule, if the carmaker recommends a periodic oil check and fill, you will see a filler plug on the car's steering box.

On cars equipped with power steering, the fluid level should be checked about once every six months. The reservoir is usually housed in the same unit as the power steering pump, near the fan belt, and is readily accessible. If the dipstick has two *Full* marks, the upper one is for a hot engine, the lower one for a cold engine.

Car model	Manual steering lubricant
AMC Ford imports	Lithium grease
Chrysler	Gear lubricant "For service GL4"
Chrysler imports	
Ford	Power steering fluid
GM (except Cadillacs)	Steering gear lubricant
Datsun	Gear lubricant "For service GL5"
Toyota	

Car model	Power steering lubricant
AMC Chrysler Ford (1973-77) GM	Power steering fluid
Ford (1978 and later)	Automatic transmission fluid, Type F
Chrysler imports Datsun Honda Toyota	DEXRON automatic transmission fluid

Lubricating the suspension and steering

Lubrication is a simple procedure that can add many kilometres to your car's life. Even though most carmakers allow long intervals (up to 60,000 km or 36,000 mi) between lubrications of the suspension and the steering systems, it is a good idea to renew the grease in the components at least once a year, or every 10,000 km (6,000 mi) if driving conditions are severe.

If you are doing it yourself, choose a chassis grease that contains molybdenum disulfide (moly) made by a reputable oil company. Most brands are available in cartridge form for use in the ordinary low-pressure, hand-operated grease guns available from hardware or auto parts stores. Most cars are equipped with nipple-type grease fittings, but some have plug-type fittings as well. When you purchase a grease gun, make sure to get nozzles that suit the fittings on your car. A flexible hose attachment and some right-angle nipples are also useful, since

standard grease fittings are often located in places that may be hard to reach with a hand-powered gun.

Lubricating your car yourself is easy if you prepare for the job before you begin. Have all the tools and materials you will need within easy reach while you are under the car. Wear old clothes and protective eye goggles, and have a good supply of rags or paper towels on hand. To avoid a messy cleanup, spread newspapers or a large piece of cardboard beneath the car to catch loose grease and dirt. Work in a well-lit area, or use a droplight. It also helps to consult a lubrication diagram in your service or owner's manual before you begin. Do not overlook any fittings that are hidden beneath heavy accumulations of road dirt and old grease.

Caution: Make sure that you have raised the car safely (see p. 98) before you begin. Set the parking brake and put the transmission in gear (automatics in *Park*).

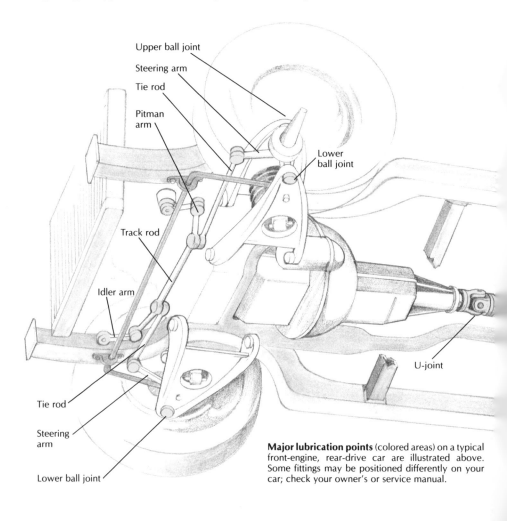

Upper ball joint

Steering arm

Tie rod

Pitman arm

Lower ball joint

Track rod

Idler arm

U-joint

Tie rod

Steering arm

Lower ball joint

Major lubrication points (colored areas) on a typical front-engine, rear-drive car are illustrated above. Some fittings may be positioned differently on your car; check your owner's or service manual.

Unless they are replacement joints, most U-joints (universal joints) are packed with lubricant and sealed for life. You can identify a U-joint that should be lubricated by noting whether or not there is a grease fitting or plug on it. If there is, lubricate the U-joint every time you lubricate the suspension and steering. Some drive shafts have more than one U-joint, so be sure not to miss any lubrication point.

U-joints

To check a U-joint for wear, grip the drive shaft with one hand and the U-joint with the other *(below)*. If there is any rattling or side-to-side movement, the U-joint is worn and should be serviced.

Lubricate the U-joint at the grease fitting on the cross. If the cross has a plug instead, remove it and screw in the fitting to lubricate it, then remove the fitting and reinstall the plug. Lubricate double U-joints in the same way as single U-joints.

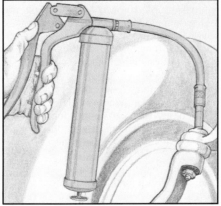

To lubricate a joint, first wipe the fitting clean of old grease and road dirt. Press nozzle over grease fitting and operate the grease gun. Watch as old grease is forced out at the joint. Stop pumping when fresh grease appears. To grease sealed joints, such as ball joints *(above)*, inject grease until you can see or feel the rubber seal begin to swell.

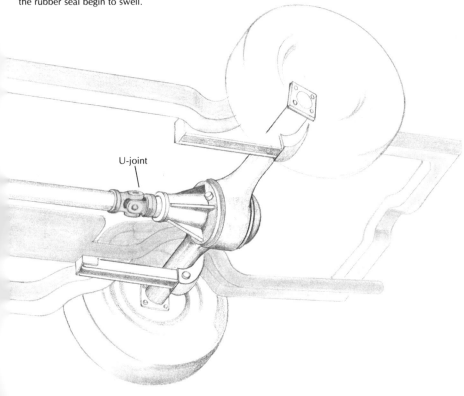

U-joint

Checking and changing your oil

Motor oil does more than simply lubricate engine parts. Special additives ward off sludge, carbon, and varnish deposits; keep the oil from becoming too thin or too thick in varying temperatures; retard rust; and control foaming when the oil is churned up by fast-moving engine parts. Other additives keep sludge in suspension until it is removed during an oil change. Since additives dissipate in time, the oil must be changed periodically.

Most carmakers recommend two oil-change intervals: a longer one for ideal driving conditions (long trips at relatively steady speeds) and a second, shorter interval for the type of driving most people do (short trips, stop-and-go driving, trailer towing). You can buy oil on sale at discount department stores or even in some supermarkets. But consult your owner's manual to make certain that the oil is the type recommended for your car and your driving conditions.

The best type of oil for post-1970 cars with gasoline engines is labeled ''For Service SE'' or ''SF.'' Oil labeled ''CC'' or ''CD'' is made for diesel engines. Most diesel engines require frequent oil changes because their very high compression forces combustion by-products past the piston rings, and this quickly contaminates the oil.

Choose a multi-grade oil that suits your driving conditions. Generally, oil with a viscosity range of 10W-40 is ideal for year-round use. For high-speed, high-altitude, or heavy-duty driving—such as pulling a trailer—heavier 10W-50 oil may be more suitable. At temperatures below -20°C (-4°F), lightweight 5W-30 or 5W-40 oil is best, unless specified otherwise by the carmaker. When using any 5W oil, avoid speeds above 80 km/h (50 mph).

Synthetic oil, though it is expensive and in some cases not recommended for use with diesels, lasts much longer than conventional mineral oils. Manufacturers claim that, because of its excellent lubricating qualities, synthetic oil decreases fuel consumption. Before switching to synthetic oil, however, check your car's warranty, if it still applies; make sure that the extra time between oil changes will not void the warranty.

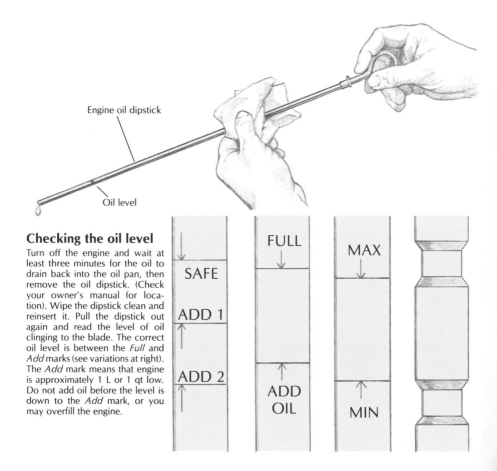

Engine oil dipstick

Oil level

Checking the oil level

Turn off the engine and wait at least three minutes for the oil to drain back into the oil pan, then remove the oil dipstick. (Check your owner's manual for location). Wipe the dipstick clean and reinsert it. Pull the dipstick out again and read the level of oil clinging to the blade. The correct oil level is between the *Full* and *Add* marks (see variations at right). The *Add* mark means that engine is approximately 1 L or 1 qt low. Do not add oil before the level is down to the *Add* mark, or you may overfill the engine.

SAFE

ADD 1

ADD 2

FULL

ADD OIL

MAX

MIN

How to change engine oil

Change your engine oil at the intervals specified by the manufacturer (usually every 5,000 to 15,000 km, or 3,000 to 10,000 mi), more often if you drive only on short stop-and-go trips or over dusty roads.

If possible, drain the oil while the engine is warm; the old oil will drain more quickly and completely, and more of the contaminants will be removed. Be careful, however, of engine parts that may be too hot to touch. If the engine is cold, let the oil drain for at least 20 to 30 minutes before replacing the drain plug.

Raise the front end of the car and support it on jack stands unless clearance is adequate (see p. 98). Place a large basin beneath the oil drain plug. Loosen the plug with a wrench, then remove it carefully by hand. **Caution:** Work to the side of the plug to avoid the stream of hot engine oil when the plug is removed. Let the old oil drain completely into the basin. Clean the drain plug and washer with clean rags (some plugs are magnetized to trap metal particles). Replace the drain plug and washer and tighten by hand as far as possible. When the plug is firmly seated, tighten it another half-turn with a wrench.

Next, move the basin beneath the oil filter (refer to your owner's manual for its location). Clamp an oil-filter wrench around the filter and loosen it. Finish unscrewing the filter by hand and discard. Wipe the engine and new filter clean. Install the new filter by hand until seated, then give it three-quarters of a turn.

A beer-can opener will do to open the oil can, and a clean funnel will serve to pour the oil. Some plastic containers have a built-in pour spout as shown. On cars with hard-to-reach filler caps, a funnel with a flexible neck may be needed. Add fresh oil through the filler atop the engine (see owner's manual for the correct amount). When full, start the engine and check for leaks at the drain plug and filter. Adjust the oil level if necessary.

Don't pour used engine oil down a drain or storm sewer or even into the ground. This not only contributes to pollution, but is illegal in many areas. Try to buy your oil from an outlet that has disposal arrangements. Some oil companies recommend straining used oil through cheesecloth and adding it to the tank of an oil-burning furnace. Special plastic drain pans that can temporarily store your waste oil are available from auto parts stores.

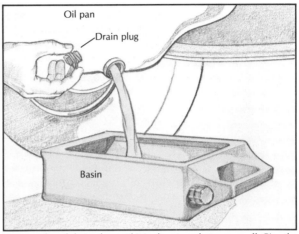

Oil pan
Drain plug
Basin

Unscrew the oil drain plug until it is almost ready to come off. Give the plug a last quick turn by hand to release it.

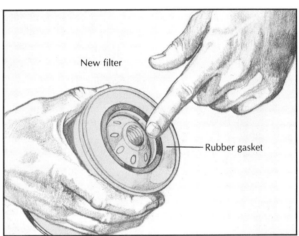

New filter
Rubber gasket

Lubricate and seal the new oil filter by applying a thin coat of fresh engine oil to the gasket with your finger.

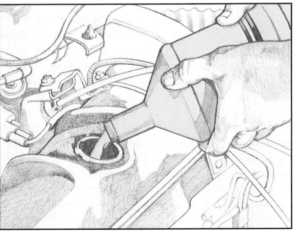

Through the filler atop engine, refill with amount of oil specified in owner's manual (1 L less if you have not changed the filter).

Periodic checks

A typical car uses 14 parts of air to every part of fuel when measured by weight; but by volume that's about 9,000 parts of air for every part of fuel. A car with an average fuel consumption of 12 L/100 km (24 mpg) needs 120 ml (4.2 fl oz) of gas and some 1,060 L (233 gal) of air for every kilometre (or 0.6 mi) driven. Because vast amounts of air are pumped through the engine, dust and dirt must be filtered out; otherwise, dirt would block the small jets in the carburetor and rapidly wear down piston rings and cylinder walls.

The usual filter is a pleated sheet of resin-impregnated paper with pores of a certain size. It is housed inside a pan-shaped metal or plastic housing called the air cleaner. The filter muffles the hissing rush of air through the carburetor, and the shape of the intake snorkel is designed to damp out the noise caused by air pressure fluctuations in the intake manifold.

The filter inside the housing should be removed and inspected every 20,000 km (12,000 mi). If the filter is wet, damaged, or very dirty, it should be replaced with a new one designed specifically for your engine. Running your car with a clogged filter could result in hard starting, stalling, and poor fuel economy. A damaged filter can cause excess engine wear. When inspecting the air filter, you should also remove and inspect the positive crankcase ventilation (PCV) filter and, if necessary, replace it with a new one.

On some cars, you may have to remove the entire air cleaner assembly, not just the filter. This usually involves disconnecting several hoses and various clamps that are attached to the snorkel, sides, and underside of the air cleaner. To make reassembly easier, label each hose and its attachment point.

The heat-controlled air cleaner system also functions as part of the car's emission-control system. Basically, it serves as a pre-heater for the carburetor. By keeping the temperature of the air that enters the carburetor within a specific range, the carburetor can run much leaner, and pollution emissions are reduced.

The heat source for the system is the exhaust manifold. A sheet-metal duct around the manifold collects the heat and directs it to the air cleaner's snorkel. The snorkel is also connected to an outside-air intake duct. A damper flap inside the snorkel controls the mix of outside and heated air that enters the air cleaner and the carburetor. The damper flap may be moved by a thermostat or heat-sensing switch. Loss of engine power or an engine that runs poorly until it warms up may indicate a poorly operating damper flap. Check the operation of the flap at every tuneup. If you cannot see the flap, reach inside the snorkel with a pencil to feel the flap move. Remove the air intake duct (if any) from the snorkel; it is usually held in place by clamps. Then gently work the flap by hand. If it sticks, clean off any dirt from the inner walls of the snorkel. Next, check the damper flap while the engine is running. When the engine is cold, the flap should be closed to outside air; when the engine is hot, the flap should be open. **Caution:** Do not touch hot or moving engine parts.

Inspecting air filters and PCV filters

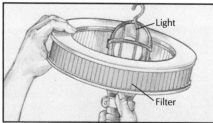

Remove the cover from the air cleaner (usually held in place by a wing nut or by bolts, nuts, or clips). If any hoses attached to the cover interfere with its removal, disconnect them first. Lift out the air filter and inspect it for dirt, tears, or damage. To inspect most air filters, hold a light to the inner side and revolve the filter around it. If you can see light through the entire filter, it is clean and can be reused. If the filter is slightly dirty, tap it sharply against a flat surface or blow compressed air through it. If the filter is so dirty that you cannot see light through it, or if it is damaged or soggy, replace it with a new one.

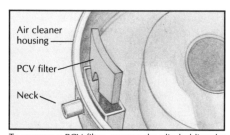

To remove a PCV filter, remove the clip holding the crankcase breather hose to the air cleaner and pull the hose away. Pull filter retainer away from the side of the air cleaner, then slip the filter from the retainer. If necessary, replace it with a new one. Reverse removal procedure to reinstall PCV filter and air filter. Chrysler and AMC V-8 systems do not have a PCV filter in the air cleaner. Instead, Chrysler has a filter in the crankcase inlet air breather (see owner's manual for location); AMC has a filter in the oil filler cap. To clean these filters, remove the breather or cap and rinse with auto parts solvent.

Inside an air cleaner

From a simple filter mounted on top of the carburetor, the air cleaner has evolved into a complex, thermo-statically controlled unit that is part of the car's emission-control system. Although most air cleaners are mounted on the carburetor, some—especially in fuel-injected or turbocharged engines—are mounted in less accessible positions. To locate these units, follow the air duct from the carburetor to the air cleaner. Dodge Omnis and Horizons, for example, have a cannister-like air cleaner next to the carburetor cover. Several imported cars have rectangular air cleaners that may be attached to the carburetor or remotely mounted. Some GM cars with four-cylinder engines have a sealed cleaner whose filter cannot be inspect-ed. Instead, the unit must be replaced at 80,000-km (50,000-mi) intervals.

When inspecting the air cleaner, also check the various hoses clamped to it. One small hose supplies filtered air to the positive crankcase ventilation (PCV) system. A large hose supplies hot air from the vicinity of the exhaust manifold to the intake snorkel. Two small vacuum hoses and a diaphragm operate a damper flap inside the snorkel that controls the amount of heated air entering the air cleaner. If the damper sticks when open, overheated air will enter the engine, causing a loss of power. If the damper sticks when closed, the car may run unevenly until the engine warms the air under the hood.

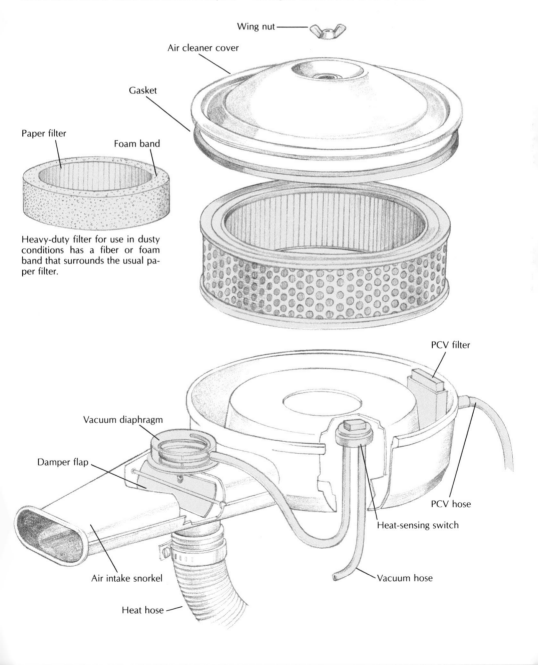

Wing nut

Air cleaner cover

Gasket

Paper filter

Foam band

Heavy-duty filter for use in dusty conditions has a fiber or foam band that surrounds the usual paper filter.

PCV filter

Vacuum diaphragm

Damper flap

PCV hose

Heat-sensing switch

Air intake snorkel

Vacuum hose

Heat hose

Inspecting for leaks and wear

Your car's exhaust system carries the hot, poisonous exhaust gases from the engine to a point where they can be released without danger to the passengers. The system also reduces the sound of combustion, and usually contains a catalytic converter (in newer cars), where pollutants are converted into less harmful emissions.

The muffler breaks up the tremendous pressure waves generated by the engine during combustion. Baffles and expansion chambers allow the exhaust gases to slow down, greatly reducing both pressure and noise. Some cars have a second muffler,

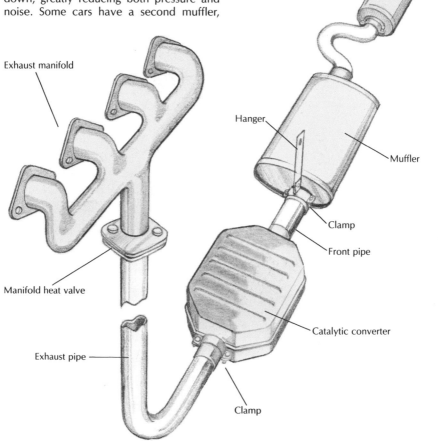

Hanger

Resonator

Exhaust manifold

Hanger

Muffler

Clamp

Front pipe

Manifold heat valve

Catalytic converter

Exhaust pipe

Clamp

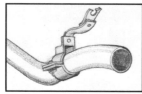

Check frequently for broken hangers or loose clamps, especially if you drive on rough roads. Vibrating components develop leaks; contact with underbody causes rattles. Severe damage can result if the exhaust droops.

Tap muffler and pipes gently with a hammer or wrench to check internal condition. Rust or collapsed inner parts will produce dull thuds or rattles. A clear, ringing sound indicates that the part is likely in good condition.

Push up on the muffler and other fixtures to check the condition of end tubes and seams. Check rust damage on all parts by jabbing with a screwdriver. If metal flakes excessively or holes develop, replace parts.

called a resonator, designed to absorb the noise not trapped by the first muffler.

Water and road salt corrode the exhaust system from the outside. Water and acid vapors eat away from inside the pipes and mufflers. When the exhaust system is fully warmed up, these vapors pass out the tail pipe with minimal damage. When the system is cold, however, some vapors condense inside the pipes and mufflers, causing corrosion. Because the exhaust system warms up from the engine rearward, components toward the back of the car tend to rust away sooner. Thus a car used only for short trips will need more frequent muffler replacement than one used mostly for highway driving trips.

Engine faults can often be detected by observing and listening to the exhaust system. Sooty exhaust smoke, for example, may indicate too rich a fuel mixture. Excessive blue smoke during acceleration points to an internal oil leak. White smoke indicates a coolant leak. Loud or unusual noises—hissing, rumbling, or rattling—coming from beneath the car are almost always signs that the exhaust system needs repair. To inspect it, place the car on jack stands (p. 98) and check each part for damage or misalignment visually and by feel. Start with the tail pipe and work forward toward the engine compartment. Do not overlook the exhaust manifolds;

they can become loose, or their gaskets may wear out. To find leaks where damage is not apparent, make the inspection outdoors with the engine idling. Have a helper partially block the exhaust pipe with a wad of rags. Without touching the hot parts themselves, carefully place your hands near the exhaust system joints or areas where hissing can be heard. You should be able to feel any jets of escaping gas.

Also inspect the exhaust pipe hangers, which suspend the exhaust system beneath the car. A stretched or broken hanger will weaken nearby joints and allow parts to rattle against the underbody. If a hanger must be replaced, try to buy an exact duplicate of the original; otherwise, improvise with universal hangers, available at auto parts stores.

Another important pollution control on the car is the positive crankcase ventilation (PCV) system, which draws vapors from the crankcase into the intake manifold, where they are mixed with the air-fuel mixture and burned in the engine. Yearly inspection and maintenance of the PCV valve, hoses, and filter help to keep the system working properly. The location of the PCV valve varies from one type of engine to another, so consult your service or owner's manual. The PCV filter in most cars is located in the air cleaner. If any parts are defective, replace them with new parts designed for your car.

Checking the PCV valve and hose

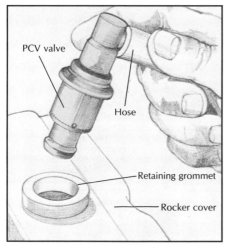

With the engine on, pull the PCV valve out of its retaining grommet (on some engines, the valve is spliced into a hose). If the valve doesn't rattle, it is plugged and should be replaced. Even if the valve rattles, it may be bad. Run the engine with the valve connected to its vacuum source. If you cannot feel a strong vacuum at the open end of the valve, replace it.

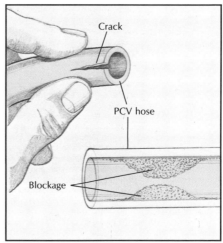

To replace a PCV valve, simply pull the valve out of its seat. It may be necessary to loosen a hose clamp before the valve will come out. Inspect the PCV hose. If it is cracked, blocked, damaged, or collapsed, replace the hose. Then reinstall the PCV valve (replace the clamp if it is damaged) and place it back into its retaining grommet or other hose section.

Manual transmission troubleshooting

The manual transmission makes it possible to match the engine's speed to that of the drive wheels, in conditions ranging from highway driving to hill climbing. The lower gears allow the engine to turn very fast in comparison to the drive wheels, thereby providing maximum torque (twisting power) to start the car from rest and accelerate. Higher gears keep the engine rpm low for maximum fuel economy at cruising speeds. Going uphill, the engine will falter and stall unless a lower gear is selected.

The gears between *First* and *High* bridge the gap between the torque required to start a fully loaded car and the power needed to keep it rolling along at highway speeds. In the days when engines were big and produced lots of torque, only three forward speeds were needed. Today's smaller engines produce less torque at higher rpm and often require four or five gears.

Manual transmission components are more accessible than those in an automatic transmission, and routine maintenance is relatively simple. About once every six months, check the oil level in the transmission and add fluid if necessary. With a manual transmission, you will have to remove a metal or rubber filler plug and check the level with your finger (facing page). Most carmakers do not recommend ever changing the oil in manual transmissions unless the car has had unusually heavy use. Only Honda and Toyota recommend a regular change of oil, about once every two and a half years.

Manufacturers are specific about the kind of lubrication that should be used in the transmission. Only Honda recommends engine oil. Consult your owner's manual for the recommended lubricant. These are graded according to viscosity—the higher the viscosity number, the thicker the oil. Select a lubricant with a viscosity number suitable for the climate in which you drive. In areas where the temperature drops well below freezing, for example, use a lubricant with a viscosity number of either 80W or 80W-90.

The various parts of the gearshift linkage and clutch should also be inspected and lubricated regularly as part of a car's normal maintenance routine. For efficiency, the job may be performed at the same time as the periodic lubrication of the steering and suspension (pp. 110-111). Use fresh, multipurpose grease and apply it to all swivel points in the shift linkage after first wiping away any road dirt and old grease.

Checking the clutch

The clutch connects the engine to a manual transmission. Stepping on a pedal disengages the clutch so that the engine can run without turning the wheels. This allows the driver to shift from one gear to another.

A friction material on both sides of the clutch disc, similar to that on brake linings, allows the disc to be engaged gradually (by strong springs) for smooth starts when the engine is turning at more than 1,000 rpm. Clutches are named after the kind of pressure springs they use. *Coil-spring* clutches, once common, are now giving way to *diaphragm clutches* which are lighter, cheaper, and reduce pedal pressure. Some coil-spring clutches have weights that increase the clamping force of the springs as engine speed increases. These are called *centrifugal clutches.*

To avoid early clutch failure, the operating linkage of the clutch should be checked and adjusted at intervals of 5,000 to 20,000 km (3,000 to 12,000 mi) or every six months, depending on the car. If the clutch slips or the transmission is hard to shift even when the pedal is pressed all the way to the floor, an adjustment is overdue and the clutch may already be damaged.

The clutch pedal should have approximately 2.5 cm (1 in.) of free play. This is most easily determined by operating the pedal with your hand *(above).* If no difference in pressure is required to depress the pedal all the way to the floor, either

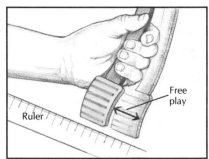

Ruler · Free play

the linkage needs adjustment or the pedal's return spring is broken or disconnected. To check the return spring (except on Ford vehicles from 1979 onward), lift the pedal. If it flips freely up and down, the spring is probably broken or unhooked.

There are three types of clutch linkages: rods, cables, and hydraulic systems. Adjustments are usually made between the engine and transmission, where the clutch-operating fork protrudes from the clutch housing. On rear-wheel-drive cars, this is under the car, usually on the driver's side. On front-drive models, adjustments can often be made in the engine compartment without jacking up the car. If you suspect a linkage problem, have the clutch assembly checked and adjusted by a mechanic.

Inside a manual transmission

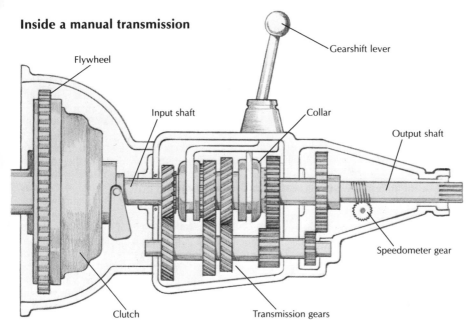

Gearshift lever

Flywheel

Input shaft

Collar

Output shaft

Speedometer gear

Clutch

Transmission gears

As its name implies, the manual transmission allows the driver to change the ratio between the speed of the engine and the speed of the drive wheels. Moving the shift lever slides collars that engage sets of gears. Most manual transmissions have three, four, or five forward speeds plus *Neutral* and *Reverse*.

Neutral disengages all drive gears so that the engine can idle while the clutch is engaged and the car is stationary. To permit smooth shifting, manual transmissions in all modern automobiles are *synchromeshed,* which allows two sets of gears to reach the same speed before they are engaged.

Adding transmission oil

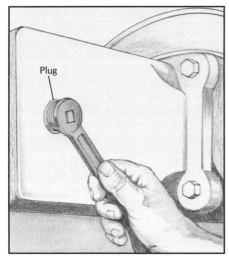

Plug

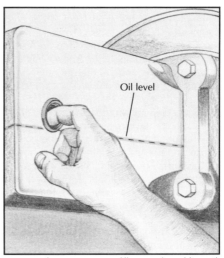

Oil level

Locate the transmission filler plug and remove it *(above, left)*. Do not confuse it with bolts on the transmission; accidental removal of a bolt may allow internal parts to spring loose. Insert your finger to check the oil level *(above, right)*. Most transmissions should be filled up to the filler hole (check the owner's manual or the carmaker's service manual). **Caution:** Beware of hot engine parts.

If oil is not up to the correct level, add more through a length of hose and a funnel. Or use a clean plastic squeeze bottle (such as a ketchup dispenser). Five-speed transmissions on some smaller

cars may have a separate filler cap for adding oil.

Repeat this procedure to check the oil level in the differential every six months. Be sure that the car is horizontal; if you want to raise it, lift and support both ends of the car so that it is level.

Use the lubricant recommended by the manufacturer, of a viscosity matched to the temperature range in which the car is driven. Special lubricants are used in limited-slip differentials—check to see if your car has this feature. Most carmakers do not recommend ever changing the oil in the differential unless the car has been subjected to unusually heavy use.

Shifting made easy

An automatic transmission works on the same principle as a manual transmission. But, instead of being connected to—and disconnected from—the engine by a manually operated clutch, the automatic transmission is linked to the engine by a fluid coupler (the torque converter), which means gears can be shifted without disconnecting the transmission from the engine. Through a network of valves, springs, pistons, and pumps, the automatic transmission uses hydraulic pressure to change gears. This pressure is transmitted by oil (transmission fluid), which fills the system.

Under normal driving conditions, it is advisable to check the level of the automatic transmission fluid every few months. Most car manufacturers recommend checking the fluid level every time you change the engine oil. If you pull a trailer, drive on steep mountain roads at high altitudes, or drive consistently in heavy city traffic (especially in hot weather), you should check the transmission fluid more often—about once or twice a month. Never run your car when the transmission fluid is low; doing so could cause serious internal damage. Check the fluid level if you notice the car slipping erratically in and out of gear, a warning sign that is most noticeable when the engine is cold or the car is being driven up a hill.

The gearbox must be at operating temperature before the fluid level is checked. Drive the car 15 to 25 km (10 to 15 mi) or for about 20 minutes. Then stop the car on level ground and apply the brakes. With the engine running, move the gearshift lever through all positions. Finally, put the transmission in *Park* on Datsuns, Hondas, and Ford and General Motors cars, or in *Neutral* on American Motors and Chrysler cars, Toyotas, and Volkswagens. Set the parking brake and leave the engine running at idle.

Caution: The parking brake must be in good operating condition; if it will not hold the car stationary on a hill, have the parking brake adjusted before checking the transmission fluid.

Lift the hood, remove the transmission fluid dipstick, and carefully touch the tip to test the heat of the fluid. The end of the dipstick should be too hot to hold comfortably: 45°C to 95°C (150°F to 200°F). Note the color of the fluid; it should be red or pink unless your owner's manual specifies otherwise. Compare the color and smell to that of new fluid. Brown or black fluid, especially if it smells burned, often indicates an overheated transmission and the need for maintenance. Wipe the dipstick with a paper towel or clean rag,

being careful not to let any lint cling to the stick. Check the stain for particles or gummy residue. If either are present, the transmission should be inspected by a specialist. Insert the clean dipstick back into the filler tube, making sure that it is seated fully or according to the instructions in the owner's manual. Then withdraw it again and note the level of the fluid clinging to the stick.

On most cars the correct fluid level is at or just below the *Full* mark when the transmission is at operating temperature. If the fluid level seems too high, the transmission may be above normal operating temperature, and you should let it cool for 30 minutes and check the level again. If the fluid seems too low, the transmission may not have been operated long enough to reach the proper temperature. Drive the car again, then recheck the fluid level. Do not rely on a single low reading and add fluid to a cold transmission. You may accidentally overfill it and cause as much damage as you would by operating the car with too little fluid. Compare the fluid level and dipstick temperature to the specifications listed in the owner's manual, and add fluid only if necessary. Use the type of fluid recommended in the manual.

Many cars with automatic transmissions no longer require regular fluid changes as part of routine maintenance. For other cars, draining and changing the fluid, cleaning the oil pan, and replacing the filter is recommended at intervals ranging from every 25,000 km to every 100,000 km (15,000 to 60,000 mi). Your owner's manual will list the maintenance requirements, if any, for your transmission.

The intricate inner workings of an automatic transmission are far less accessible than those of a manual gearbox, and maintaining them is best left to a transmission specialist. Have your automatic transmission serviced periodically, according to the manufacturer's recommendation (usually every 40,000 km or 25,000 mi). If your transmission needs servicing, the garage will change the transmission fluid, if necessary; adjust the bands, if this can be done externally; replace the transmission filter; and replace the gasket around the pan and change the oil it holds. If the front seal is leaking, the mechanic must remove the transmission but will not have to take it apart. However, if the transmission needs to be overhauled, it must be disassembled so that defective seals, clutches, bands, and bushings can be replaced. Transmission repairs can run from $10 for a new vacuum modulator to several hundred dollars for a major overhaul.

Inside an automatic transmission

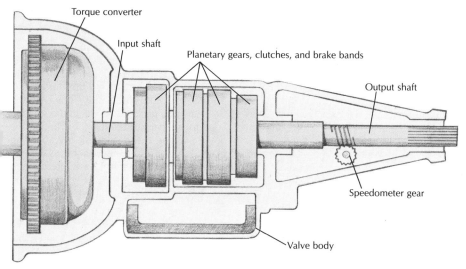

The automatic transmission uses hydraulic pressure to shift gears and transmit power from the engine to the drive train. Only a small part of an automatic transmission is taken up by the gears. Most of the space is filled by the torque convertor and a system of clutches and brake bands that activate the proper gear ratios to provide power to the output shaft. When the shift lever is set in *Drive*, pressurized oil flows through a series of valves in the valve body. The valves, which open and close automatically in response to the engine's speed and load, tighten or loosen the bands and clutches to provide the various gear ratios required for driving. Thus the transmission can shift to higher gears as the car's speed increases, and downshift for climbing hills or passing, when power is needed.

How to add automatic transmission fluid

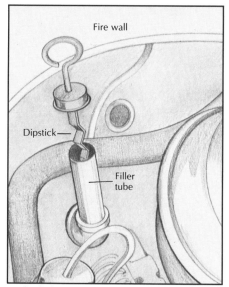

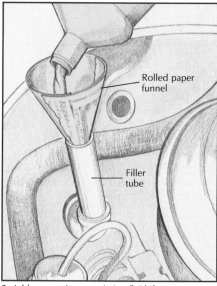

1. Check the transmission fluid level only when the car is fully warmed up. The transmission dipstick is located in a filler tube behind the engine. Do not confuse it with the engine-oil dipstick. Note the dipstick temperature (it should be hot to the touch) and level of fluid. Transmission oil expands when hot, so consult your owner's manual to determine the accuracy of the reading. A low fluid level may be correct if the transmission temperature is below normal.

2. Add automatic transmission fluid if necessary. Use a clean, flex-neck funnel to reach an awkward filler tube. Use only fluid recommended by the manufacturer, add it in small amounts, and check the level frequently. Be careful not to overfill the system. You can add fluid in an emergency by using rolled up paper as a funnel (a magazine cover works well). Use caution in makeshift situations to avoid contaminating the fluid with dirt or water.

Inspecting the brake system

Brakes stop a car by forcing a high-friction material against spinning metal discs or drums bolted to the wheels. This friction slows the car and eventually stops it. Over time, the friction material wears away.

Checking and maintaining your car's brakes need not be intimidating, even if you are not an experienced mechanic. Although they are of vital importance, brakes are normally maintained by relatively inexperienced mechanics. In many shops, apprentices do a majority of the brake repairs.

Disc brakes work by forcing friction pads against the sides of a spinning disc. Drum brakes use a pair of semicircular shoes with linings that rub against the inside surface of a metal drum to slow and stop the car. Of the two, disc brakes are more effective because the disc is exposed to a cooling flow of air. When brakes get so hot that the pads or linings lose their friction qualities, brakes fade. Because disc brakes are less inclined to fade, they are used on the front wheels of most cars, where they supply up to 80 percent of the stopping power.

Brake maintenance involves three steps: inspecting the system for damage or wear, replacing pads or linings (which are designed to wear and be replaced), and—rarely—completely overhauling and replacing parts that fail. Fortunately, most brake problems develop gradually and can be spotted before they become serious.

To check for fluid leaks, apply the brakes with the engine off and the transmission in *Neutral.* On cars equipped with power brakes, start the engine; the brake pedal should move down slightly under your foot as the power-boost system activates. The pedal should not move more than halfway to the floor, and it should hold firm for at least 30 seconds. If the pedal sinks slowly to the floor, there is probably a leak in the system. Look for seepage at the master cylinder, the brake calipers (disc brakes), the backing plates (drum brakes), and the hoses leading to each wheel. Some leaks are internal and therefore difficult to trace. If you can't find the leak yourself, have the system checked.

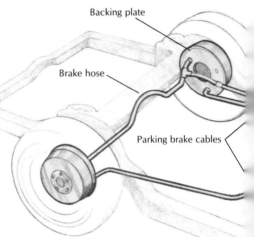

Backing plate

Brake hose

Parking brake cables

Inside a drum brake

Drum brakes are enclosed, so that checking their condition on most cars is difficult. Some brakes have inspection holes in the drum or backing plate so you can check lining wear without removing the drum. Look for a hole or a rubber plug near the edge of the drum. (Some have a knockout plug, like those in an electrical wiring box, in the backing plate. This is an adjustment hole, not an inspection opening.) By turning the drum, you can check the entire lining for thickness and wear. New drum-brake linings are about 0.5 cm (3/16 in.) thick. If they are riveted to the shoes, have them replaced when the lining wears down to just above the rivet heads. If linings are bonded to shoes, they can wear down to 1.6 mm (1/16 in.).

Drum-brake backing plates may show signs of brake fluid leakage where the wheel cylinder is mounted, at hose connections, or near bleeder valves. Tighten these fittings; if the leak does not stop, have defective parts replaced.

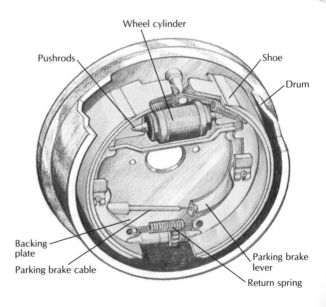

Wheel cylinder

Pushrods

Shoe

Drum

Backing plate

Parking brake cable

Parking brake lever

Return spring

Inside a disc brake

Once the wheel of a car has been removed, its disc brake can easily be inspected. Disc-brake calipers usually have an inspection hole that lets you see the lining thickness of at least one pad without disassembling the brake. The lining thickness of the outer pad can be checked by looking along the side of the disc. Minimum pad thickness should be 1.6 mm (¹⁄₁₆ in.). The rubbing surfaces of the disc should be smooth and have no deep scores or ridges. Obvious surface wear calls for a professional check. Also inspect disc brakes for hydraulic leaks. Calipers on disc brakes may leak where the flexible hose is screwed in, at the bleeder valve, or around the piston. Tighten leaking bleeder valves or fittings. Replace hoses that are mushy, brittle, or damp with brake fluid.

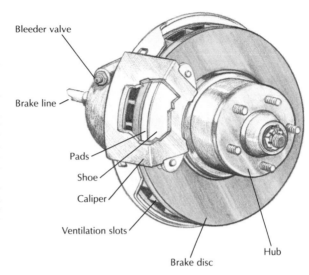

Bleeder valve

Brake line

Pads

Shoe

Caliper

Ventilation slots

Brake disc

Hub

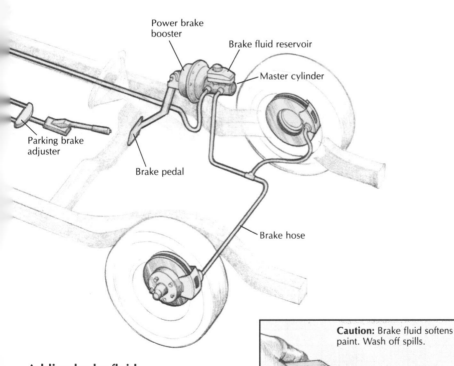

Power brake booster

Brake fluid reservoir

Master cylinder

Parking brake adjuster

Brake pedal

Brake hose

Caution: Brake fluid softens paint. Wash off spills.

Adding brake fluid

To check the brake fluid level, first locate the brake's master cylinder. In most cars it is under the hood where the pedal linkage comes through the fire wall. On some cars the brake fluid reservoir is translucent, which allows you to see the level without removing the top. The brake fluid reservoir on many other North American cars is an aluminum or iron casting with a stamped-metal cover secured with a bail. To check the level, pry the bail aside; lift the cover and the rubber diaphragm. Fill reservoir to the *Full* mark or within 1.5 cm (½ in.) of the top, using new brake fluid marked DoT 3 or DoT 4.

Electrical system troubleshooting

A car's electrical system can be a complicated and frustrating source of problems for the non-mechanic. Even minor problems such as a defective switch or frayed wire can be difficult to trace and repair unless you understand some of the basics of an electrical system. For example, the 60 m (200 ft) of wire that links the electrical components in a modern car—with the exception of grounding straps, battery leads, and high-voltage ignition wires—is wrapped with insulation of various colors to permit quick recognition. Manufacturer's repair manuals (and some owner's manuals) usually include a complete diagram of the different car circuits—ignition, starter, charging, lighting, and accessory—keyed to these colors. The battery supports the system by supplying current to the lights and accessories when the engine is not running, and by supplying

How to use this chart

Find problem at top of chart. Look down column to locate possible causes. First check repairs that you can do yourself. If none of these procedures work, consult a competent mechanic.

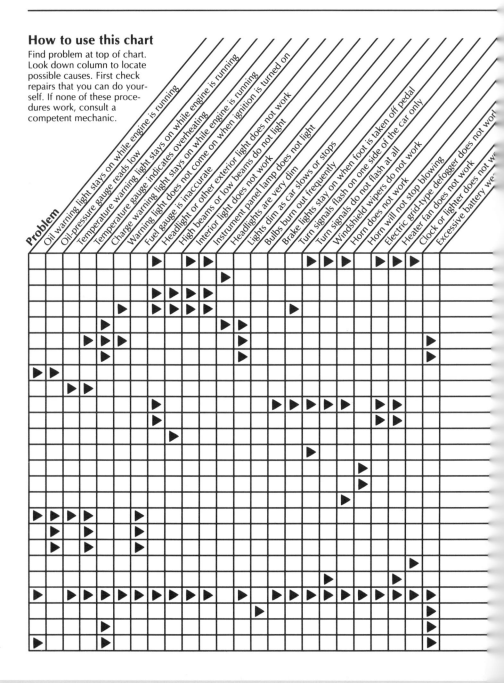

the power that starts the engine. After the engine is running, the alternator takes over, recharging the battery and meeting all the other electrical requirements of the car.

When a light or accessory does not work, the fault is either a short circuit or an open circuit somewhere in the system. Shorts cause fuses to blow, so check the fuse box first. Damaged insulation, broken wires, or open connections can cause short circuits.

Burned-out bulbs or motors, faulty switches, loosened connections, broken wires, or corrosion commonly cause open circuits. Accumulations of dirt, oil, or corrosion at the terminals and light bulb sockets can also interfere with the flow of electricity. Any of these faults can appear almost anywhere in the system. When looking for defects, first check and clean all connections; you may avoid a costly trip to the garage.

Replacing fuses

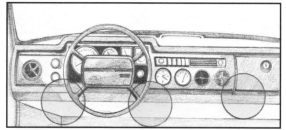 

Replace a blown fuse with one that matches the rating printed on the fuse panel, located in one of the areas indicated above. If the replacement fuse also blows, check for a short.

Use an inexpensive fuse puller *(above)* to remove and install glass tube fuses.

Possible cause	Cure
Fuse blown or circuit breaker tripped	Replace fuse or reset circuit breaker *(above)*
Lights dirty	Clean lights with water and detergent
Poor electrical contact at bulb socket	Clean bulb base and socket with wire brush
Bulb burned out	Replace bulb or headlight (pp. 130-131)
Battery low or defective	Recharge or replace battery (pp. 128-129)
Fan belt loose or broken	Tighten or replace fan belt (pp. 134-135)
Alternator overloaded	Reduce use of accessories, or use heavy-duty alternator
Oil problem in engine	Check oil level; investigate oil problem (pp. 112-113)
Engine overheating	Check cooling system (pp. 132-133)
Defective switch	Replace switch
Defective relay	Replace relay
Faulty dimmer switch	Replace dimmer switch
Defective flasher	Replace flasher
Sticking horn switch	Repair or replace horn switch
Sticking horn relay	Replace horn relay
Defective horn or horn relay	Replace horn or horn relay
Faulty sending unit	Replace sending unit
Defective gauge	Replace gauge
Faulty instrument voltage regulator	Replace instrument voltage regulator
Defective lighter or clock	Replace defective part
Faulty electric motor	Replace motor
Faulty wiring or ground connection	Locate and repair poor ground, short, or open circuit
Defective voltage regulator	Adjust or replace voltage regulator
Alternator charging poorly	Repair or replace alternator
Shorted diode in alternator	Replace diode assembly or alternator

Checking and changing spark plugs

Modern spark plugs handle electricity at up to 40,000 volts and temperatures as high as 2500°C (4500°F) for up to 48,000 km (30,000 mi). Hundreds of kinds of plugs are manufactured to fit various engines and driving conditions. When replacement is needed, do not use just any plug that fits. Plugs are classified by an important factor called *heat range*—their ability to transfer heat from the insulator tip to the engine block. A *hot plug* transfers heat slowly and therefore stays hot. A *cold plug* transfers heat quickly and remains cooler. A plug that is too hot may glow and ignite the fuel mixture before it should, causing pinging. A plug that is too cold may not burn away deposits that will eventually bridge the gap between the electrodes, a result called *fouling*.

The way you drive affects the heat range required. The recommended plug for your car is intended for a "normal" mixture of city and highway driving. If your car is used mostly for short trips, for stop-and-go driving, or at low speeds, you may need a hotter-than-normal plug to burn off deposits. If your car is used mostly for long-distance, high-speed highway driving, you may need a cooler-than-normal plug to avoid overheating, which can wear plugs rapidly. At your next tune-up, ask your mechanic to recommend the best plug for your driving needs, or consult your owner's manual.

Inside a spark plug

Spark plugs ignite the air-fuel mixture that powers your car. Each plug consists of a metal rod, called an *electrode*, surrounded by a ceramic insulator. The lower end of the insulator is encased in a threaded metal shell that screws into the cylinder head. Another electrode is welded to the shell, and is separated from the center electrode by a narrow gap. High-voltage current from the distributor flows down the center electrode and jumps this gap in the form of a spark.

For top engine performance, this spark must be large enough and last long enough to ignite the fuel mixture efficiently. The wider the gap, the bigger the spark. But wider gaps require higher voltage to produce a spark. Every engine has a specified spark plug gap, which ranges from 0.5 mm (0.02 in.) to 2 mm (0.08 in.). This gap can be adjusted by bending the side electrode. If the gap is too wide, the plug may not fire at all. If the gap is too small, the spark may not be big enough to ignite the fuel mixture. The gap should be checked periodically because the electrodes erode with use.

Other causes of weak or erratic sparking are dirt, oil, or water on the ceramic insulator; a cracked insulator; or fouled electrodes. All these faults can create an alternate path for the high-voltage current between the ignition cable and the cylinder head. Such current shortcuts are called short circuits. Most important, a misfiring spark plug can increase fuel consumption by as much as 10 to 15 percent in a V-8 engine and 25 to 35 percent in a four-cylinder engine. Plugs that last up to 80,000 km (50,000 mi) have been developed, but they have such expensive features as platinum electrodes.

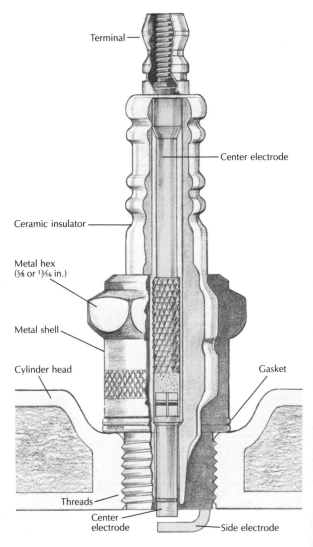

Terminal

Center electrode

Ceramic insulator

Metal hex (⅝ or ¹³⁄₁₆ in.)

Metal shell

Cylinder head

Gasket

Threads

Center electrode

Side electrode

Cleaning, adjusting, and installing plugs

Spark plugs should be inspected every 8,000 to 12,000 km (5,000 to 7,500 mi) and replaced whenever they are worn or fouled, usually every 16,000 to 24,000 km (10,000 to 15,000 mi).

To remove spark plugs, you will need a spark plug socket. This is a socket deep enough to fit over a plug; it usually has a rubber insert that grips the plug's ceramic insulator and lifts the plug from the cylinder head. Spark plug sockets are made in two sizes to fit the most common plugs: 13/16-inch and 5/8-inch.

Caution: Always disconnect the ground cable from the battery before beginning work on any electrical parts. Failure to do so may result in sparks that can damage equipment and burn hands.

To avoid confusion, label all plug cables. On V-type engines, add "D" for the driver's side and "P" for passenger side. Use a ratchet wrench, a U-joint, and a spark plug socket to remove plugs. If a plug is hard to reach, add an extension. To jar a plug loose, hit the end of the wrench with the heel of one hand while holding the other end of the ratchet. But be careful: the ceramic insulators are easily broken if forced sideways.

If the plugs can be reused, wash them with parts-cleaning solvent and a stiff bristle brush; do not use a wire brush. After the plugs have dried, carefully pry their side electrodes away from their center electrodes. File the electrodes until their surfaces are flat and horizontal, and their edges are sharp. Use a plug file thin enough not to bend the electrodes.

Measure the electrode gap on used plugs with a wire feeler gauge. For extra-wide plug gaps, use a bar-type gauge designed to measure gaps up to 2 mm (.08 in.). A blade feeler gauge can be used to measure the gap of new plugs, whose electrodes have not become worn. Compare your measurement with the correct gap for your engine (use manufacturer's specifications) and adjust if necessary. To change the gap, bend the side electrode using the tang on the gap gauge.

Before installing new plugs, check their gaps first and make any necessary adjustments. A plug should screw easily into the cylinder head until it seats. Be careful not to cross-thread a plug by screwing it in at an angle. To ensure a durable electrical connection between the spark plug's terminal and cable, spray silicone lubricant or dab an electrically conductive grease on the inside of the connector in the cable boot.

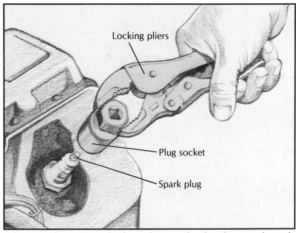

Locking pliers

Plug socket

Spark plug

If there are obstructions, slip the socket over the plug, then turn the socket with a wrench or locking pliers.

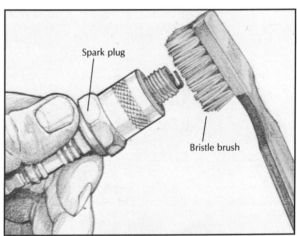

Spark plug

Bristle brush

Wash used plugs with parts-cleaning solvent. Be careful not to leave bits of bristle on the plug, as these will impair its operation.

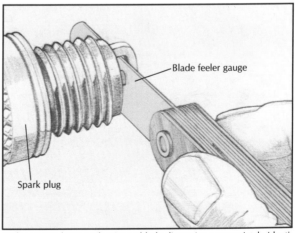

Blade feeler gauge

Spark plug

Feeler gauges have each wire or blade dimension appropriately identified. Slide the gauge firmly but not forcefully.

Checking and maintaining the battery

The battery provides the electricity for the ignition system and starter motor, and for the lights and other electrical equipment when the engine is off. During the few seconds that the starter turns the engine over, it may be drawing as much as 400 amperes from the battery. (Headlights, in comparison, draw about 15 amperes, the taillights only 1.5 amperes.) Because of this high current drain, the starter should never be operated for more than 30 seconds at a time; it should then be allowed to rest for a minute, to reduce the chance of draining the battery completely. After the engine is running, the alternator takes over, recharging the battery and meeting all the other electrical demands of the car.

The battery is made up of a number of cells, each supplying just over two volts, with terminals linked by metal bars. Modern car batteries have six cells giving twelve volts. Each cell consists of two plates, or *electrodes,* in a solution of water and sulfuric acid (called the *electrolyte*). When a cell is functioning, the acid reacts with the plates, converting chemical energy into electricity. A battery will eventually go dead and cannot be recharged for several reasons: The plates may disintegrate or become so encrusted with sulfate that a charge cannot get through to them. Or current leakage may cause a short circuit.

All batteries require maintenance, even the so-called maintenance-free type. This is particularly important in winter, when even a well-maintained battery may deliver no more than 40 percent of its normal power. If the battery has removable caps, check the water level once a month and, if necessary, add distilled water. Do not add water in winter unless you intend to drive immediately. Otherwise, the water will not mix with the acid but will freeze and damage the battery.

Remove powdery deposits that form on the top of the battery terminals with a wire battery brush, or by scrubbing them with a baking soda and water solution. To prevent any further deposits from forming, smear the

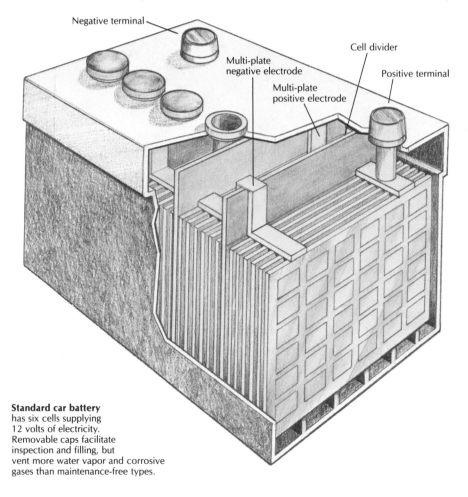

Negative terminal

Cell divider

Multi-plate
negative electrode

Positive terminal

Multi-plate
positive electrode

Standard car battery
has six cells supplying
12 volts of electricity.
Removable caps facilitate
inspection and filling, but
vent more water vapor and corrosive
gases than maintenance-free types.

terminals with grease. Also check for frayed wires leading to the terminals. Do not delay replacing damaged wires or cables, or the battery may short circuit. Grit and fluid on the battery case can act as a medium for electrical current to seep between the terminals and drain the battery. Clean and inspect the case, terminals, clamps, and support at least once a month.

Caution: Work carefully when maintaining the battery. Batteries emit explosive hydrogen gas; never smoke or light a match around one. Also remove rings and other jewelry in order to prevent sparks. If you spill battery fluid (sulfuric acid) on yourself, wash immediately with water. Seek prompt medical help if any acid gets into your eyes (flush them first with water).

Checking the charge

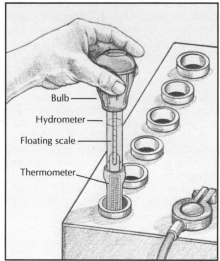

Bulb
Hydrometer
Floating scale
Thermometer

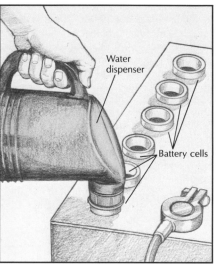

Water dispenser
Battery cells

If a battery has removable vent caps, its charge can easily be checked with a hydrometer. Squeeze the bulb and draw up enough fluid to float the scale inside. Record the reading, then correct the results for temperature (most hydrometers also have a thermometer). In temperate climates a reading of 1.265 or more indicates that the battery is fully charged.

Once a month, check the level of fluid in all six cells. It should cover the metal plates inside and come to within about 0.5 cm (¼ in.) of the bottom of the filler hole. On some batteries the correct level is specified on the case. Add distilled water to battery cells that are low on fluid. Use a small funnel or the special dispenser shown above.

Recharging a battery

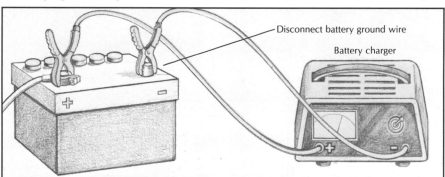

Disconnect battery ground wire

Battery charger

A battery with a low charge can be recharged either by running the engine (assuming that the alternator and voltage regulator work properly) or by connecting a trickle charger to the battery for several hours or overnight. Leave the charger connected until its meter drops to a reading of less than 1 ampere. If the charger does not have a meter, but the battery has vent caps, check the battery once every hour using a hydrometer. When the hydrometer gives the same reading for three consecutive hours, the battery cannot be charged further. If the battery cannot be brought to a full charge, replace it. Never try to charge a frozen battery; bring it indoors for several hours to warm up first.

See and be seen

Your car is required to have headlights, side marker lights, taillights, a rear license plate light, flashing turn signals, four-way hazard warning flashers, backup lights, and stoplights that turn on when the brakes are applied. By law these must be working properly at all times.

Most newer cars are equipped with sealed-beam headlights. The reflector and lens is made as one piece, vacuumized, and sealed. The entire unit, therefore, functions as one large bulb. Sealed-beam lights are widely available and inexpensive, but they generate only about 75,000 candelas of yellowish light. Quartz-halogen headlights can produce over 150,000 candelas of a bright, white light, but they cost much more than conventional lights. Quartz lights are available in two types: sealed-beam units and European-style lights with a separate bulb and reflector. All headlights are mounted in brackets that are adjusted by screws so that the beam can be aimed.

Separate bulbs can be used for the taillights and stoplights, but they are often incorporated into a single bulb containing two filaments. Each taillight filament draws about 1.5 amperes of current. The brighter stoplight filaments draw about 4 amperes. Taillights are enclosed by red lenses with built-in prisms that reflect the headlights of an approaching car.

Turn signals on new cars have amber lenses both front and rear. When turned on, the lights are set to blink on and off at a rate of 60 to 120 times per minute. This is accomplished by a flasher unit in the turn signal circuit. Another flasher unit activates all four amber lights at once as an emergency hazard warning.

A typical car also has 15 to 20 interior bulbs, and procedures for replacing them range from simple to very difficult. The most difficult involve the instrument panel bulbs, as arrangements of these lights vary widely from one make to another. Some of the more direct ways to reach instrument panel bulbs are: reaching under and behind the dashboard; reaching through the top of the dashboard after removing the screws and top panel; taking the bulbs out of the front after removing the panel trim and instrument lens. One type of bulb is simply pulled from its spring-clip socket; another type must first be pushed in and turned counterclockwise.

Caution: Always disconnect the ground cable from the battery before working on electrical parts.

Replacing exterior bulbs

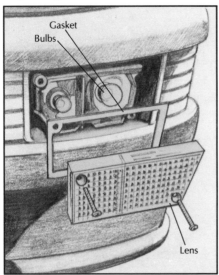

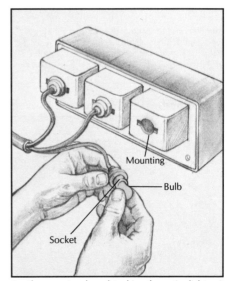

Exterior car lights vary from one car to another, but it is common to find several bulbs grouped together in one housing. A typical example is a taillight assembly that may also include the stoplight, backup light, and turn-signal light. There are basically three kinds of light housings and three ways to get at a defective bulb. One way is to take off the lens after removing a number of exposed lens-mounting screws *(above)*.

Another way involves detaching the entire light unit and then removing the bulb, with its socket, from the back of the unit *(above)*. The third method does not require disassembly of the light unit; the bulb is reached from behind via the trunk, the fender, or the bumper. The bulb and socket mount are removed from the back of the housing. Buy a correct replacement from an auto parts store or car dealer.

Inside a headlight

Aside from burning out completely, headlights can become less effective with age. (This problem does not affect halogen headlights.) If a light darkens markedly it should be replaced. If a high-beam filament in a four-headlight system burns out, three headlights remain to illuminate the road ahead, so that it is possible not to notice the loss. High beams should light up not only the road but also any adjacent tree or pole for about 100 m (330 ft); low beams should be aimed to cover the road only or the road and its right-hand margin, where a pedestrian may walk.

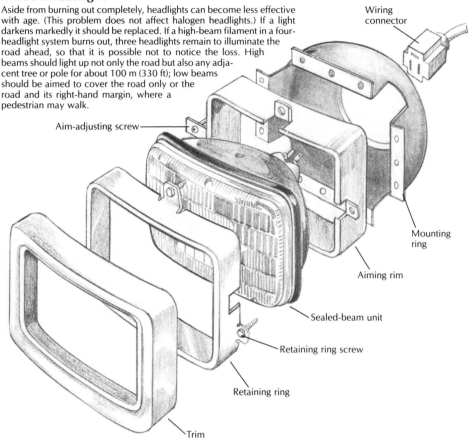

Wiring connector

Aim-adjusting screw

Mounting ring

Aiming rim

Sealed-beam unit

Retaining ring screw

Retaining ring

Trim

Replacing and aiming a headlight

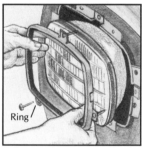

Ring

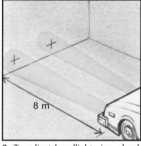

8 m

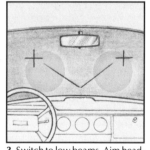

1. Remove the screws or clips that secure the headlight trim to the car body, and remove the trim. Do not disturb the aim-adjusting screws (accessible through a hole in the trim on many models). Remove the retaining ring screws, and lift off the retaining ring. In some cases the screw need only be loosened. With the retaining ring off, the sealed-beam unit is free to be lifted out. To disconnect the wiring, pull the wiring connector off its terminals on the back of the lamp.

2. To adjust headlight aim, check the light pattern that the beams cast on a smooth, vertical wall. Park the car on a level floor near the wall, and mark a point opposite the center of each headlight. Draw or tape a cross through each mark. Back the car away from the wall in a straight line until the headlights are 8 m (25 ft) from the wall. To aim, turn adjusting screws on headlight mounting ring. On some models, these screws are directly accessible. On others, trim must be removed first.

3. Switch to low beams. Aim headlights (outer pair of four-headlight system) so that beams cast a light pattern as shown, with almost no light appearing above horizontal line. On four-headlight system, switch to high beams and mask the outer lights. Aim the inner lights to cast a bright spot on wall that is centered and 5 cm (2 in.) below crosses. If the headlights are arranged one above the other, aim the top pair on low beam only. Then mask the top pair and aim the bottom pair.

Cooling system checks

Fuel burns inside the engine cylinders at temperatures above 2500°C (4500°F). In even the most efficient engines only 20 to 25 percent of this heat energy is used to drive the car. Much of it must be carried away by the cooling system in order to keep oil from evaporating and engine parts from seizing (jamming) or melting. On most cars this is done by circulating a mixture of water and antifreeze through the engine, where heat is absorbed, and then through a radiator, where the heat is given up.

The liquid, called *coolant*, is kept in circulation by the water pump, which is located in the front of the engine and is driven by a rubber V-belt from the crankshaft. A fan is attached to the water pump pulley, and keeps air flowing through the radiator when the car is stopped or moving slowly. Cars with front-wheel drive and transverse engines use a small electric motor to run the fan.

The parts of the cooling system that require periodic maintenance are the hoses and clamps, the drive belt, a few mechanical parts, and the coolant. **Caution:** Do not perform any check of the cooling system (except circulation checks) unless the engine is off and cool. If the car is equipped with an electric fan, be especially wary of a warm engine—it can cause the fan to start unexpectedly, even though the engine is off.

The most neglected element of the cooling system is the coolant. Insufficient coolant or a low proportion of antifreeze can lead to overheating and corrosion in parts of the system. Coolant loss can be minimized with a coolant recovery tank. Most new cars have a recovery tank, which catches and stores coolant overflow. Older cars have an overflow tube that allows any boilover to spill out onto the ground. Kits are available for installing recovery tanks on older cars.

Coolant loss can also result from a leak in the system, usually caused by a faulty seal, broken hose, rust-through, or physical damage to a part such as the radiator. A leak reduces the pressure in the cooling system, which lowers the boiling point of the coolant and leads to overheating.

White stains or rust on a radiator are sure signs of a coolant leak. Add a sealant to the radiator or have the system checked by a cooling specialist. Coolant leaks can also occur if the radiator drain plug or petcock is loose. To stop the leak, simply tighten the valve. Also check for leaks at engine core plugs (freezeout plugs), head gasket, hoses, and water pump. Tighten clamps or replace leaking parts. Minor leaking (called weeping) at the water pump is normal.

Heater hoses. When the engine is running, the inlet and outlet hoses circulate heated coolant through the heater core, which warms and distributes air to the passenger compartment. To inspect the heater hoses, turn on both the engine and heater and feel the hoses. If the temperatures are not similar, suspect a clogged hose or a defective heater core or heater control valve. Have the system checked and any defective part replaced. **Caution:** Since the engine must be running to perform this check, beware of the fan.

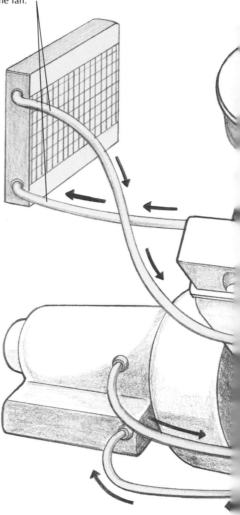

Recovery tank. Less coolant is lost through boilover if the coolant recovery system is in good working order. For a recovery system to function properly, the tank and hose must be free of cracks and leaks, and the hose must not be clogged. One end of the hose should be fastened securely to the neck of the radiator, the other end to the cap of the recovery tank. If replacements, both the radiator cap and the recovery tank cap should be those specified for the system. The coolant, when cold, should be at the *Normal* or *Cold* mark on the side of the tank. If necessary, add pure antifreeze or a mix of antifreeze and water to top up the system.

Thermostat. The thermostat blocks the flow of coolant to the radiator when the coolant temperature is below 85° to 103°C (185° to 217°F). If your car overheats, takes a long time to warm up, or if the air in the heating system does not warm up, suspect a faulty thermostat. To replace it, drain the radiator below the level of the thermostat. Unfasten the housing where the upper radiator hose meets the engine block. Lift out the old thermostat and gasket. Install the new thermostat—valve end up—and new gasket. Coat the gasket with sealer and replace the housing.

Radiator. Check the radiator cap and fins periodically. The cap's seal (or seals) should be clean, pliable, and free from cracks. Rust deposits along the neck of the radiator mean that the coolant should be replaced. While the radiator cap is off, check the condition and level of the coolant. If the level is low (below the metal fins), look for "solder bloom," a formation of deposits in the radiator core that blocks the flow of coolant. If it is present, have the system serviced by a mechanic. To ensure that a maximum amount of air passes through the radiator, keep its surface free from dirt, insects, and litter. Clean the radiator fins, both front and back, using full pressure from a garden hose.

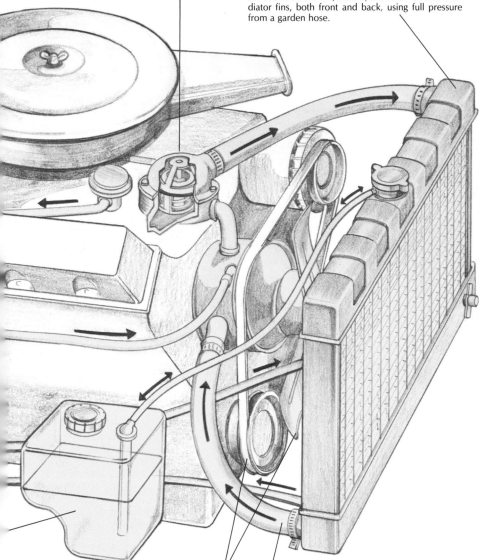

Fan and belts. Inspect and test the radiator fan only when the engine is off and cold. Replace any fan that has a bent or broken blade or rivet. An electric or clutch fan should rotate with some drag or resistance when pushed. Silicone in the clutch should not leak. Replace either fan or clutch if defective. A direct-drive fan should not move easily when pushed. If it does, it may mean that the drive belt needs tightening. Test belt tension (p. 135).

Radiator hoses. With the engine running, squeeze the upper radiator hose to check for coolant flow (the hose should become hot to the touch within a few minutes). If you do not feel the coolant flowing, check for a clogged hose, a faulty thermostat, or a broken water pump. Next look at the lower radiator hose. If it flattens out, it has either lost its resilience or the spring inside it has collapsed. Replace it with a new hose. **Caution:** Beware of the fan.

Maintaining hoses

Most cooling systems are equipped with only four hoses—an upper and lower radiator hose and a heater inlet and outlet hose. Some systems also have a bypass hose near the water pump. The radiator hoses are most prone to wear or damage and may have to be changed at least two or three times during the life of your car.

Cooling system hoses should be checked at least every six months. Any hose that is cracked, leaking, oil-soaked, or that feels hard or spongy when squeezed should be replaced immediately. Early replacement of a weak hose will prevent the overheating and possible engine damage that a leaking hose can cause. Follow the instructions below when replacing a hose, and be sure that the replacement is the correct size, length, and shape for your car.

Hoses come in many different diameters, lengths, and shapes to fit particular car models. Lower hoses have an internal spring that helps maintain their shape. Many replacement hoses are pleated to allow the hose to be bent to fit different engine and radiator combinations. No matter what hose you use, be sure that it hugs the neck tightly. If the hose does not fit snugly, coolant could leak out, even if the hose clamp is tight.

Hoses are held in place by hose clamps, which should be inspected periodically. If they are loose, tighten them. If a spring-type clamp is loose, it must be replaced, preferably with a worm-drive clamp. As with hoses, clamps come in different sizes to fit the hose and neck to which they are attached.

Caution: Inspect and replace hoses only when the engine is cool. Coolant is sweet-tasting and poisonous. Avoid contact with the eyes and keep out of reach of children and pets. Drive belts, too, must be inspected only when the engine is off. If the car has an electric fan, disconnect the battery or wait for the engine to cool off; any heat may turn the fan on unexpectedly.

Removing and replacing a hose

The directions here deal with radiator hoses, but also apply to heater hoses. **Caution:** Never attempt to replace air-conditioning hoses. Air conditioners and their hoses contain a special type of refrigerant, under pressure, that can cause serious injury.

If the upper radiator hose must be replaced, drain about two litres (two quarts) of coolant from the system into a clean container. If you are replacing the lower hose, drain the radiator below the level of the hose. Save the coolant; if it is clear, it can be reused.

Loosen the clamp at each hose end and slide the clamp back onto the hose. Gently twist and pull the hose free of the metal connecting joints. If the hose is stuck to the neck, do not force it. Doing so could damage the neck, radiator or heater core. Cut the hose with a utility knife and peel it back with a screwdriver.

Clean the neck with a stiff wire brush, and scrape off bits of the old hose with a putty knife. Coat the connecting joints with a film of water-resistant adhesive. Slip two new hose clamps (preferably the worm-drive type) onto the replacement hose. Push each hose end onto a neck (dipping hose ends in coolant will make them slip on easier). Slide the clamp toward the end of the hose, past the joint's ridge. Position the clamp so that the screw or bolt is easy to reach. Carefully tighten the clamp screws.

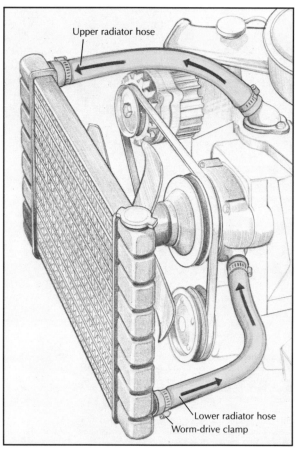

Upper radiator hose

Lower radiator hose
Worm-drive clamp

Drive belts

Drive belts operate various engine accessories such as the fan, water pump, power steering pump, air conditioner, alternator, and air-injection pump. All these belts are driven by the crankshaft pulley. The most basic drive belt is often called the fan belt, which usually drives the fan, the water pump, and the alternator. If a car is equipped with optional accessories, such as power steering and air conditioning, there will usually be one or more additional belts to drive them *(right)*.

Frequent checks of a belt's condition and tension will help to avoid problems. At least once a month, examine each belt for wear and tension. Replace a belt that is cracked, brittle, oil soaked, badly glazed, or slippery.

To check for tension, press down on the belt with your thumb. If there is more than 1.5 to 2 cm (½ to ¾ in.) of play, it is too loose.

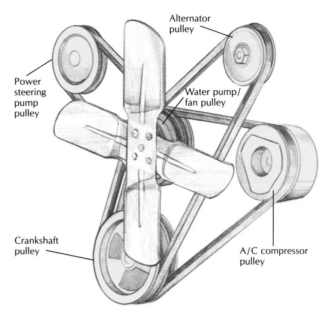

Alternator pulley

Power steering pump pulley

Water pump/ fan pulley

Crankshaft pulley

A/C compressor pulley

How to tighten or replace a drive belt

When buying a belt, be sure that it is the same size and type as the original. If the accessory is driven by a matched pair of belts and only one breaks, buy a new, matched set. Position any replacement belt on the same pulleys and tracks as the original. Once the belt is in place, tension it properly. The belt must be tight enough so that it will not slip but not so tight that it will exert excess pressure on the accessory's bearings. The tension may need readjustment after the belt has been in place for a few weeks, since new belts stretch with initial use.

First, loosen the mounting bolts on all accessories driven by the belt to be replaced. Reduce the tension on the drive belt by gently pushing the accessory toward the engine block. If it sticks, loosen the mounting bolts further and push again. If it remains stubborn, use a tire iron as a pry bar. Always lever against the part to which the pulley is attached, never against the pulley itself.

When there is enough slack in the belt, pry it off its pulleys. If there are other belts in the way, they must be removed first. Roll the new belt into its pulley tracks. To exert tension on the belt, pry the accessory away from the engine and partially tighten its mounting bolts. Do not pry against fins, power steering pump reservoir, or other fragile parts. Check for proper belt tension, then tighten bolts fully.

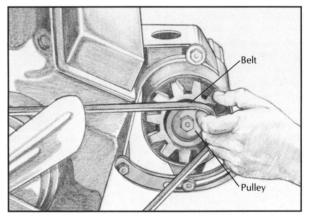

Belt

Pulley

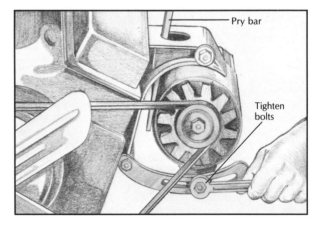

Pry bar

Tighten bolts

Air conditioning troubleshooting

Your car's air conditioning system works on the simple principle that heat flows from a warmer surface to a colder one. Heat from the warm air inside the car is transferred to the cold metal fins of the evaporator. The working fluid—Freon-12 or Refrigerant-12—flows through the evaporator, where it vaporizes, collects the heat and carries it to the compressor. There the gas is pressurized, which concentrates the heat by raising the temperature of the gas. The gas then goes to the condenser, which looks like a thin radiator. Here the Freon gives off its heat to the cooler air flowing through the grill and condenses into a liquid. The liquid flows into a tank called the receiver-dryer, where excess fluid is stored and any water is removed. From here the liquid flows through a hose to the expansion valve, then back into the evaporator. Here it expands from a cool, high-pressure liquid into a cold, low-pressure gas. This evaporation absorbs heat and cools the fins that, finally, cool the air in the car. The warmed gas then returns to the compressor.

Besides cooling the air, an air-conditioning system dehumidifies it by removing moisture that condenses on the evaporator fins. The condensed water drains through a tube and is released underneath the car. It is normal to find a small puddle of water under an air-conditioned car on a warm, humid day. (Make sure, however, that it is not a leak from another component.)

For an average driver, work on a car's air-conditioning system should be limited to the simple maintenance jobs shown here. Any other problem is best left to a CAA-approved or equivalent air-conditioning specialist, not just the average home mechanic. One important maintenance routine is to operate the air conditioning at least once a week whenever the outside temperature is above 10°C (50°F). This circulates the refrigerant and keeps the many seals in the system moist and free from cracks. Determine if your system is low on refrigerant (see box at right). If the level is low, have the system recharged. Cooling efficiency can also be improved by vigorously cleaning the surface of the condenser with a garden hose.

If your system is not cooling properly, a broken compressor may be the cause. All compressors are belt driven, and are operated by a magnetic clutch in the center of the compressor pulley. First, with the engine off, check the compressor belt drive; if necessary, adjust its tension or replace it (pp. 134-135). If the belt is all right, check to see that all electrical connections are tight. Then, if

necessary, test the fuses and relays in the system; if these are working, have an air-conditioning expert inspect the system and make any necessary repairs.

Although all auto air-conditioning systems work in basically the same way, each differs slightly in its components and layout. Use this illustration to locate those parts necessary for determining the charge and trouble-shooting the system.

Every system has a high-side (pressurized) and a low-side (depressurized) service port

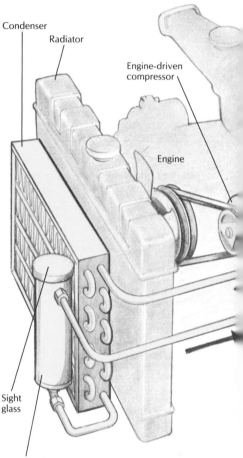

Condenser
Radiator
Engine-driven compressor
Engine
Sight glass
Receiver-dryer

at which the pressure in both sides of the system can be measured. A service port is actually a valve, either a Schrader or a Rotalok type, protected by a removable cap. Schrader valves (the type found on tires) are easy to use; Rotalok valves require special tools to operate and should be left to a professional mechanic. If your system has a sight glass (see box), pressure readings are not necessary.

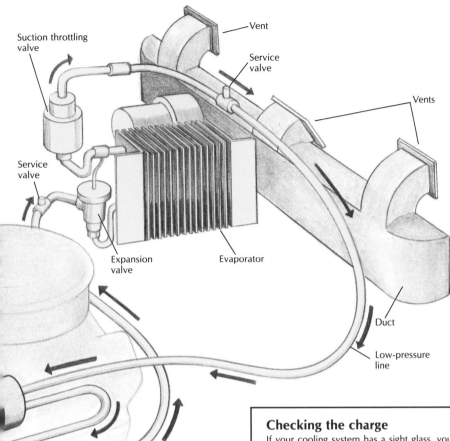

Suction throttling valve

Vent

Service valve

Vents

Service valve

Expansion valve

Evaporator

Duct

Low-pressure line

High-pressure line

Taking pressure readings

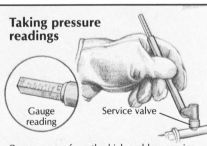

Gauge reading

Service valve

Remove caps from the high and low service valves; if valve leaks or hisses, replace cap and have an A/C mechanic service the system. With engine off, press the gauge into each valve. If the readings are equal and close to the outside air temperature, the system is charged; if readings are lower than the outside temperature, the system needs a charge. Turn on the engine and the A/C; take a second set of readings. The high side should read about 965 kPa (140 psi); low side about 70 to 200 kPa (10 to 30 psi).

Checking the charge

If your cooling system has a sight glass, you can determine the amount of refrigerant simply by looking at the fluid as it passes under the glass. A sight glass is often in the receiver-dryer, but in some cars it is in a pressure line on the high side of the system. To read a sight glass, turn on both the engine and air conditioning. After five minutes, examine the refrigerant closely for the following signs and symptoms:

If clear, the system is either fully charged or empty. If the A/C emits cool air, or if bubbles appear when switched off, the system is charged.

A few bubbles means that the system needs a charge or the clutch is off. Wait for the clutch to go on, then check again.

If foamy, there is very little refrigerant in the system. Oil streaks mean that the system is empty and must be recharged.

If cloudy, the drying agent in the receiver-dryer is breaking up and being circulated through the system. Have the A/C checked by an expert.

How to identify leaks

There are more than a dozen liquids that can leak out of your car. Of the fluid leaks, brake fluid is the most serious and windshield washer solution the least. Leakage of other fluids, if not corrected, can lead to an expensive breakdown.

Some leaks affect driving safety. Gases seeping from the exhaust pipe can let deadly carbon monoxide enter the passenger compartment. Air leaking out of a tire can create serious handling problems.

A puddle of water under your car on a warm day is probably condensation from the air conditioner—the only desirable leak that cars produce. If no condensation is formed, the air conditioner is not dehumidifying the air inside the car.

Not all fluid leaks show up as puddles, but if you notice a stain on the pavement or garage floor, find its source. Place a small container under the car in the spot where the leak occurs and catch some of the fluid. If the leak is very small, place a piece of white paper under it to identify its color. Compare this to the color of various fluids in your engine and other components.

The distinctive odor of most car liquids can also help pinpoint the source of a leak.

Although small leaks are harder to find, they may be much easier to repair. If you are lucky, simply tightening a clamp or a few loose bolts or replacing a coolant hose may effect a permanent repair. However, fluid leaks do not always show up in obvious places. Sometimes oil or brake fluid can run along the outside of a pipe or body flange and drip at a point some distance away from the source.

Some leaks are even less obvious. For example, a leaky master cylinder can let brake fluid enter the vacuum power booster, where it can be sucked into the intake manifold and burned in the engine. The fluid level will drop but there are no visible leaks. You can spot this by checking inside the power booster's vacuum hose for traces of wetness.

The illustration below shows where to look for leaks beneath most front-engine, rear-drive cars, and identifies each leaking fluid or gas. **Caution:** Beware of hot or moving engine parts.

How to find the source of a leak

1. Radiator: Check seams on bottom or side tank, drain plug, lower hose, and heater hoses. Leak: antifreeze.

2. Water pump: Check vent hole and gasket joint. Leak: antifreeze.

3. Power steering: Check pump and hoses. Leak: power steering fluid or automatic transmission fluid (ATF).

4. Steering gear: Check seals at Pitman arm or steering rack boots. Leak: gear oil.

5. Battery: Look for cracked case and loose, cracked, or missing caps. Leak: battery acid (sulfuric acid and water).

6. Windshield washer: Check all plastic lines, pump, nozzles, and reservoir. Leak: water or washer fluid.

7. Oil pan: Check drain plug, pan gasket, timing chain cover, and front crankshaft oil seal. Leak: engine oil.

8. Oil filter: Check for tightness of filter and adapter, especially after oil change. Leak: engine oil.

9. Fuel pump and lines: Check fittings, hose connections, filter, carburetor. Flooded engine may cause temporary leakage. Leak: gasoline. Engine oil can leak from pump gasket.

10. Bell housing: Check for engine oil at bottom inspection cover. Check for automatic transmission fluid (ATF) or gear oil from front seal. Leak may be engine oil, ATF, or gear oil.

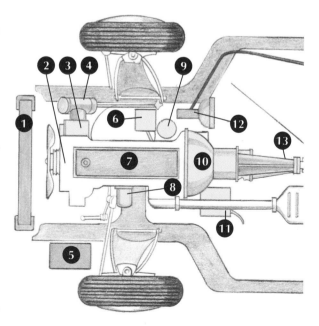

What can leak from your car

Air: Tires (and windshield washer bottles on some cars) contain air under pressure up to 450 kPa (65 psi). Slow leaks may hiss audibly. Harmless when pressure is released slowly.

Antifreeze: Clear or tinted (usually green or yellow) liquid slightly thicker than water, with faint, sweet odor. Confirm identification by checking coolant reservoir or top of cold radiator. *Poisonous.*

ATF (automatic transmission fluid): Light oil, usually red, with a distinctive odor. Confirm identification by matching to fluid on transmission dipstick. *Poisonous, somewhat flammable.*

Battery acid: Sulfuric acid and water solution with a distinctive odor. If acid touches your clothes or skin, immediately flush with water. *Poisonous, corrosive.*

Brake fluid: Clear, slightly oily liquid, usually with a distinctive odor. Confirm identification by looking into master cylinder reservoir and sniffing. *Poisonous, somewhat flammable, dissolves paint.*

Diesel fuel: Light oil, like home heating oil, has distinctive odor. Confirm by sniffing fuel filler neck on diesel cars. *Poisonous, flammable.*

Exhaust gas: Hot, pressurized gas with distinctive odor. Makes hissing or other noises when it leaks out of holes in the exhaust system. *Poisonous.*

Gasoline: Thin, volatile liquid with distinctive odor. Sniff fuel filler neck to confirm identification. *Poisonous, highly flammable explosive vapors.*

Gear oil: Heavy oil, light tan when new, may turn dark or black with use. Lubricates manual transmissions, axles, differentials, and steering gearboxes. *Poisonous, somewhat flammable.*

Heavy grease: May be black with dirt or additives such as lithium or graphite. *Poisonous, somewhat flammable.*

Power steering fluid: Light oil with distinctive odor. Sometimes ATF (automatic transmission fluid) is used, which is often dyed red. Sniff power steering pump reservoir and check fluid color for identification. *Poisonous, somewhat flammable.*

Shock absorber fluid: Light oil that usually appears as a dark stain on lower section of tubular shock absorbers. *Poisonous, somewhat flammable.*

Water: Air conditioning condensation is water that drips from A/C in hot weather. *Non-poisonous, non-flammable.*

Windshield washer fluid: Water solution containing detergent as well as alcohol to prevent it from freezing. May be tinted various colors. Slightly slippery. *Poisonous.*

---

11. Air conditioner: Clear water under front of passenger compartment is normal if A/C has been in use, especially on hot, humid days when condensation drips from system. Leak: water.

12. Brake master cylinder: Look for wetness around fittings, push-rod, and power brake vacuum hose. Leak may also be internal and difficult to notice. Leak: brake fluid.

13. Transmission: Check drain plug (if any), gaskets of cover plate or side plate, and rear seal. On automatic transmissions, check bolts and gasket on oil pan, and rear oil seal. Leak: gear oil or ATF.

14. Exhaust system: Check for pinholes and rust perforation, especially at joints.

15. Shock absorbers: Check for dripping or wetness and replace leaking front or rear shocks. Leak: shock absorber oil.

16. Brakes: Look for stains on drum backing plates, disc calipers, hoses, and fittings. Make sure leak is not grease or gear oil. Leak: brake fluid.

17. Differential housing: Check drain plug (if any) and filler plug, cover-plate gasket. Leak: gear oil.

18. Rear wheel seals: Check drum-brake backing plates, axle ends of differential housing. Leak: gear oil.

19. Fuel tank: Check seams, drain plug, pipe fittings, and any dents caused by road debris. Leak: gasoline or diesel fuel.

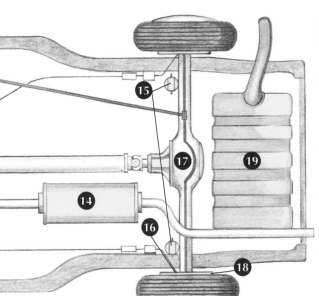

The ten most serious car noises

Before you can analyze strange sounds, you must be aware of how your car normally sounds. Walk around your car as it idles and listen to the noises it makes. Also listen to it as you drive. Open the windows as you pass by a wall or through a tunnel to hear the sounds that are reflected back to you.

Drive the car at different speeds on different road surfaces and analyze the results. If a noise occurs all the time, even when the car is in *Neutral,* the source is probably the engine or one of its belt-driven accessories. If the noise occurs only while the car is moving, it is probably coming from the transmission, chassis, or suspension.

Sometimes the source of a noise is not so obvious. A sound can travel through a car's body and chassis in the same way that a leak can appear far from its source. Some sounds are intermittent or may disappear when the car warms up. A noise that you might describe as a harsh rapping sound might be regarded as a mild clicking by a mechanic. Here is a breakdown of the ten most serious car noises and what they signal. **Caution:** If you raise the car, support it properly (see p. 98); beware of hot engine parts.

Squeal. If you hear a noise like the grating screech of a rusty gate, and it appears to be coming from the front tires, stop your car and investigate. If the noise comes as you make a turn, it may be something simple such as low tire pressure. If the noise is accompanied by a drifting of the car to the right or left, it may mean that the wheels are out of alignment as well. A squeal from under the hood could mean a slipping or worn drive belt; have it tightened or replaced if necessary. If the squeal comes from the very front of the engine, check to see if there is water dripping from the water pump just behind the fan. This could mean a water-pump bearing is failing.

Howl. If you hear a loud, prolonged howl coming from below your car, you will need the help of a transmission specialist. He can usually tell what is wrong by driving the car, without tearing the transmission apart.

Hiss. If you hear a sound like escaping steam coming from under your hood, it could mean a leak in the car's vacuum system. A rapidly repeating ''hiss-hiss-hiss'' could indicate a loose spark plug. A hiss in the car's rear end often points to an obstruction or pinhole in the exhaust system.

Clang. If you hear a clang from the car when you stop or start, especially one accompanied by a buzz or whir when you are moving, you can suspect a universal joint. Don't delay repairs; if a U-joint fails, the drive shaft may drop free and whip around, causing extensive damage.

Grind/growl. Imagine two pieces of metal rubbing together, causing a deep, grating sound. If you hear a persistent grind or growl from any wheel, have your wheel bearings inspected. A grind or growl from under the hood also requires prompt attention. It may indicate a low level of hydraulic fluid in the power steering pump or a defective clutch throw-out bearing.

Knock (ping). A soft knock from within the engine could be a signal to change to a higher-octane fuel or have the timing checked. It also could mean a loose piston pin. A light, metallic rapping that diminishes when the car is coasting and out of gear often signals a worn connecting-rod bearing. If the engine also seems to struggle and emit a heavy, thudding sound, suspect the main crankshaft bearings. As a rule, knocks coming from places other than the engine are not very serious and generally involve body work or bolt tightening.

Click. If you hear clicking from the top of the engine, ask your mechanic to check the valve train and rocker arms. Clicks can also be caused by a broken valve spring or a sticking valve. Clicking from the wheels may be another indication of wheel-bearing failure. Check first to see if stones or other debris are caught behind the wheel cover.

Thump/thud. This heavy noise may be nothing more than a spare tire bouncing around in the trunk. Or a perfectly good tire may be cold and temporarily ''flat-spotted.'' If the tire has an unusual bump or blister, however, replace it at once. A thump or thud from the engine compartment can mean anything from a loose battery or flywheel to worn crankshaft main bearings. If you see nothing obviously loose under the hood, check with a mechanic.

Rattle. In most cases, a rattle suggests loose trim or bodywork, and is not serious. But if a rattling sound is coming from near the front wheels, you should pull into a garage and have the car lifted. The noise may indicate a defective wheel bearing. Another cause of a rattle is a loose shock absorber, which will also throw off the car's handling. The exhaust system is a prime source of rattles—an inexpensive clamp may be all that is required to put things right.

Hum. Coming from the car's drive wheels, a humming sound may be caused by snow tires or by an unusual road surface and is no reason for alarm. Otherwise, have the lubricant in the differential checked. If it is low, the gears or bearing could fail.

What your car is telling you

SOUND/LOCATION	POSSIBLE CAUSES
Bang. A sharp, heavy, loud explosion *from the exhaust or intake manifold*	Incorrect ignition timing or fuel mixture; cracked distributor; defective valve, valve spring, or air pump
Buzz. A beelike hum *from around the dashboard*	Loose dashboard or heating component
Chatter. A steady, rapid, tapping sound *From the rear* in cars with limited-slip differentials *From the engine*, the sound varies with engine speed	Limited-slip differential may have incorrect fluid Defect or wear in valve train
Chirp. A shrill, pulsating sound *from the front wheels* of cars with power steering	Loose drive belt on the power steering pump
Clang. A metallic bang *from the drive train*	Faulty U-joint
Click. A sharp, tapping, metallic sound *From the front wheels,* the sound intensifies as speed increases *From the engine compartment,* the sound changes with engine speed *From the inside of a cold engine,* when it is started *From inside the engine,* while it is running *From inside the engine,* the noise decreases as it warms up	Loose hubcap or stone in hubcap; defective wheel bearing Bent or loose fan blade is hitting the radiator Engine low on oil; loose manifold heat-control valve Hydraulic valve lifter fails to fill with oil Broken valve spring or sticking valve
Clunk. A dull, thumping sound *from beneath rear drive cars*	Defective U-joint
Grind/growl. A grating, scraping sound *From the clutch* as it is depressed *From the front wheels,* the sound lessens when brakes are applied *From the rear end* of cars with rear differentials, the sound occurs during turns *From the rear end* of cars with rear differentials, especially during acceleration *From the rear end* of cars with rear differentials, the sound is steady while the car is coasting	Defective clutch throw-out bearing Worn front-wheel bearings Worn differential Differential end play (may be normal); snow tire hum (normal) Worn axle shaft bearings
Hiss. A sharp, buzzing hum *from any component* under pressure (e.g. tires, valves) or vacuum (hoses)	Leak in the component; defective gasket
Knock/ping. A light, regular sound *from the engine* during acceleration	Fuel too low in octane; improper ignition timing; defective spark plug; overheating; worn connecting-rod bearing or main crankshaft bearings
Put-put. Flat, short, regular explosions *from the tail pipe*	Leaking exhaust valves; over-rich fuel mixture; faulty air pump system
Rap. Metallic tapping noises *from the engine* while the car is coasting	Worn connecting rods or crankshaft bearings
Rattle. Irregular tapping noises *from near the front wheels*	Loose shock absorber, steering linkage, or exhaust component
Scrape. A sharp, grating sound *from the wheels* as the brakes are applied	Worn brake pads or linings. Some disc brakes scrape or squeak when pads need replacement
Screech. A high-pitched, shrieking sound *from the engine compartment* as the engine is revved	Loose drive belt; defective bearing in a belt-driven accessory
Squeak. A high-pitched, shrill noise *From the wheels,* as the brakes are applied *From the chassis or body,* as the car goes over a bump or dip in the road	Defective drum-brake lining or disc-brake pads Chassis points require lubrication; worn suspension bushings
Thump/thud. A dull, heavy bang *From the engine,* the sound occurs regularly *From the engine,* when it is under a heavy load *From under the car,* when driven on rough roads	Loose flywheel Loose or worn main bearings Loose or misaligned exhaust system
Whir. Fluttering vibrations *from under the car*	Unbalanced drive shaft

Lubricating body parts

To ensure quiet, smooth, and reliable operation, all moving body parts *(below)* should be lubricated twice a year (more frequently if your car is stored outside). Hoods, trunk lids, and hinges can be damaged if they seize and then are forced. First, clean away any dirt or old lubricant, then apply new lubricant where the parts pivot or where they contact other components. Work the parts several times to distribute the lubricant, then wipe away any excess. Use engine oil or a waterproof white grease on the hinges and latches on the doors, hood, and trunk. If the parts are likely to touch your clothing, use a nonstaining waterproof white grease. Do not apply too much lubricant to the hold-open mechanisms on the door hinges, or the door might not stay open. Nylon or plastic parts are not usually lubricated; consult your owner's manual for the carmaker's recommen-

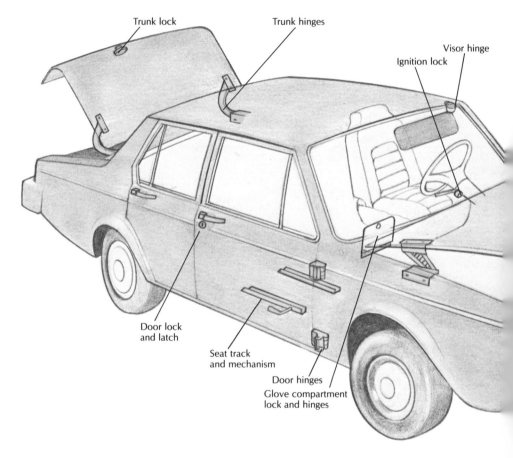

Trunk lock

Trunk hinges

Visor hinge

Ignition lock

Door lock and latch

Seat track and mechanism

Door hinges

Glove compartment lock and hinges

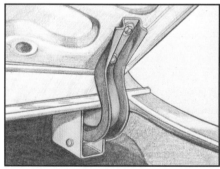

Apply lubricant to the pivot points susceptible to the most wear, such as trunk hinges.

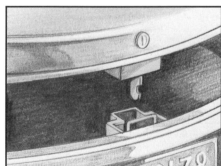

Shaded areas indicate where lubricant is recommended (trunk latch and release).

dations. Don't forget the small or out-of-the-way mechanisms. Lubricate the seat tracks as well as the hinges on the sun visors, glove compartment door, and movable license-plate holders.

To lubricate the door and trunk lock cylinders, use silicone spray or a graphite-based lock lubricant. Do not use oil on a lock cylinder; oil may make the tumblers sticky and hard to operate. Once the lubricant is in the cylinder, work it around by inserting the key into the lock and turning it back and forth several times. If the lock has a seal, use the tip of the key to hold it open. Remember to clean the key before putting it back into your pocket or purse.

To discourage rust and corrosion, most cars have drains along the bottom of any body part that could collect water, such as doors, rocker panels, quarter panels, heater housings, the trunk, and the passenger compartment. The drain is often a simple hole through which water can flow, unless the opening becomes clogged with dirt or debris. Sometimes drain holes are fitted with a rubber or plastic plug. To remove it, gently pry on its edges with a screwdriver. Use a whisk broom to sweep accumulated water out, then carefully hammer the plug back into place. Drain plugs should always be reinstalled to prevent poisonous exhaust fumes from entering the car.

Hood hinges

Hood latch and release

If you lock yourself out of your car

If your car has button-type locks that have a head, or crown, wider than the shank, you can use a wire coat hanger to hook and lift the lock. Straighten the hanger, then make a hook on the end just large enough to go around the button. Slide the hanger past the weather stripping as close to the lock as possible.

New-car keys have code numbers, either on the key itself or on attached tags. Copy this number and keep it with you. A locksmith can make a key from this number, but you must have the registration to prove you own the car. If all else fails and you must break a window, choose the window that is smallest and cheapest to repair.

To remove a broken key, insert a broken coping saw blade into the keyhole. Position the blade so that its teeth are against the cut edge of the key. Catch the key with the teeth, and draw it out.

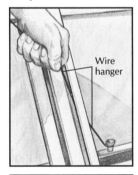

Wire hanger

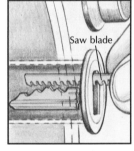

Saw blade

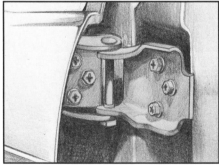

On door hinges, which might touch clothing, use a non-staining, waterproof white grease.

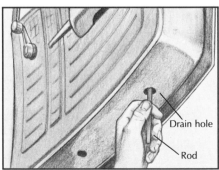

Drain hole

Rod

To clear a drain hole, insert a narrow rod into the opening and gently ream out dirt and debris.

Hinges, latches, and stops

There are several standard ways to adjust the fit of doors, hoods, trunk lids, and other body panels on a car *(below)*. Sometimes two or more of these are used in combination to align a body panel correctly.

In order to seal properly, the doors of a car should fit flush with the body with a gap of about 5 mm (¼ in.) all around. The primary support for a door is its hinges, and these should always be adjusted first. Two people are needed to move a heavy door into position; one person must hold the door steady while the other tightens the bolts.

When the hinges have been adjusted, close the door and note whether it is lifted up, pulled down, forced in, or left too loose by the latch assembly. If so, the striker—the part of the latch mounted on the body—needs to be adjusted. There are two types of strikers: bolts and plates. Both are adjusted by shifting in or out and up or down until the door closes tightly without being forced.

Adjusting movable parts

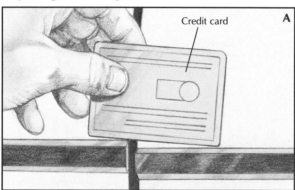

Credit card   A

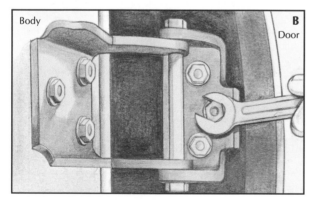

Body   B
Door

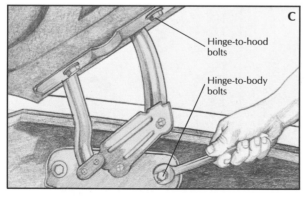

C

Hinge-to-hood bolts

Hinge-to-body bolts

Before making any hinge adjustments, check to see if the door is sagging (the most common problem with door alignment). Place a ruler or credit card along adjacent trim sections (A). Or try to move a sagging door up and down. If it moves, one or more of the hinge bolts is loose and must be tightened. When all the bolts are tight, close the door to determine what hinge adjustments are necessary. Always make hinge-to-body adjustments first, then hinge-to-door adjustments.

To move the door forward or back, or up or down, loosen all the bolts holding the hinges to the body. To move the door in or out, loosen the bolts holding the hinges to the door (B). Loosen the bolts only enough so that two people can move the door. Push and pull the door into position, then gently close it and check the fit. Readjust as necessary until the alignment is correct, then have an assistant hold the open door steady while you tighten the bolts.

If the door is pulled out of position when it is closed and the hinges are properly adjusted, the striker is out of alignment. Loosen the striker bolt or plate just enough so that you can move it with light hammer taps. Tap the striker carefully into position. Close the door gently to check the alignment before retightening the striker bolt or striker plate completely.

Examine the closed hood carefully to determine what adjustments are necessary. If the hood needs to be lowered or raised, loosen all the bolts holding both hinges to the body (C) just enough so that two people can maneuver the hood into position. Welded hinges, of course, are not adjustable. If it needs to be moved forward or back, loosen all the bolts holding the hinges to the hood. Partially tighten the bolts. Carefully lower the hood and check the new alignment before tightening the bolts fully.

A hood should fit flush with the surrounding bodywork with an even gap all around. Three support mechanisms keep the hood in place: the hinges position the hood and attach it to the car; adjustable stops keep the hood level with the fenders; and the latch keeps the hood closed and supports its opening end. As the main hood supports, the hinges must always be adjusted first.

Trunk lids, like doors, must fit evenly with about a 5-mm (¼ in.) gap all around in order to seal properly. Generally, only the parts of the hinges bolted to the lid are adjustable. Slotted bolt holes allow the lid to be moved forward or back on the hinges. The height of the lid is often adjusted by adding or subtracting shims between the hinges and the lid. Trunk latches can usually be adjusted from side to side so that the striker is centered in the latch, and up and down so that the lid closes tightly without excessive slamming.

When the hood hinges are adjusted, note whether any corners or edges are higher or lower than the fenders. If so, one or more of the adjustable stops is too high or too low. Pry the rubber bumper off the stop, loosen the locknut with a wrench (D), and screw the stop up or down. Tighten the locknut and replace the bumper when the stop is at the correct height. Repeat on all the stops until the hood is flush with the body.

To move the trunk lid forward or back, loosen the hinge bolts just enough to push the lid into position. If the lid must be raised, close it and pile shims on it until they reach the height of the fender (this will approximate how many shims to add). If the lid should be lowered, pile shims on the fender until they reach the lid. Loosen the hinge bolts just enough to slip U-shaped shims on or off (E). Remove the bolts to add or remove washers.

To determine whether the striker is centered on the hood or trunk latch, put a lump of clay on the latch and slowly lower the hood or lid until the striker leaves an indentation in the clay. If the mark is off-center, loosen the screws holding the striker, and shift it until it is centered on the latch. On most hoods the latch assembly is mounted on the radiator support, and the striker is mounted on the hood. Trunk lids vary; the latch assembly may be mounted on the lid or on the body.

Close the hood or lid and note whether it is either difficult to close or still loose enough to move when it is latched. In either case, loosen the locknut; then screw the striker bolt to tighten or loosen the latch (F). Or, loosen the bolts holding the latch on the radiator support, then lower or raise the entire latch assembly to tighten or loosen the latch. The hood should close tightly without being slammed too hard (all require some slamming).

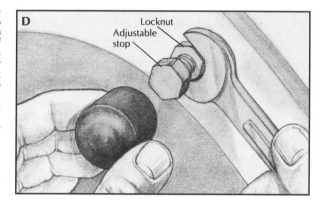

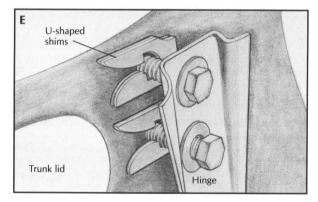

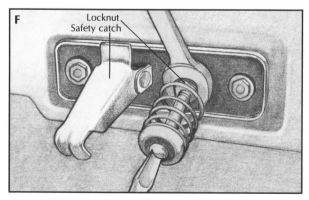

Finding and fixing body leaks

Water, air, and dust leaks can be annoying and uncomfortable. An unchecked water leak can start a serious rust problem, ruin carpeting, or render the trunk unfit for storing anything except the spare tire. However, finding leaks can be tricky, since they do not always originate at the points where water appears inside the car. Before trying to stop a leak, use one or more of the tests illustrated below to locate all problem spots. Because several water leaks may be collecting at one point, or several air leaks may sound like a single noise, always continue testing until all possibilities have been checked.

Small air leaks that whistle when the car is moving can be especially hard to pinpoint. In this case, use masking tape to seal the windows completely. Drive the car at the speed at which the noise usually occurs. Have a helper slowly peel off the tape until you hear the noise again, then mark the spot that was just uncovered. The water test *(below)* is the only way to find leaks around the windshield, the rear window, or any fixed glass. It can also be used around doors and the trunk lid. Be sure the stream of water is gentle, since strong water pressure could actually cause a leak. Both the paper test and the air test can help determine whether a seal is too tight or too loose. After you have found a leak, mark the exact spot with masking tape so that you can locate it later.

While you are checking, keep in mind some common problems. Damaged weather stripping is the most frequent cause of leaking doors and trunk lids, but poor align-ment may also be at fault (see pp. 144-145). Leaks in the trunk often come from the tail-light housings or the rear window as well as from the trunk lid. Body leaks can develop at seams or where trim is screwed into holes in the body panels.

Products available at auto parts or hardware stores make sealing most small leaks fairly simple. Clear plastic sealer or silicone caulking compound, available in black or clear, is squeezed directly into the gap between the windshield or other fixed glass and the gasket. Caulking compound is also useful for sealing seams and screw holes in the car body. If repositioning the weather stripping does not stop a leak, self-adhesive household weather stripping can be used to shim up uneven auto weather stripping that does not seal properly.

Weather stripping seals the doors and trunk against leaks. If it is badly worn, dried out, cracked, or torn, it cannot seal properly and must be replaced. Auto weather stripping is not simply glued in place; various combinations of tabs, clips, screws, and studs fit into specific holes in the car body. The cross-sections and thicknesses of these seals vary widely from car to car. Since the weather stripping made for one car will not fit most others, buy weather stripping that is identical to the original from a new-car dealer, or have custom replacements made for your car at a body shop. Weather stripping obtained from wrecking yards is likely to be as old, worn, or dried out as the weather stripping you want to replace.

Testing for leaks

1. Slowly run a gentle stream of water over all the window gaskets. Start at the bottom and move up both sides, then across the top. Have a helper inside the car mark any points that leak.

2. Close the car door on a strip of paper about 5 cm (2 in.) wide. Pull the paper out; it should drag as you pull on it. If it comes out easily, the seal is too loose. If the paper tears, the seal is too tight.

3. Turn the heater fan on *High*. Roll up all the windows and close the doors tightly. Feel along the outside of all doors and windows for escaping air, and mark each spot where the seal is loose.

Repairing leaks

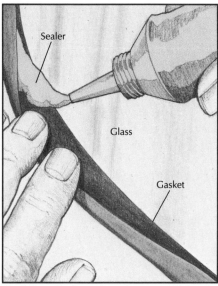

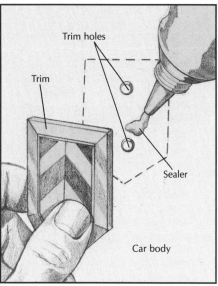

Fixed glass: Gently pry the gasket away and clean the leaking area thoroughly so that the sealer will adhere properly. Squeeze an even bead of silicone or plastic sealer into the gap. If many spots leak, apply a thin, even bead all around the glass. Work quickly before the sealer has time to set.

Body trim holes: Remove the trim and repair any small rust spots that have developed (pp. 148-149). When the touch-up paint is completely dry, squeeze a dab of silicone caulking compound around each trim hole, then replace the trim. Dab the screw or bolt with caulking compound.

Weather stripping

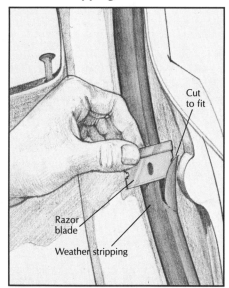

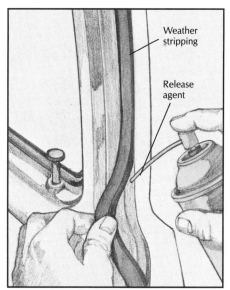

Adjustments: Small body irregularities can be corrected. In low spots, add household weather stripping under the original or fill depression with body filler. In high spots, shave down back of weather stripping with a razor. Reglue with weather-strip adhesive. If high spot still causes leak, grind it down with a power drill and grinding wheel. **Caution:** Always wear eye protection when using a grinding wheel. Fill slight depression with body filler. Prime and paint the repair, and replace weather stripping.

New weather stripping: Remove all fasteners in the old weather stripping. Spray weather-strip release agent under the seal. When adhesive softens, pull stripping off. Carefully check correct position of new stripping by mounting it in the body holes. Remove it and apply thin coats of adhesive to both door and weather stripping. Push weather stripping in place on door (work quickly or adhesive may dry). Push clips or tabs into their holes. Screw in retaining screws. To improve the seal, spray with silicone lubricant.

Professional bodywork or amateur touch-up

The most important ingredient in bodywork is patience. Mistakes are difficult and sometimes costly to correct, so always work slowly and carefully. Small scratches and rust spots can be repaired by a competent amateur mechanic who is willing to take the time to do the job right. However, large dents and major paint jobs are best left to a garage specializing in bodywork.

Some dents, such as those made by flying gravel, are so small that they do not need hammering or pulling out. In such cases, an average do-it-yourselfer can repair the damage with body filler and a couple of cans of spray paint. But do not use filler in deep dents—it should never be applied more than 3 mm (⅛ in.) thick.

Before starting work on a dent, take off any easily removable chrome or lights near the area. Use masking tape to cover any trim you cannot remove. Clean the area around the dent thoroughly with solvent and clean rags to remove any wax or grease. If there is any paint left in the dent, sand it down to bare metal with coarse sandpaper or a wire brush attached to a drill. **Caution:** Wear safety goggles.

To prepare the filler, carefully follow the directions on the can. Apply an even coat with a squeegee and allow the filler to cure for the length of time specified on the label—as much as 48 hours. With a flat file, lightly stoke the hardened filler until it is level with, and contoured to, the surrounding surface. Wrap fine sandpaper around a block and buff the filler until it is smooth.

Because paint does not adhere well to bare metal, you must apply a coat of primer before painting. Primer is used to cover plastic body filler and bare metal as well as a margin of the old paint, so it also provides a uniform surface for new paint. **Caution:** Always wear a face mask when spray painting; work carefully with volatile, toxic solvents.

Instead of using masking tape to limit the spray on a small area, cut a nickel-size hole in a piece of cardboard, hold it about 2.5 cm (1 in.) from the surface, then spray. This way you won't end up with the sharp edges left by masking tape.

It is important to match the primer to the paint you will use. Use only lacquer primer for lacquer paint and enamel primer for enamel paint. Spray on several light coats of primer in even strokes, moving the can constantly to avoid runs and sags. Wet-sand the dried primer just enough to roughen its surface. Hold the sandpaper flat in your hand and keep water flowing on the surface by squeezing a sponge over it so that the sandpaper does not clog. If bare metal shows anywhere, spot-prime those areas.

The basic difference between the two types of paint used on modern cars—lacquer and enamel—is that lacquer can be dissolved by thinner no matter how long it has been on the car, while enamel hardens to form a tough, almost impermeable finish after about six months. For this reason, lacquer can be painted over an enamel finish that is at least six months old, but the solvents in some enamels can ruin an original lacquer paint job.

For a car owner making his own repairs, acrylic lacquer has several advantages. It dries quickly, so dust and dirt will not ruin the finish; it blends well with the old paint; and runs and mistakes can be sanded when dry, and repainted. If yours is a new car with an enamel finish, however, take it to a body shop for repainting. Metallic finishes, which are applied in several carefully blended layers, are also best left to professionals.

Before applying any primer or paint, test it on an inconspicuous spot such as under the bumper—preferably on the same panel you will be painting. Do not test the inside of the trunk or hood, where a different kind of paint is often used.

Aerosol cans of paint in colors corresponding to those of most car makes and models are available from dealers and auto supply stores. However, these spray paints seldom match a car's color exactly, as the original paint will have faded. (For an exact match, paint must be custom mixed at a body shop and applied with a spray gun.)

For large areas, keep the can 20 to 25 cm (8 to 12 in.) from the surface and paint with a sweeping, back-and-forth motion, spraying constantly. Start at the top of the repair area, then move downward to the bottom. Apply four to five light, semi-transparent coats until the surface is completely covered. Let each coat dry for three to four minutes before applying the next coat.

Allow the paint to dry for at least 24 hours, then apply rubbing compound over and slightly beyond the painted area. Work in the compound with a damp cloth, then buff it with a clean, dry cloth. This will blend the finishes so that the repair will not show.

Use touch-up paint to fill in chipped spots (opposite page). If you take care of tiny nicks and scratches right away, they will not develop into rust spots. However, such touch-ups always show—if you want a better finish, wet-sand the area, prime it, sand it again, then spray-paint.

Touching up small scratches and chipped spots

1. Cut away any blistered paint around the damaged spot with the point of a razor blade, being careful not to cut into the good paint. Blisters are evidence of hidden damage and must be removed. With the flat edge of the razor blade, gently scrape off any loose rust. Keep the repair area as small as possible.

2. Wipe the area with metal conditioner, then wipe it off before it dries. Metal conditioner is a chemical that etches remaining rust from metal and helps the primer to adhere better. (Conditioner will blacken metal.) Next, wipe with pre-cleaning solvent to remove any wax, grease, or tar.

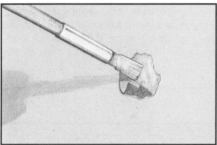

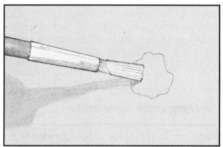

3. Apply the primer only when the solvent has dried completely. Use a small paintbrush to paint on the primer. Try to fill in just the repair spot without going over onto the paint, but be sure to cover all the metal—paint does not adhere well to bare metal. Let the primer dry completely.

4. Shake the touch-up paint until it is thoroughly mixed. With a small brush, paint in the spot as neatly as possible, completely covering the primer. A touch-up will show no matter how careful you are; the repair is mainly to prevent serious rust damage from spreading.

The cost of corrosion

One of the most insidious and costly hazards of winter driving in Canada is corrosion. The use of road salt not only produces meltwater where none might have existed but also increases its corrosiveness. Fortunately, a number of steps can be taken to prevent or reduce corrosion.

Rustproofing the car will help in many instances, provided that the job is carried out by a reputable firm and is done while the car is still new. The procedure consists of coating all rust-prone surfaces with an oily, wax-like substance. Holes are drilled to reach hard-to-get areas, such as the interior of doors, and the rustproofing substance is sprayed inside. The holes are then plugged with plastic. The underside of the car (chassis and suspension) is also sprayed. Because of the equipment required, this type of rustproofing is not a job you should attempt yourself. However, if you own a paint spray gun you can use the following do-it-yourself method: Strain used engine oil through a rag and spray it twice a year—in spring and fall—on the underside of your car and in the wheel wells. The coat of oil keeps corrosive salt and water from making contact with the metal surfaces.

A few other simple maintenance chores also help to prevent rust. Inspect the painted surfaces of your car; any scratches or chips should be treated immediately. Clear out drain holes and ventilation holes in the trunk, along the bottoms of doors, and under the hood. Wipe chrome-plated parts, such as bumpers, with kerosene. This will seal surface pores against salt.

Spray rubber parts (such as trim, bumper guards, and weather stripping) with silicone as soon as cold weather sets in to keep the rubber from getting brittle.

Once winter arrives, wash the car at least once a week. After each wash, wipe door, hood, and trunk lid edges and openings with a cloth dampened with windshield washer fluid to remove caked salt.

Cleaning and repairing upholstery

To keep vinyl tops and vinyl upholstery looking new, wash them regularly with mild soap and water or with a special foam cleaner made for vinyl. Do not use harsh detergents, abrasives, or cleaning fluid on vinyl, as they will damage the surface.

Sooner or later cloth upholstery will begin to look dull and grimy. The best treatment is to wash the seats with clean face towels soaked in warm, sudsy water. Rinse by wiping with clear water. If the cloth is stained, treat the stain as indicated in the chart below. Don't use gasoline, naphtha, acetone, or other solvents on synthetics; they will permanently weaken or discolor the fabric. Leather upholstery should be cleaned only with saddle soap and treated with preservatives made especially for leather. To restore faded leather, dust the seats lightly with baby powder and buff with a soft cloth. **Caution:** Many commercial cleaning products are flammable or toxic.

Torn cloth upholstery can sometimes be mended. However, if it is badly torn or worn out, cover it with a new seat cover; these are made to fit virtually every size and shape of seat, in a variety of colors and patterns. To repair torn vinyl upholstery, you must insert a patch of the same material between the padding and the cover. If you merely glue the vinyl, the adhesive will destroy the foam rubber padding.

A vinyl top is more delicate than the painted body of the car. After washing, apply one of the waxes specifically made to protect vinyl. If your top has already become faded or discolored by weathering or improper cleaning, you can restore it with a vinyl-dying kit or conditioner.

If your vinyl top has begun to peel, you may be able to fix it by melting the old glue with a hair dryer or a heat lamp and pressing the vinyl back in place. If this does not work, reglue the top with automotive trim cement.

Cleaning cloth upholstery

Stain	Treatment
Ball-point ink	Use rubbing alcohol. If stain remains after repeated applications, do not try anything else. Ink eradicator will ruin upholstery.
Blood	Wipe with a cloth and cold water. Do not use soap.
Butter, crayon, oil, grease	Scrape off excess with a dull knife blade. Use cleaning fluid sparingly.
Candy	Use cloth soaked in lukewarm water for chocolate. Flush other candies with lukewarm water, allow to dry. If necessary, rub lightly with cleaning fluid.
Ketchup	Wipe with cloth soaked in cool water. Use mild detergent if more cleaning is needed.
Chewing gum	Harden gum with ice cube, then scrape off with a dull knife blade. Moisten with cleaning fluid and scrape again if necessary.
Coffee, fruit, ice cream, milk, soda, liquor, wine	Wipe with cloth soaked in cold water. If necessary, rub lightly with cleaning fluid. Do not use soap and water, which may set the stain.
Lipstick	Cleaning fluid works well on some brands. If stain remains, do not try anything else.
Mustard	Rub with a warm, dampened sponge, then rub mild detergent on stain and work into fabric. Rinse with clean, damp cloth. Repeat several times.
Shoe polish (paste)	Use cleaning fluid sparingly.
Tar	Scrape off excess with a dull knife blade. Moisten with cleaning fluid; scrape again. Rub lightly with more cleaning fluid.
Urine	Sponge with lukewarm soapsuds from a mild soap, rinse with clean cloth soaked in cold water. Soak a cloth in a solution of 1 part ammonia to 5 parts water. Hold it on stain for 1 min. Rinse with a clean, wet cloth.
Vomit	Sponge with a clean cloth dipped in cold water. Wash lightly with lukewarm water and mild soap. If odor persists, treat area with a solution of 1 teaspoon baking soda to 1 cup warm water.

Repairing torn vinyl upholstery

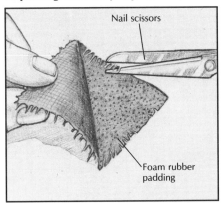

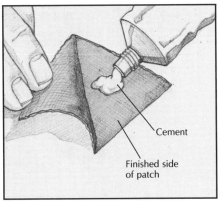

1. Use nail scissors to trim off loose threads along the edges of the tear. Cut a patch at least 1.5 cm (½ in.) larger all around than the tear to be sure no cement contacts the padding. Fold the patch and carefully insert it under the tear.

2. Open the patch so that it lies flat with its finished side facing up. Apply auto trim cement evenly to the bottom of the tear and to the top of the patch. Press the torn vinyl gently into place, keeping the edges as close together as possible.

Removing bubbles from a vinyl top

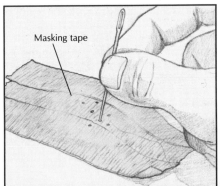

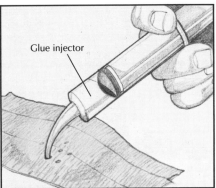

1. To eliminate a bubble, first cover it with masking tape; any cement that oozes out will get on the tape, not the vinyl. Puncture the bubble with a darning needle in several places (An ordinary needle makes too small a hole.)

2. Heat the area with a hair dryer or a 250-watt heat lamp. Press down with a wood block until the cement rehardens. If the old cement will not hold, inject more with a glue injector, available at hobby shops. Press down again.

Repairing a burned carpet

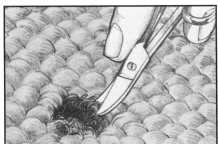

1. To repair a small burned spot, first trim away all the charred carpet loops using curved nail scissors. Then, from an area that will not show, such as a section under the seats, cut a sufficient number of loops to replace the charred ones.

2. Fill in the hole with a clear-drying, waterproof glue. Position the newly cut loops in the hole with tweezers and hold them upright until the glue has set. To protect carpets from burns and stains, cover them with rubber floor mats.

Improving visibility

Bad weather brings on a host of severe visibility problems. These range from salty slush kicked onto the windshield by other vehicles to whiteouts in snowstorms, glazings of freezing rain, and wipers caked with ice.

Good windshield wipers and a sturdy plastic scraper are essential, but there are other techniques that can improve visibility. If snow is expected and driving is unavoidable, carry a large, stiff-bristled broom in your trunk. It is much easier to push snow off your car with a broom than it is to flick it away with a scraper. Check all your lights—parking lights, flashers, and turn signals as well as headlights. It can be just as important to be seen as it is to see. Not only should all the lights be working, but they should be clean. Dirty, snow-covered brake lights, for example, may be dangerous.

Windshield wipers keep the windshield clear in bad weather and are essential for safe driving. To keep the wipers working efficiently, wash both the windshield and the wipers about once a week. Wash the inside of the windshield as well.

The squeegees—the parts of the wiper system that actually clean the windshield—are made of natural rubber, which deteriorates with time. Squeegees must be flexible enough to follow the contour of the glass, and have edges sharp enough to cut through water and snow cleanly. Air pollution, weather, and time will make the rubber brittle. Road grease can soften the rubber until the squeegees' edges are no longer sharp. Generally, squeegees (often called refills) should be replaced every 6 to 12 months, or sooner in harsh conditions.

The blade assembly should distribute pressure evenly along the entire length of the squeegee. If the metal is bent or if the swivel joints are corroded, pressure may be uneven, so that the wiper misses some areas of the glass. If so, replace the blade. Wiper arms contain tension springs that exert the correct pressure on the blades. If the spring breaks, the arm must be replaced. Whenever you have to replace a part, take the old part with you to make sure you obtain the correct replacement.

Wiper blade replacement

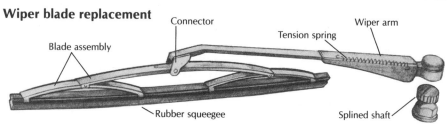

There are three basic lock designs for attaching the squeegee to the blade assembly, and the type of refill you need depends on the lock. Anco or Trico-type refill squeegees fit all North American cars and some foreign cars. One or the other of these types is available at most service stations. Many foreign cars use a clip system requiring special refills that may be available only from the dealer. However, in many cases, the more readily available blade assemblies can be fitted to these foreign cars.

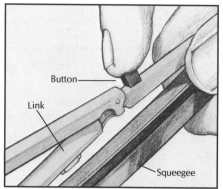

Anco type. Push the red button on either link. Pull out the squeegee along with the released link. Thread the refill through the free link, then through the link attached to the blade assembly. Snap the free link back into place.

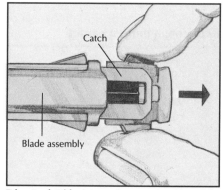

Trico (and Tridon) type. Squeeze the sides of the spring catch together and pull the squeegee out. Thread the end of the refill without the spring onto the blade assembly first. Push on the end of the squeegee until the catch snaps into place.

Common windshield wiper problems

The patterns of smears, streaks, or beads left on your windshield by faulty wipers can help you diagnose the problem *(below)*. However, to clean the windshield adequately, not only the wipers but the washer must be in good condition. The wipers alone will simply smear road film or rain, dangerously reducing visibility. In winter, plain water will freeze and crack the reservoir; you should use washer fluid even in summer because it contains special cleaners. Never use engine antifreeze in the washer—it will damage car paint. Clean the washer nozzles with a needle or pin, taking care not to enlarge the holes.

Smearing can be caused by a dirty windshield or wipers, by improperly mixed washing solution, or by worn-out squeegees. Before replacing the squeegees, try cleaning the glass and wipers and adding the correct amount of solvent in summer or antifreeze in winter. The fluid reservoir in most cars is a large plastic bottle connected to the washer by a hose. Do not confuse it with the coolant recovery tank. Premixed washer solution (usually colored blue or green) is readily available at garages and service stations.

Smearing in only one direction occurs when the squeegee does not flip back and forth, often caused by extreme cold. Expose wipers to warm air or rinse them in warm water. If the squeegees have hardened from age or are the wrong size, replace them. Snow and ice can jam wipers, preventing them from flexing properly. Special winter wiper blades are made with a protective rubber boot that covers the entire blade assembly and keeps snow and ice out. These can be installed and replaced in the spring and fall.

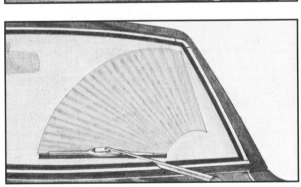

Chattering can be caused by a bent wiper arm that is no longer parallel to the glass, or by a frozen squeegee. Turn the defroster on *High* to warm the windshield and prevent freeze-over. Thaw a frozen squeegee with warm air or warm water. If your wipers clog while you are driving, open the window and place your hand on the windshield so that the wiper runs up onto your fingers. Flip the wiper away from the glass to snap off ice and slush. A bent arm can sometimes be straightened with pliers; if not, replace the arm.

Water beads on the glass result from an accumulation of grease, oil, wax, or silicone. Spray-wax treatments applied in automatic car washes—which coat the windows as well as the body with a thin film of wax—are a typical source of such buildup. Clean the windshield and wipers thoroughly with rags dipped in solvent normally used to clean bodywork before painting. Rinse the windshield and wipers until no trace of solvent remains. Otherwise, the solvent will eat away the wipers and window gaskets.

Shopping for a garage

Regular maintenance at a good garage by a skilled mechanic can save you many motoring dollars. Picking a repair facility is difficult, but the auto repair business is highly competitive, and there are many choices. Before you take your car to any shop, consider these factors:

1. The shop's reputation. Consult friends or relatives who may have dealt with the shop. Check with the local consumer group or the Better Business Bureau. It is generally best to deal with a facility that has existed for awhile and has built up a good reputation. True to the old cliché, a shop's best advertising is a group of satisfied customers.

2. How does the shop look? A good shop is usually clean and well organized. An efficient facility will probably be busy, but not necessarily overburdened with work.

3. Repair shops throughout Canada that have been certified by the Canadian Automobile Association provide guaranteed service at a reasonable price. All such approved garages have been investigated by qualified inspectors and have agreed that the CAA, or an affiliate club, will arbitrate any disputes involving CAA members. For further information, contact the closest CAA club office (listed in the telephone book) and ask for a directory of Approved Auto Repair Services (AARS).

4. A cooperative attitude. A good mechanic will solicit information about you and your car in a businesslike fashion, without badgering or pushiness.

5. Does the shop engage in ethical business practices? The garage should be willing to give you a written estimate and an itemized bill for service. All work should be guaranteed in writing for 100 percent of parts and labor for a specified period of time or distance driven. Minor repairs should be guaranteed for 30 days or 1,600 km (1,000 mi); major overhauls, for up to six months or 10,000 km (6,000 mi).

Listed below are the kinds of shops that exist and the services they provide.

An auto dealer's service department is the best place to go if your car is under warranty or needs work on such complex items as power seats, fuel injection, or electronic gadgetry. The dealer usually has the specialized tools and the latest information needed for work on new cars. And you might void your warranty if you allow unauthorized parts to be used in your car.

An independent garage is often your best bet for adequate and reasonably priced car care. The owner of such a shop depends on establishing and maintaining a good reputa-

tion. The work will not be as expensive as a dealer's, and you can often talk directly to the mechanic who will work on your car. The mechanics are more likely to repair than to replace parts, and the cost of parts is often less than at a dealer's service department. There are certain disadvantages to using an independent garage. Some parts may not be on hand and will have to be ordered. Labor charges are relatively high because only licensed mechanics may be employed to do customer repair work. However, if your car needs a routine tuneup, or work on the transmission, brakes, cooling, electrical, or suspension systems, get a written estimate from an independent garage and compare it to those from the shops listed below.

The local gas station is still used most often because of its accessibility. Gas stations continue to provide routine lubrication, tuneups, and parts replacement. Labor charges are low because the mechanics do relatively simple work that does not command high pay. Frequenting a good gas station makes as much sense as patronizing a reliable garage. You and your car will get special attention.

Specialty shops are often the best equipped to deal with specific components or complex problems. There are two types of specialty shops: franchised and independent. The franchised operator advertises heavily and must pay franchise fees; the result is often an added cost to the consumer. Compare the prices and guarantees offered by both operators. Below is a list of various specialty shops.

Muffler shops. Always check your exhaust system before you go to a muffler shop. Such shops prefer replacing large sections of the system to making small repairs that could save you money.

Radiator shops. These garages concentrate on cooling-system and air-conditioning work, and on repairing and rebuilding radiators. You can save up to 50 percent of the service station's charge by removing a radiator yourself and taking it to the shop.

Automatic transmission shops. Because of its complexity, the transmission is probably the most misdiagnosed part of your car. Be wary of shops that push for a complete overhaul or use hard-sell tactics to promote a rebuilt transmission when less expensive repairs might suffice. Ask a few local gas stations where they have their transmission work done. They are not likely to farm work out to incompetent or dishonest shops.

Body shops, whether independent or part of a large operation, concentrate on repairing and repainting vehicles. If your car needs bodywork, this is the only place to go to get this kind of specialized attention.

Auto glass shops specialize in replacing cracked or broken glass. They do cheaper work than auto dealers or general repair facilities, who farm their work out anyway.

Diagnostic centers—which provide objective evaluations of automotive problems—were once regarded as the answer to consumers' needs. However, motorists were often reluctant to pay the rising costs for just a checkup, and, as a consequence, many commercial diagnostic centers have gone out of business. Private organizations, such as the Canadian Automobile Association, continue to run inspection centers, usually open to club members only.

Explaining your problem

The key to service satisfaction is good communication between motorist and mechanic. The solution to an automotive problem depends, more often than not, on an accurate description of the symptoms. Often, a car is not repaired properly because the mechanic has been provided with a sketchy and unclear description of the trouble. The following guidelines should help bridge the communication gap.

1. You are the only one who can describe your car's symptoms. Since the car cannot speak for itself, proper repair depends on your ability to explain the problem clearly and accurately.

2. Keep written records of previous work done on your car; use the *Logbook* of *Canadian Driver's Handbook*. All records should be kept in the glove compartment for inspection by the mechanic. Unnecessary work can be avoided by checking to see what work was recently done on the vehicle.

3. Before visiting the garage, write down the things you want checked or repaired. Note any symptoms you have observed. For instance, how long has the problem existed? Does it happen constantly or only under certain conditions? Is a sound or odor associated with the problem?

4. Call ahead and make an appointment. Most reliable shops are busy and will have to schedule a date in advance.

5. Describe the problem accurately and give the person you're dealing with a written copy of the symptoms. Often, the first person you deal with is not going to work on the car, so make sure you have the vehicle's problem in written form, and keep a copy.

If you are sure what the problem is, have the shop draw up a service order. Before you authorize the work, however, make certain the order includes only necessary repairs. If you are not sure what is wrong, have the service order made out for a diagnosis only. Ask the shop to call you before any repair work is begun.

6. Try to have your car serviced by the same mechanic each time. If you can establish a rapport with him, you'll have a much better chance of having your car worked on correctly. Not only will he be familiar with your car and its particular quirks, but he will also be more likely to service your car professionally if he knows you personally.

7. Be polite but firm in your dealings with mechanics. Stick to the facts. Don't offer opinions unless you are knowledgeable. Try to explain symptoms in simple language.

8. Do not be intimidated by a shop or mechanic. You are entitled to know what the problem is and what you are paying for. If you learn something about your car, you can ask intelligent questions and understand the mechanic's explanations. Also, the mechanic will listen more closely to your descriptions of the car's problems.

9. If you have difficulty in adequately describing a technical problem, or if past maintenance records are not available, get an unbiased opinion from an independent diagnostic center.

10. Before you sign any service order, ask for an estimate of the job, and be sure it is written down on the work order. If the shop is uncooperative about writing out the estimate, take your car elsewhere. You are not bound by law to have any shop work on your car until you authorize it in writing.

11. Make sure that all work is guaranteed before you authorize it. The guarantee is valid only if it is written out. Always save both the bill and guarantee in case the repairs prove to be faulty.

12. After the work has been completed, take the car out for a road test. If the problem persists, bring the car right back to the shop. If the shop balks at fixing a recurring problem, or tries to charge you again to fix the same problem, let them know this is unacceptable. Your recourse would be to contact the Better Business Bureau or local consumer groups if the garage is independent. In the case of new-car dealers or oil-company service stations, send your complaint in writing to the manufacturer or corporate headquarters. If the garage is CAA-approved, telephone the nearest CAA office. However, you should not have to go this far. If you have dealt with the shop fairly, an honest shop will respond to you in kind.

accelerator: Controls the amount of air/fuel mixture entering the carburetor, and therefore engine speed.

additive: Any product added to oil or gasoline to improve its performance.

aftermarket: Industry term for auto parts that are not supplied by the carmaker but added to a car after it has been purchased.

afterrunning: Condition in which the engine continues to operate after the ignition switch is turned off.

air bag: Passive restraint device in front of the driver and passengers. The bags automatically inflate with gas to provide cushioning against the impact of a collision.

air cleaner: Filter assembly ordinarily mounted in a housing on top of the engine to remove dust from the air being drawn into the carburetor.

air-cooled engine: Engine that radiates heat by means of cooling fins rather than through a liquid cooling system.

air filter: Usually refers to the air cleaner's filter that captures and holds harmful particles and dust. There are other air filters in the PCV and air-injection systems.

air-injection system: Emission-control design in which fresh air is mixed with hot exhaust gases to consume unburned fuel.

alternator: Belt-driven generator on the engine that produces a flow of alternating current and converts it to direct current. Current is stored in the battery and used to supply all electrical needs of a car.

antifreeze: Additive that lowers the freezing point of a liquid, such as coolant and windshield washer fluid.

arcing: (1) The jumping of a spark from one electrode to another, as on a spark plug. (2) The undesired sparking between electrical conductors or between a conductor and ground.

automatic choke: System that enriches the air-fuel mixture in a cold engine when the accelerator is first depressed. As the engine warms, the choke is opened automatically.

axle: Metal rod, extending from the differential, that transfers power to drive wheels.

backfire: Undesirable ignition of the air-fuel mixture in the intake of the exhaust manifold.

backflush: Method of cleaning the cooling system by pumping water through it in a direction opposite to the normal flow of coolant.

ball joint: Ball-and-socket design that permits rotation in all directions; used in suspension and steering systems.

battery acid: Solution of sulfuric acid and water used in car storage batteries.

bearing: Device fitted between two moving parts to reduce friction.

belt: (1) Flat band of material beneath the tread of a tire. (2) A drive belt.

bias-belted tire: Combines the crisscross plies of a bias-ply tire with the reinforcing belts of a radial.

bias-ply tire: Tire in which the body plies are set at an angle, or bias, to the centerline.

bleeding: Removing the air from hydraulic brake lines.

blow-by: Leaking of gases from the combustion chamber past the piston rings into the crankcase, usually due to worn rings or excess pressure.

brake drum: Metal housing bolted to a car wheel against which the brake shoes apply pressure.

brake fade: Loss of braking effectiveness due to excessive heat.

brake fluid: Liquid with a high boiling point used to transmit force through brake lines.

brake lines: Pipes and hoses filled with fluid that transmits force from the master cylinder to the wheel cylinders or pistons.

brake pads: Pads of friction material on a disc brake that are periodically replaced when worn.

brake shoe: Curved metal plate that holds the brake linings in a drum-brake system.

breaker points: Switch in the distributor that opens and closes the ignition circuit.

butterfly valve: Pivoting metal plate that controls the flow of air or fuel mixture within a carburetor.

camber: Vertical wheel alignment. Positive camber is created when a wheel leans out at the top; negative camber when it leans out at the bottom.

carbon-fouled: Buildup of carbon desposits on engine parts or spark plug electrodes. Fouled plugs may misfire, causing a loss of power and wasting fuel.

carbon monoxide: Deadly substance in exhaust gas. Abbreviation is CO.

carburetor: Device that mixes air and fuel for burning in cylinders.

catalytic converter: Component of the exhaust system that converts certain exhaust pollutants into harmless substances.

charging: Filling a container or system, such as a battery or air-conditioning system.

chassis: Frame, running gear, steering, and suspension of a car.

choke: Device in most carburetors that enriches the air-fuel mixture by choking off, or restricting, the airflow.

circuit breaker: Device that opens contacts when an electrical flow is excessive; used in place of a fuse.

clutch: Mechanical device used to engage or disengage the flow of power from one component to another, such as from the engine to the transmission.

coil: Device in a transformer that steps up low-voltage current to the high levels needed to produce an ignition spark.

coil spring: Steel rod or wire bent into a spiral; widely used in car suspensions.

combustion chamber: Portion of the cylinder between the piston and cylinder head in which the air-fuel mixture is burned.

condenser: Device in a distributor that absorbs electrical surges and prevents arcing.

contact points: see breaker points.

coolant: Liquid (water and antifreeze) that carries excess heat away from the engine to the radiator.

coolant recovery tank: Receives the overflow when coolant in the radiator expands. When coolant contracts, the overflow is drawn back into the radiator.

crankcase: Metal housing of the crankshaft and related components.

crankshaft: Shaft in a piston engine that converts the reciprocating power produced by the pistons into rotary power.

cylinder: Hole in the engine block in which a piston moves and combustion takes place.

diesel engine: Engine that achieves ignition from the heat generated by extreme compression of the air-fuel mixture and without an electrical spark.

dieseling: See afterrunning.

differential: Gear unit that allows the outside drive wheel to revolve faster than the inside one during a turn.

dipstick: Metal rod, round or flat, that indicates the level of oil in a container such as the crankcase, automatic transmission, and power steering reservoir.

disc brake: Brake design in which stopping power is applied by two friction pads that are squeezed against a steel disc by a caliper.

displacement: The total volume (expressed in cu in., cm^3, or L swept by the pistons during their compression strokes.

distributor: Device that routes high-voltage electricity to the individual spark plugs.

drive belt: A reinforced rubber belt, usually with a V-shaped cross section, used to drive various engine accessories such as the alternator, air conditioning compressor, and water pump. Also called fan belts.

drive shaft: Metal tube that transmits power from the transmission to the differential.

drive train: All power-transmitting components between the engine and the wheels, including the clutch, transmission, drive shaft, differential, and axles.

drum brake: Brake design in which stopping power is applied by friction linings on metal shoes pressing against the inside of a metal housing (drum).

dynamic balancing: balancing a wheel while it is turning in order to eliminate uneven tire wear and wheel shimmy.

electrode: Conducting rods in a spark plug, separated by a gap across which the ignition spark leaps.

electrolyte: Mixture of sulfuric acid and water in a battery that helps produce and store electricity.

exhaust manifold: Collector that connects the exhaust ports of the engine to the exhaust pipe.

exhaust pipe: Pipe that leads from the exhaust manifold to a catalytic converter, muffler, or resonator.

exhaust system: All components involved in controlling, converting, and carrying away an engine's exhaust gases.

expansion tank: See coolant recovery tank.

feeler gauge: Tool used to measure clearances between automotive parts.

flasher: Device in the turn-signal system that opens and closes the circuit to produce flashes of light, as for a turn signal.

flooding: Condition in which the air-fuel mixture is too rich to permit combustion.

four-wheel drive: Design in which all four wheels of a vehicle are driven by the engine.

frame: Steel components that support the car's body and engine and are in turn supported by the suspension.

Freon: Trademark for a refrigerant used in most car air-conditioning systems.

front-end alignment: The correction of the relationship between the front wheels and steering components and the road.

frozen: Condition in which a mechanical part is unable to operate because its parts are corroded or heat-warped.

fuel injection: System in which the carburetor is replaced by jets that inject fuel directly into the cylinders or intake system.

fuel pump: Mechanical or electrical device that moves fuel from the fuel tank into the carburetor.

fuse: Metal link in a circuit that melts when the current flow is excessive, breaking the circuit.

gasket: Compressible material that makes a leak-free seal between mating surfaces.

generator: Electromagnetic device that converts mechanical power into electricity.

grounding: Connecting one side of a car's electric circuit to the chassis, body, or engine, providing a path back to the battery to complete the circuit.

horsepower: Measurement of an engine's capacity to perform work; one unit equals 33,000 foot-pounds of work per minute.

hydraulic brakes: Design in which fluid in tubes transmits force to operate the brakes.

hydrometer: Instrument used to measure the specific gravity of liquids, such as battery fluid or radiator coolant.

idler arm: Component of the steering system that transmits steering force.

ignition system: Part of the electrical system that produces and distributes the spark that ignites the air-fuel mixture.

jack stand: Safety device that is placed under a car to guard against jack failure.

km or KM: Abbreviation for kilometre.

knock: Sound produced when a car's fuel mixture is ignited by something other than the spark plug, such as a hot spot in the combustion chamber. Light knock is normal during heavy acceleration.

leaded gasoline: Gasoline to which tetraethyl lead has been added.

leaf spring: Suspension device consisting of several strips of spring steel.

lean mixture: Mixture in a gasoline engine with a relatively high ratio of air to fuel.

limited-slip differential: Differential unit that transfers power to the drive wheel with the best traction.

linkage: An assembly of rods or levers designed to transmit motion.

master cylinder: Piston and cylinder assembly that forces brake fluid to the wheel cylinders.

misfiring: Condition of an engine when one or more cylinders are not producing power.

muffler: Chamber between the exhaust pipe and the tailpipe that reduces noise and cools exhaust gases.

negative terminal: Post on a positive-ground battery from which the current flows.

net horsepower: Power developed by an engine after the power used by such accessories as the water pump and alternator has been subtracted.

octane rating: Index of antiknock properties in gasoline; the higher its octane rating, the less likely that the gas will cause knock.

odometer: Instrument, set in the speedometer, that measures distance traveled.

oil filter: Replaceable device that traps foreign particles in recirculating oil.

oil pan: Metal housing at the bottom of the engine that serves as an oil reservoir.

oil pump: device that forces lubricating oil under pressure through an engine.

overdrive: Gear ratio that causes the drive shaft to turn faster than the crankshaft.

overflow tank: See coolant recovery tank.

overhaul: Major disassembly of an engine or other mechanism, and the replacing or reconditioning of its parts.

oversteer: A handling characteristic in which a car's rear wheels will begin to skid in a turn at a lower speed than the front wheels.

pad: Friction material in a disc brake which is pressed against the disc by a piston.

parking brake: Mechanical brake system for locking the rear wheels when the car is parked. Some designs lock the drive shaft.

PCV: Positive crankcase ventilation.

piston: Sliding metal part fitted to operate within a cylinder under hydraulic, mechanical, or combustion pressures.

plenum: Chamber containing an air supply in a heating system or intake manifold.

ply: the fabric layers of a tire.

positive crankcase ventilation: Emission-control system that routes engine crankcase fumes into the intake manifold, where they are drawn into the cylinders and burned with the fuel mixture.

power brakes: Brake system that employs vacuum or hydraulic pressure to augment the force applied to the brake pedal.

pre-ignition: Undesirable ignition of the air-fuel mixture before the spark. Also called knocking or pinging.

pressure cap: Radiator cap designed to permit a limited buildup of pressure.

rack and pinion: Steering system that uses a pinion gear at the end of the steering column to move a toothed bar (rack) left or right to transmit steering movement.

radial tire: Tire design in which the cords of the body plies run at right angles (radially) to the tire's centerline.

radiator: Component of the cooling system that dissipates excess engine heat.

recapping: Tire-renewal process in which a new tread (cap) is bonded to a used-tire carcass. Also known as retreading.

recharge: (1) To restore energy to a battery by means of an electric current. (2) To restore the proper level of a fluid or gas in a system, such as recharging an air conditioner with refrigerant.

recirculating ball: Steering design in which movements are transmitted by ball bearings placed between a worm gear and a nut.

resonator: A second, muffler-like, sound-reduction device located behind the muffler in an exhaust system.

retreading: See recapping.

rich mixture: Air-fuel mixture with a high proportion of fuel.

roll bar: Safety device, usually a pipe, mounted over the driver's head to protect him if the car turns over.

rotary engine: An engine, such as the Wankel rotary engine, whose power is developed by a rotor moving in a circular pattern within a combustion chamber.

R&R: Abbreviation for remove and reinstall.

Schrader valve: Type of spring-operated pressure valve; found on most tires.

sealed-beam: Headlight design incorporating filaments, a reflector, and a lens in a unit with no separate bulb.

seized: See frozen.

service rating: Grading system that identifies the kind of service for which automotive lubricants are intended.

shim: Thin strip used to separate one component from another or to change the angle of a part.

shimmy: Undesirable side-to-side motion of the front wheels.

shock absorber: Device that limits the travel of a spring and prevents its continued oscillation.

short circuit: Defect in an electrical circuit in which electricity flows directly from one conductor to another rather than through the intended circuit.

sight glass: Small window that opens into a fluid line (such as an air conditioner) to allow a visual check of level or flow.

slow charge: Charging a battery over several hours or overnight, as with a trickle charger.

socket wrench: Wrench with a hood (socket) designed to grasp a nut or bolt head. A ratchet or handle provides a grip for turning the socket.

spongy pedal: Brake pedal that does not give firm resistance to foot pressure; often indicates air in the brake system.

stabilizer bar: A bar linking the two front suspension systems in order to help them resist sway. Also called an anti-roll bar, roll bar, anti-sway bar, and sway bar.

starter: Electric motor and drive mechanism used to start an engine.

steering column: Shaft between the steering wheel and steering gearbox.

suspension: System of springs, arms, shock absorbers, and related components that connect a car's body and frame to its wheels and axles.

synchromesh: Transmission design that matches the speed of the gears before they are meshed.

tachometer: Instrument that measures engine speed in revolutions per minute.

throttle: Valve that controls the flow of air-fuel mixture and, therefore, engine speed.

tie rod: Steering system component that moves the steering arms.

timing: Regulation of the spark impulse so that the spark occurs at the precise instant for ignition.

tire rotation: systematically changing the location of tires to different wheel positions in order to equalize wear and extend tire life.

toe-in: the amount that a front wheel points inward.

toe-out: the amount that a front wheel points outward.

torque: A twisting or turning force measured in Newton-metres or foot-pounds.

torsion bar: Suspension component making use of a special steel rod's resistance to twisting to achieve spring action.

transmission: System of gears, shafts, and other components that multiplies engine torque and allows the engine to run at efficient speeds.

tread: Outside part of the tire that contacts the road.

trickle charger: Device designed to charge a battery at a slow rate.

turbocharger: Air compressor, powered by exhaust gases, that increases the supply of air-fuel mixture to the intake manifold.

understeer: Handling characteristic in which the front wheels tend to resist the turning forces applied by the driver and continue in a straight line. Understeer is common in front-drive cars.

universal joint: Flexible joint between two rotating shafts that allows one shaft to be at an angle to the other.

vacuum: The absence of air, or the condition of less-than-atmospheric pressure.

valve: Mechanical device designed to open, close, or restrict the flow of fluid or gas.

vehicle identification number: The serial number of a vehicle (VIN).

viscosity: The resistance of a liquid, such as oil, to flow.

viscosity rating: Numerical rating of oil viscosity. Common readings run from 5W to 60 for engine oil and to 140 for gear oil. The higher the number, the thicker the oil.

voltage regulator: Device that prevents excessive voltage on, or overcharging of, the battery by the generator or alternator.

water pump: Engine-operated pump that circulates coolant.

wear indicator: Strip of material built into the tire tread, brake lining, and the like to give a visual or audible signal when the component is worn.

wheel alignment: See front-end alignment.

wheelbase: Distance between the centers of the front and rear wheels.

Zerk fitting: Brand name for one type of grease fitting.

PART III

Coping with accidents and breakdowns

Emergencies

What you must do—and need *not* do

Accidents are an unfortunate fact of life on Canadian highways. More than 4,000 Canadians are killed in auto mishaps every year and the annual toll has been mounting steadily. Almost a quarter of a million people are injured in each 12-month period, some so seriously that they spend the rest of their lives in hospitals or wheelchairs. The cost is staggering—more than $1.25 billion a year in property damage alone. And this does not include medical costs, lost production, loss of human resources, or the time and money involved in legal battles.

Sooner or later you will come upon an automobile accident, or be involved in one yourself. At such a time, the most important thing to remember is to keep calm and follow the steps below.

1. Stop immediately, as close to the scene as possible without blocking traffic. Get everyone out of the car and to a safe place. If the vehicles involved cannot be moved out of the traffic lanes, put out flares, reflectors, or some other warning (see pp. 172–173), or enlist bystanders to direct oncoming cars. Turn off the ignition. Since gasoline may be leaking, do not smoke.

2. Get assistance for the injured. Do not move anyone who may be hurt, except to avoid further injury. Call an ambulance rather than a doctor; it is best equipped to give emergency care. Unless you are familiar with first-aid techniques, the less you do for the injured, the better off they are likely to be. Such lifesaving methods as cardiopulmonary resuscitation may be dangerous if incorrectly applied.

3. Notify police immediately if anyone has been injured, or if property damage appears to exceed $400.

4. Exchange identification with the other driver. You are both required by law to show your licenses for verification. Give the other person the name of your insurance company, but don't reveal the amount of coverage you hold. Be sure to get the names and addresses of all occupants of the other car and to note their apparent physical condition.

5. Control your temper and think before you say anything. Time and again trivial accidents have ended in brawls, even in manslaughter cases, because tempers flared. Do not argue, no matter how much you are provoked. Leave the determination of blame to the police and the insurance companies.

6. Get witnesses. All too often drivers who have been reassured at the scene that there was little or no damage find themselves sued for "whiplash" injuries or extensive repairs to the other car—or cited for negligence or traffic violations. Therefore it is important to record the names, addresses, and phone numbers of witnesses to the accident. If they are uncooperative, write down their license numbers to submit to the police or your insurance company.

7. Make a record of all pertinent facts. If a police officer is at, or comes to, the scene, take down his name, badge number, and the station to which he belongs, especially if the other driver was at fault. (Your insurance company will want to get in touch with him.) If you suspect that the other driver has been drinking, ask that the police officer give both of you a chemical test. If no testing facilities are available, ask the officer to note your request in his report.

Try to write down all the essential circumstances: date, hour, location, visibility, weather and road conditions, status of traffic-control devices, direction each car was going, estimated speeds. Draw a diagram showing the type of intersection, if any; the point of impact; the position of the cars when they came to rest. Sample diagrams are supplied in the *Car Logbook*; many insurance companies also provide such forms. If anyone is taken to a hospital, get its name and location. Note the apparent extent of any injuries suffered by casualties.

There are two reasons for making a detailed record of the accident. Many months after the event you may have to go to court, and by then the details are likely to be hazy in your memory. In addition, you must report to your insurance company and to the appropriate police station without delay. A report is mandatory if there was any personal injury, minor or major, or if property damage exceeded a specified amount.

Your report to your insurance company should be comprehensive. If you were at fault, say so. If you receive a letter or phone call of any kind from the other party, his lawyer, or his insurance company, forward it immediately to your insurance company for handling. Do not deal directly with the other party in such circumstances.

Here are four things you are *not* required to do in the event of an accident:

1. You need not make any admissions to the police either at the scene or at the station house. Agree only to give your name, address, and license number and, if requested, to certify the exact facts for such things as position of vehicles and number of passengers. If you are detained for questioning, you can decline to answer other questions until you have consulted a lawyer.

2. You need not admit fault. Even if you are in the wrong, insurance companies urge strongly that you make no such admission publicly, especially at the scene of the accident. This is a precaution against saying anything that can be twisted to your disadvantage later.

3. You are not required to sign anything at the scene for anybody but the police. In most provinces, they may prepare a statement in your presence. Do not make any statement to alleged "investigators" or lawyers other than your own.

4. You are not required to say whether you are hurt. Do not make any statements at the scene about your physical condition. If anyone wants to know if you have been hurt, just say, "I'm not sure—I won't know until I have seen a doctor."

It is unfortunate that an accident, with all its inconvenience or worse, should call for such legalistic action on the part of its victims. But the fact is that both parties are not necessarily cooperative. If the worst does happen, be courteous, cooperative, and reasonable. But use your common sense.

The aftermath
The legal results of a highway accident can be as serious as the injuries and property damage it causes. They are even more serious if you have an accident while breaking a traffic law, especially if you were intoxicated. In this case, you will have points assessed against your record if your province uses a point system. Your driver's license may be suspended or revoked. Worse, you may be fined or put in jail. Thus, having an accident while violating a traffic law can involve you in a criminal case.

There can be other repercussions. If someone is injured in the accident, you may be held responsible and sued for damages. Where there is property damage, you may also be sued. Whether you have to pay or not, and how much, must be decided in court as a *civil case*. For serious accidents, this sum may be much more than your insurance policy covers. You may be required by

the court to pay part of your wages or salary for many years, and lose your driving privileges forever.

Another consequence of an accident—even a fender bender—is the possibility of an increase in your insurance premium for at least three years. In the case of minor accidents, ask your agent to do a cost analysis to see how a claim will affect your insurance costs over the next few years. When filing an accident report, make sure your insurance company knows whether or not you are claiming any damages for your car. You may decide that it's cheaper to pay for a small repair from your own pocket. (You will have to pay the equivalent of the deductible in any case.) It is a good idea to keep a copy for your records of any report you send to the authorities or your insurance company.

The good Samaritan
You witness a head-on collision on a little-traveled side road. Should you stop and help, or will your good intentions be rewarded with a lawsuit?

Canadian highway legislation imposes no legal obligation to help—or even stop—at the scene of an accident unless you were involved, nor do you even have any legal obligation to report it or to send for help. (The situation is slightly different in Québec, where the Charter of Human Rights and Freedoms obliges *everyone* to aid anyone whose life is in peril.) There is a moral obligation to help, however. Someone's life could depend on your ability to take quick, positive action.

Unless there is an obvious and immediate need—to pull an injured person from a burning car, for example, or to stem a flow of blood—the most sensible course of action is to make an accident victim comfortable, calm him or her as much as possible, and summon help. Moving an injured person unnecessarily, or performing first aid incorrectly, may cause further injury. If this occurs, or if you accidentally hasten the death of an accident victim, you will leave yourself open for a lawsuit charging you with negligence. You assume a "duty of care" when you assist an injured person. In causing further injury, you may have neglected that duty.

A basic knowledge of first-aid techniques can equip you to cope with highway emergencies, and minimizes the possibility of making a costly mistake if you find yourself at an accident scene. Consider taking one of the many first-aid courses offered by such groups as the Canadian Red Cross Society and St. John Ambulance.

How to avoid a collision—or lessen its consequences

Emergency situations threaten even the best drivers. Driving *out* of trouble depends on two things: your ability to stay calm, and your knowledge of defensive driving techniques. At all times, expect the unexpected: the dump truck ahead of you that spills part of its load; the oncoming car that suddenly swerves into your lane; a blowout that sends your car into a skid. Scan the road and its shoulders for potential hazards. Glance in your mirrors every few seconds, and look back over your shoulder occasionally to check the blind spot. Make sure your conversation with passengers is secondary to thoughts about driving. Keep music strictly in the background, and concentrate on driving rather than the passing scenery. Maintain proper following distances, which should be increased if the weather or road conditions are poor (see pp. 46–47). Remember that, even at 70 km/h (45 mph), the 25 m (85 ft) in front of you will be gone before you can move your foot from the gas pedal to the brake. Work to remedy the bad habits that creep into everybody's driving: riding the brake pedal or clutch, failure to signal, tailgating, impatience, and inattention.

An emergency may force you to make sudden and extreme changes in your car's speed and direction. Driving experts recommend the following techniques. Which of them you should use depends on the situation, road conditions, and your room to maneuver.

• *Threshold braking.* If your following distance has left you enough room, threshold braking should bring you to a controlled stop in your own lane. Under the stress of trying to stop quickly, most drivers overreact and simply ''slam on the brakes,'' which locks the wheels and results in loss of directional control. To maintain such control, apply steady, but not full, pressure on the brake pedal. Once the wheels start to lock, ease up immediately, but quickly reapply slightly less pressure. Repeat this squeeze-and-release process until the car comes to a full stop.

• *Four-wheel lock.* Use this braking method when you must stop the vehicle in the shortest possible distance, and only at low speeds (up to 65 km/h or 40 mph). Keep full pressure on the brake pedal until the car comes to a complete stop. The vehicle will usually continue in a straight line in the direction it was traveling when the brakes were applied. But remember, when the wheels are locked, you lose directional control.

• *Evasive steering.* Swerving to the left or right to avoid collision is preferable to panic braking. At speeds over 40 km/h (25 mph),

it takes less time to steer around an object than to brake to a stop. However, in some situations—driving on a busy, two-lane road, for example—it may be safer to brake than to weave into an oncoming lane.

With your hands at the 10-and-2-o'clock position, you should be able to quickly turn the steering wheel up to 180 degrees in either direction. This is important because evasive steering is really two actions: avoiding an obstacle and recovering your course. Turn the wheel only as far as necessary to avoid collision. After making a sharp emergency turn, immediately turn the wheel in the opposite direction to recover, then back again to the center. While out of your lane or on the shoulder, try to stay parallel to your original path of travel. Often, the best way to avoid an accident will be a combination of evasive steering and threshold braking.

• *Acceleration* may also be an effective defensive driving tool. At busy intersections, highway entrance and exit ramps, and other places where traffic merges, a quick burst of speed may be your only means of escape. However, such action will be safe only if you have a clear path ahead.

Choosing how to collide

You can't always predict and avoid collisions. But you can minimize their consequences. By practicing basic car safety, you can also reduce the possibility of death or injury. Seat belts and child-safety restraints prevent you and your passengers from being thrown around within the car. Statistics show that you are far less likely to be injured if you remain in the car during an accident.

Grip the wheel tightly. You might bruise or even break your arms in a high-speed crash, but it is better to stay put by holding the steering wheel than to be thrown forward into the steering column or windshield. You may need to regain steering control.

Even if a crash is imminent, the rules of defensive driving apply right up to and beyond the moment of impact. Keep your head and be prepared to choose *what* to hit, and *how,* using these guidelines:

• Choose any alternative to a head-on collision. If another vehicle is approaching and time allows, brake hard (but avoid locking the wheels—you need maneuverability) and use evasive steering. If there is time, lean on your horn and flash your headlights to warn the other driver. Do not try to outguess the driver of an oncoming car by swerving to the left. If asleep or drunk, he or she may ''come to'' and instinctively pull back into the correct lane—to hit you head-on.

Car in your lane—what would you do?

1. Slam on the brakes and try to stop before hitting the oncoming car?

2. Steer into the left lane, and off the road if necessary?

3. Try to squeeze by the oncoming car on the right side, easing two wheels off the road if necessary?

4. Jerk the steering wheel hard to the right and head off the road rather than risk a head-on collision?

1. At highway speeds, it takes less time to avoid a collision by evasive steering than with panic braking, even if both drivers react quickly. In this situation, don't slam on the brakes.
2. If the other driver has drifted into your lane through inattention, his reaction will be to swerve back into his lane—and directly into your path. Or he may be passing a slower car or truck which you have not noticed. By moving to the left, you will be heading directly for the second vehicle.

3. When the other driver sees you, he will probably try to move back into his lane, even if it is partially blocked by another vehicle. If you edge toward the shoulder, you will likely avoid a head-on collision. Even if the vehicles sideswipe, you should be able to recover control. Squeezing right is the best alternative.
4. Should you react by jerking the steering wheel to the right, you will go completely off the road, risking a serious accident. Panic steering has the same risk as panic braking—loss of control.

• On a two-lane road, never swerve to the left to avoid a collision with a car or object. This places you in the path of oncoming traffic. Dodge to the right, even if it means leaving the road. Driving into a guard rail or ditch is preferable to colliding with another vehicle, even at slow speeds.

• If a small animal crosses your path, use threshold braking or evasive steering, but don't risk a skid or collision with a guard rail or another car. The options aren't pleasant, but often the lesser evil is to hit an animal rather than injure yourself or others. (Remember that an animal may "freeze" in the glare of your headlights.)

• To minimize damage and injury, choose to: 1. hit something going in your direction (such as another vehicle) rather than a stationary object; 2. hit something stationary rather than something coming toward you; 3. aim for something soft and flexible (a ditch rather than a tree); 4. hit another vehicle rather than a pedestrian. Car passengers have at least some protection in a crash; pedestrians have none.

Schools for skids

Every moment you are behind the wheel your life—and those of your passengers—is at stake. Canada's highway death toll remains high partly because some drivers have forgotten what they learned, but chiefly because most drivers were never taught what to do in emergencies.

The first advanced driving course in North America was launched in 1967 by BP (now Petro-Canada) in Oakville, Ontario. Today, this program has expanded to include the Petro-Canada Skid Control School in Montréal. Both of these offer a defensive driving and skid-control course year-round to any licensed driver. Expert instructors evaluate the student's skills in both normal and emergency situations, and seek to remedy poor driving habits. Most of the one-day session is spent behind the wheel.

For more information, contact the Petro-Canada Skid Control Schools at 9155 Metropolitan Boulevard East, Ville d'Anjou, Québec, H1J 1K2; or 576 Bronte Road, Oakville, Ontario, L6J 4Z3.

Coping with highway hazards—large and small

Tire blowout

Keeping good tires on your car and checking them frequently will reduce your chances of having a flat or blowout on the highway. A blowout will be sudden, often accompanied by a loud bang. The tire instantly loses its cushion of air, the wheel rim drops to the pavement, and the car is thrown out of balance. A front-tire blowout will drag your car to the side of the bad tire. A rear-tire blowout may cause your car to skid or fishtail. A tire going flat will be felt more gradually—the ride will become unsteady and the steering heavy and unnatural.

Should you have a blowout, lift your foot off the accelerator and keep a firm grip on the steering wheel, which will start to wobble. The car will begin to wander to the side of the blowout, so steer to the opposite side to maintain a straight course. Once the car is under control, gently apply the brakes to slow down. Turn on your emergency flashers, and pull off the road to a safe spot where you have enough room to park without danger to yourself or other motorists. (To change a tire, see pp. 182–183.)

Loss of steering

Power-steering failure is the most common type of steering loss. Fortunately, it is only partial. Your car can still be steered, but with extra effort due to the loss of power assist. Keep a firm grip on the steering wheel, reduce your speed, and pull off the road as soon as possible.

When a front wheel collapses because of a broken control arm or ball joint, you will still have some control over the car's direction. But use of the brakes could send the car into a skid. Instead, use the parking brake (which affects only the rear wheels) to slow the car. Hold the parking brake release open with one hand so that you can release and apply pressure as needed. Pull off the road.

In the rare case of total steering loss, let up on the gas pedal and brake *gently*. If you slam on the brakes you will risk a dangerous skid—with no way to correct it. If your car has a manual transmission, downshift to let the engine help slow the vehicle. Blow your horn, put on your flashers, flash your headlights, or use hand signals to warn other drivers or pedestrians. When you finally stop, set up flares or other warning devices. With help from passengers or passersby, turn the front wheels by hand and push the car off the road if it is safe to do so.

Brake failure

Newer cars have a split braking system to reduce the possibility of total brake failure. A warning light on the instrument panel glows when pressure in one set of brakes falls to a dangerous level. If the brake light comes on while you are driving, slow down, pull off the road, and check under the hood. If the problem is simply a low brake-fluid level, you may drive carefully to the nearest garage. If, however, there is an apparent leak or other serious problem, wait for help.

To drivers accustomed to power brakes, a malfunction in the power-assist system may lead them to think that the brakes have failed. If the brakes do not respond when

When your hood flies up

Should your hood fly open suddenly and block your vision, resist the urge to jam on your brakes and thereby risk a rear-end collision. Instead, hunch down and see if you can peer beneath the open hood. Otherwise, lean out the window and look around the hood. Switch on your emergency flashers, brake gradually, and pull off the highway. The next time your hood is open at the garage or service station,

check which vantage point is best in your car—beneath the hood or around it.

A frequent cause of popped hoods is the failure of a service station attendant to close the hood properly. Become accustomed to the sound made by your hood when it closes firmly. Then, if you fail to hear the familiar ''thunk,'' check the hood yourself before driving away.

When fire strikes, take these precautions

Most automobile fires are caused by a short circuit in the electrical system or by leakage in the fuel system. Others, such as ashtray or upholstery fires, are caused by carelessness. If you see or smell smoke coming from your car, immediately pull off the road, turn off the ignition, and get everyone away from the car. Warn motorists and passersby of the danger, have someone call the nearest fire department, and set up flares or warning triangles.

Even if you have a fire extinguisher (it should be an automobile-approved type), whether or not you should try to put out the fire is a matter of judgment depending on the risks. If the fire is severe or is fuel-fed, or if it is near the gas tank, stand clear and wait for the fire department. If not, use a rag to carefully open the hood (it will be hot), just enough to aim the extinguisher at the base of the fire. Turn your head aside as the hood is released, to prevent facial burns from flashing flames. Dirt or sand (shoveled with a

hubcap), or a heavy blanket can also be used to smother the flames. Never use water on an automobile fire. Try to flag down a trucker; they usually carry heavy-duty extinguishers.

If you see that the problem is caused by insulation burning on electrical wiring, try cutting the wire or disconnecting the battery. In an emergency, the quickest method is to wrap the jack handle with a piece of cloth or other non-insulating material, then rip loose any burning wires.

A fire in the passenger compartment can be caused by a half-burned cigarette that has fallen behind a car seat, or by waste paper igniting in the ashtray. Cover the seat or carpet, or close the ashtray, to smother the fire. When it is out, saturate the material with water. Otherwise, smoldering may continue without any hint of smoke or odor. Do not drive until you are positive that the fire is out. Open the windows to allow toxic fumes to dissipate.

you touch the pedal, simply apply greater pressure to slow the car. Drive carefully to the next garage, or pull off the road.

If your brakes fail completely, first pump them hard. Often you can build up enough pressure to get back at least partial braking. Shift to a lower gear, permitting the engine to help slow the car. Gently apply the parking brake. Use your horn, flashers, and lights to warn other drivers and pedestrians that you have lost your brakes. Look for a safe place to steer the car.

Stuck accelerator

A stuck gas pedal often triggers panic—you want to reduce your speed, but you can't. First, try to pull the pedal up with your toe, or have a passenger do it. (Never take your eyes off the road, and do not reach down with your hand to free the pedal.) If this doesn't

work, shift into *Neutral* and hit the accelerator pedal two or three times with your foot.

If the pedal refuses to come unstuck, turn the ignition to the *Off* position to cut the engine. (Be careful not to turn it to *Lock*, which will freeze the steering.) Be prepared for stiff braking and steering if these are power assisted. Coast to a safe place and pull off the road to investigate the problem.

If your accelerator sticks in heavy traffic, do not switch off the engine—you will need power-assisted brakes and steering to maneuver. Shift into *Neutral* or, if you have a manual transmission, depress the clutch. Then apply the brakes. Once you have safely pulled off the road, switch off the racing engine before it is damaged. Determine what is holding down the pedal linkage and free it if possible. If you cannot find the problem, call for help.

Headlights go out

A total loss of lights is usually caused by the burnout of a fuse, by a short circuit, or by a loose battery cable (in which case all electrical power will be lost). If only one headlight goes out, the problem may be a circuit breaker which has opened. These are heat-activated to open and close, so the light may work intermittently.

If you are suddenly plunged into darkness while driving in light traffic, brake as hard as you can without skidding. The idea is to pull your speed down quickly before a slight steering error sends you off the road. Then ease onto the shoulder as far from traffic as possible. Since other motorists will be blind to you, set out flares or use a flashlight to warn oncoming cars. Use your emergency flashers if they are operable, or even your dome light. Never drive at night without headlights or taillights. (See pp. 130–131.)

Dropped driveshaft

One of the most dangerous mechanical emergencies is a dropped driveshaft. When a universal joint fails, the driveshaft—which connects the transmission and differential in rear-drive cars—may drop to the roadway. If the rear U-joint fails, power will be lost but you will be able to steer carefully to safety with the driveshaft dragging beneath you. However, if the front U-joint fails and that end of the driveshaft drops, it may dig into the pavement and throw the car out of control. The most important thing to remember is to slow down *before* pulling off the road to prevent the driveshaft from digging into the rough shoulder.

U-joints will vibrate noisily before they fail completely. Have them inspected and lubricated periodically (see pp. 110–111). If you hear a rattle coming from beneath your car, stop and investigate.

Stalled on railway tracks

You have about 20 seconds from the time bells, flashers, and crossing gates are activated until the train arrives at a crossing. If you are in the middle of the tracks when the gate starts to drop, keep going.

Should your car stall on the tracks when a train is approaching, get everyone out of the car immediately. Don't waste time trying to get the car started or pushing it off the tracks. Run alongside the tracks toward the train so that you won't be hit by flying metal in the event of a collision. Wave your arms and point to the crossing to warn the engineer.

If there is no train coming in either direction, and the car has a manual transmission,

shift into first gear or *Reverse* and hold the starter switch to inch the car off the tracks. If yours is an automatic, get passengers or passersby to help you push it to safety. But be alert for approaching trains.

Out of gas

If the engine begins to miss or sputter, check the fuel gauge. If it reads "empty," pull into a slower lane and switch on your emergency flashers. If you have a manual transmission, stretch what little fuel remains by gently accelerating to about 50 km/h (30 mph). Shift into *Neutral* and let the car coast until it slows to about 15 km/h (10 mph), then accelerate back to 50 km/h. If you have an automatic transmission, coast downhill whenever possible, but stay in high gear. In either case do not shut off the engine while coasting; it may be difficult to restart.

If the road is dry and clear of other traffic, wiggle the steering wheel to slosh fuel toward the pickup inside the fuel tank. If you are not likely to find a service station within the next few kilometres, pull off the road *before* you run out of gas (see p. 176).

Wheel wobbles

If one of your wheels begins to wobble, or you hear a creaking or rattling noise coming from a wheel at low speeds, the cause may be a loose or missing lug nut. The problem is often caused by improper wheel replacement or by stripped lug bolt threads, which will not hold the nuts tightly. Fix such a problem before you lose a wheel. Pull off the road, remove the hubcap, and check the tightness of all lug nuts. If they are secure, the sound could be caused by a faulty or burned-out wheel bearing. Drive carefully to the nearest garage.

If you have already lost two or more nuts from a wheel, borrow one nut from another wheel so that you can tighten the wheel adequately. At the first opportunity, replace all the missing lug nuts. If two or more of the lug bolts are too stripped to permit retightening, do not risk the loss of a wheel by driving.

Locked bumpers

This problem is common on busy city streets, where parking room is at a premium. There are two remedies. One driver can stand on the bumper of the lower car while the other person pushes up on the bumper of the upper car. If this doesn't work, place a jack under the upper car, and raise it high enough so that the lower car can pull away. Be careful not to pinch your fingers with either technique.

How to escape from a submerged car

This frightening emergency is more common than most drivers imagine. Each year many unwary motorists drive off wharves, break through thin ice, or lose control of their vehicles while backing down boat ramps. Should your car go into deep water, panic is your worst enemy. You must remain calm in order to plan your escape. Before the water reaches window level, you may be able to release your seat belt, crawl out an open window and swim to safety. Remove your shoes and heavy clothing so that their extra weight will not drag you down.

If the car is almost submerged, however, close the windows completely. A car with sealed doors and windows will float for three to ten minutes. (But roll down power windows immediately; otherwise, water may short-circuit the electrical system, making it impossible to open the windows.) The passenger compartment will hold enough air for you to breathe while you prepare to abandon the vehicle. The car will not drop like a stone, but will sink relatively slowly, heavy end first. In these few minutes, you should take the following steps:

1. Free yourself and all passengers from seat belts and child-safety restraints. Use as little energy as possible in order to conserve the air in your lungs. Turn on the headlight and emergency flashers, if they are still working; they may attract help.

2. Go where the air is. There will be an air pocket on the ceiling of the passenger compartment for several minutes. Hold the heads of children and injured passengers above the water as it rises. Kick off heavy shoes and restrictive clothing.

3. Release all door safety locks and slowly wind down the windows to allow water pressure to equalize inside the car and out. If you can't get a window open, don't panic. Lift the door handle and lean against the door. When the pressure has equalized, the door will open and you will be able to escape (open only one door or window).

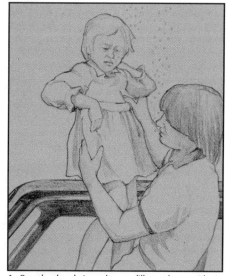

4. Breathe deeply in and out to fill your lungs with air, and wait until the last second before taking the final breath. Once out of the car, with your lungs full of air, you are bound to float upward even if you cannot swim. Air trapped in your clothing will have the same effect. Hold hands with other passengers to form a human chain, and push children to the surface.

When your car goes out of control

No good driver should ever find his car skidding unintentionally. A skid is usually the result of poor observation, too high a speed, harsh use of the controls, an improperly maintained car, or the sudden action of another vehicle. Knowing how to control a skid is essential, however, since even a good driver may skid sometime.

A skid is caused when a tire loses its grip on the road surface and starts sliding instead of rolling. The area of contact between tire and road is very small—no bigger than the sole of a man's shoe. It is critical that this small area remains effective. The condition of the tread is therefore important in retaining grip, particularly if the surface is wet.

Wet weather driving demands gentle use of all the car's controls—steering, brakes, accelerator, and clutch—and a greater-than-normal allowance for errors and emergencies (see pp. 46–47). The presence of rain means reduced visibility and increased risks of skidding and hydroplaning.

To avoid and control skids, pay proper attention to the road surface and its bumps, dips, and curves. In good weather, dust or gravel on the surface can reduce tire adhesion, as can mud on country roads. Rain is most dangerous when it falls after a long dry spell. The water then mixes with oil and rubber deposits on the road surface to form a coating which greatly increases the risk of skidding. The faster you are moving, the poorer the grip of your tires on the road surface. This, plus over-powering, over-braking, and over-steering, can lead to one of the following types of skids.

Four-wheel skid. When hard braking locks all four wheels, the only way to regain control is to release the brakes and then reapply them more gently. This allows the tires to roll again and reestablish their grip on the road. If the car is skidding sideways out of the lane, straighten out the front wheels before trying to get back on course.

Wheelspin. The definition of a skid, in which the grip of the tire on the road surface is lost, could include wheelspin. It is usually caused by a too-heavy foot on the accelerator, particularly at stops, and can only be remedied by easing off on the gas pedal until control is regained.

Hydroplaning: riding a wedge of water

If your car is driven at high speed into surface water, a cushion of water builds up ahead of the rolling tire. If the tread grooves cannot allow sufficient water to pass through them, the tire will lose road contact and float up on a wedge of water. This undesirable action—called *hydroplaning*—is much like water skiing.

Once you are hydroplaning, applying the brakes and steering is dangerous, because the car can easily begin to skid. If the car is still heading straight, ease off the gas pedal and brakes until the speed drops sufficiently for the tires to make road contact again.

Conditions of hydroplaning will be reached at different speeds for different types of tires. Where there is 3 mm (1/8 in.) of water on the road, a car with bias-ply tires in good condition would probably start to hydroplane at speeds of 90 km/h (55 mph). A vehicle with smooth tires, whether bias-ply or radial, could start to skid at only 65 km/h (40 mph). Radial tires with drainage channels in their treads perform best in wet conditions—instead of building up beneath the tread, water is displaced to either side. Contrary to popular belief, lowering the tire pressure merely brings on hydroplaning at lower speeds.

On a dry road, the tire tread grips enough of the surface to keep the car on course and provide braking action.

Puddles can form a wedge of water in front of a rolling tire, causing it to ride up like a water ski. The result is loss of control.

This driver steered too sharply on a rain-soaked road. The result: a rear-wheel skid.

Front-wheel skid. The car tends to travel in a straight line in this type of skid, despite the driver's attempt to turn the car. It is usually brought about by entering a corner too fast, when the front wheels lose their grip. It may seem at first that the steering has failed, but do not react by steering even further. The first thing to do is take your foot off the gas pedal. Then reduce the angle of the front wheels so that they can start rotating again. Once tire grip has been restored, steer carefully in the direction you wish to take. The steering correction must be applied very briefly. Over-correction could lead to rear-wheel skid as the rear wheels swerve outward into the curve.

When a front-drive car goes into a front-wheel skid, take your foot off the gas ped-al—this will shift some of the car's weight onto the front wheels for better traction. Reduce the angle of the front wheels until their grip is restored, then steer carefully in the direction you want to go.

Rear-wheel skid. When driving too fast on slippery surfaces, or around a corner or bend, the rear of the car may swerve away and cause a rear-wheel skid. How much corrective steering you must apply depends on how far you have skidded. Since motorists are taught to drive with extreme caution in poor conditions, most tend to under-react when they start to skid. Instead, you must react quickly and decisively (see below) and be prepared to deal with a secondary skid. Most important, do not panic. (For basic driving techniques, see pp. 28–35.)

Controlling a rear-wheel skid

Whether the car skids to the left *(above)* or the right, the corrective action is exactly the same. Suppress the instinct to brake, and lift your foot off the accelerator. Now, steer in the direction of the skid. This common advice is sometimes hard to interpret in an emergency situation. In layman's terms, it simply means that if the rear of the car skids to the left, you must steer to the left. If the car skids to the right, steer right. Act quickly; if excessive steering causes the car to skid in the opposite direction, stay calm and steer in this direction to regain control. When correcting a rear-wheel skid, always be prepared to deal also with a secondary skid.

Always steer with two hands (see pp. 28–29). It is not necessary to grip the steering wheel more tightly than usual during skid control, although this may be your first reaction. A light but firm grip is preferable, and allows the car's course, once it starts to wander, to be corrected with less risk of over-correction. Make your movements quick but deliberate.

Early warnings of mechanical breakdown

Even if your car has been well maintained and properly driven, there will probably come a time when something goes wrong. The problem may announce itself with a loud backfire or blowout, or it may appear as a flashing warning light on the dashboard. Or perhaps the car simply won't start when you turn the ignition key. Mechanical problems are often expensive and always irritating, but they need not turn into major emergencies. With a few simple tools and troubleshooting techniques, you should be able to diagnose, and often solve, what is wrong with your car.

If your engine dies, your hood pops open, or your headlights fail, you have no choice but to pull off the road immediately. But your car may give you less drastic indications that something is wrong. On the cars of yesteryear, dashboard instruments measured the performance of the various systems. Replacing them, in most of today's cars, are "idiot lights"—so called because they merely announce the fact that the system is performing poorly, or has failed. Three of these lights warn of trouble with the oil pressure, the engine temperature, and the alternator. A fourth light, found in most new cars, warns of a problem in the braking system. (All these lights come on momentarily when you turn the ignition key, to indicate that they are functioning.)

• *If the oil light comes on*, or the oil-pressure gauge reads low, pull off the road to investigate—coasting in *Neutral*, if possible. Turn off the engine the moment you come to a full stop. Running an engine when its oil pressure is low can damage it in minutes.

• *The temperature light* signals when the engine is overheating and may soon stall. Pull off the road immediately and allow the engine to cool before tracing the problem.

• *A glowing alternator light* indicates that the electrical system is not recharging—a problem but not necessarily an emergency. Turn off whatever electrical accessories you can to conserve power—radio, air conditioning, fan—and continue driving to the nearest service station.

• *The brake light* flashes on when either of the car's separate braking systems fails. Usually, the hydraulic pressure in one of the systems has been reduced to a point where it can no longer activate the brakes for two wheels. Even though the warning light stays on, you probably have enough braking power to drive to the nearest garage. Slow down and test the brakes. If they are sufficient, increase your following distance and begin braking earlier than you normally would.

• *A sudden or unusual noise* may also warn of mechanical trouble (see pp. 140–141). Generally, the louder the noise, the more critical the problem. A humming transmission, whining axle, or metallic hammering from the engine should tell you to reduce speed and proceed with caution to the next service station. If the noise gets louder or the car's performance changes, pull over and call for a tow. Continued driving may severely damage your car.

• *Strange odors*, especially from the engine compartment or wheels, should be investigated as soon as possible. A brief misfiring accompanied by the smell of gas may indicate that the gas tank is almost empty. Overheated brake linings, oil leaking on hot engine parts, and spilled coolant all give off characteristic odors that signal mechanical problems. Most dangerous of all is a fuel-fed fire. You will usually smell smoke before you see it. Don't wait to trace its source—pull off the road immediately and follow proper fire safety procedures (see p. 167).

The moment you realize your car is in trouble, switch on your emergency flashers and scan the roadside for a safe place to stop. If the engine has stalled, try to coast off the road while the car still has momentum. Do not stop on a curve or the crest of a hill if at all possible. If you need help, tie a white cloth or handkerchief to the antenna or door handle, and raise the hood—both are universally recognized signals of distress. At night, leave the low beams and taillights on, as well as the dome light, to make your vehicle as visible as possible to other motorists. Set up flares and reflectors *(right)*.

It is best *not* to leave your car unless you know that a service station or telephone is only a short walk away. On most Canadian highways, help will arrive within 30 minutes. If the breakdown cannot be repaired at roadside, you will need a tow to the nearest garage. Most cars should be towed with the drive wheels raised. Do not have your vehicle pulled or pushed by another car—serious damage can result.

Before your car is hitched to the tow truck, find out how far the truck will take you, and exactly how much it will cost. If you are asked to sign for the towing service, read the fine print first. Do not authorize any repairs until you know precisely what is wrong with your car. If you are a CAA member, towing and other emergency services are provided free of charge (see pp. 92–95). Your insurance policy may also cover towing charges and provide for a "loaner" car while yours is in the shop.

Warning other motorists

If your car stops dead on a busy highway before you can pull over to safety, flash your taillights to warn any vehicles immediately behind you, then switch on your emergency flashers. At the first break in traffic, move all passengers away from the vehicle.

Even if you have pulled a stalled car well off the road, set up flares or other warning markers to warn other drivers. The positioning of flares depends on the location of your car. On a two-lane highway *(right)*, place the first flare 3 m (10 ft) behind the car, the second about 90 m (300 ft) back, and the third 30 m (100 ft) *ahead* of the car, to warn approaching traffic.

On a divided highway, where the primary danger is vehicles approaching from behind at high speeds, place flares well back from your car. Position the first flare about 3 m (10 ft) behind the car, a second flare about 60 m (200 ft) back, and a third at 120 m (400 ft). If there are curves or rises in the roadway, place the flares between them and oncoming drivers.

Set the flares on the shoulder as close to the road surface as possible. If your car is stalled on the road—or if there is no shoulder—stick the flares into cracks in the pavement or simply lay them on the road at the proper intervals.

Flares and reflective red triangles can be used interchangeably. Flares are easier to see both day and night, but they burn for only 15–20 minutes and cannot be reused. Reflectors are less visible, but more practical if your car is likely to sit by the road for longer than your supply of flares will last.

30 m (100 ft)

3 m (10 ft)

90 m (300 ft)

To light a flare, pull up on the cloth or plastic tab, which frees the cap and exposes the matchlike head.

Point the head of the flare away from you and strike it with the top of the cap.

As soon as the flare ignites, press its spiked end firmly into the ground or pavement.

Fix it yourself—or know when to call for help

Some emergency car repairs are no more difficult than wrapping a gift or reading a thermometer. You need to know where to look, what to look for, and most important, what to do when you find a problem. Proper maintenance, including well-spaced tune-ups, will make a lot of troubleshooting unnecessary by heading off most malfunctions before they reach the critical stage.

To use the troubleshooting guide that follows, first find the symptom, then follow the repair procedures outlined. If you cannot find or fix the problem, do not run the risk of driving—call for a tow. If you do manage a temporary patch, have a proper repair made by a mechanic as soon as possible.

Problem: Oil-pressure light goes on

Pull over immediately and turn off the engine. Oil may be leaking from the engine, or a mechanical defect may be causing a drop in the oil pressure. Even a few minutes of driving with insufficient oil or a defective pump can destroy an engine. Lift the hood and check the level on the oil dipstick (see pp. 112–113).

• If the dipstick reading is low, add a litre of oil if you have it. If not, and the oil light was only flickering before you stopped, drive on slowly to the next service station to add oil. If the oil light starts to glow steadily while you drive, pull over and wait for help.

• If the oil light glows steadily, even though the oil level is adequate, it indicates an engine problem more complex than a simple leak. Pull over immediately.

• If the oil level drops again soon after you have added oil, your problem is probably a leak. You can continue driving with a small leak, as long as you check the level frequently, and top it up when necessary. Have the leak repaired as soon as possible.

Problem: Temperature light comes on

If the temperature light starts to glow, if you smell hot oil or coolant, or if steam is rising from under the hood, pull over immediately. You may be able to cool an overheated engine by revving it, or by turning on the heater (see pp. 54–55). If your car overheats in cooler weather, the problem is likely a mechanical defect.

The engine may overheat for a number of reasons: a low coolant level, inadequate pressure in the cooling system, a leak in the radiator or hose, or a blocked radiator. **Caution:** Let the engine cool for at least 10 minutes before opening the hood; 30 minutes before opening the radiator cap.

• If the level is low, top it up with coolant through the radiator or coolant recovery tank. If you have no spare coolant, use water—straining it through a cloth if it is particularly dirty (have the cooling system flushed later to prevent blockage or deposits). Do not add cold liquid to a hot engine—you might crack the block. If you have a coolant recovery system, check its coolant level against the *Hot* marking on the side of the reservoir (see pp. 132–133).

• Squeeze the two main radiator hoses. If either is soft or collapses easily, replace it.

Makeshift repairs—for experts only

"Mexicaneering" is the term used by competitors in the famous Baja 1000 road race to describe temporary repairs made to keep their vehicles rolling. They use boulders to straighten bent steering arms, substitute pieces of cactus for coil springs, and solder electrical connections using battery sparks. Such creative jury-rigging is *not* recommended for the average motorist, however. Improvised repairs, although they may get you to the next service station, may be harmful to your car and dangerous to you and your passengers. One exception is the following "fashionable" solution to a broken fan belt.

In an emergency, a nylon stocking or pair of pantyhose will substitute for a broken fan belt. Twist the stocking into a rope.

Slip it under the lower pulley, then around the fan pulley. Stretch it as tightly as possible to apply friction to both pulleys.

Tie securely, then trim off loose ends close to the knot with a knife or scissors. Drive slowly to the nearest garage for a replacement.

Where to troubleshoot for engine problems

The mass of hoses, wires, pipes, and accessories under the hood of a modern car presents a hopelessly bewildering picture to most people. However, the essential moving parts that make a car start, stop, and turn are relatively few and comparatively simple. All car engines may not look identical, but the parts should be basically the same. Check your owner's manual for specific details, and study this diagram to locate those parts that you can simply (and safely) troubleshoot when breakdown occurs.

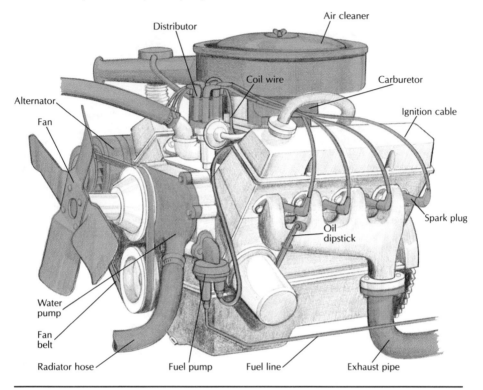

Install a spare hose if you have one (see pp. 134–135). Otherwise, leave the radiator cap open one notch to relieve pressure on the system. A loose radiator cap reduces the efficiency of the cooling system, but may let you drive farther before the engine overheats than a fast leak would. Drive to the nearest service station.

• Next, check for leaks in the radiator and heater hoses. If a hose has burst completely, do not attempt to repair it. Call for help unless you can install a proper replacement.

• If you find a leak near the hose clamp, remove the clamp, trim off about 2.5 cm (1 in.) of the defective end, and reinstall the hose. Have this shortened hose replaced as soon as you can.

• If you find a leak in the middle of a hose, wrap the hose with waterproof tape (heating duct tape is best) at least 8 cm (3 in.) on each side of the leak. Wind the tape tightly around the hose and overlap each wrap. Leave the radiator cap open one notch and have the taped hose replaced soon.

• If you find no leaks, look for water in the exhaust pipe, especially if overheating was preceded by roughness and loss of power. Water in the exhaust would point to a leaking engine gasket.

• Check the oil level, and add oil if necessary. If the level is unusually high, coolant may have leaked into the crankcase.

• Check the fan belt, especially if you heard a high-pitched squeal coming from under the hood before you stopped. If there is too much free play, the belt must be tightened or replaced (see pp. 134–135).

• If your car has an electric fan, inspect and replace the fuse, if necessary.

• If the temperature light comes on again after you have topped up the coolant and driven a short distance, the source is probably a radiator leak. A can of "stop leak" poured into the cooling system will mend a minor leak temporarily. Top up the coolant again and have the radiator checked soon.

Caution: If you cannot pinpoint the source of overheating at roadside, do not drive.

Problem: Alternator light comes on

A glowing alternator light reports that the alternator is not recharging the battery. Sooner or later (sooner if the air conditioning or headlights are on), the engine will stall because the battery will be drained.

The alternator may not be rotating fast enough to produce the necessary voltage, it may be defective, or there may be a problem in the circuit, which prevents electricity from reaching the battery.

• If the alternator light is on, you can make it to the next service station. Turn off all electrical accessories, especially air conditioning. You should have enough power stored in the battery to drive two to four hours, if necessary. With the headlights on, you have 30 to 60 minutes. Do not stop the engine, or you may not be able to start it again.

• If you do not think you can reach a garage in time, stop and investigate. Check the fan belt first; if it is loose, tighten or replace it (see pp. 134–135). If a quick check under the hood reveals no obvious problem, call for help. Tampering with the electrical system can be dangerous and can damage your car.

Problem: Engine dies on the highway

Engine failure can be both frightening and mystifying. If your engine dies with a sputter, there may be trouble in the fuel system—or you may be out of gas. Sudden loss of power is usually associated with the ignition system or battery. Check your fuel gauge *and* your tank before opening the hood *(below)*.

• Inspect the fuel lines that extend from both sides of the carburetor. Be sure that the connections at each end are tight and that the hoses are not cracked or punctured. If you find a leak, seal it with waterproof tape until you can have the hose replaced.

• If it is a hot day, your problem may be vapor lock in the fuel system. Heat can make gasoline vaporize in the fuel lines or pump, sending bubbles of gas instead of liquid fuel to the carburetor. Cooling is the only answer—pull over and wait for the engine to cool down, or try wrapping the fuel pump and lines with wet rags.

• Make sure the ground strap of your battery has not come loose; tighten it if necessary. If the cable is broken, replace it *temporarily* with a battery jumper cable. Route the cable so that it is clear of hot or moving engine parts, and tape or wire it in place.

• If you drive through a deep puddle or during a heavy rainstorm, the ignition system may short circuit, causing the engine to stall. Turn off the ignition, and wait a few minutes for the heat of the engine to dry out the system. If the car will not start, use a rag to dry the distributor, spark plugs, and cables (especially the connection inside the rubber boot that fits over the spark plugs).

Problem: Engine cranks but will not start

Starting a car's engine involves three components: the starter motor, the ignition system, and the fuel system. Begin troubleshooting a starting problem by seeking the simplest possible cause, however obvious.

• If the engine cranks normally but will not start, remember that the correct way to start most cars is to press the gas pedal to the floor, release it, then turn on the ignition. If this does not work, do not run down the battery with continued cranking.

• If you smell gasoline, the engine may be flooded. Excessive pumping of the accelerator to start a reluctant engine draws so much gasoline through the carburetor that the fuel mixture reaching the cylinders is too rich to

Problem: Out of gas

If your car stalls on the highway, check the gas gauge. If it reads *Full*, look to see if there is actually gas in the tank (the gauge may be broken). Remove the gas cap and rock the car by pushing on the rear bumper. You should hear the sloshing of fuel. If the tank is empty, walk to the nearest gas station. You should have an empty 4-litre (1-gallon) gas can or collapsible container for such emergencies. When you return to your car, put most of the gas into the tank. Save a cupful and pour part of this directly into the carburetor *(right)*. **Caution:** Be careful not to drip gasoline on hot engine parts.

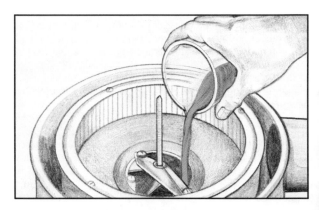

Quick fix for a flooded engine

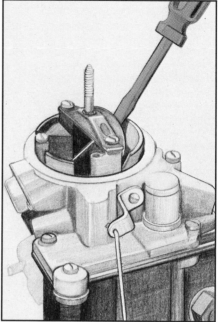

If your engine is flooded and refuses to start, open the air cleaner cover (see pp. 114–115) and check the position of the choke plate (butterfly valve). If it is closed, the air-fuel mixture may be too rich. Wedge it open with a pencil or screwdriver *(above)* and try starting again. **Caution:** Keep hands and face clear while the engine is being started. Do not attempt to repair a fuel-injection system.

If the engine won't start but is *not* flooded, make sure the choke plate is fully *closed.* (The engine may be getting too much air.) If the valve is open, push the gas pedal to the floor to close it. If this does not close the valve, hold it closed with a pencil or screwdriver while someone starts the engine. Replace the air cleaner cover. Use carburetor solvent to free a sticky butterfly valve.

---

ignite. Try pressing the accelerator slowly to the floor and turning the key for ten seconds (no longer). If the engine still won't start, turn off the ignition and wait at least 15 minutes for the excess fuel to evaporate, or open the choke plate *(above)*.
● See that ignition system cables are free from moisture or greasy dirt, which can cause a short circuit. Check that all spark plug cables are firmly seated in the distributor cap and pushed tightly onto each plug. Inspect the distributor cap for cracks. If you have a wrench and spark-plug socket, remove one or two plugs and see if they are dry and clean. Plugs wet with gasoline or water will not fire. Dry them over the car defroster, or wipe with a rag.
● If none of these procedures works, the engine's timing may be improperly set or there may be a hidden defect in the ignition system. **Caution:** Do not attempt any electrical test or repair beyond the steps described above. Jury-rigging today's high-performance engines can be dangerous to both you and your car.

Problem: Light does not work
● When some bulbs or headlights work and others do not, check the unlit bulbs. Replace any bulbs that are burned out (see pp. 130–131), and clean any corroded sockets.
● When none of the lights work, look for a blown fuse in the fuse box under the dashboard. If a fuse is burned out, replace it with one of the same capacity. Do not try to by-pass the fuse with a wire or other conductor. Running without a fuse in a defective circuit is dangerous.

Problem: Dragging exhaust pipe
A scraping sound from beneath your car could mean a loose muffler or tailpipe. If it is dragging, flying sparks in combination with gasoline could cause a serious accident. Use baling wire, a coat hanger, or anything at hand to lash the pipe tightly to the bumper or the underside of the car. Wind the wire at least three turns around the broken pipe and the chassis. Remember that, no matter how secure, this is a temporary measure only.

Problem: Engine does not turn over

• If your car has an automatic transmission, be sure that the gearshift lever is set in *Park*. If this doesn't work, try *Neutral*. Jiggle the gearshift lever in each gear—a safety switch may have become misaligned.

• Next, test the battery. Turn on the headlights and try to start the car. If the lights burn brightly, the problem is *not* likely to be with the battery, but in some other part of the starting system. However, if the headlights dim or flicker out when you try to start the car, the battery is probably discharged. (To jump-start a car, see pp. 184–185.)

• Follow the heavy cable from the battery's positive terminal to the starter and make sure that the connection is tight. Then trace the cable from the negative side of the battery. Check its connection to the engine and tighten if necessary.

• A clicking sound when you turn the key often points to a problem within the starter. Try tapping the starter casing with a shoe or tool. This often does the trick by realigning a loose connection.

Caution: Do not try to start a car with automatic *or* manual transmission by getting a push from another vehicle. Cars with automatic transmissions cannot be started in this way, and cars with manual tranmissions can be damaged.

Problem: Engine runs poorly or backfires

• If the engine is sluggish or knocks excessively, switch to a higher-octane fuel to improve its performance.

• Open the air cleaner cover and inspect the air filter (see pp. 114–115). Replace if clogged, oil-stained, or wet.

• Make sure the spark plug cables are securely attached to the correct plugs (check your owner's manual).

• When the engine has warmed up, remove the air cleaner cover. While a helper pushes the accelerator to the floor, check if the choke plate (butterfly valve) is open all the way. If not, have it adjusted.

Problem: Car is hard to steer

• Pull over to a safe spot, and inspect the tires and wheels. Low tire pressure can affect handling, making a car slow to respond to steering corrections.

• Check the fluid level in the power-steering pump (see pp. 108–109); add fluid if the level is low.

Stuck horns and errant wipers

If your horn refuses to stop blaring, or sounds only part of the time when it is pushed, lift the hood and let your ears lead you to two round, trumpetlike speakers. They are usually located at the front of the engine compartment, often near the radiator. Tiny plugs connect wiring to each horn. Pull out these plugs, then reattach them. The short that most likely caused the trouble may have corrected itself. If not, leave the plugs detached and have a mechanic trace the problem. Do not drive without a horn.

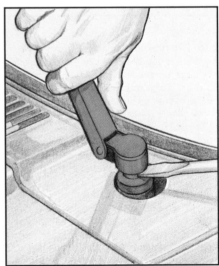

If your wipers collide or do not cover the windshield properly, one or both wipers is probably set incorrectly on its drive shaft. Grasp the wiper arm with one hand and lift it away from the windshield. Gently pry the wiper off its arm with a screwdriver. Reposition it so that it does not collide with the other wiper and press or tap it firmly back onto the splined shaft. If necessary, lift off and reposition the other wiper. If the problem recurs, have a mechanic check the splined shaft and wiper arm.

• Inspect the drive belt that connects the crankshaft to the power-steering pump. A loose or glazed belt may slip, turning too slowly to provide adequate pump pressure; steering will become more difficult. Tighten or replace the belt.

• On very cold days, lubricants in the steering and suspension may have congealed. When engine heat raises the temperature under the hood, the lubricants will thin out and steering should become normal.

• Other causes of steering problems include faulty alignment, binding in the steering linkage, and insufficient lubrication—all jobs for a professional mechanic.

Problem: Car tends to drift or wander

Strong crosswinds, roads with high crowns, the buffeting effect of passing trucks—as well as steering and suspension defects—can cause a car to veer even though the steering wheel is held steady.

• Check the tire pressures. If one or more tires are low, this is the likely cause of drift.

• See that the tires on all four wheels are of identical type (radial, bias-ply, or bias-belted) and size, and that they show about the same amount of wear.

• Make sure the brakes, including the parking brake, are not dragging. Have them adjusted or repaired if necessary. If you leave your car overnight in very cold weather, put the transmission in gear (automatics in *Park*) but do not set the parking brake. If the parking brake becomes frozen in the locked position, wait for it to thaw. Do not crawl under the car to release it.

• Wet brakes—especially on one side—can cause a car to veer when you try to stop. (Disc brakes are less susceptible to this problem than drum brakes.) If you drive through a deep puddle or in heavy rain, apply light pressure on the brake pedal to generate heat from the friction to dry the brakes.

An emergency kit for your car

Whether you use it or not, a well-stocked emergency kit will bring peace of mind on car trips. Store the following tools and materials in a box in your trunk, and remember to replace spare fluid, belts, hoses, or fuses as they are used.

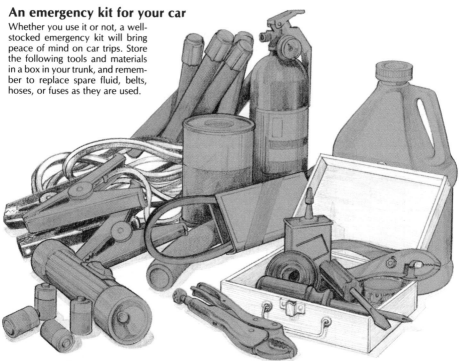

- Fire extinguisher (car-type)
- Six flares, or three reflectors
- Heavy-duty flashlight and spare batteries
- Quarters (phone calls)
- Square of plywood (to support jack)
- Wheel chocks
- Tire pressure gauge
- Jumper cables

- Pocketknife
- Set of screwdrivers
- Adjustable wrench
- Utility pliers
- Rubber mallet
- Funnel
- 4-L (1-gal) plastic container (for water or gas)
- Waterproof tape
- Length of wire

- Clean rags
- Penetrating oil
- Spare can of engine oil
- Spare container of coolant
- Spare fan belt
- Spare radiator hose
- Spare fuses
- Spare windshield washer fluid
- Jar of assorted nuts and bolts
- First-aid kit (see pp. 186–187)

When your engine backfires, misses, or stalls

How to use this chart
Find problem at top of chart. Look down column to locate possible causes. First check repairs that you can do yourself. If none of these procedures work, consult a competent mechanic.

Problem (columns, left to right):

1. Starter does not work
2. Starter clicks but does not turn
3. Engine turns over but does not start
4. Engine stalls when cold
5. Engine stalls when hot
6. Engine runs roughly
7. Engine misfires at highway speeds
8. Engine rattles or pings
9. Engine lacks power
10. White smoke from exhaust
11. Black smoke from exhaust
12. Blue smoke from exhaust
13. Engine backfires
14. Engine smells of gasoline
15. Engine smells of oil
16. Poor fuel economy
17. Excessive oil use
18. Temperature light comes on
19. Oil pressure light comes on
20. Alternator light comes on
21. Brake warning light comes on
22. Engine makes unusual noise
23. Engine vibrates excessively
24. Engine boils over

1	2	3	4	5	6	7	8	9	10	11	12	13	14	15	16	17	18	19	20	21	22	23	24
►																							
►	►																►						
		►	►	►																			
		►	►	►						►													
		►	►																				
		►	►	►	►																		
		►	►	►	►	►		►															
		►			►	►		►															
		►	►	►			►		►				►										
				►	►																		
			►	►	►	►	►		►				►										
			►		►			►															
			►	►	►	►	►																
			►	►	►			►															
		►	►	►	►			►							►								
			►	►	►			►															
			►	►	►			►															
			►				►	►			►												
						►	►																
			►	►	►						►				►								
►	►																						
		►			►	►		►			►												
		►			►	►					►												
			►	►	►	►				►					►								
			►	►	►		►					►	►										
													►	►	►				►				
																►							
																			►				
										►							►						
																►					►		
																►	►	►			►		
																►	►	►	►				
																►							
																►							
																►					►		
																►					►		
							►			►		►	►		►		►				►	►	

CAA emergency service—a phone call away

The Canadian Automobile Association answers some 1.5 million emergency calls annually, coming to the aid of members with car trouble. The service is free of charge to CAA and affiliated members, and available around the clock throughout Canada. Emergency call boxes along most Canadian highways provide direct lines to CAA member clubs. Elsewhere, help is a phone call away with a toll-free number. In response to a distress call, the Emergency Road Service dispatcher will arrange for a CAA-approved mechanic and service vehicle to:

• deliver gas, oil, or water;

• boost a dead battery, or perform minor repairs such as replacing a clogged air filter or freeing a stuck horn;

• remove a flat tire, and install the member's spare;

• tow the car to the nearest service station if it cannot be fixed at roadside;

• tow or winch a car stuck in mud or snow, as long as the vehicle can be reached safely by one mechanic and service vehicle;

• open a car door when the keys have been locked inside, unless a locksmith is needed. (However, you must have proper identification and proof of ownership before a locked car can be opened.)

Emergency road service is a benefit to members traveling abroad, too. Britain's compact highway system, for example, is patrolled regularly by Automobile Association (AA) service vehicles. These "mobile garages" are often at the scene of a breakdown before the stranded motorist has time to call for help.

Possible cause	Possible solution
Transmission in gear	Shift into *Park* or *Neutral*
Battery weak or dead	Clean cable connections; jump-start engine (pp. 184–185)
Out of gas	Add at least 4 L (1 gal) of gas to tank (p. 176)
Carburetor flooded	Wait a few minutes, then try again; open choke plate (p. 177)
Poor gas vaporization	Spray starting fluid into carburetor; use engine heater (pp. 48–49)
Faulty ignition cables	Clean and dry cables, coil, and distributor; replace if damaged
Faulty breaker points	Have points adjusted or replaced
Faulty condenser	Have condenser replaced
Choke plate stuck	Close choke plate manually; clean and lubricate
Vapor lock (warm weather)	Let engine cool; wrap fuel lines and fuel pump with wet rags
Clogged air filter	Clean or replace filter (pp. 114–115)
Carburetor icing	Add a can of gas-line antifreeze to the tank; use engine heater
Heat control valve stuck	Free valve, saturate with penetrating oil
Vacuum hose disconnected	Locate and reattach disconnected hose
Faulty spark plugs	Remove plugs, check for damage, or improper gap (pp. 126–127)
Damaged distributor cap	Inspect cap; replace if cracked
Faulty coil	Have coil tested; replace if necessary
Incorrect ignition timing	Have timing set to manufacturer's specifications
Incorrect grade of gasoline	Switch to a higher octane gasoline
Incorrect carburetor adjustment	Have idle speed and mixture adjusted
Faulty starter, relay, or solenoid	Have ignition system inspected and repaired
Clogged fuel filter; faulty pump	Have filter and pump inspected and repaired
Dirt or water in gas	Replace fuel filter; have tank and lines cleaned
Worn or dirty carburetor	Have carburetor cleaned; rebuild or replace if necessary
Faulty PCV system	Check PCV filter (p. 115); check hoses for leaks (p. 134)
Oil leakage	Tighten oil filter, drain plug; check oil pan (pp. 112–113)
Coolant level too low	Top up with proper antifreeze/water mix (pp. 132–133)
Inadequate pressure	Add brake fluid; check for leaks (pp. 122–123)
Incorrect grade of oil	Change oil and filter (pp. 112–113)
Incorrect antifreeze mixture	Drain cooling system; refill with proper antifreeze mixture
Slipping drive belt	Adjust belt tension; replace worn or glazed belt (pp. 134–135)
Faulty gauge	Check gauge and connections
Leaking radiator or heater hose	Tighten hose clamps or replace hose (pp. 134–135)
Faulty thermostat	Have thermostat tested; replace if necessary
Leak or blockage in radiator	Add a can of "stop leak"; have radiator inspected (pp. 132–133)
Internal engine damage or wear	Have engine inspected and repaired by a mechanic

How to change a tire

Thanks to space-age materials and strong, reinforcing belts, tires do not puncture or leak as easily as they used to. Eventually, however, most motorists do get stuck with a flat tire. To make the changing both safer and easier, practice jacking up your car and changing a tire at least once *before* you need to deal with a flat at night, in winter, or beside a busy highway.

Always carry a spare in the trunk, and check its condition and pressure whenever you check your other four tires. Make sure your car is equipped with a good jack and a lug wrench (usually this doubles as the jack handle). Also carry a square of plywood large enough to support the jack on mud or sand; two bricks or heavy blocks to chock the wheels; a can of penetrating oil to loosen the lug nuts; and a tire gauge to retest the spare tire pressure before installing it.

Jacks are usually stored disassembled in the trunk. Be sure you know how to put your own model together. Assembly directions are printed in your owner's manual, or on a decal in the trunk. The owner's manual will also locate your car's specific jacking points, grooves, or fittings—those places where the vehicle can be safely raised and supported. On most cars, these are located beneath the bumpers or on the chassis below the rocker panels. A bumper jack has a hooked jaw which fits into the jacking point under the bumper. Both side-lift and scissors jacks are designed to fit beneath the rocker panels.

Run your hand along the underside of your car beneath the doors until you find the four jacking points for your type of jack. If you cannot locate them, ask your car dealer or mechanic to help you.

Should one of your tires go flat—or blow out completely—slow down, switch on your emergency flashers, and pull well off the road onto solid, level ground. If the shoulder is not safe to change a tire, keep driving slowly until you find a suitable spot. Turn off the ignition, apply the parking brake, and leave the transmission in gear (shift an automatic transmission into *Park*). Get everyone out of the car and safely away from the road. Have one passenger direct traffic. Before you raise the car, check the pressure of the spare tire. If it is adequate, remove the tire, tools, and jack, and carefully follow the procedures on the opposite page.

Raising the car

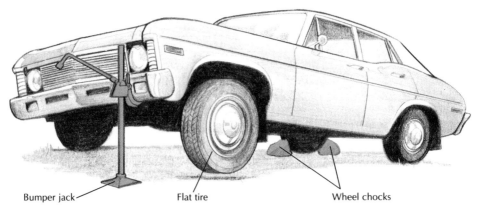

Bumper jack   Flat tire   Wheel chocks

The base of a bumper jack must be positioned so that, at first, the jack is angled slightly under the car. As the car is raised, the jack will become vertical *(above)*. Set the ratchet-control tab on the jack hook to its *Up* position. Using the lug wrench as a handle, pump up and down to raise the car. Be sure to allow enough clearance to replace the flat tire with the fully inflated spare. To lower the car, flip the ratchet-control to its *Down* position and pump slowly until the jack hook is disengaged. Be sure to place chocks on both sides of the wheel diagonally opposite the flat tire.

A scissors jack *(right)*—which has a wide, flat base and U-shaped top—is more stable than a bumper jack or side-lift jack. Place it below the jacking point closest to the flat tire.

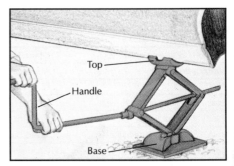

Top

Handle

Base

Replacing a flat

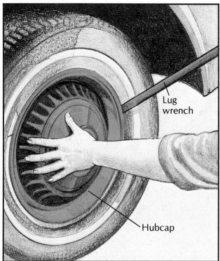

Lug wrench

Hubcap

Lug wrench

Wheel nuts

1. Move the car to a safe, level spot as far off the road as possible to change a flat tire. Set up flares or warning triangles, or have someone direct traffic while you concentrate on the repair. Put the transmission in gear (*Park* for automatics) and apply the parking brake. Remove the spare tire, jack, and lug wrench from the trunk. A screwdriver, a rubber hammer, and penetrating oil will be useful if you have them. Use the screwdriver, or the flat end of the lug wrench, to pry off the hubcap or wheel cover and expose the wheel nuts. Do not raise the car until the wheel nuts are loosened at least two turns.

2. Loosen the wheel nuts with the lug wrench. Get a good grip on the wrench and push down on it—never pull up. If the nuts are stubborn, loosen them with a squirt of penetrating oil or push on the wrench with your foot. Most nuts have right-hand threads and are loosened by turning them counterclockwise. However, if the stud is marked with an "L," the nut has left-hand threads and must be loosened in a clockwise direction. Loosen each nut two turns; *do not* remove them until you have raised the car. Assemble the jack, following the instructions in your owner's manual or the decal on the trunk.

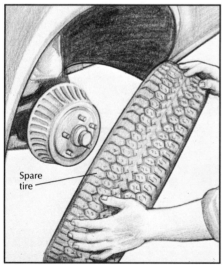

Spare tire

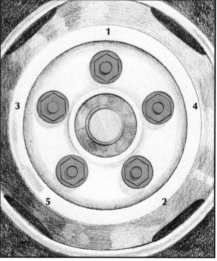

3. Chock the tire diagonally opposite to the flat, and carefully raise the car *(opposite page)*. Remove the lug nuts and place them in the overturned hubcap to prevent their loss. Pull off the wheel and tire with both hands. Make sure the jack is stable, then roll the spare into position. If the wheel is heavy, lower the car slightly or improvise a ramp with a piece of board and a rock. Align the holes in the wheel with the studs and put on the spare. Hold the wheel firmly in position with one hand and screw the nuts in (tapered end toward the wheel) with the other.

4. Lower the car slowly and remove the jack. Tighten the nuts with the lug wrench, in the sequence shown above. Tightening the nuts in the correct order ensures that the wheel is properly aligned, and that stress is distributed evenly. An improperly mounted wheel can shimmy or even crack. Place the tire valve through the hole in the hubcap, then hammer the hubcap securely onto the wheel with a rubber mallet or the heel of your hand. Put away the jack and tools, remove the wheel chocks, and have the flat tire repaired or replaced as soon as possible.

How to jump-start a battery

If your car refuses to start, eliminate the obvious possibilities before flagging down a passing motorist for a boost. Make sure the transmission is in *Park* or *Neutral*, and check the gas supply. Next, open the hood and inspect the battery cables and terminals. Tap the terminals with a piece of wood or the heel of your shoe. (**Caution:** Do not use an uninsulated metal object.) Or drive the tip of an insulated screwdriver between the battery post and clamp. You may improve the connection enough to start the engine. If this does not work, remove and clean the battery cables (see pp. 128–129), reconnect them, and try again. If your headlights do not work, or grow very dim when the ignition is switched on, you will need to jump-start the battery as described below.

Normally, the alternator recharges the battery while the engine is running. But freezing temperatures, too many attempts to start a reluctant engine, or headlights left on while the engine is off can drain the battery's stored current. Over a period of weeks, numerous engine starts with insufficient mileage between these starts can also drain the battery.

Be prepared for a dead battery by reading in your owner's manual how to jump-start your particular model (details sometimes vary from one make to another). Carry a pair of jumper cables in your trunk year-round—they cost less than $20 and will pay for themselves if they save the cost of one service call. The cables should be made of four-gauge wire so that they will pass current

Boosting a battery step by step

1. If either car has an automatic transmission, put it in *Park*. Shift a manual transmission into *Neutral*. Turn off both ignitions and switch off all accessories.

2. Remove the vent caps from both batteries. If the fluid level in the dead battery is low, top it up with water. Cover the open vents with clean rags.

3. Determine which of the battery terminals in each car is positive, and which is negative. The positive post is generally fatter than the negative post, and may be marked with a plus sign or "POS." On negative-ground cars, this terminal is connected to the car's starter. The negative post may be marked with a minus sign or "NEG," and is grounded to the chassis.

4. Attach the red booster cable to the positive terminals of both batteries, in the sequence shown at right (first donor, then dead battery). Force the booster cable jaws through any grease or corrosion with a rocking motion to obtain a firm contact.

5. Attach one of the black clamps to the negative terminal of the donor battery. Attach the other black clamp to a good ground (such as an unpainted bolt or flange) on the engine or chassis of your car. The attachment point should be at least 30 cm (12 in.) from the battery to minimize the risk of sparks.

6. Make sure all hands and cables are clear of all moving parts on both cars, then start the engine of the donor car. Have a helper rev it moderately.

7. Start your engine. If it turns over but still will not start, check for additional problems in the ignition or fuel systems, or call a mechanic.

8. Keep your car running while you carefully disconnect the jumper cables in the reverse order from which they were attached—black cable from the dead car, then from the booster car; red cable from the dead car, then from the booster car.

9. Remove the rags and replace the vent caps. Drive your car for at least 30 minutes after jump-starting to recharge the battery.

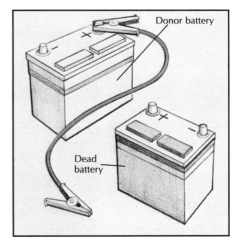

Donor battery

Dead battery

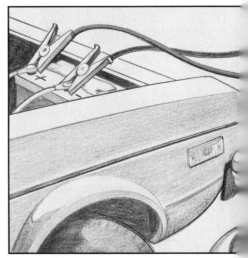

easily. Cables 5 m (16 ft) long will reach from one battery to another even if the cars cannot be positioned nose to nose. Be sure that the cables are color-coded.

Caution: Jump-starting your car can be dangerous. Car batteries are filled with a sulfuric acid solution that generates hydrogen gas. Leaking acid can cause severe burns, and a stray spark can cause the battery to explode. Follow all procedures carefully, and observe the following precautions:

• Make sure that both car batteries have the same voltage (12-volt batteries have six filler holes; 6-volt batteries have three filler holes). Next, check to see that both batteries have identical grounding. Most cars have negative grounding (with the negative terminal connected to the vehicle ground). If your car is an older model, it may have positive grounding. If you are uncertain, check your owner's manual, or trace the cable leading from each terminal. On a negative-ground battery, the cable leading from the negative (−) terminal will be bolted to the chassis. The positive (+) cable will lead to the starter.

• Remove the vent caps (if any) from both batteries and allow any built-up gases to escape. In extremely cold weather, look into the vent and check the electrolyte. If it is frozen, call for help. Pockets of hydrogen gas may be trapped in the frozen fluid; boosting could ruin the battery or cause an explosion.

• Wear gloves and safety goggles if you have them. After you attach the cables, beware of moving engine parts. Be prepared to remove the cables in the event of fire.

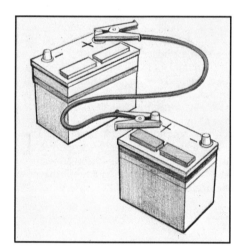

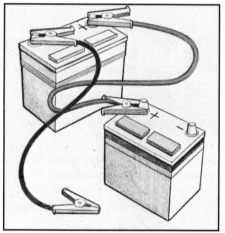

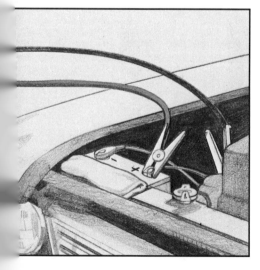

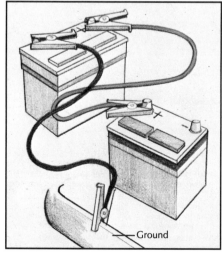

Ground

Be prepared for the worst

Almost half of all accidental deaths in Canada result from motor vehicle collisions. When someone is injured or becomes suddenly ill, there is a critical period before medical help arrives. What you do or do not do during this time may mean the difference between life and death. The following pages give you vital first-aid guidelines in concise, convenient form, from first responses to coping with bee stings. Study this part of *Canadian Driver's Handbook* carefully—before an emergency arises.

From the very beginning, your conversations with victims can help them relax—and lower their breathing and pulse rates. Stay as calm as you can, and reassure them that help is on the way. If a victim behaves abnormally or appears unaware of what is happening, watch the person carefully. Be alert for failing respiration, weakening pulse, and the onset of shock. The patient's *vital signs*—pulse, respiration, and temperature—will tell you a lot about his or her condition and alert you to new problems as they develop.

The pulse rate of a healthy adult at rest varies from 50 to 100 beats per minute, averaging about 70 beats per minute. In children, the rate is higher; a ten-year-old child's may be 90 beats per minute, an infant's as high as 140. Injury can cause the heart to pump faster or slower. A pulse rate below 50 beats per minute or above 120 beats per minute is cause for concern. If the victim is unconscious, there is little you can do to change the pulse rate other than to treat obvious injuries. However, if the patient is conscious, reassuring conversation can change the pulse rate by ten beats per minute. This margin could help save a person's life.

Stopped breathing is a life-threatening medical emergency, especially when accompanied by heart failure. The normal breathing rate for an adult is 12 to 18 breaths per minute (for children, 20 to 30 breaths per minute). Normal breathing at rest is regular, quiet, and moderately deep. The chest rises and falls with each breath, and air movement can be heard or felt at the nose and mouth. (The rate and depth will increase with exertion.) If a victim is unconscious, or if his breathing is shallow or uneven, be prepared to administer artificial respiration (see pp. 190–191).

Skin temperature is measured at the victim's forehead—as long as this area is not injured. Use the back of your hand to feel if the skin is warm, cool, or normal. At the same time, notice if the skin is dry or moist. Look for "goose bumps," which are associated with chills. Cool, moist skin can indicate such conditions as shock, fever, drug reaction, or heat illness.

Keep track of these vital signs as you care for an injured person, and report them to the ambulance team when help arrives. Also note any *symptoms*—feelings of discomfort due to heat, cold, pain, nausea, or other abnormal sensations. (A total lack of sensation is also a symptom.) Even if you cannot treat an injury, your careful observations may save a doctor precious minutes in diagnosis and treatment.

Taking a pulse rate

 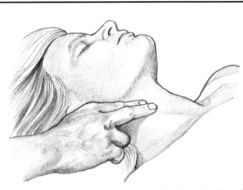

The pulse of an accident victim should be taken for a full minute. Note its strength and rhythm as well as its speed. The *radial pulse (above)*, taken at the wrist, is the most common point for measuring a conscious adult's pulse. Place the tips of one or two fingers on the thumb side of the forearm, about 2.5 cm (1 in.) above the creases of the wrist and about 1.25 cm (1/2 in.) from the top of the forearm. Press down lightly until a pulse is felt. Do not use your thumb; it has a pulse of its own and may confuse the reading.

The *carotid pulse* is preferred when checking the heart rate of an unconscious person, during artificial respiration, or when there are injuries to the arms (and a radial pulse would be inaccurate). To take a carotid pulse, locate the Adam's apple at the front of the neck with two fingertips. Slide the fingers back along the side nearest you to locate the carotid artery between the neck muscle and the trachea (windpipe). Do not feel for or compress both carotid arteries at the same time.

Checklist of first-aid supplies

Assemble a car first-aid kit *now*, before you need it in an emergency. Don't add these items to the jumble in the medicine cabinet. Instead, gather medical supplies in a suitably labeled box so that everything will be handy when needed. A tight plastic container, such as a fishing-tackle box or small tool chest, will protect medicine and sterile dressings from dust and moisture.

Clearly label everything in the box, and indicate what each item should be used for. Do *not* lock the box; otherwise, you may have to hunt for the key when seconds count. Tuck the kit into the glove compartment or trunk, away from children, and keep it there. On long car trips, be sure to include medicines for any particular ailments of individual family members, such as allergies, asthma, or motion sickness. Most important, know how and under what circumstances to apply each treatment. A small dab of petroleum jelly, for example, may soothe a minor burn or chafe. However, greasy lotions should never be applied to serious burns.

Remember that drugs do not last indefinitely. They may lose their potency, or they may evaporate to concentrations that can be harmful. Keep all bottles tightly stoppered. Don't keep any prescription drugs left over from a previous illness. Discard any drug that has changed color or consistency, especially old iodine, eye drops, cough remedies, and ointments. Check your first-aid kit before each long trip, and remember to restock any items you use.

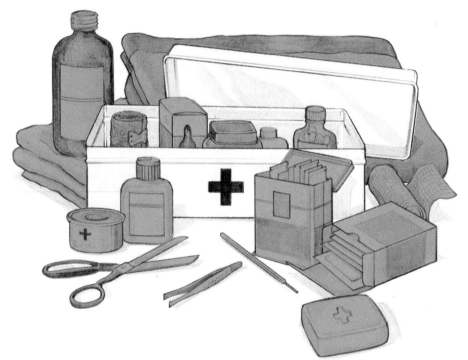

Dressings. Sterile gauze, 10 x 10 cm (4 x 4 in.) for cleaning and covering wounds.

Adhesive tape for securing dressings.

Bandages. Large triangular bandage for sling and head injuries; gauze roller bandage for securing dressings over other wounds; wide elastic bandage for sprains; box of assorted adhesive bandages for minor cuts and scrapes.

Tourniquet. Use only as a last resort for badly wounded or severed limbs.

Antiseptic. Mild cleansing agent such as iodine or mercurial antiseptic (mild solution), or rubbing alcohol. Replace with fresh antiseptic occasionally.

Calamine lotion or baking soda for relief from sunburn, insect bites, and rashes.

Petroleum jelly for minor burns and scrapes, sunburn, chapped lips, and dry skin.

Aromatic spirits of ammonia for fainting spells.

Scissors for cutting gauze, bandages, and clothing.

Tweezers or packet of needles for removing splinters.

Thermometer (oral) for measuring a victim's temperature.

Aspirin or aspirin substitute for headache or fever.

Disinfectant soap to clean and sterilize hands.

Wooden splints. Two boards or pieces of heavy cardboard measuring 10 x 75 cm (4 x 30 in.) for leg fractures; two measuring 8 x 35 cm (3 x 14 in.) for fractured arms.

Blanket to cover an injured person or serve as a makeshift stretcher.

Medicine dropper (eye dropper).

The critical first few minutes

You need not stand helplessly by at the scene of an automobile accident. Knowing what to do—as well as what *not* to do—could help save someone's life.

If you come upon a serious automobile collision, your first priority is to prevent further accidents. Switch off the vehicle's ignition and warn people not to smoke. Alert oncoming traffic, and set up flares or other signals if the location is dangerous and victims cannot be immediately moved (see pp. 172–173). If possible, send someone to call for an ambulance and notify the police. Be sure they tell the dispatcher:
- the exact location of the incident;
- the nature of the injuries, if known;
- whether people are trapped in a vehicle;
- whether other rescuers have been called to the scene. Should a trained first-aider, nurse, or doctor arrive, turn the responsibility over to him or her and offer your help.

If you are the only one who can help, exercise your own sound judgment. As a general rule, do what you can for the injured at the scene, but wait for police or an ambulance before moving the victims.

Quickly examine the casualties to determine the extent of injuries, then help each one in order of urgency. Give *first priority* to those victims requiring immediate treatment for such life-threatening conditions as stopped breathing, severe bleeding, and unconsciousness. Give *second priority* to those whose injuries are serious but for whom treatment may be deferred. These include victims with burns, fractures, and back problems. The *third priority* is for those with minor fractures, minor bleeding, behavioral problems and other lesser injuries.

As you approach each injured person, think of these ABC's:

A is for airway. Make sure that the victim's airway has not been blocked by the tongue or some foreign object (such as chewing gum or food). If the victim has vomited and there is no evidence of neck injury, turn the head to one side to prevent choking. If you suspect the airway is blocked, lift the tongue away from the back of the throat to let air reach the lungs and restore spontaneous breathing. Wipe the mouth clean of vomit, food, or saliva. If the victim has dentures and they are loose, remove them.

B is for breathing. Lean close to the victim's face and check for signs of breathing. Look, listen, and feel for air exchange. If respiration has stopped, apply mouth-to-mouth resuscitation immediately (see pp. 190–191).

C is for circulation. Check the victim's responses by tapping on the shoulder and shouting, "Are you all right?" Consciousness means the blood is circulating. If there is no response, check the pulse. If there is no pulse, administer cardiopulmonary resuscitation, *but only if you are trained to do so* (see p. 199). The well-meaning but untrained person who attempts this procedure may do more harm than good. Finally, stop all heavy bleeding (see pp. 192–193). Remember that *any* bleeding, if allowed to continue, will eventually prove life-threatening.

Examine all victims for injuries, even those who appear only "shaken up." Listen to complaints of pain and descriptions of how the injuries occurred, and gather pertinent information about allergies, medical problems, and medications. This can provide valuable information to pass on when medical assistance arrives. Carefully cut clothing away from cuts and fractures if necessary, but avoid abrupt movement, which may add to the victim's pain. *Never* pull clothing away from serious burns.

Give necessary first aid at once, inside the vehicle whenever possible. Do not move the injured person unless necessary to avoid further danger, such as fire, explosion, or the threat of a second accident. Movement increases pain, causes bleeding, and, if the injury involves the spine, may result in paralysis. If you must extricate a trapped victim, or move him away from the vehicle, always keep his neck and back as straight as possible (see pp. 206–207).

Keep the injured as comfortable as possible. To prevent shock, see to it that the victim is warm, but do not apply external heat. If the ground is cold, lay a heavy coat or blanket beneath the person. Elevate and support the legs 20 to 25 cm (8 to 10 inches) to promote circulation. Do not give fluids, alcohol, or medication of any kind unless directed by a doctor. Remember that your calmness can allay the victim's fears, and convince him or her that everything is under control. Protect and reassure the victim until assistance arrives.

Unless there is no alternative, only qualified first-aiders, nurses, doctors, and ambulance attendants should transport an injured person to the hospital. Even a short trip in the back of a station wagon or the bed of a truck can result in more serious injury.

Finally, never assume that an accident victim is dead—this is an assessment for the authorities to make. Coming upon a serious accident can be a shocking experience. Even if you are unable to help the injured, you can be of great help by warning other drivers and sending for help.

The recovery position

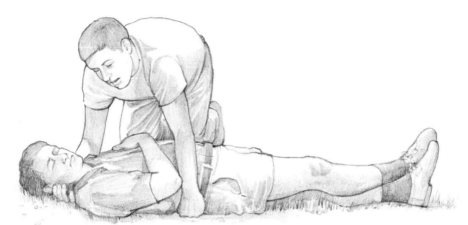

An injured person may suffocate if left lying in the face-up position. If their injuries permit, victims who must be left unattended should be placed carefully in the *recovery position*. Kneel at the person's side and bring the far leg toward you to cross at the ankles.

Tuck the arm and hand nearest you along the victim's side; lay the other arm across his chest. Make every movement slowly and gently. **Caution:** If the victim's pain is too great, or if spinal injuries are suspected, do not continue.

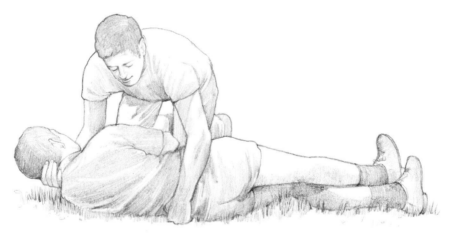

Place your knees close to the victim, reach under the head to support it, and grip the clothing or belt at the hip on the opposite side. Roll the person toward you in one smooth, firm motion, protecting the head and

neck during the roll. Bring the chest and abdomen to rest on your thighs. Move back and bend the victim's upper leg slightly toward you to prevent the body from rolling forward.

Position the head so that the neck is extended and the airway remains open. Bend the arm nearest you at the elbow to support the upper body. Lay the other arm alongside the victim to keep him from rolling over on

his back. Wait a moment, then check the victim's breathing and pulse rate. If they appear stable, he may be left unattended while you summon help or attend to other casualties.

The breath of life

Every second counts when an accident victim has stopped breathing. If you cannot feel or hear air being inhaled or exhaled, and the person's chest does not move up or down, act quickly. When oxygen is not being circulated to the body, permanent damage may occur within minutes.

Opening the airway may be all that is needed to clear the tongue from the back of the throat and restore breathing. Place the edge of one hand on the victim's forehead and press backward. Place the other hand under the neck and lift gently. If possible, place a firm object high up between the shoulder blades to help extend the victim's neck. If neck injuries are suspected, do not tilt the head back. This may cause further injury to the spine. Instead, use the jaw thrust without head tilt (see p. 196).

"Direct" methods of artificial respiration supply the lungs with the greatest volume of air, and should be considered first. *Mouth-to-mouth* resuscitation, the most basic procedure, is described below. The *mouth-to-mouth-and-nose* method is preferred for small children and infants. The key to this technique is to make a tight seal over *both* the mouth and nose. Use gentle puffs of air rather than full breaths, and repeat the procedure about once every three seconds (20 times per minute).

Whatever direct method is used, always start by giving four full breaths as quickly as possible to inflate the victim's lungs. If the

---

Mouth-to-mouth artificial respiration

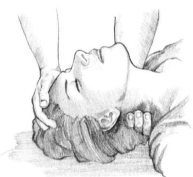

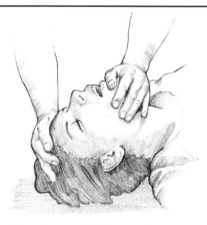

1. Place the victim on his back, and loosen restrictive clothing around the neck, chest, and waist. Remove any foreign matter from the mouth with your fingers. Place your hand under the victim's neck and lift gently to tilt back the head.

2. Lift the chin upward. This moves the tongue away from the back of the throat and clears the air passage. If breathing does not start spontaneously when the airway is cleared, begin mouth-to-mouth technique immediately.

3. Press your open mouth firmly over the victim's mouth, making a tight seal, and pinch the nostrils. Deliver four quick breaths without allowing the patient's lungs to deflate between breaths. This forces them to fill rapidly and saturates the blood with oxygen.

4. Break contact with the victim's mouth, allowing air to flow from the lungs. Listen for air coming out of the mouth and look for the fall of the chest. Breathe again, then check for exhalation. Repeat this cycle every five seconds (12 times per minute) for an adult.

chest does not rise, start again by repositioning the head and making a tight seal over the victim's mouth (or nose and mouth). If the lungs inflate after four quick breaths, check the carotid pulse (see p. 186) to determine if there is a heartbeat (and recheck it every five minutes). If a pulse cannot be felt, administer cardiopulmonary resuscitation, but only if you are trained to do so.

"Indirect" or manual methods of artificial respiration supply air to the lungs by physical compression and expansion of the chest. Although these methods are not as effective as direct artificial respiration, they can be life-saving alternatives.

The *Holger Nielson method* (described below) is recommended for casualties with severe facial injuries. It should *not* be used for obese persons, women in advanced stages of pregnancy, or casualties with back injuries. For children age five and over, pressure on the shoulder blades should be reduced and applied with the fingertips only. For children under five, the arms should be placed at the sides. Hold the child's shoulders between your thumbs and fingers, and apply thumb pressure to start exhalation. Then lift the shoulders to expand the chest. Repeat this cycle every four seconds (15 times per minute).

Don't give up—some victims have been revived only after several hours. Once revived, the injured should be covered with a blanket and kept quiet until help arrives.

Holger Nielson (back-pressure—arm lift) method

Place the victim face down with the hands under the forehead. Turn the head to one side. Placing soft padding under the head will tilt the chin and help maintain an open airway. Clear the nose and mouth of obstructions, and position yourself on one knee at the victim's head. Place your hands on the victim's back, spreading your fingers between the shoulder blades, and begin the following cycle:

1. Lean forward slowly until your arms are vertical. Apply just enough pressure to force air out of the lungs (*right*).

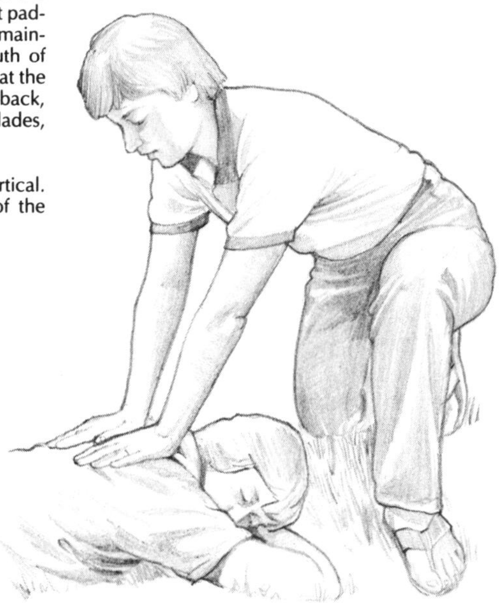

2. Rock back, sliding your hands past the shoulders, and grip the upper arms near the elbows.

3. Continue rocking back, raising and pulling the victim's elbows until you feel tension (*left*). Do not lift the victim's chest from the ground.

4. Lower the victim's arms and slide your hands back to the shoulders to begin the expiration phase again. Each cycle should take about five seconds (12 per minute) for an adult.

Four steps to control severe bleeding

The average adult's body contains five and a half to seven litres of blood. Since the loss of more than a half litre can be life-threatening, severe bleeding must be controlled quickly. First, have the victim lie down to reduce circulation, and be alert to signs of shock. Keep him or her calm—this will reduce the pulse rate and slow the flow of blood from the wound. Use one of the following procedures, and whatever materials are at hand, to control severe external bleeding:

• *Direct pressure.* Most external bleeding can be stopped by applying direct pressure to the wound *(below).* Ideally, a sterile dressing or clean cloth should be used, but don't waste precious time searching for a clean bandage. If immediate action is necessary, place your hand directly over the wound and apply firm pressure.

• *Elevation.* If the wound is on the hand, arm, leg, or head, carefully raise and support it above the level of the heart to reduce the flow of blood. **Caution:** Elevate a wound only if injuries permit.

• *Pressure points.* If bleeding from an arm or leg cannot be stopped by direct pressure or elevation, try shutting off circulation in the artery supplying the blood by pressing firmly against it with your hand or fingers *(below).* **Caution:** Do not use arterial pressure for wounds of the head, neck, or torso.

• *Tourniquet.* If all other methods fail to stem the bleeding, use a tourniquet only as a last resort. A tourniquet is a hazardous first-aid measure; you run the risk of causing the eventual loss of the limb from which you are cutting off the blood.

Internal bleeding may result from fractures, puncture wounds, or blows to the head, chest, or abdomen. Although its effects are serious, internal bleeding is difficult for a first-aider to detect and care for. Bleeding from the nose, mouth, or ears; vomiting; and the symptoms of shock all point to internal injuries. The most important step is to prevent shock by placing the victim in the recovery position (see p. 189); loosening clothing around the neck, chest, and

Steps to control bleeding

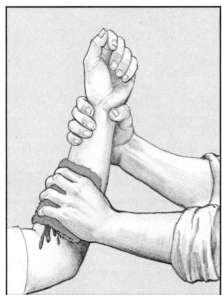

Direct pressure and elevation. For severe external bleeding, try this method first. Apply firm, constant pressure directly to the wound using a sterile dressing, or the cleanest cloth at hand. If the wound is on the arm or leg, elevate the limb (if injuries permit). Do not dab at the wound, and do not lift the dressing every few seconds to see if the bleeding has stopped. If the dressing becomes soaked with blood, lay a fresh cloth over the saturated one and continue pressure. When the bleeding stops, bandage the dressings firmly in place—but not so tightly that you cannot feel the pulse below the wound.

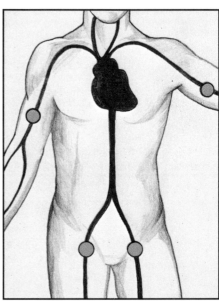

Pressure points. There are four points *(above)* where arterial pressure is practical for first-aiders. For bleeding from the arm, extend the victim's arm and lay it at a right angle to the body. Place your fingers in the groove below the bicep muscle, and press against the artery here. Bleeding should stop, and you should no longer feel a wrist pulse.

For wounds of the leg, locate the femoral artery, midway along the crease where the thigh joins the torso. (You should feel a pulse here.) Apply firm pressure with the heel of your hand. Bleeding should stop, and you should no longer feel a foot pulse.

waist; and keeping the victim quiet until help arrives. If possible, keep a record of the injured person's breathing and pulse rates, and any changes in condition.

Puncture wounds require special care, because the object may have damaged internal tissues and carried contamination deep into the wound. Some puncture wounds may have both an entry *and* exit wound. Such injuries usually cause internal damage and severe bleeding. Do not remove objects that are deeply embedded. Instead, spread your fingers around the object and apply pressure to the wound site, or use a ring pad (see p. 196). Cover the wound loosely with several layers of dressings, cloths, or handkerchiefs (take care not to put pressure on the object). If you have ice, apply a cold compress to reduce swelling, relieve pain, and slow absorption of toxicity. Get the patient to a doctor, who will clean the wound and take steps to prevent tetanus.

Cuts, scratches, and abrasions may not appear serious, but dirt imbedded in the skin may cause infection. If possible, wash your hands thoroughly with soap and water before treating any wound. Clean the skin around the wound, and then the wound itself, in the same way. To avoid contamination, wash away from the wound, not toward it. If it is necessary to use tweezers to remove debris, boil them for ten minutes, or sterilize them in the flame of several matches and wipe the carbon away with sterile gauze. Cover the wound with sterile gauze, or the cleanest cloth available, held in place by a bandage or adhesive tape.

With any wound there is always a danger of tetanus (lockjaw); in deep wounds, the threat is serious. Try to find out if the victim has been immunized, and how recently, so that the doctor can determine proper treatment. Tell the victim to watch for these signs of infection (which may not appear for several days): a reddened, painful area surrounding the wound; swelling around the wound; chills or fever. If infection should appear, he or she should see a doctor at once.

Tourniquet—bandage of last resort

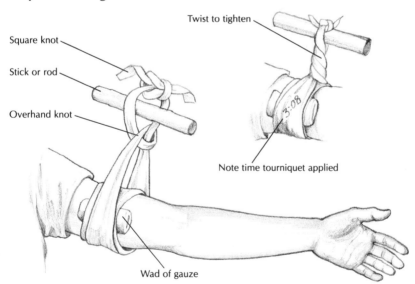

Twist to tighten

Square knot

Stick or rod

Overhand knot

Note time tourniquet applied

Wad of gauze

Use a tourniquet—which cuts off the blood supply to the wound site—for severe injuries such as amputations, and only after other measures have failed. Apply a tourniquet as close to the wound as possible.

Place a thick wad of gauze or cloth over the artery on the inside of the arm or thigh. Do not allow the tourniquet to touch the wound. Wrap a long strip of fabric tightly around the limb, and make a simple overhand knot. Put a strong stick (or similar object) on the knot, and tie a square knot.

Slowly twist the stick to tighten the tourniquet just enough to stop the flow of blood to the wound. Tie the stick to the injured limb with the loose ends of the cloth strip, and make a written note of the time (preferably on the tourniquet itself). This step is important—the physician will want to know how long the blood flow has been stopped. Do not loosen the tourniquet if the victim will receive medical aid within one hour. Otherwise, loosen the tourniquet hourly. When the tourniquet is loose, apply constant pressure to the wound. If bleeding does not resume, leave the tourniquet loose but in place until help arrives. If you can estimate how much blood has been lost, this information may help the doctor.

Protecting an Injury

Before bandaging a wound, you should cover it with a sterile (or clean as possible) dressing. Dressings should be compressible, thick and soft (so that pressure can be applied evenly to the wound), and absorbent (to keep the wound dry). Gauze, cotton, or linen dressings will not stick to the wound; wool or other fluffy materials—such as cotton balls—are not suitable.

A bandage may be any prepared or improvised material that is used to hold a dressing in place, secure a splint, or support a limb. It should be snug enough to hold the dressing securely in place, but not so tight that it restricts circulation. Never place a bandage directly on a wound—especially a severe burn—without a dressing. Be careful, too, not to leave any loose ends. When the patient is moved, loose tape, dressing, or cloth might snag and tear open the bandage. As a general rule, do not cover the tips of fingers or toes—they are good indicators of circulation. Cold skin and complaints about numbness, pain, or tingling all indicate that the bandage is too tight and must be loosened immediately.

Arm and leg injuries

The *roller bandage,* either the clinging or open-weave type, may be used in various ways to hold a dressing in place over a wound. When it is applied in a simple spiral, each turn of the bandage should overlap the previous turn. Anchor the bandage at the first turn by holding the end of the bandage, making one wrap, and allowing a corner to protrude. Fold the corner over the first wrap, then make another wrap to secure it.

Foot injuries. Wind a narrow (2.5 cm or 1 in.) bandage two or three times around the instep and up around the ankle. When the injury is covered, split the bandage for about 25 cm (10 in.). Secure the ends with an overhand knot. Bring the ends around the ankle and secure with a double knot.

Leg and arm injuries. Make several turns around the injured limb, then twist the bandage after each revolution. This herringbone pattern will not slip or loosen as easily as a conventional wrap. When the injury is covered, again make several straight turns, then split the bandage and secure the loose ends. Bring the ends around the bandaged limb and tie them.

Another indispensable first-aid item is the *triangular bandage,* two of which can be made by cutting a one-metre square of cloth from corner to corner. When open, the bandage can be used as a sling or to hold a large dressing in place. Folded, it can serve as a bandage or ring pad.

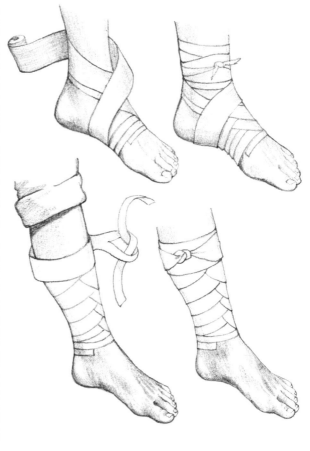

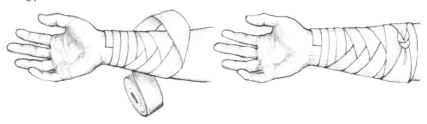

Hand injuries

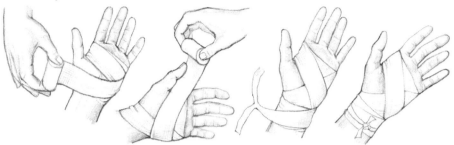

Cover the wound with a thick dressing and wrap a narrow roller bandage around the palm, then around the wrist for several turns. Split the bandage and secure the ends with an overhand knot. Bring the ends around the bandaged wrist and secure with a double knot. As an alternative, have the victim close his fingers over the dressing and make a fist to put pressure on the wound. Bandage the clenched hand.

Head injuries

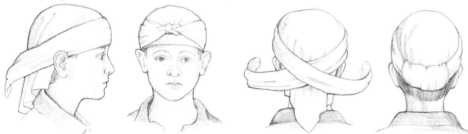

Make a 5-cm (2-in.) fold along the base of a triangular bandage. Put the bandage, point downward at the back, on the victim's head, covering the dressing. Bring the two ends around the back of the head and above the ears. Cross the ends and continue around the head to tie them with a secure knot above the eyes. Draw the point of the bandage down to put the desired pressure on the dressing.

The St. John tubular sling

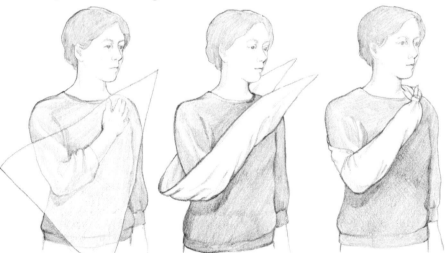

This sling, which transfers weight to the uninjured side, is used to support the hand and forearm in a raised position. Place the injured forearm diagonally across the chest, fingers pointing toward the opposite shoulder. Next, lay an open triangular bandage over the hand and forearm, with its point hanging well below the elbow. Support the forearm and ease the base of the bandage under the hand, forearm, and elbow.

Pass the lower corner across the back and over the shoulder of the uninjured side. Gently adjust the height of the arm as you tie off or pin the ends of the bandage above the collarbone.

Improvised slings can be made by placing the hand inside a buttoned jacket; supporting the arm with a scarf, belt, or necktie; or pinning up the sleeve of a shirt or jacket.

How to recognize and care for broken bones

A fracture is any break or crack in a bone, and is a common consequence of an automobile collision. Fractures can be caused by direct force (an arm or leg smashing into the dashboard), or by indirect force (such as fractures of the collarbone caused by a fall on an outstretched arm). *Closed fractures* are breaks over which surrounding skin is unbroken. *Open fractures*, in which the broken bone protrudes through the skin, are more serious. The bone ends may have torn open veins, arteries, or internal organs, causing further injury that is often more serious than the fracture itself.

Suspect a fracture if the injury was caused by some external force, such as being thrown from the car, or if any of the following symptoms are present:

• pain and tenderness near the injury, aggravated by movement of the injured part;
• swelling in the tissues surrounding the fracture (which may camouflage other signs);
• loss of function of the injured part, usually caused by pain or swelling (even if the victim can move an injured arm or leg, don't assume that it is not broken);
• deformity (any unnatural shape or angle of a limb or joint);
• grating—a painful sensation felt when the ends of the bones accidentally rub together;
• shock, increasing with the severity of the injury;
• loss of foot or wrist pulse.

The first priority for fracture injuries is to keep the victim still and treat for shock (see p. 204). Do not move the person unless absolutely necessary, even if it means treating the fracture in the automobile. Do not try to set a broken bone, or to push a protruding bone back under the skin. If it is necessary to remove clothing, cut it away or fold it back. Do not remove clothing by pulling it over an injured arm or leg. Stem any bleeding by applying indirect pressure to the wound, or use a *ring pad*. Make a large loop around one hand by passing one end of a narrow bandage twice around the four fingers. Pass the other end through the loop and wrap around it until the entire bandage is used and a firm ring dressing is formed.

Emotional support is as important as first aid in treating a fracture victim, whose injuries are often painful and frightening. Remind the person that fractures can be set in the hospital and that bones will heal with time. This reassurance may help the victim rest, and will lower the blood pressure and breathing rate. If you must move a victim yourself, immobilize a fractured bone by splinting it *(right)*. Use whatever rigid ma-

terial you have at hand—a piece of wood or stiff cardboard, a broom handle, an umbrella, or a firmly folded newspaper or magazine. An uninjured part of the body makes an excellent natural splint.

Pad the splint with soft cloth and bind it firmly in place with bandages, belts, or strips of cloth. The bandages should be wide enough to provide support without discomfort, and knotted on the uninjured side or over the splint. Check the limb every 15 minutes or so to make sure the bandages have not become too tight because of swelling. Loosen the bandages if the injured part becomes more painful or cool to the touch, or loses color. Parts of the body that are bandaged together should be separated with soft padding to prevent friction and discomfort.

Head and spine injuries.
First aiders should be quick to recognize injuries to the head and spine because of their life-threatening complications. Proper handling of such injuries in the first minutes after an accident could mean the difference between a fracture and paralysis or death.

Symptoms of skull fracture include a swollen, bruised or lacerated scalp; blood or straw-colored liquid coming from the ears or nose; black eyes; swelling and bruising of the lower jaw; and unconsciousness. First, check the victim's breathing and make sure that the airway is open. If neck injuries are suspected, however, do not tilt the head back. Instead, place the hands on both sides of the casualty's head, keeping the head and neck in a fixed position. Place the index finger of each hand alongside the lower jaw and lift upward. Use the thumbs to depress the lower lip and to keep the mouth open. Control bleeding with direct pressure, and protect any bumps or depressions with a soft, thick dressing. If blood or fluid is coming from the ear, apply a sterile dressing, and tape or bandage it lightly in position. Lean the victim's head to the injured side to allow fluids to drain.

If there is a head injury, suspect a back injury. Spinal fractures may be accompanied by a loss of sensation in the arms and legs. Touch the victim's hands and feet and ask if there is feeling. If the victim is unconscious, monitor the breathing closely and continuously. If breathing stops, open the airway without tilting the head (as described above) and give artificial respiration. Do not attempt to straighten the victim. Any unnecessary movement could cause permanent damage. Loosen restrictive clothing, cover the person, and wait for medical help.

Immobilizing a fracture

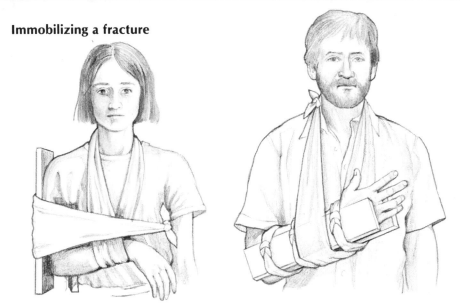

A properly applied splint should prevent movement of the bone ends, reduce damage to surrounding tissue, and lessen pain. It can also help closed fractures from becoming open fractures. Make a splint long enough to reach beyond the joints above and below the fracture, and wide enough to fit comfortably against the limb.

For fractures of the shoulder, collarbone, and upper arm *(above left)*, a sling and bandage are recommended. Tuck the wrist into a sling to ease the weight on the injured arm (the tubular sling is best). Then immobilize the fracture with a splint secured by a bandage tied around the victim's chest.

Fractures of the forearm or wrist can be immobilized in a simple splint *(above right)* and supported with a sling. Be sure to secure the knots away from the injury so they will not cause pain or interfere with circulation. For a finger fracture, simply tape the broken finger to an adjacent, uninjured finger, or use a tongue depressor or ice cream stick as a splint.

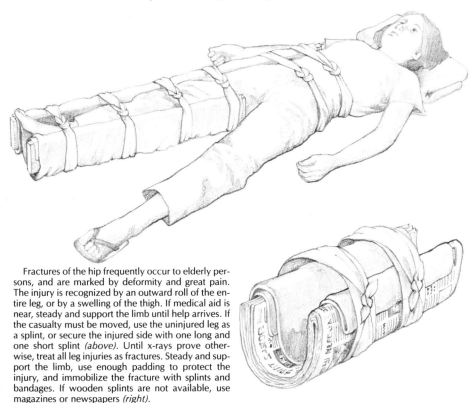

Fractures of the hip frequently occur to elderly persons, and are marked by deformity and great pain. The injury is recognized by an outward roll of the entire leg, or by a swelling of the thigh. If medical aid is near, steady and support the limb until help arrives. If the casualty must be moved, use the uninjured leg as a splint, or secure the injured side with one long and one short splint *(above)*. Until x-rays prove otherwise, treat all leg injuries as fractures. Steady and support the limb, use enough padding to protect the injury, and immobilize the fracture with splints and bandages. If wooden splints are not available, use magazines or newspapers *(right)*.

Emergency medical care

Amputation

The violent impact of an automobile collision can sever limbs and other body parts. Treatment of such terrifying injuries depends on your ability to control panic—both yours and the victim's.

First, stem the flow of blood, which may be severe, from the wound (see pp. 192–193). If a limb has been severed, a tourniquet may be necessary. Once the bleeding has been reduced, you can care for the amputated part, which should be preserved, regardless of its condition. Surgeons may be able to reattach a finger, hand, or foot if the part is well preserved. A partially ampu-

tated part should be kept as near as possible to its normal position; covered with a sterile dressing, bandaged, and supported; and kept cool with an ice bag or cold compress.

A completely amputated part should be gently wrapped in sterile gauze or the cleanest cloth available and placed in an airtight container such as a plastic bag or sandwich box (do not moisten the tissue). If it's summer and there is ice in the picnic cooler, pack it around the bag to keep the severed part cool. In winter, snow will work just as well. Make a record of the time at which you cared for the injury.

Behavioral problems

Victims of automobile accidents can sometimes behave abnormally—possibly as a result of alcohol or drug intoxication. Hysteria, overactivity, depression, or aggressive behavior can mask serious physical injuries and hinder treatment. First aid for psychological casualties is limited, however. The first-aider should calm a disturbed victim *before* caring for injuries or sending for help. If there are several casualties involved and one begins to panic, isolate him or her from the group to prevent mass hysteria. If it is necessary to restrain a victim for the safety of others, act quickly but humanely with the help of bystanders.

Emotional anxiety or stress can frequently trigger *hyperventilation*. In this condition, a victim unknowingly breathes too rapidly, upsetting the normal oxygen and carbon dioxide balance in the body. The result is tingling and spasms of the fingers and toes, and numbness around the mouth. These symptoms often make the victim still more anxious, and more hyperventilation results. Try to calm and reassure a person who is hyperventilating. If this does not help, have him or her breathe slowly for ten minutes into a paper (not plastic) bag held firmly over the mouth and nose. If this does not work, get the victim to a hospital.

Bites and stings

In most people, an insect bite or sting produces only a mildly painful swelling, accompanied by redness and itching. However, an allergic person reacts violently to insect stings and may display signs of shock, including breathing difficulty, nausea and vomiting, and coldness. Help the person to take any prescribed allergy medication, remove the stinger by carefully scraping it from the skin (avoid squeezing the stinger, which will inject more venom), and treat the wound with cold compresses. If the sting is in the mouth or throat, watch carefully for

breathing difficulties. Place the victim in the recovery position—or any position that makes breathing easier. Seek medical help immediately.

Soothe the discomfort of minor insect bites with calamine lotion or antihistamine lotion. For bee stings, carefully scrape the stinger out with a clean knife, razor blade, or fingernail. Apply a solution of ammonia and water to ease the pain. For wasp stings, apply a solution of lemon juice or vinegar. If the sting is in the mouth, have the victim swill a solution of baking soda and cold water.

Burns

To treat localized surface burns, gently remove clothing from around the wound (but leave it if it sticks to the burn). Remove rings, bracelets, or shoes before swelling begins. Immerse the burn immediately in cold water to relieve pain and reduce swelling and blistering. Alternatively, soak a clean cloth in water and apply it directly to the injury.

Cover the burn with a sterile dressing or clean, lint-free cloth. Do *not* apply lotions, ointments, or oily dressings. Doctors must always scrape away such applications. If the burn is major, monitor the victim's breathing and give artificial respiration if needed, cover the burned area lightly with a clean dressing, and treat for shock.

Corrosive chemicals continue to burn as long as they remain on the skin. Flush a chemical immediately with water. Continue flooding until the chemical has been completely washed away. Apply a clean dressing as for thermal burns and get medical help. Do not apply chemical neutralizers to the burn unless advised to do so by a doctor.

Electrical burns can be more serious than they appear because of their internal effects. *Never* touch a casualty before disconnecting him or her from the electric current, and do not go near a live high-voltage line (call the police or electric company). If you cannot shut off the current, push the victim away with a non-conducting object (such as a long stick), or drag him away with a rope. Check for breathing and give artificial respiration if needed. If a pulse cannot be felt, give cardiopulmonary resuscitation if you are trained in this procedure. Burns, where the current entered and exited the body, should be treated. Finally, check for fractures; electrical-shock victims are often thrown violently.

Cardiopulmonary resuscitation

Caution: Cardiopulmonary resuscitation (CPR) should be applied only by rescuers trained to Canadian Heart Foundation standards. If you are untrained and attempt the technique, you may fracture a patient's ribs or damage internal organs. Approved CPR courses are offered nationwide by the Canadian Heart Foundation, St. John Ambulance, and the Canadian Red Cross.

If an accident victim's heart has stopped and he or she is no longer breathing, you and a helper—or you alone, when no one else is available—must apply CPR.

Even if you are untrained, you can still assist in an emergency: A CPR-trained rescuer may need your help to administer artificial respiration while he or she attempts to maintain circulation. To be of help, you should at least know the fundamentals of the combined technique. With the victim lying face-up, the CPR rescuer will first confirm that there is no heartbeat. (Applying CPR while the heart is still pumping can result in death.) She will then kneel beside the victim's chest and place the heel of her hand (never the palm) against the center of the breastbone. She will rest her other hand on top of the first and interlock her fingers. With a quick, firm thrust, the rescuer will push down with enough pressure to compress the lower breastbone. She will repeat the rhythmic compression approximately once per second to squeeze the victim's heart, forcing blood out to his body.

You, meanwhile, should kneel at the victim's head. Tilt the head back to maintain a clear airway, then give mouth-to-mouth resuscitation once every five chest compressions. You can also assist in CPR by monitoring the carotid (neck) pulse after each compression. Once a strong, regular pulse returns, advise the CPR rescuer. Continue artificial respiration until the victim can breathe normally on his own.

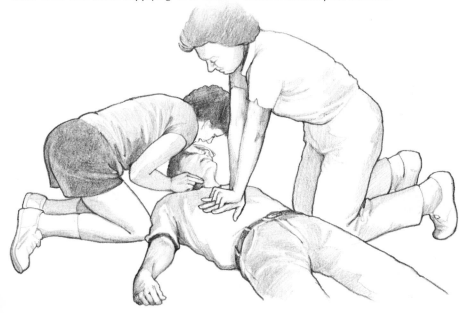

Choking

From the moment that food or other objects are lodged in the windpipe and cut off oxygen, the victim has four to five minutes to live. If the person cannot talk, he is probably choking and you must take immediate action. Treatment consists of three maneuvers: back blows, manual thrusts, and finger sweeps. The methods are described separately; in practice they are applied in rapid sequence.

Back blows are a series of four sharp blows given with the heel of the hand to the area between the victim's shoulder blades. (Remember to use less force for children or older people.)

Abdominal thrusts *(below)* are a series of four quick, inward and upward compressions of the upper abdomen. If the victim can stand, get behind him and wrap your arms around his waist (and under his arms). Make a fist with one hand and place it, thumb side in, above the victim's navel and below the rib cage. Grasp your fist with the other hand and press into the victim's upper abdomen with a quick, upward thrust. Repeat this maneuver four times. If the victim is sitting, stand behind him and proceed in the same manner. **Caution:** Do not use abdominal thrusts on pregnant women or obese people, or for choking infants or children.

If the victim becomes unconscious, place him on his back, open the airway, and try to ventilate the lungs with four quick breaths. If the lungs do not inflate, roll the victim against your knees and give four back blows. Next, roll the casualty on his back and give four chest thrusts *(below)*. Finally, sweep the mouth clear of loose objects, open the airway, and ventilate the lungs. If the lungs fail to inflate, repeat the back blows, chest thrusts, finger sweeps and ventilations until successful or until medical help arrives.

If you are alone and choking, try anything that applies force to your abdomen or chest. Press down onto the edge of a table or sink, or use your own fist to force air from the lungs and ''pop'' the obstruction.

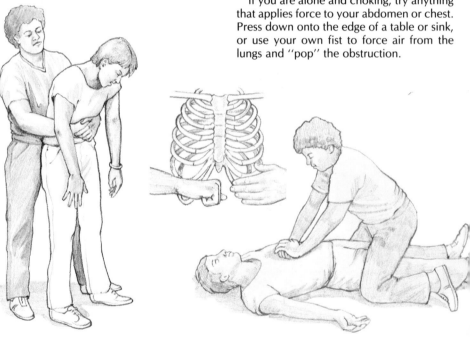

Convulsions

Convulsions, or seizures, are violent attacks. They may be triggered by head injuries, brain diseases, drug reactions, or by chronic conditions such as epilepsy. In convulsive attacks, the victim's lips may turn blue, the eyes roll upward, the teeth clench tightly, and the body may be wracked by uncontrollable spasms. Such seizures usually last only a minute or two; they rarely last more than five minutes.

First aid for such patients is aimed at preventing injury. Do *not* try to restrain convulsive movements, although this may be your first reaction. Place the victim on the floor, and turn the head to one side to allow saliva to drain. Move sharp objects or any source of danger away from the victim. Do not force the teeth apart, or put anything in the victim's mouth. After the seizure, the victim may be in need of reassurance and rest.

Diabetic emergencies

If someone becomes confused, incoherent, or unconscious for no apparent reason, the person may be a diabetic who is either having an insulin reaction or going into a diabetic coma.

Insulin shock occurs suddenly when the victim has more insulin in the system than is needed and the blood-sugar level becomes dangerously low. Symptoms include paleness, shallow breathing, trembling, confusion; later, rapid pulse, "intoxicated" or aggressive behavior, faintness, and unconsciousness. If the victim is conscious and can swallow, give orange juice or a soft drink; if neither is available, give pure sugar or candy. If the person is unconscious, do not try to force-feed solid or liquid food—this could cause choking. Get the victim to a doctor immediately.

Diabetic coma can occur when a diabetic has taken too little insulin or too much food, or has had much more or much less physical activity than usual—all possible effects of long car trips. Symptoms include a flushed face, dry skin and tongue, great thirst, a weak and rapid pulse, and labored breathing. The breath may smell of acetone (not unlike the odor of nail-polish remover). If the diabetic is in a deep coma and cannot be awakened, keep him warm, monitor his breathing, give artificial respiration if necessary, and rush him to a hospital.

Eye injuries

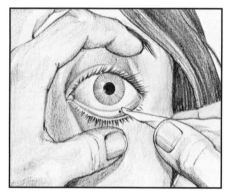 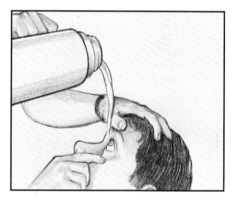

To examine an injured eye, gently pull down the lower lid and turn back the upper lid by grasping the eyelash. If a speck of dust or glass is lodged on either lid, try to remove it by touching it gently with the moistened corner of a clean cloth. If the speck is on the eye itself, do not try to remove it. Place a clean cloth over the eye and hold it lightly in place with tape. See a doctor immediately.

If gasoline, battery acid, or other strong chemical splashes on the eyes, flush them with water gently but thoroughly from the nose outward. If only a basin is handy, have the victim immerse the entire face and blink repeatedly. Milk or melted ice from the picnic cooler will also work. Cover the eyes with a clean dressing and take the patient immediately to a doctor or hospital.

Bruises to the eye are darker than on other parts of the body because of the large number of blood vessels there, and the transparency of the skin. Ease pain and swelling by applying cloths soaked in cold water. A milk, ice, or snow compress will also work. If the eyeball is bloody or the pupil is a different size than the uninjured eye, or if the victim complains of vision problems, seek medical help immediately.

Fainting

Fainting may be caused by a wide range of conditions: overheating, fatigue, hunger, or sudden emotional upset. Before a person faints, the breathing is usually weak, the face pale, and the forehead covered with beads of perspiration. Place the person on his or her back, with the head lower than the feet. Make certain that the airway is clear and that the victim is breathing. Loosen tight clothing and apply cold cloths to the face. When the person revives, give sips of warm liquid until fully recovered.

Fainting spells usually last only a minute or two. If the patient does not recover and cannot be aroused, keep him warm and covered and call for an ambulance immediately.

Frostbite and hypothermia

With frostbite, the skin turns numb and white and may even freeze solid without a person being aware of it. Thawing, however, is painful, and care is needed to avoid further damage. Keep a frostbite victim warm (but not near a stove or heater) and give warm drinks. If the frostbite is severe, get the victim to a doctor immediately.

Hypothermia results when the body temperature drops below 35°C (95°F), and is ac- companied by shivering, slowed breathing, a weak pulse, and eventual loss of con- sciousness. Remove any wet clothing and wrap the victim in dry blankets, coats, or a sleeping bag. Warm those areas where heat loss is greatest—the head, neck, chest, arm- pits, and groin. Monitor breathing and circu- lation closely and be prepared to administer artificial respiration. Carefully transport the victim to a hospital.

Head injuries

Head injuries can occur whenever there is a severe blow to the head. A conscious victim may experience dizziness, headache, nau- sea, and confusion. Other symptoms include bleeding from the mouth, nose, or ears; pu- pils of unequal size; double vision; and vom- iting. Or the victim may appear uninjured— only to lose consciousness later.

If someone has suffered a blow to the head, have him or her lie down—this re- duces the chance of hemorrhage. If the per- son is conscious, keep the head slightly raised. If the victim is unconscious, and there is no apparent spinal injury, turn the head to one side so that blood or mucus can drain from the corner of the mouth. If the scalp is bleeding, place a clean dressing over the wound and bandage it gently in place. In treating head wounds, take advan- tage of the fact that the victim's blood- soaked hair forms a natural primary dressing. Therefore, do not wash the wound or set the hair aside. In fact, if the victim's hair is long enough, take strands of hair on either side of the wound and tie them firmly together to help close the wound.

Heart attack

Automobile accidents are occasionally the result of heart attacks suffered at the wheel. The most frequent cause of such attacks is a blood clot blocking a coronary artery. The victim may complain about a tight, immobi- lizing pain across the chest, as though it were held in a vise. This pain can also extend to the arms, neck, and jaw. Symptoms may in- clude gasping and labored breathing; a weak, irregular pulse; cold, clammy skin; weakness and restlessness. Breathing may stop and the victim lapse into unconsciousness.

Your primary goal in caring for a heart attack victim is to lessen the load on the heart and ease the breathing. Do not move the patient unnecessarily, but prop up the head and shoulders in a semi-sitting position. Loosen restrictive clothing. Ask if the victim is carrying prescribed medicine. If there is no response, look for a Medic-Alert bracelet or tag, or a medical card, which may identify the exact nature of the victim's condition. If breathing stops, administer mouth-to-mouth resuscitation and monitor the carotid pulse.

If the victim's heart stops beating, the cause is cardiac arrest. The appropriate emergency treatment is cardiopulmonary re- suscitation (CPR—see p. 199). **Caution:** CPR is too hazardous to be used by anyone who has not had special training.

Heat injuries

To avoid heat injuries, resist the urge to overdo summer driving or outdoor activ- ity. Dress properly for hot weather—light- colored clothing reflects heat and sunlight, and helps your body maintain normal tem- peratures. Drink plenty of liquids. Unless you are on a salt-restricted diet, take an occasional salt tablet or salt solution when you have worked up a sweat. However, never take salt when drinking water is in short supply; the kidneys cannot handle too high a concentration of salt.

Heat cramps, characterized by painful muscle spasms and profuse sweating, are caused by excessive loss of body salts and fluids. Replace fluids by giving lightly salted water, and relieve muscle spasms by having the victim rest quietly in a cool place.

Heat exhaustion is more serious. The vic- tim, whose temperature may be about nor- mal, feels cold and clammy. Move the person out of the sun, but protect against chilling with a blanket or jacket. Have him or her lie down, with the feet elevated. Give sips of a mild salt solution. Place an unconscious victim in the recovery position and monitor breathing. Seek help immediately.

Heatstroke is the total failure of the body's temperature-control mechanism and, if left untreated, can be fatal. Symptoms include headache, dizziness, nausea, and a flushed, hot appearance. The casualty will stop sweating and the body temperature rise rapidly to a dangerously high level. Until medical help arrives, reduce the victim's body temperature as quickly as possible. Remove most of the victim's clothing, and immerse him or her in a cool bath, or sponge the body freely with rubbing alcohol or cool water. Check body temperature frequently and get the victim to a hospital at once.

Poisoning

The victim of carbon monoxide poisoning should be dragged into the open air and kept quiet to minimize oxygen consumption. If the casualty is not breathing or is breathing irregularly, use artificial respiration (see pp. 190–191). If the heart, too, has stopped, apply cardiopulmonary resuscitation, but only if you are trained in CPR.

Poisons taken by mouth often cause nausea, cramps, and vomiting. First, identify the poison. If the victim is conscious, ask what was taken, how much, and when. If the victim cannot answer, look around for the container. The best procedure is to call the local poison information center or hospital emergency room for guidance.

A person who has swallowed a corrosive poison (such as battery acid, or cleaning fluid) or a petroleum product should *not* be induced to vomit as tissues may be further damaged. Give a conscious victim water to drink; rush an unconscious victim to hospital.

If the poison is identified as nonalkaline and nonacidic—such as amphetamines, tranquilizers, sleeping pills, or antifreeze—have the victim drink as much water as possible to delay absorption. Touch the back of the throat to induce vomiting, or give syrup of ipecac—a nonprescription medicine available at any drugstore—as directed by a doctor. Get medical aid immediately.

Ensure that all poisonous chemicals around your house and garage are properly marked as such. Refer to the standard labeling system for hazardous substances *(below)*. And make certain that your children—even those too young to read—can recognize a poison by its label.

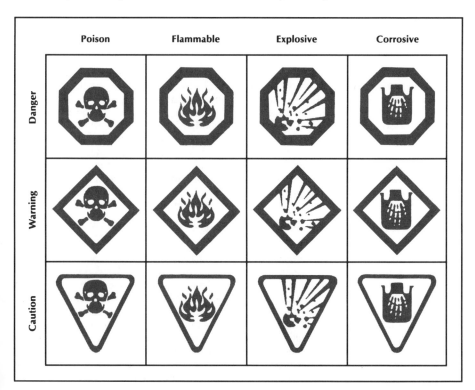

	Poison	Flammable	Explosive	Corrosive
Danger				
Warning				
Caution				

Shock

Expect some degree of shock, whether immediate or delayed, with any traffic accident or medical emergency. Symptoms of this life-threatening condition—in which the circulatory system cannot supply sufficient blood to all parts of the body—include pale and clammy skin, faint and rapid pulse, thirst, nausea, and shallow or irregular breathing. Some victims feel unusually weak or faint, others restless and apprehensive. Some lose consciousness altogether.

Since stress could trigger hyperventilation, reassure the victim. If there is breathing failure, profuse bleeding, fractures, or unconsciousness, treat these injuries immediately. Otherwise, loosen clothing around the neck, chest, and waist. Place the victim lying down with the feet higher than the rest of the body to encourage blood flow to the brain. However, if there is an injury to the head, chest, or abdomen that does not involve the spine, the head should be raised slightly, supported, and turned to one side.

Try to maintain the victim's body at normal temperature with blankets or heavy clothing. Do not use a hot-water bottle or warming pad; they dilate the blood vessels and draw blood away from vital organs (the casualty may also be unaware of excessive heat and could suffer burns). If the victim complains of thirst, wet the lips and mouth. Place an unconscious victim in the recovery position if there is no spinal damage (see p. 189). Do not give anything by mouth.

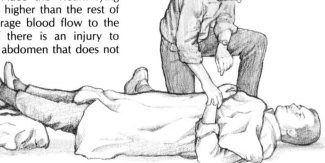

Snakebite

Because most people are terrified by snakes, anyone bitten by a snake will likely be upset and frightened. Have the victim lie quietly—movement will stimulate the blood circulation and hasten the spread of venom throughout the body. Try to identify the snake. While most Canadian snakes are harmless, poisonous snakes are found in some parts of the country.

Thoroughly flush the wound with soapy water, then support and immobilize it, keeping it lower than the heart to minimize absorption of the poison. Apply a constrictive bandage immediately between the bite and the victim's heart. Tie it tight enough to retard blood flow in the surface vessels, but not tight enough to shut off deeper vessels. If the bandage is properly adjusted, you should see some fluid oozing from the wound. Do not open the wound further, or attempt to suck the venom from the wound.

A bite from a venomous snake will cause almost immediate pain, swelling, and skin discoloration; later may come nausea, weakness, shortness of breath, and unconsciousness. Rush the victim to a hospital for an injection of anti-snakebite serum.

Stroke

A burst blood vessel in the brain (cerebral hemorrhage), or blockage in a brain artery (cerebral thrombosis and cerebral embolism), can trigger a crippling stroke. The victim may temporarily lose consciousness, suffer paralysis on one side of the body, and have difficulty speaking, swallowing, or breathing. Other symptoms include confusion, loss of bladder and bowel control, unequal pupil size, and convulsions.

Call a doctor or ambulance immediately. Before help arrives, place the victim in a semi-sitting position and prop up the head and shoulders. Loosen restrictive clothing, and keep the patient quiet and reassured. Place an unconscious victim in the recovery position (see p. 189). Make sure that the air passage is clear by bringing the tongue forward. Never use smelling salts or other stimulants to arouse a stroke victim.

Unconsciousness

Loss of consciousness indicates that something has interfered with the nervous or circulatory system. Among the many possible causes are choking, shock, drug overdose, stroke, heart attack, and loss of blood. In a state of deep unconsciousness, the pupils may be dilated and unresponsive. (If the victim does not have these symptoms and responds to gentle shaking, he or she may have merely fainted.)

First, determine the cause of unconsciousness. If you smell alcohol, the victim may be seriously intoxicated. If one side of the body is numb, stroke may be the problem. Check for heavy bleeding, fractures, concussion, or other serious injury. Examine the victim's wrist, neck, purse, or wallet for a Medic-Alert tag or medical card which specifies a medical problem. However, do not disturb or remove an unconscious stranger's personal effects or anything that may be evidence of a crime or attempted suicide.

Next, make the victim comfortable by loosening tight clothing and covering him or her with a blanket. Keep the airway clear and monitor the pulse and breathing. The unconscious casualty's muscles will relax and, if the person is lying face upward, the tongue may fall back and obstruct the airway. If there is no injury to the skull, neck, or spinal cord, move the victim to the recovery position (p. 189). Turn the head so that vomit or blood can drain from the mouth. Do not give anything to drink. If breathing fails, apply artificial respiration. If there is no pulse, apply cardiopulmonary resuscitation, but only if you are trained to do so.

The modified Glasgow Coma Scale (below) was developed to describe levels of consciousness more precisely. The assessment is based on the victim's ability to open the eyes, to speak, and to use the muscles. Use the scale to describe an injured person's condition to a doctor or ambulance attendant, such as: "Eyes open to pain, speech is confused and at times incomprehensible, and muscles flex slightly when the forearm is pinched."

Also note any changes in the victim's level of consciousness, including whether the onset was sudden or slow, or if the patient drifted in and out of consciousness.

Eye response
• Open spontaneously
• Open to speech or pain
• Do not open at all

Vocal response
• Oriented and alert
• Confused, incomprehensible
• No response at all

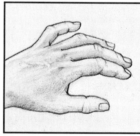

Motor response
• Obeys commands to move
• Responds to pain
• No response at all

First aid training

Canadian Heart Foundation
• *Heart Saver:* One-day course (six to eight hours) which teaches how to apply cardiopulmonary resuscitation (CPR) and other first-aid measures to heart-attack victims.

For more information, contact a branch of the Canadian Heart Foundation, or write the Canadian Heart Foundation, Suite 1200, 1 Nicolas Street, Ottawa, Ontario, K1N 7B7.

Canadian Red Cross Society
• *Standard:* About 15 hours of first aid and medical emergency instruction.
• *Emergency:* Six hours of instruction dealing with life-threatening situations.

For more information, contact a local branch or provincial office of the Red Cross, or write to Canadian Red Cross Society, 95 Wellesley Street East, Toronto, Ontario, M4Y 1H6.

St. John Ambulance
• *Standard:* A 15-hour course for those who want more than the basics of first aid.
• *Emergency:* An eight-hour course covering basic first-aid skills.
• *Lifesaver:* A 2½-hour survey course on coping with breathing failure, loss of consciousness, bleeding, and choking.
• *Advanced:* Forty or more hours of comprehensive first-aid training.
• *Cardiopulmonary Resuscitation:* A 4- or 12- hour course.
• *First Aid for Drivers:* This innovative four-hour course covers not only medical emergencies, but how to manage the scene of a car accident. Highly recommended for all motorists.

For more information, contact a local branch of St. John Ambulance, or write to P.O. Box 388, Terminal A, Ottawa, Ontario, K1N 8V4.

Moving a victim when danger threatens

Moving a seriously injured person can be dangerous, even life-threatening. Wherever possible, keep a victim stable, tend to his injuries, reassure him, and wait for medical assistance to arrive. Ambulances and rescue vehicles are equipped with such special equipment as stretchers and spine boards. Head and spinal injuries are especially susceptible to further damage if handled improperly. However, there are times when moving an accident victim is absolutely necessary. Consider moving someone *only* under one of the following circumstances:

• *The scene is hazardous.* Uncontrolled traffic, fire or the danger of fire, possible explosion, live electrical wires, or the threat of a second accident may make it necessary to move a patient immediately from the scene of an accident.

• *First aid requires repositioning.* You may have to move or turn over an injured person to reach a bleeding wound, or to administer artificial respiration. If their injuries permit, unconscious victims should be placed in the recovery position (see pp. 188–189).

• *You must gain access to other victims.* You may have to move a victim with minor injuries in order to reach another patient requiring lifesaving care.

• *Medical aid cannot come to the scene.* You may have no way of summoning aid, or

may be on an isolated road with no help in sight. In this situation, the victim must be moved to a doctor or emergency room with as little disturbance as possible. Improvise a stretcher, if possible—use a door or a wide plank, or two poles and blankets or buttoned jackets. Pick up and carry a victim only if there is no other alternative.

Even if the victim must be moved the slightest distance, select the rescue method that will best protect his particular injury. The safest techniques are done with the help of other rescuers—the more, the better. If the victim has injured his foot or hand and is conscious, a simple four-hand carry *(right)* should work. If you are alone with an unconscious victim who must be moved a short distance, place her carefully on a blanket or coat and drag her to safety *(right)*.

Support an injury as best you can before the victim is moved. Fractures should be splinted with whatever materials are at hand, wounds bandaged, and back injuries immobilized. If you can reach a victim in the vehicle, treat him there instead of attempting to drag him out. If extrication is necessary—in the case of a burning car, for example—follow the procedure described below. Always be careful not to strain yourself when lifting or carrying a casualty. An injured rescuer is of little help to accident victims.

Emergency extrication

If there is grave danger from fire or traffic and you must move a victim alone, carefully follow these steps:

1. Disentangle the victim's feet from the wreckage and bring the feet toward the door.

2. Ease your hand and forearm under the person's armpit nearest you and up to support his chin and prevent head movement.

3. Gently ease the victim's head backward to rest on your shoulder, keeping the head and neck as rigid as possible.

4. Slide your other forearm under the armpit on the opposite side. Grasp the wrist of the victim's arm nearest the exit. Let the other arm remain limp.

5. Get a firm footing and pivot with the person, keeping the head and neck as rigid as possible.

6. Drag the victim from the vehicle to safety with the least possible movement of the spine.

Blanket rescues and human carries

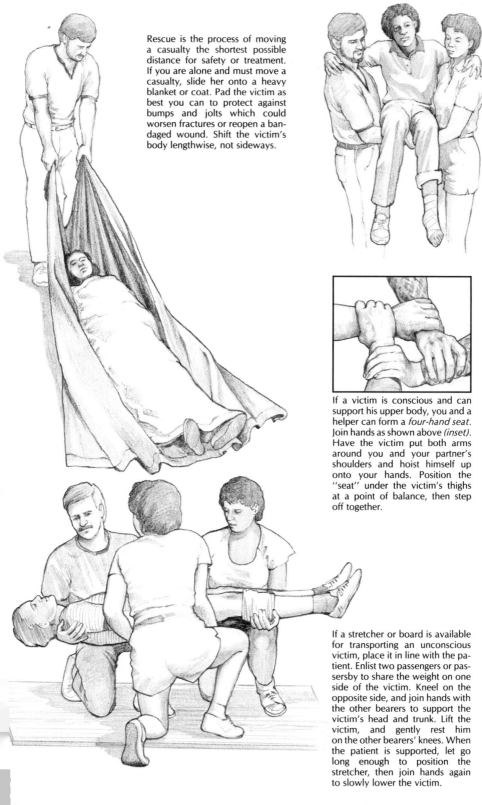

Rescue is the process of moving a casualty the shortest possible distance for safety or treatment. If you are alone and must move a casualty, slide her onto a heavy blanket or coat. Pad the victim as best you can to protect against bumps and jolts which could worsen fractures or reopen a bandaged wound. Shift the victim's body lengthwise, not sideways.

If a victim is conscious and can support his upper body, you and a helper can form a *four-hand seat*. Join hands as shown above *(inset)*. Have the victim put both arms around you and your partner's shoulders and hoist himself up onto your hands. Position the "seat" under the victim's thighs at a point of balance, then step off together.

If a stretcher or board is available for transporting an unconscious victim, place it in line with the patient. Enlist two passengers or passersby to share the weight on one side of the victim. Kneel on the opposite side, and join hands with the other bearers to support the victim's head and trunk. Lift the victim, and gently rest him on the other bearers' knees. When the patient is supported, let go long enough to position the stretcher, then join hands again to slowly lower the victim.

Stay calm—and with your car

Every year many motorists become stranded—and some perish—because their cars have broken down on camping or skiing trips. Whenever you travel away from civilization—even for a few hours—tell someone where you are going and when to expect you back. Take along a detailed, up-to-date map and guidebook. Consult weather forecasts (see pp. 212–213) and dress accordingly. Wear several layers of loose-fitting clothing, and sturdy boots or shoes. Take more food and water than you plan to use. Bring an emergency repair kit (p. 179), a first-aid kit (p. 187), and assemble an outdoor survival kit (below). If you become stranded, follow these guidelines:

● Experts agree on one thing—*stay with your car.* If you have a breakdown on a major route, help usually arrives quickly. But in isolated areas be prepared for a long wait. Unless you can see a house or service station, don't leave the car. It is easier to spot than a person on foot.

● Distress signals rely on units of three—three whistles, three flashes of headlights, or three flares set in a triangle. Fire is one of the most effective signals, readily spotted from the air. Build signal fires at least 30 metres (100 feet) apart in a triangle or in a row along a riverbank or ravine. To conserve fuel, light fires only when you hear a rescue party or aircraft. Keep a small fire—even a candle—going at all times to provide a ready flame. In winter, use rubber, evergreen boughs, or oily rags to generate black smoke—highly visible against snow.

● A human can live for up to three weeks without food but can survive only three or four days without water. Fast-flowing water in isolated areas is usually safe to drink, as are melted snow, water drawn from a frozen lake, and rainwater. Near marshes, dig a hole and allow it to fill with water. Let the water stand until any sediment has settled. If in doubt, boil the water for about five minutes, or add 20 drops of tincture of iodine to four litres (one gallon) of water.

● Most injuries suffered on camping trips are minor. But you should be prepared for serious emergencies (see pp. 186–207). Treat all injuries; don't let pain influence your plans for survival.

● Hunger weakens a person's resistance to cold, pain, and fear. Conserve the food you have brought and use whatever fish, game, and edible plants you can scavenge. Almost all Canadian fish, birds, and mammals are edible—if not pleasant-tasting. Avoid eating plants—especially wild mushrooms—that you don't recognize.

A survival kit for your car

- Matches dipped in wax or stored in a watertight container to keep out moisture
- Knife
- Ball of string
- Wire (picture-hanging type)
- Needles and thread

- Chlorine or iodine tablets for purifying water
- Salt
- Sugar, raisins, nuts, chocolate
- Whistle
- Compass
- Candles

Optional
- Small cooking pot
- Blanket
- Fishing hooks and line
- Safety pins
- Small signal mirror
- Aluminum foil

Your car as survival tool

More campers become stranded in their cars than are lost on foot in the wilderness. When help is far away, common sense and a cool head can mean the difference between life and death.

The motorist above is snowbound, but knows what to do. She is keeping the exhaust pipe clear (**1**) to prevent poisonous carbon monoxide fumes from seeping into the passenger compartment. While outside the car, she is wearing a plastic bag as protection against the wind (**2**). She has opened the window slightly to provide ventilation (**3**), and has left the dome light on to check on her passengers (**4**). Finally, she has put out a flare so that the car can be more easily seen (**5**).

If you become stranded in snow and the engine is working, use the heater to stay warm. Run the engine at a speed equivalent to about 50 km/h (30 mph)—not at idling speed—to warm it up quickly and recharge the battery. After the engine has run a few minutes, turn the heater on *High* for five minutes. Then shut off the engine to save gas. Restart it only when the cold becomes unbearable. A lighted candle will also help warm the passenger compartment.

To keep warm it may become necessary to damage your car. You can line your clothing with insulation from the roof and seats, or use interior carpeting as a blanket *(below)*. To start a fire without matches, attach one end of each jumper cable to the positive and negative leads of the battery and carefully cross the other ends to generate sparks. Have plenty of dry tinder, such as paper or peeled birch bark, on hand to catch the sparks. A headlight lens can be used to focus sunlight on paper or other tinder. If the ground is wet, build a small fire in a hubcap or oilpan.

Signal rescuers by burning tires or floor mats—these create dense, black smoke. Oil burned in a hubcap also generates a highly visible smoke. Flashing headlights and sunlight reflected by rear-view mirrors may attract attention.

Rainwater can be collected in hubcaps, taillight covers, and windshield washer reservoirs (rinse them first). Boil all water collected in this way, or purify it with several drops of tincture of iodine. Wires can be used to make snares, tourniquets, or fishing lines. A hubcap can serve as a frying pan or shovel; license plates are useful for digging and cutting. In an emergency, a spare tire will serve as a life preserver, even with the wheel attached. Several tires can be lashed together to form a makeshift raft.

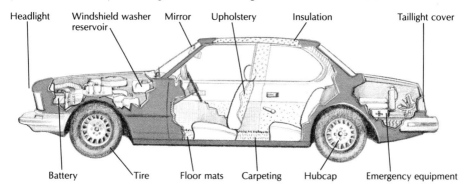

Headlight   Windshield washer reservoir   Mirror   Upholstery   Insulation   Taillight cover

Battery   Tire   Floor mats   Carpeting   Hubcap   Emergency equipment

Test your first aid knowledge

You may think that you know what to do if someone is bleeding badly, has a heart attack, or swallows poisonous cleaning fluid. But do you? Test your reactions to the following emergency situations. For more detailed information, refer to the first aid pages (pp. 186–207).

Questions

1. You are first at the scene of a multi-car collision. Several seriously injured victims need your attention. After warning traffic and summoning an ambulance, which victim should you help first?
a. A man, apparently thrown some distance by the force of the crash, who is bleeding profusely.
b. A woman, lying by the side of the road, who has stopped breathing.
c. A child, still trapped in the car, who is conscious but appears to have multiple fractures.

2. A passenger suddenly clutches her heart and gasps for breath. You realize that she is having a heart attack and pull over to call for help. What should you do until the ambulance arrives?
a. Have her lie down flat and keep her warm with a blanket or jacket.
b. Give her a mild stimulant, such as coffee or tea; encourage her to walk around to keep her heart pumping.
c. Support her in a sitting position and loosen tight clothing.

3. While you are cleaning your car upholstery and are not looking, your young child swallows some cleaning fluid. The *first* thing to do is:
a. tickle his throat to encourage vomiting;
b. give him water to drink to dilute the poison and delay absorption;
c. take the child to the hospital.

4. What first-aid treatment would you apply for a serious burn?
a. Apply petroleum jelly.
b. Apply butter or oil.
c. Soak in cold water.

5. What is the first thing to do for a serious wound that is bleeding badly?
a. Press on the nearest pressure point.
b. Press directly on the wound.
c. Apply a tourniquet.

6. A cyclist is knocked off her bicycle at an intersection and is unconscious. After providing safety from traffic, what do you do?
a. Carefully carry her to your car and rush her to the nearest emergency room.
b. Support her in a semi-sitting position.
c. Turn her to one side and cover her with a blanket while you wait for the ambulance.

7. After several hours of driving in a hot, stuffy car, a passenger complains of headache, dizziness, and nausea. His skin is cold and clammy and he appears to be suffering from heat exhaustion. How do you treat him?
a. Have him lie down in a cool place; give him cold drinks.
b. Raise his legs, or put his head between his legs, to encourage blood circulation to the brain.
c. Mop his forehead with cool, wet compresses.

8. An accident victim has apparently broken her leg. While waiting for the ambulance, you should:
a. carry her to another vehicle and have her sit with her leg supported on the car seat;
b. keep the injured leg from moving, by splinting it if possible;
c. gently tug the foot and ankle to reset the fracture and reduce pain.

9. You step on a rusty nail, puncturing your foot. Although the bleeding is not heavy, you should:
a. wash the foot with plenty of soap and water, apply antiseptic, and bandage;
b. go to an emergency room or doctor for treatment;
c. soak the injured foot in a mild salt solution for at least ten minutes.

10. You are having a roadside picnic and come in contact with a three-leafed plant you believe to be poison ivy. How do you avoid the itching and discomfort that accompany a rash?
a. Apply a soothing lotion to moisturize your skin.
b. Apply rubbing alcohol with a cotton ball or clean cloth.
c. Wash the areas of contact with laundry soap and water.

11. It is a bitterly cold, windy day. The air temperature is −10°C, but when this figure is combined with 50-kilometre gusts, the effect is −33°C. You notice that the tips of your fingers have turned white and are numb. You should:
a. rub the affected areas with snow;
b. warm the injured hand under your coat;
c. exercise to increase circulation.

Answers

1. b. In a serious emergency, when there are several badly injured people, it is often difficult to determine who is in most immediate need of your help. In this situation, the victim whose breathing has stopped has only a few minutes to live and desperately needs artificial respiration (see pp. 190–191). Bleeding injuries are the next priority (see pp. 192–193). Unless the trapped child is in imminent danger, he must be left until last (see pp. 196–197).

2. c. A failing heart works more economically if the patient is in a sitting or semi-sitting position. She should be supported to prevent her from falling forward. Loosen tight clothing around the neck, chest, and waist. Do not move heart-attack victims unless they are in danger. Get medical attention immediately. (See p. 202.)

3. c. Take the child to the hospital at once (or better still, call a poison control center if there is one in your area). If possible, give water on the way. Bring the container or the remains of the substance your child has swallowed, so that an antidote or treatment can be found quickly. Never induce vomiting if a petroleum product or a caustic substance such as cleaning fluid has been taken. Remember that prevention is better than cure. Keep all poisonous substances out of reach of children. (See p. 203.)

4. c. Cool water relieves the pain of burns without interfering with treatment. A clean cloth soaked in cool water can be applied to areas that cannot be submerged in water. Do not apply salves or lotions to burns, or attempt to remove clothing that sticks to a burn injury. (See p. 198.)

5. b. Provided the wound is free of any foreign matter, press directly over the bleeding area with anything that is available—gauze, towels, or your bare hand if necessary. Bandage the dressing securely once the bleeding is under control. Such direct pressure can even cope with a cut artery. Arterial pressure should be used only when direct pressure fails to reduce the flow of blood. A tourniquet is a last-ditch measure that can sometimes do more harm than good. (See pp. 192–193.)

6. c. If there is no apparent spinal injury, place the cyclist in a position halfway between side and face down (the recovery position; see p. 189). This prevents the air passage from being blocked by blood, regurgitated food, dentures, or other foreign matter. Monitor the victim's breathing, pulse rate, and temperature and administer artificial respiration if needed. Do not move an unconscious person if at all possible—wait for an ambulance. (See p. 205.)

7. a. If it is not treated, heat exhaustion may develop into a serious heatstroke. The first priority is to restore the body's fluids and salts, which are lost through perspiration. Give the victim sips of cold liquid, preferably lightly salted water. Have him lie quietly out of the sun until he returns to normal. Elevate the legs and treat as for shock. (See p. 204.)

8. b. Keep the injured leg from moving, unless the victim is in danger. Splinting is the best way to stabilize an injured arm or leg and prevent additional injury if the victim must be moved. If you do not know how to splint, just keep the casualty quiet and reassured until help arrives. Do not attempt to realign a fractured limb unless you are trained in this procedure, and *never* try to straighten injured shoulders, elbows, wrists, knees, or ankles. (See pp. 196–197.)

9. b. A puncture wound should be treated immediately by a doctor, who will administer an anti-tetanus shot. It is good to wash the injury and apply a light dressing, but more important to prevent the spread of infection. (See pp. 192–193.)

10. c. It is the oily secretion of poisonous plants that causes rash, blisters, and itching. The best way to prevent skin irritation is to wash the affected area with strong soap or laundry detergent as soon as possible. Then wipe the area with rubbing alcohol to prevent infection, and apply calamine lotion to sooth the irritation. Better yet, learn to recognize and avoid poisonous plants.

11. b. Frostbite of the fingers, face, ears, or toes is most often superficial and can be recognized by the white appearance of the skin. The area may also be numb and firm to the touch. Gradual rewarming is the best remedy. Breathing on the frostbitten area or placing the injured part in close contact with a warm area of your body may be all that is needed. When the frozen part is white and waxy, and cold and hard to the touch, the frostbite is deep and medical aid is required. The casualty should be carried if possible—especially if the legs are affected. (For transportation methods, see pp. 206–207.)

Where to call *before* you travel

British Columbia

Road conditions
Vancouver-Burnaby (604) 525-0961
Kamloops (604) 374-4112
Nelson (604) 352-2211
Prince George (604) 562-8131
Terrace (604) 635-6254
Nanaimo (604) 758-3991

Highway patrol
Royal Canadian Mounted Police
Telephone: (604) 732-4511

Alberta

Road Conditions
Medicine Hat (403) 529-3640
Lethbridge (403) 329-5480
Hanna (403) 854-4451
Calgary (403) 261-6311
Stettler (403) 742-4495
Red Deer (403) 340-5200
Vermillion (403) 853-2811
Lac La Biche (403) 623-5250
Edmonton (403) 463-7227
Edson (403) 723-3341
Athabasca (403) 675-2656
High Prairie (403) 523-3545
Grande Prairie (403) 539-2310
Peace River (403) 624-6125
High Level (403) 926-2241

Highway patrol
Royal Canadian Mounted Police
(Provincial headquarters)
Telephone: (403) 479-9414

Saskatchewan

Road conditions
Regina (306) 565-7623
Moose Jaw (306) 694-0555
North Battleford (306) 445-3825
Prince Albert (306) 764-5100
Rosetown (306) 882-3791
Saskatoon (306) 244-9500
Swift Current (306) 773-2955
Weyburn (306) 842-6561
Yorkton (306) 782-2400

Highway patrol
Royal Canadian Mounted Police
Telephone: (306) 359-5813

Manitoba

Road conditions
All regions (204) 945-3704

Highway patrol
Royal Canadian Mounted Police
Telephone: (204) 949-5420

Ontario

Road conditions
Bancroft (613) 332-3621
Barrie (705) 835-3014
Chatham (519) 354-7504
Cochrane (705) 272-5775
Hamilton (416) 639-2427
Huntsville (705) 789-4483
Kenora (807) 548-5910
Kingston (800) 267-0284
 (613) 544-2523
Lindsay-Peterborough (705) 277-3333
London (800) 265-6070
 (519) 681-2047
Niagara Falls (416) 682-6641
North Bay (800) 461-9523
 (705) 474-0044
Orillia (705) 835-3104
Ottawa (613) 745-7049
Owen Sound (519) 376-9683
Port Hope (416) 885-6351
Sarnia (519) 542-7718
Sault Ste. Marie (705) 256-2855

Weather (Environment Canada)

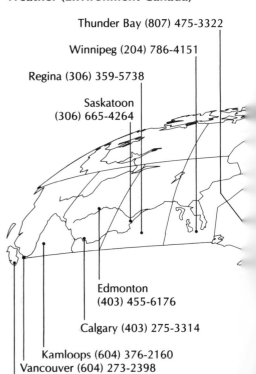

Thunder Bay (807) 475-3322

Winnipeg (204) 786-4151

Regina (306) 359-5738

Saskatoon
(306) 665-4264

Edmonton
(403) 455-6176

Calgary (403) 275-3314

Kamloops (604) 376-2160
Vancouver (604) 273-2398
Victoria (604) 656-3377

Stratford (519) 271-8321
Sudbury (705) 522-0388
Thunder Bay (800) 465-6934
   (807) 475-3561
Toronto (416) 248-3561
Windsor (519) 253-3536

Highway patrol
Ontario Provincial Police
Telephone: (416) 965-4401

Québec

Road conditions
Québec City (418) 643-6830
Montréal (514) 873-4121
Chicoutimi (418) 549-2966
Drummondville (819) 478-4644
Gaspé (418) 368-2389
Hull (819) 776-0059
Rimouski (418) 722-3702
Rivière-du-Loup (418) 862-7244
Sherbrooke (819) 562-4738
Trois-Rivières (819) 375-7344

Highway patrol
Sûreté du Québec
Telephone: (514) 395-4161

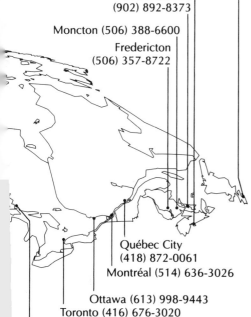

St. John's (709) 737-5532

Halifax (902) 861-2302

Charlottetown
(902) 892-8373

Moncton (506) 388-6600

Fredericton
(506) 357-8722

Québec City
(418) 872-0061
Montréal (514) 636-3026

Ottawa (613) 998-9443
Toronto (416) 676-3020
Sault Ste. Marie (705) 779-2240

New Brunswick

Road conditions
All regions (506) 454-6720

Highway patrol
Royal Canadian Mounted Police
Telephone: (506) 452-3400
New Brunswick Highway Patrol
Telephone: (506) 453-2714

Nova Scotia

Road conditions
All regions (902) 424-3933

Highway patrol
Royal Canadian Mounted Police
Telephone: (902) 426-3950

Prince Edward Island

Road conditions
All regions (902) 894-7059

Highway patrol
Royal Canadian Mounted Police
Telephone: (902) 892-2451

Newfoundland

Road conditions
Eastern region (709) 737-2382
East-central region (709) 466-7952
Central-west region (709) 489-2293
West and Labrador (709) 635-2162
St. John's (709) 737-3641

Highway patrol
Royal Canadian Mounted Police
Telephone: (709) 737-5405

Northwest Territories

Road conditions
All regions (403) 873-7328

Highway patrol
Royal Canadian Mounted Police
Telephone: (403) 920-8320

Yukon Territory

Road conditions
All regions (403) 667-5811

Highway patrol
Royal Canadian Mounted Police
Telephone: (403) 667-5555

Communicate your way out of car trouble

At the garage

Please fill it up with regular (premium) leaded (unleaded).
Le plein d'essence ordinaire (super) avec plomb (sans plomb), s'il vous plaît.
Leh plan day-sonce ordee-naire (sooper) avek plonn (sonn plonn), seel-voo-play.

Check the oil (coolant).
Vérifiez l'huile (l'antigel).
Vay-ree-fee-ay leh-weel (lantee-jel).

I have a flat. Can you fix it?
J'ai une crevaison. Pouvez-vous la réparer ?
Jay oon creh-vay-sohn. Poo-vay-voo la ray-par-ray?

My radiator is overheating.
Mon radiateur surchauffe.
Monn ra-deea-teur sur-show-ff.

My battery needs charging.
Ma batterie a besoin d'être rechargée.
Ma ba-tree ah beuz-wan dett-reh reh-shar-jay.

My car will not start.
Ma voiture ne veut pas démarrer.
Ma vwa-toor ne veh pah day-ma-ray.

The steering pulls to the right (left).
La direction tire sur la droite (la gauche).
La dee-rex-eeon teer soor la drwat (la goshe).

My brakes scrape.
Mes freins grincent.
May frenn grannss.

I need brake fluid.
J'ai besoin de liquide de freins.
Jay beuz-wan deh lik-eed deh frenn.

My engine is backfiring.
Le moteur a des retours de flamme.
Leh mo-teur ah day reh-toor de flam.

My transmission won't shift.
Ma transmission ne change pas de vitesses.
Ma trons-miss-eeon neh chonge pah de vee-tess.

One of my lights has burned out.
Please replace the bulb.
Un de mes phares ne fonctionne plus. Je voudrais le remplacer.
An deh may farr neh fonk-see-onn ploo. Jeh voo-dray leh rom-plass-ay.

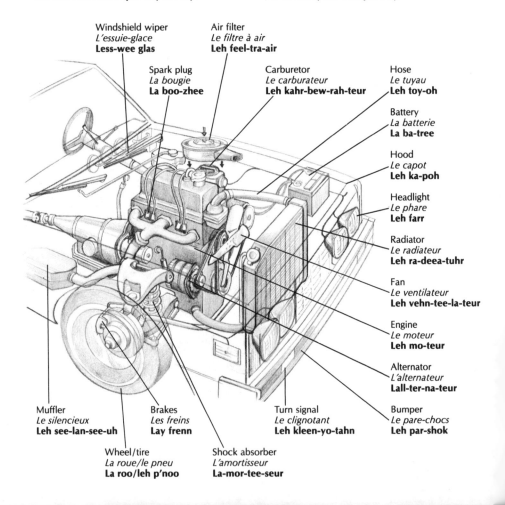

Windshield wiper
L'essuie-glace
Less-wee glas

Air filter
Le filtre à air
Leh feel-tra-air

Spark plug
La bougie
La boo-zhee

Carburetor
Le carburateur
Leh kahr-bew-rah-teur

Hose
Le tuyau
Leh toy-oh

Battery
La batterie
La ba-tree

Hood
Le capot
Leh ka-poh

Headlight
Le phare
Leh farr

Radiator
Le radiateur
Leh ra-deea-tuhr

Fan
Le ventilateur
Leh vehn-tee-la-teur

Engine
Le moteur
Leh mo-teur

Alternator
L'alternateur
Lall-ter-na-teur

Muffler
Le silencieux
Leh see-lan-see-uh

Brakes
Les freins
Lay frenn

Turn signal
Le clignotant
Leh kleen-yo-tahn

Bumper
Le pare-chocs
Leh par-shok

Wheel/tire
La roue/le pneu
La roo/leh p'noo

Shock absorber
L'amortisseur
La-mor-tee-seur

On the road

My car has broken down.
Ma voiture est en panne.
Ma vwa-toor ett on pan.

I need a tow.
J'ai besoin d'une dépanneuse.
Jay beu-zwan doon day-pa-neuz.

My car is out of gas. Can you give me a lift to the nearest gas station?
Je n'ai plus d'essence. Pouvez-vous m'amener à une station-service ?
Jeh nay ploo day-sonns. Poo-vay-voo ma-meh-nay ah oon sta-seon ser-veece?

My battery is dead.
Can you give me a boost?
Ma batterie est à plat.
Pouvez-vous la survolter ?
Ma ba-tree ett ah pla.
Poo-vay-voo la soor-voll-tay?

Is there a gas station (open)?
Y a-t-il une station-service (ouverte) ?
Ya-teel oon sta-seon ser-veese (oo-vert)?

Am I far from town?
Suis-je loin de la ville ?
Swee-jeh lwan deh la vill?

Is there a hotel (motel) near here?
Can you point the way?
Y a-t-il un hôtel (motel) près d'ici ?
Pouvez-vous m'indiquer le chemin ?
Ya-teel an no-tell (mo-tell) pray-dee-see?
Poo-vay-voo man-dee-kay leh cheh-man?

Is there a grocery store (open) near here?
Y a-t-il une épicerie (ouverte) près d'ici ?
Ya-teel oon ay-piece-ree (oo-vert) pray dee-see?

Can you show me on the map where I am?
Pouvez-vous m'indiquer sur la carte où je suis ?
Poo-vay-voo man-dee-kay soor la cart oo jeh swee?

How far is it to . . . from here?
A quelle distance sommes-nous de... ?
Ah kell dee-stons sum noo deh...?

Can you point the way to . . .
Pouvez-vous m'indiquer...
Poo-vay-voo man-dee-kay...

the police station?
le poste de police ?
leh poss-teh deh poh-leece?

the hospital?
l'hôpital ?
loh-pee-tahl?

the bank?
la banque ?
la bonk?

the washroom?
les toilettes ?
lay twa-let?

Can I park there?
Puis-je me stationner là ?
Pwee-jeh meh stah-see-onay la?

In an emergency

I need help.
Pouvez-vous m'aider?
Poo-vay-voo may-day?

There has been an accident.
Il y a eu un accident.
Eel-ee-ah oo an ak-see-don.

I need a doctor.
J'ai besoin d'un médecin.
Jay beu-zwan dan may-dsan.

Is there a telephone near here?
Y a-t-il un téléphone près d'ici ?
Ya-teel an tay-lay-fon pray dee-see?

Is anyone hurt?
Y a-t-il des blessés ?
Ya-teel day bleh-say?

Don't move.
Ne bougez pas.
Ne boo-zhay pah.

Call a doctor quickly.
Appelez d'urgence un médecin.
Ah-puh-lay dur-jence an maid-san.

Please call the police.
Appelez la police, s'il vous plaît.
Ah-puh-lay la poh-leece, see-voo-play.

Traffic signs

Most provinces have adopted standard North American traffic symbols to indicate road conditions, speed limits, crossings, tourist services, and prohibitions

(see pp. 84–87). A few signs, however, have written instructions only. The following terms are therefore worth noting when you drive in Québec:

Arrêt interdit: No stopping

Entrée interdite: Do not enter

Stationnement interdit: No parking

Arrêt: Stop

Cédez: Yield

Dépassement interdit: No passing

Déviation: Detour

Poste de péage: Toll booth

Péage exact: Exact change

Sans monnaie: Without exact change

Sens unique: One way

Reculez: Go back

Production credits

Typesetting   Reader's Digest Text Processing Center

Engraving   R.P.J. Litho Inc.

Printing   Pierre Desmarais Inc.

Binding   Harpell's Press Co-operative

Some of the text in *Canadian Driver's Handbook*
has been adapted or reproduced from the following Reader's Digest publications:
Complete Car Care Manual, You and the Law, Complete Buyer's Guide,
and *Family Health Guide and Medical Encyclopedia.*